ARMED SERVANTS

Peter D. Feaver

Armed Servants

Agency, Oversight, and
Civil-Military Relations

HARVARD UNIVERSITY PRESS

Cambridge, Massachusetts, and London, England   2003

Library of Congress Cataloging-in-Publication Data

Feaver, Peter D.
  Armed servants : agency, oversight, and civil-military relations / Peter D. Feaver.
    p. cm.
  Includes bibliographical references and index.
  ISBN 0-674-01051-5
  1. Civil-military relations—United States. 2. Civil supremacy over the military—United
States. I. Title.

JK330.F43 2003   2002192215
322'.5'0973—dc21

Contents

Preface

This project has spanned a significant portion of my academic career, and throughout its meandering course I have accumulated a series of intellectual debts that I can never repay. The project originated in my dissatisfaction with the state of civil-military relations theory, which I had earlier used in *Guarding the Guardians* (Feaver, 1992) to explore civilian control of nuclear weapons in the United States. In that book, as in this one, I realized I was wrestling with some of the most basic questions of democracy, the same ones that some forty or so years earlier had engaged the formidable mind of one of my dissertation mentors, Samuel Huntington. I know I am no Sam Huntington, but I was nevertheless motivated to see whether I could push civil-military relations theory in a new direction, beyond some of the problems that I thought one encountered in his landmark *Soldier and the State*. Because he has suffered this project with only occasional flashes of exasperation, and has taken it in the spirit in which it is given—reformation as the highest form of flattery—I owe my first and deepest intellectual debt on this project to Samuel Huntington.

The project was shaped at an early stage by my experience as director for defense policy and arms control on the National Security Council staff in 1993 and 1994. I was there courtesy of a Council on Foreign Relations International Affairs Fellowship, and this experience gave me an unparalleled window into civil-military relations both in the trenches and at the highest levels. Along the way, I was tutored by some of the finest men and women with whom I have ever had the privilege to work. I suspect they will shake their heads in dismay at some of "lessons" I think I learned, but I am forever in their debt. In this regard, I would especially like to thank: Steven Andreason, Robert Bell, Hans Binnendijk, Joseph Bouchard, Kurt Campbell, Keith Hahn, Brent James, Steven Jones, the late Joseph Kruzel, Daniel

Poneman, James Seaton, Joseph Sestak, George Tenet, and Anne Wittkowsky. Of course, I am grateful to Anthony Lake, Sandy Berger, and Nancy Soderberg for the risk they took in allowing a practicing academic on the staff.

I am likewise grateful for the extraordinary window into civil-military relations that I have been provided as an officer in Navy Reserves. The requirement of putting on and taking off the uniform has ritually inscribed in me the understanding that civil-military relations is not just a field of scholarly inquiry. It involves real live human beings who are worthy of more respect than academic theory can give them. Over the years, I have met hundreds of men and women in uniform, and my respect for their service is deep and profound.

The project's conceit was to address civil-military relations with a realism that practitioners would recognize as authentic, while using an approach that would also resonate with the most academic of political scientists. I hope to bridge various epistemic divides: civilian and military, policymaker and academic, American politics and national security. The insights of the principal-agent framework seemed especially well suited to this ambition, and I am very grateful to the scholars who helped me tease out a useful theory from this sprawling literature: Deborah Avant, Steve Balla, Robert Bates, William Bianco, John Brehm, James Hamilton, Emerson Niou, Kenneth Shepsle, and David Spence. I am also in the debt of Bruce Bueno de Mesquita, James Morrow, Clifton Morgan, and the rest of the Hoover "boot camp," for tutoring me in the limits and utility of even very basic formal methods.

I have started and completed many other research projects in the interim, and every time I returned to this I found myself thinking about the problem in new ways. My collaborators and advisors on all those projects have thus profoundly shaped my thinking on civil-military relations, none more so than my good friend and trenchant intellectual critic Richard Kohn. I am proud to be a part of a renaissance of academics and practitioners who take seriously the study of the politics of national security. I want to thank in this regard: Andrew Bacevich, Stephen Biddle, Bernard Boene, James Burk, Eliot Cohen, Chris Dandeker, Cori Dauber, Michael Desch, Thomas Donnelly, Benjamin Fordham, Christopher Gelpi, Hein Goemans, Ole Holsti, Gerhard Kuemmel, Thomas Langston, Laura Miller, Charles Moskos, Mack Owens, Albert Pierce, Thomas Ricks, Peter Roman, David Rosenberg, Scott

Sagan, David Segal, Don Snider, Paul Stockton, Hew Strachan, David Tarr, Pascale Venneson, Michael Vickers, and Jay Williams.

Of course, this project would not have been possible without the considerable financial investment of several institutions. I am especially grateful for the generous support given by the John D. and Catherine T. MacArthur Foundation. Some of the research here came out of a separate project looking at the gap between the military and American society funded by the Smith Richardson Foundation, and I thank that foundation heartily for its support. I have also benefited from the support of the Arts and Sciences Research Council at Duke University. The book manuscript was finally finished while I was on sabbatical as a visiting fellow at Corpus Christi College and a visiting scholar at the Centre of International Studies, Cambridge University.

This book would not have been finished without the prodigious efforts of a stable of thoroughbred research assistants: Erin Abrams, Anne Marie Boyd, Ajin Choi, Shin-Hai Michael Chu, Lindsay Cohn, Damon Coletta, Roger Cooper, Kirk Hawkins, Carrie Liken, Al Malbon, Edmund Malesky, Mary Martin, Jennifer Martinez, Michael Noonan, Tammy Meyer, Anne Richardson, Christopher Shulten, and Christine Young.

I have had the rare and at times excruciating privilege of seeing my work in progress dissected, critiqued, and ultimately improved by teams of Duke undergraduate and graduate students in several successive courses built around the project. I tried to hold those students to the highest possible standards, and they repaid the favor in spades by showing me many (though not all) of the mistakes and lapses with which my own work is afflicted. I thank them all, and hope I have not committed yet another goof by omitting a name: Lauren Aronson, Carol Atkinson, Robyn Barnett, Jen Bassler, Kate Brennan, Devlin Casey, Bill Chen, Phillip Demske, Alyssa Dragnich, Jennifer Ezring, David Filer, Robert Gallagher, Amy Gravitt, Jen Greenough, Christy Hamilton, Carrie Hayes, Matthew Hoffman, Adam Hudes, Eugene Hsu, Tom Jones, Richard Kells, Dan Kocab, Claire Kunstling, Kevin McGee, Alec Miller, Ingrid Moeller, Ross Montante, Dennis Nuxoll, Matt Pittman, Matt Sample, Jamie Satnick, Leah Scholer, Melanie Shirley, Victoria Snabon, John Snyder, Daniel Thompson, Elizabeth Tolle, Kulbir Walha, Whitney Walker, and John Wyatt.

There are numerous people, too numerous to mention, who gave penetrating feedback on portions of the text. I thank, of course, the anonymous reviewers at Harvard University Press as well as my encouraging editor, Michael Aronson, and his staff, especially Benno Weisberg and my eagle-eyed copy editor, Julie Hagen. I also thank: John Aldrich, Eva Busza, Kurt Dassel, John Duffield, Colin Elman, Joseph Grieco, Hal Klepak, Peter Lange, Jeff Legro, Mariano Magalhaes, Jim Miller, David Priess, Brian Taylor, Harold Trinkunas, Sharon Weiner, and the participants in the National Security Seminar of the Olin Institute for Strategic Studies, the Program on International Security Policy at the University of Chicago, and the Ohio State University Department of Political Science.

Portions of Chapter 1 and Chapter 3 build on an article originally published in *Armed Forces and Society*, "The Civil-Military Problematique: Huntington, Janowitz, and the Question of Civilian Control," *Armed Forces and Society* 23, no. 2 (Winter 1996): 149–178. Portions of Chapter 6 also build on an article originally published in *Armed Forces and Society*, "Crisis as Shirking: An Agency Theory Explanation of the Souring of American Civil-Military Relations," *Armed Forces and Society* 24, no. 3 (Spring 1998): 407–434. Copyright for both articles is held by Transaction Publishers. Material from these articles is used by permission of the publisher. Other portions of Chapter 1 were originally published as Peter D. Feaver, "Civil-Military Relations," *Annual Review of Political Science* 2 (1999): 211–241, and the material is used with the permission of the publisher. Other portions of Chapter 6 were originally published as Peter D. Feaver, "Civil-Military Conflict and the Use of Force," in Donald Snider and Miranda A. Carlton-Carew, eds., *U.S. Civil-Military Relations: In Crisis or Transition?* (Washington, D.C.: Center for Strategic and International Studies, 1995), and the material is used with the permission of the Center for Strategic and International Studies. Still other portions of Chapter 6 were originally published as Peter D. Feaver, "Book Review of *Civilian Control of the Military: The Changing Security Environment*, by Michael C. Desch," *American Political Science Review* 94, no. 2 (June 2000): 506–507; that material is used with the permission of the American Political Science Association.

Finally, I acknowledge my everlasting debt to the co-conspirators who held up the personal side while I labored on the academic side of the project. I am blessed with the best collection of friends, work distractors, and prayer partners a man could ever have, and they carried me over the hump: Ian Baucom, Robert Beschel, Luke Condra, Josh Crossman, David Fott, Paul Gronke, Timothy Prinz, William Walker, Connie Walker, David Welch, and Paul Yanosy. None deserves more praise than my family, my sweet Karen, Samuel, and Ellie; any interest they had in civil-military relations would have been satisfied without a completed book, but they let it be a family project even so.

I dedicate this book to my college mentor, Carey Joynt, who got me started on the rewarding quest of intellectual discovery that engages me still.

ARMED SERVANTS

CHAPTER 1

Introduction

The tragic events of 11 September 2001 and America's response thereto underscored the centrality of military power, even in a modern liberal democracy. The brutal return to something of a war footing after a decade of comparative peace reminded Americans that freedom comes at a price. At times liberty must be defended with its antithesis: coercion and military force. If they had ever forgotten, Americans remembered just how much they depend on the men and women who train to use military force and who pledge their lives in defense of the nation. These men and women are the nation's armed servants, empowered but subordinate, capable of wielding astonishing levels of coercive force, but expected to wield it only within narrow confines dictated by others. They wear a uniform to mark their special status, and since 11 September 2001, no one can ever doubt their importance. This book, which was conceived and largely written before that dramatic turn of events, is nevertheless a book for the future, because it addresses a question that has only grown in significance as Americans have begun to wrestle with the new global security environment.

How do civilians control the military? This most basic of political questions has two meanings. On the one hand, given that military institutions enjoy an overwhelming advantage in coercive power, how is it that civilian institutions are able to impose their will on their more powerful military agents? On the other hand, given that civilians in mature democracies enjoy general supremacy over the military, how does the control relationship play out on a day-to-day level? This book explores the second aspect of the question, developing a new theory of civil-military relations called agency theory, which is based on the principal-agent framework and which I use to illuminate changes in U.S. civil-military relations during the Cold War and post–Cold War eras.

Understanding how civilians exercise control—identifying the factors that shape civilian control on a day-to-day basis and the trade-offs inherent in the relationship—is central to the democratic enterprise. The civil-military challenge is to reconcile a military strong enough to do anything the civilians ask with a military subordinate enough to do only what civilians authorize. How much autonomy can the military enjoy without violating the principle of civilian control? Alternatively, how much control can civilians wield without interfering disastrously in the conduct of the military mission? Civilian leaders decide these normative questions every day, for better or for worse.

This long-standing challenge for democracy resurfaced with the end of the Cold War in the form of an alleged crisis in American civil-military relations. Soon after the post–Cold War era began, participants in and observers of the American political scene noted that relations between the uniformed military and their civilian masters had reached their stormiest level in decades (Cushman 1994; Dunlap 1992–93, 1994; Kohn 1994; Luttwak 1994; Powell et al. 1994; Weigley 1993). The public vitriol directed at the president and commander in chief was only the most obvious manifestation. Perhaps more serious still were the questions raised about whether senior military leaders were challenging the civilian role in decisionmaking for the use of force in places like Bosnia, Somalia, Haiti, and eventually Kosovo. The new war on terrorism put the question of civil-military relations in especially sharp relief, simultaneously raising the stakes and underscoring the importance of civilian control to the day-to-day workings of the government.

Civil-military relations theory is supposed to help us make sense of these questions, but the theoretical literature has progressed little since Samuel Huntington introduced his classic model of U.S. civil-military relations more than four decades ago (Huntington 1957). The tradition inspired by Morris Janowitz provides an important counterweight to Huntington, but on the crucial question of how civilian institutions control military institutions on a day-to-day basis the Janowitzean school does not represent a significant alternative to Huntington (Janowitz 1971).

In this book, I advance such an alternative theory, drawing on relatively recent advances in the study of political oversight of the nonsecurity bureaucracy. I argue that the essence of civil-military relations is a strategic interaction between civilian principals and military agents. Civilians decide how to monitor the military, based on varying expectations they hold about whether or not the military will obey them faithfully in the particulars of what they ask—what I call "working" and "shirking." (The working and shirking typology comes from the jargon of the principal-agent literature, and the terms have an unfortunate connotation in the military setting. Shirking, as I use the term, does *not* mean what it typically means in the military vernacular: lazy or desultory behavior, or possibly treasonous treachery. Rather, as I use it, it is a technical term defined precisely and at length in Chapter 3. The reader is urged to treat the term as such, giving me the benefit of the doubt that all plausible alternative terms were considered and rejected as presenting equally problematic connotational or definitional challenges.) The military decides whether to obey in this way, based on military expectations of whether shirking will be detected and, if so, whether civilians will punish them for it. These expectations are a function of many factors, including the costs of monitoring, the degree of overlap between the preferences of the civilian and the military players, and the political strength of the actors.

This book, then, provides a theory for answering one important question: How do civil-military relations in the United States play out on a day-to-day basis? In the conclusion of the book, I turn to other related and interesting questions—for instance, Is civilian control of the military a good thing for American national security? For reasons of scope, however, these other questions are deferred as a next step for scholarly research, an agenda made more tractable by the improved understanding of civilian control that agency theory represents.

This is primarily a book about civil-military relations theory. I draw on the principal-agent framework to derive a specific theory, agency theory, that specifies the conditions under which we would expect civilians to monitor the military intrusively or nonintrusively and the conditions under which we would expect the military to work or shirk. Within the limits of probabilistic social science, and the equally limiting constraints of measurement and operationalization of difficult concepts, agency theory allows for contingent predictions about the likely conduct of day-to-day civil-military relations. I use the existing empirical literature on U.S. civil-military relations to demonstrate the utility of the theory, and in doing so suggest new interpretations of the empirical record. But the book is not another primary history of post–World War II civil-military incidents, and its chief contribution is not original source data.[1] Rather, the primary contribution is at the theoretical level, reconceptualizing American civil-military relations in an explicitly deductive fashion. For all the empirical critiques of Huntington's civil-military relations theory,[2] there are remarkably few deductively grounded alternatives that have sufficient analytical scope to challenge Huntington.[3] It is my hope that the agency theory developed here meets that latter and more demanding contest.

The Civil-Military Problematique;
or, Why Look at Civil-Military Relations?

As I discuss at greater length in Chapter 3, civil-military relations is at the heart of a central concern of democracy: How can people organize themselves politically so as to preserve their liberties and advance their interests?[4] Political philosophers since Plato have understood that politics involves the management of coercive power because the human condition involves conflicts of interests. This coercive power may take the form of a military organization established to protect the interests of one political group against the predations of others. Once established, however, the coercive power is itself a potential threat to the interests of the political group it is meant to protect. Managing the coercive power of the military—making sure that those who govern do not become a tyranny to the governed—is the central focus of civil-military relations.

The civil-military problematique is thus a simple paradox: the very institution created to protect the polity is given sufficient power to become a threat to the polity.[5] This follows from the agency condition inherent in civilization. We form communities precisely because we cannot provide for all our own needs and therefore must depend on other people or institutions. Civilization involves delegation to agents, assigning decisionmaking to the collective (in the form of a leader or leaders), and consigning the societal protection function to specialists and institutions responsible for violence.

The civil-military problematique is so vexing because it involves balancing two vital and potentially conflicting societal desiderata. On the one hand, the military must be strong enough to prevail in war. One purpose behind establishing the military in the first place is the need, or perceived need, for military force either to attack other groups or to ward off attacks. The military primarily exists as a guard against disaster and should be always ready even if it is never used. Moreover, its strength should be sized appropriately to meet the threats confronting the polity. It serves no purpose to establish a protection force and then to vitiate it to the point where it can no longer protect. Indeed, an inadequate military institution may be worse than none at all. It could be a paper tiger inviting outside aggression: strong enough in appearance to threaten powerful enemies, but not strong enough in fact to defend against their predations. Alternatively, it could lull leaders into a false confidence, leading them to rash behavior and then failing in the ultimate military contest.

On the other hand, the military must conduct its own affairs so as not to destroy or prey upon the society it is intended to protect. Because the military must face enemies, it must have coercive power, the ability to force its will on others. But coercive power often gives the holder the capability to enforce its will on the community that created it. A direct seizure of political power by the military is the traditional worry of civil-military relations theory and has been a consistent pattern in human history. Less obvious but just as sinister is the possibility that a parasitic military could destroy society by draining it of resources in a quest for ever greater strength. Yet another concern is that a rogue military could involve the polity in wars and conflicts contrary to society's interests or expressed will. And, finally, there is the simple matter of obedience: even if the military does not destroy society, will it obey its civilian masters, or will its latent strength allow it to resist civilian direction and pursue its own interests?

The tension between the two desiderata is inherent in any civilization, but it is especially acute in democracies where the prerogatives of the protectee are thought to trump the protectors at every turn, and where the metaphorical delegation of political authority to agents is enacted at regular intervals, through the ballot box.[6] Democratic theory is summed up in the epigram: the governed should govern. People may choose political agents to act on their behalf, but that should in no way mean the people have forfeited their political privileges. Most of democratic theory is concerned with devising ways to ensure that the people remain in control even as professionals conduct the business of government. Civil-military relations are just a special extreme case, involving designated political agents controlling designated military agents.[7]

It follows that in a democracy the hierarchy of de jure authority favors civilians against the military, even in those cases when the underlying distribution of de facto power favors the military (Kohn 1997). Regardless of how strong the military is, civilians are supposed to remain the political masters. While decisionmaking may in fact be politics as usual—the exercise of power in pursuit of ends—it is politics within the context of a particular normative conception of whose will should prevail. Civilian competence, in the general sense, extends even beyond their competence in a particular sense. That is, civilians are morally and politically competent to make the decisions even if they do not possess the relevant technical competence in the form of expertise (Dahl 1985). This is the core of the democratic alternative to Plato's philosopher king. Although the expert may possibly understand the issue better, the expert is not in a position to determine the value the people will attach to different issue outcomes. In the civil-military context, this means that even if the military is best able to identify the threat and the appropriate responses to that threat for a given level of risk, only the civilian can set the level of acceptable risk for society. Of course, it is doubtful that the military is always best able to identify the threats and responses. In some circumstances, civilian experts on national security may know more than military experts. But the claim of democratic theory is that even when civilians are less expert, they are still rightfully in charge. The military can propose the level of armaments necessary to have a certain probability of being able to defend successfully against one's enemies, but only the civilian can say for what probability of success society is willing to pay. The military can describe in some detail the nature of the threat posed by a particular enemy, but only the civilian can decide whether to feel threatened and, if so, how or even whether to respond. The military assesses the risk, the civilian judges it.

The democratic imperative insists that this precedence applies even if civilians are woefully underequipped to understand the technical issues at stake. Regardless of how superior the military view of a situation may be, the civilian view trumps it. Civilians should get what they ask for, even if it is not what they really want. In other words, civilians have a right to be wrong.

The two central desiderata—to have protection *by* the military and to have protection *from* the military—are in tension because efforts to assure one side complicate efforts to assure the other. If a society relentlessly pursues protection from external enemies, it can bankrupt itself. If society minimizes the strength of the military so as to guard against a military seizure of political power, it can leave itself vulnerable to predation by external enemies. It may be possible to procure a goodly amount of both—certainly the United States seems to have had success in securing a large measure of protection both by and from the military—but trade-offs at the margins are inevitable.

Even if a society succeeds in simultaneously achieving adequate levels of assurance against utter collapse at either extreme—battlefield collapse and coup—there is still a range of problematic activities in which the military can engage. The challenge of ensuring that the military is both capable of doing *and* willing to do what is asked of it remains difficult. Thus, "solving" the problem of coups does not solve, in the sense of neutralize, the general problem of control on an ongoing basis (Kohn 1997, Nelson 2001). Since the two sides of the problematique are intertwined, some theorists, notably Samuel Huntington, have attempted to address both simultaneously. As I will show in Chapter 2, however, this effort, though rich and influential, is ultimately not supported by the available evidence. Accordingly, the agency theory alternative I propose addresses just one side of the problematique, the day-to-day exercise of control over the military; in Chapter 8 I suggest a research agenda that would build on these insights to address the other side of the problematique, the consequences for national security.

Why Begin with Huntington's Theory?

I develop my explanation of civil-military relations as an explicit alternative to Huntington's approach. Why bother with a model that is over forty years old? The answer is that Huntington's theory, outlined in *The Soldier and the State*, remains the dominant theoretical paradigm in civil-military relations, especially the study of American civil-military relations.[8] The Janowitzean alternative may have produced more research, and in some ways its assumptions of what is important and what is not have a firmer grip on the field (Feaver 1999). But it is Huntington's institutional approach that continues to frame analyses of democratic control over the military. Huntington's model is widely recognized as the most elegant, ambitious, and important statement on civil-military relations theory to date. Moreover, Huntington's prescriptions for how best to structure civil-military relations continue to find a very receptive ear within one very important audience, the American officer corps itself, and this contributes to his prominence in the field.

Huntington's theory survives despite repeated attempts to repeal it. Consider just three core claims that Huntington makes: (1) that there is a meaningful difference between civilian and military roles; (2) that the key to civilian control is professionalism; (3) that the key to professionalism is military autonomy. These all have been challenged, but they get revived by successive generations while the challengers drift into obscurity. Take, for example, Huntington's claim that there is a difference between civilian and military roles. Huntington emphasized this distinction because he sought to challenge the then-popular view, which he labeled "fusionist." Fusionists claimed that the emergence of the grand coalitional warfare of World War II meant that military and civilian political functions would be hopelessly entangled ever after. Huntington argued that fusionist approaches fundamentally misunderstood the nature of civil-military relations and, if followed, would lead the United States to disaster (Huntington 1957, pp. 350–354 and 459–460).

Janowitz subsequently challenged Huntington's reification of the civil-military divide, suggesting that the emergence of nuclear weapons and limited war was blurring the distinctions between the two sides. Significantly, however, Janowitz always talked about civilian versus military; his disagreement with Huntington concerned whether the old divisions of labor were still desirable, not whether there was any essential difference between the two roles.[9] After Janowitz, the civil-military distinction was repudiated as finally overtaken by events in the immediate post-Vietnam era (Lovell and Kronenberg 1974, Russett and Stepan 1973, Sarkesian 1981). In recent years, it has again been challenged as now finally and thoroughly overtaken by events since the Cold War (Roman and Tarr 2001, Schiff 1995, Dunlap 1994). In each phase, critics note that the functional logic undergirding the distinction has changed with the changing technology of war and the changing patterns of elite expertise and political interaction.[10] The trend at least since World War I has been for a civilianization of the military sphere and a militarization of the civilian sphere. Each era thinks it has reached the apotheosis, but then technology or some other development pushes the envelope further.[11] Each time, the Huntingtonian civil-military distinction has survived, only to be "slain" a few years later, often in nearly identical language and rarely with any reference to the earlier Huntington-slayers.[12]

There are at least two reasons for this phoenix phenomenon. First, for all their supposed descriptive precision, accounts that emphasize the blurring of civilian and military roles miss an inescapable and important fact that it is obvious to anyone who has participated in a national security policymaking session. It is true that military officers may be sitting in civilian chairs (and vice versa) and that participants may talk about a "team approach" or "partnership in policymaking," or use other buzzwords meant to imply the fusion of civilian and military roles. Nevertheless, the players have different moral and political competencies (on which more in Chapter 3) that differ in systematic ways depending on whether they are military or civilian. The military officer is promising to risk his life, or to order his comrades to risk their lives, to execute any policy decisions. The civilian actor is promising to answer to the electorate for the consequences of any policy decisions. The military officer is expected to obey even stupid orders, or to resign in favor of someone who will. The civilian is claiming the right to be wrong. This forms a subtextual civil-military discourse for all policymaking in the national security realm. Of course, the roles are not observed cleanly. But it is the distinction itself that makes such behavior interesting and worthy of study.

Second, and more fundamentally, the civil-military distinction survives because critics confuse empirical observations about role overlaps with the dissolving of the distinction itself. Pushing the envelope does not erase the distinction between those who fight and those who remain behind. It is democratic theory that distinguishes between the instruments of coercion and the people, and requires that the former be the servant of the latter. Thus, democratic theory motivates not only the distinction but also the focus on "control." One cannot have a theory of civil-military relations applicable to democracies that does not address in some measure the means by which civilians supervise the military.

Huntington survives all these challenges, then, because he grounded his theory in a deductive logic derived from democratic theory while his critics have not. The most successful alternative, the Janowitzean paradigm, is an exception that proves the rule. Despite a large and vibrant literature investigating the relationship of the military to the society (Moskos 1970, 1971, 1977; Larson 1974; Sarkesian 1975; Goldman and Segal 1976; Segal et al. 1974; Segal 1975, 1986; Bachman, Blair, and Segal 1977; Moskos and Wood 1988; Edmonds 1988; Burk 1993; Sarkesian, Williams, and Bryant 1995), the Janowitzean tradition has not focused on answering political questions about control and decisionmaking. Indeed, when it comes to understanding the day-to-day political management of the military, the Janowtizean approach does not differ from the Huntingtonian on any fundamental issue (Feaver 1996b).

An alternative that could replace the Huntington model would have to go beyond an empirical critique, beyond showing that Huntington's model makes claims that do not seem to stand up to the historical record. It would have to provide an alternative theory that is grounded as firmly in the deductive logic of democracy and that can therefore generate as rich a menu of interesting researchable empirical and theoretical questions. Agency theory does precisely that.

Agency theory shares an institutional point of departure with Huntington, exploring how civilian and military actors relate on political decisions in a democracy. Agency theory uses the tools of the rationalist method, and is able to subsume Huntington's best empirical insights without being dependent on the rest of the Huntington model, which, as argued in Chapter 2, is not supported by the empirical record. Agency theory preserves the civilian-military distinction—the sine qua non of all civil-military theory—but without reliance on an ideal-type division of labor. And it preserves the military subordination conception essential to democratic theory, without assuming military obedience.

Agency theory has one further desirable feature: although Huntingtonian in orientation, it offers the possibility of linking Huntington's institutional analysis to at least some of Janowitz's sociological point of view. By institutional, I mean a theory that focuses on the interaction of political actors played out in the specific institutional setting of government. The institutional lens directs attention to the top layers of the governmental hierarchy, and tolerates aggregations like "military" or "civilian" that obscure a rich sociological diversity. The sociological lens advanced by Janowitz points to many other important questions that are for the most part ignored by the institutional orientation, for example, what is the role of women or minorities in the military, how do the enlisted ranks conceive of their service to the country, and, above all, how different is military culture from civilian society? The chief focus of the institutional approach is the relationship of the military (qua institution) to civilian political leaders; the chief focus of the sociological approach is the relationship of the military (qua individuals) to civilian society. The two approaches are not in fact diametrically opposed, however, and agency theory provides a way of linking Janowitzean variables like the difference between civilian and military attitudes to Huntingtonian variables like military obedience.

Agency theory, then, is broad enough to address a range of civil-military issues, and specific enough to be useful in illuminating the political give and take involved in any single one. It has, in short, at least the necessary ambition if not the necessary prominence to be considered a rival paradigm of civil-military relations.

Why Look at Civil-Military Relations
in the United States?

The traditional preoccupation of the civil-military relations literature is the coup d'état, the direct seizure of political power by the military. In many parts of the world, a military coup is a realistic possibility, and so the study of civil-military relations has the same urgency and centrality that, say, a study of interest group voting might have in American politics. Coups are *not* a particularly realistic possibility in this country. There has never been a serious coup attempt, let alone even a temporarily successful coup in the United States.

Ironically, this proud record might be misinterpreted as a sign that there is no point in studying U.S. civil-military relations. If there is no coup, can there be anything interesting to explain, beyond the easily explained absence of a coup? After all, the literature that delineates why coups happen in other countries readily accounts for the absence of a coup in the United States. The American military has internalized the view that to be professional means that it does not directly challenge civilian political authority for control over the government (as I explain in detail throughout the book, this is not the same thing as saying that the American military always acts so as to obey without challenge any civilian order). At the same time, the United States has avoided all of the environmental conditions that foster coups in other countries: catastrophic defeat in battle, collapse of the civilian political order, persistent underfunding of the military coupled with cronyism and corruption in the military personnel system, and so on (Huntington 1957, Finer 1962, Janowitz 1971, Welch 1976, and Perlmutter 1977).

From a crass political-science point of view, the American case seems uninteresting, occupying with dreary regularity the "stable," "harmonious," or "balanced" cell in whatever two-by-two table the comparative civil-military typology generates (Finer 1962, especially pp. 88–89; Welch 1976). Consequently, political scientists interested in civil-military problems have been uninterested in American politics and those interested in American politics have been uninterested in civil-military relations. There tend to be few exchanges between the two sides, and the political science discipline tends to park scholars of American defense politics in the international relations subfield. A secondary goal of this book is to bridge the divide, to use insights from the study of American politics to inform the study of American defense politics and vice versa.

The first step in bridging the divide is recognizing that politics pervade civil-military relations even if there is no coup. Politics is about deciding who gets what and how, and even more about deciding how a group of actors is going to decide who gets what and how. A coup is one extreme form of this, but far less drastic examples include deciding whether to allow gays to serve openly in the military, or deciding whether to intervene to stop a civil war and, if so, whether to begin with a measured application of airpower or to use massive force. And in the politics surrounding these choices, the American case is replete with interesting conflict, albeit conflict that stops short of a coup. Indeed, despite the relatively harmonious experience America enjoys compared with that of the rest of the world, by far the dominant theme in the literature on U.S. civil-military relations is the presence of conflict (O'Meara 1978, Feaver 1995). The American experience thus poses an interesting challenge to civil-military relations theory: to develop an explanatory model that is sufficiently broad as to encompass the problematique, but also sufficiently nuanced as to detect and explain variations in even the "stable" American civil-military tradition.

My application of agency theory is limited to the American case. In Chapter 8, I explore ways that agency theory might be extended to apply to other political settings. At least in principle, agency theory should have relevance to any liberal democracy, although the values of the key variables in agency theory would undoubtedly change with different cultural settings. One would expect, for instance, that French political culture might have a different tolerance for autonomy in government bureaucracies and so the give and take of day-to-day civilian control would differ accordingly, even though the basic logic of agency theory should obtain. Nevertheless, for obvious reasons of scope, I do not prove the relevance with comparative case studies in this book. Even if future research establishes that agency theory only "works" in the U.S. case, at least it is a case that is intrinsically important.

Why Use a Rationalist Framework?

My approach to explaining American civil-military relations draws on insights developed in the study of American politics more generally. My agency theory comes out of the principal-agent analytical framework, which has been widely used to study American politics, and I use the rationalist method, which has wide currency in the American subfield of political science.

The principal-agent framework is designed to explore problems of agency, how political or economic actors in a superior position (principals) control the behavior of political or economic actors in a subordinate position (agents). Agency relationships are ubiquitous: for example, stockholder-board, employer-employee, voter-politician, or Congress-bureaucracy. As I explain in Chapter 3, this framework can be readily adapted for use in the civil-military domain, and indeed the civil-military problematique constitutes an interesting special case of the general problem of agency.

I adopt a rationalist method as a fruitful point of departure, not out of an ideological commitment to rational choice theory. I would expect that an important critique of the argument developed in this book could come from the bounded rationality approach, such as a "logic of appropriateness," as developed in March 1978, or "ritualized behavior" as developed in Scott and Meyer 1983. The bounded rationality critique, however, depends on at least some prior explication of the rationalist baseline, which opens the door for the agency theory developed here.

The use of the rationalist method cuts against a trend in the general political science literature to focus on nonmaterial determinants of behavior, be they identity, norms, beliefs, or ideas. A similar trend can be found in organization theory (Brehm and Gates 1997). Paradoxically, this focus on the nonmaterial determinants of behavior is where civil-military relations theory has more or less remained for the past forty years. Huntington's conception of civilian control is largely identity driven and centers on an ideology of professionalism; on this point, Janowitz is not different.

Huntington's original emphasis on professionalism owed much to Carl Friedrich's general arguments about how professionalism enhanced the control of a bureaucracy (Friedrich 1935, 1941). It also reflected, although not explicitly, the work of Chester Barnard, who argued that coercion was largely ineffective in inducing desirable behavior within an organization and, further, that other systems based on material incentives were likewise flawed (Barnard 1938; Etzioni 1961, pp. 12–19). Barnard argued that nonmaterial incentives and, above all, the morale of the workforce were the critical determinants of behavior. Huntington's stress on the *norm* of military subordination to the civilian was consistent with Friedrich and Barnard's privileging of ideational over material factors. The bulk of the theoretical literature since Huntington has concerned debates about professionalism, the nature of the military vocation (is it an institution or an occupation?), and so on.

If anything, then, civil-military relations theory needs to make room for material factors. Agency theory does that. By reintroducing factors like the costs of monitoring and the likelihood of punishment, I am not arguing that material factors are the only important concerns. Indeed, the theory I advance here can profitably incorporate identity issues, and follow-on work could use it to weigh the relative influence of these different factors. Other principal-agent treatments of bureaucracy have incorporated cultural norms variables (Kreps 1990, Brehm and Gates 1997), and the argument I present could be extended along similar lines. Rather, I am simply bringing back into view a basic concern with the incentives that press upon political actors, a concern that is remarkably absent from most existing civil-military relations theory. In a sense, my approach revives an earlier tradition, found in the older public administration literature, to which much of the sociological approaches to organizational behavior from the 1950s on has been a reaction, and which the original modern theorists of civil-military relations were themselves attacking.

Thus, agency theory is at once remarkably intuitive and yet also remarkably surprising. On the one hand, it is plausible and even obvious to think of civilians and the military as political actors responding to basic incentives like costs and benefits. On the other hand, the dominant theoretical paradigms for understanding American civil-military relations do *not* think of civilians and the military in this way. Agency theory emphasizes strategic interaction and punishment—how civilians anticipate military behavior, how military obedience itself is not foreordained, and how the likelihood that civilians will detect and punish military misbehavior shapes interactions. To my knowledge, these considerations are nowhere to be found in Huntington, Janowitz, or most other models of American civil-military relations.

There is a secondary benefit to using models and methods that are relatively familiar to students of American politics: it further integrates the study of American civil-military relations into the study of American politics. But there is a risk in bridging the fields this way. People attracted to the civil-military topic may find the principal-agent approach foreign and ungainly.[13] People attracted to the principal-agent framework are unlikely to have much familiarity with civil-military relations. It is left to the reader to determine whether this is an unhappy marriage of convenience or a felicitous coupling of strengths.

Road Map

The book proceeds as follows. In Chapter 2, I explore the empirical puzzle raised by the end of the Cold War: did civil-military relations unfold as Huntington's theory demands? In Chapter 3, I explore the deductive logic behind the alternative agency theory I propose, showing how civil-military relations can be understood with reference to insights drawn from the principal-agent framework. In Chapter 4, I use basic tools of formal rational choice theory to analyze a simple civil-military principal-agent game and thereby derive the basic expectations about civilian and military behavior that comprise agency theory. In Chapter 5, I use the insights of agency theory to reinterpret the Cold War puzzle. In Chapter 6, I offer an agency theory interpretation of post–Cold War civil-military relations. In Chapter 7, I use agency theory as a heuristic to investigate in greater detail the conduct of civil-military relations in several important post–Cold War uses of force. Chapter 8 closes the book with a brief conclusion summarizing the argument and suggesting extensions to agency theory. The book is basically an existence proof for the utility of the agency framework, and the conclusion lays out potentially fruitful ways to build on the spare model presented here.

CHAPTER 2

Huntington's Cold War Puzzle

In subsequent chapters, I will introduce the agency model and use it to explore the strategic interaction at the heart of day-to-day civil-military relations. Before showing the utility of agency theory, however, it is necessary to show that for all its elegance and appeal, the prevailing model, Huntington's framework, does not adequately explain the record. I will do this by way of exploring an empirical puzzle raised by Huntington's theory. Huntington's core claim in *Soldier and the State* is that the increased external threat confronting the United States during the Cold War would drive U.S. civil-military relations into a pathological condition that would cause the United States to lose the Cold War *unless* this natural tendency was counteracted by remedial steps prescribed by Huntington. Now that the Cold War is over, it is possible to evaluate whether the United States prevailed *because* it followed Huntington's prescription or *despite* ignoring his advice. The evidence strongly suggests that the latter is true, hence the need for an alternative explanation: agency theory.

Huntington's Cold War Diagnosis and Remedy

Huntington's theory mixed empirical and normative elements. At the empirical level, Huntington argued that civil-military relations were shaped by three explanatory variables: the level of external threat (his functional imperative), the constitutional structure of the state (one of his societal imperatives), and the ideological makeup of society (the other societal imperative). At the normative level, Huntington argued for a specific approach that he thought best addressed problems that his empirical model predicted at the dawn of the Cold War.

The motivation for his study, the "crisis of American civil-military relations," was a clash between the functional and societal imperatives brought on by the Cold War. The Soviet threat (functional imperative) imposed a requirement on the United States for a large military establishment, but the traditional liberal, antimilitary ideology (societal imperative) precluded building up the military forces and granting the military autonomy he thought necessary for national security. Huntington recognized that liberal society could mobilize to protect itself to meet a spasm threat, as in World War II. Liberal society could do so, however, only by temporarily suspending its "liberalness," effectively ceding control temporarily to the military; hence Huntington's disapproval of the way civilians ran World War II.

Roosevelt, Huntington claimed, gave too much power and authority to the military during World War II, letting it make all strategic policy decisions (Huntington 1957, p. 315). The real challenge to a liberal society would be in confronting a long-term threat. Huntington assumed that the Soviet threat would be a "relatively permanent aspect of the international scene," so, unlike in World War II, the mismatch between what the state needed and what society's ideology would provide would also be long-running (p. 456). He concluded, therefore, that the United States was doomed unless the societal imperative was changed: "The tension between the demands of military security and the values of American liberalism can, in the long run, be relieved *only by the weakening of the security threat or the weakening of liberalism*" (p. 456, emphasis added). The American embrace of liberalism, Huntington averred, was "the gravest domestic threat to American military security" (p. 457). In short, unless America changed its ideology, it could not meet the Soviet threat over the long run.

Ideology is the linchpin for Huntington's model and, consequently, the focus of the empirical analysis in the rest of this chapter. Huntington defined America's "ideological constant" as liberalism (Huntington 1957, p. 143), by which he meant "individualism," an approach that emphasized "the reason and moral dignity of the individual and oppose[d] political, economic, and social restraints upon individual liberty." Liberalism believed the natural relation among men was peace and that "the application of reason may produce a harmony of interests." The liberal celebrated free expression and thought that human nature could be "improved through education and proper social institutions" (all quotes p. 90). These core features led liberals to be hostile to the exercise of state power and to military institutions, especially professional armies (pp. 91, 153–155). A liberal would assume national security as a given and reject the need to guard it vigilantly.

Huntington thus had a very broad ideology in view when he referred to liberalism. While he was most concerned about the liberal's attitude toward foreign policy and military affairs, Huntington considered liberalism's foreign platforms to be inextricably linked to its domestic platforms: "Magnificently varied and creative when limited to domestic issues, liberalism faltered when applied to foreign policy and defense" (p. 148).

Huntington's primary contribution, by his own reckoning, was the identification of a way of meeting the Soviet threat without surrendering the bedrock democratic principle of civilian control: "objective control," which simultaneously maximized military subordination and military fighting power. The key to objective control was military professionalism. Any action that furthered the professionalization of the military could be thought of as part of the objective control endeavor; all other actions belonged to objective control's antithesis, subjective control, which produced a transmutation of the military into an institution incapable of defending the state against a determined and capable foe like the Soviet Union. The primary objective control mechanism was "the recognition of autonomous military professionalism"—respect for the independent military sphere of action. Interference or meddling in military affairs undermined military professionalism and so undermined objective control. Objective control weakened the military politically without weakening it in military terms, that is, without degrading its ability to defend society, because professionalizing the military rendered it politically sterile or neutral (Huntington 1957, pp. 83–85).

The causal chain for Huntington's prescriptive theory runs as follows: autonomy leads to professionalization, which leads to political neutrality and voluntary subordination, which leads to secure civilian control. The heart of his concept is the putative link between professionalism and voluntary subordination. For Huntington, this was not so much a relationship of cause and effect as it was a definition: "A highly professional officer corps stands ready to carry out the wishes of any civilian group which secures legitimate authority within the state" (Huntington 1957, pp. 74, 83–84). A professional military obeyed civilian authority. A military that did not obey was not professional. Fully specified, Huntington's causal chain from ideology to security runs as depicted in Figure 2.1.

Objective control was thus the remedy for the disease diagnosed by Huntington's empirical theory. His empirical theory, however, admitted of only one way to get to this remedy. Since external threat was likely to be constant

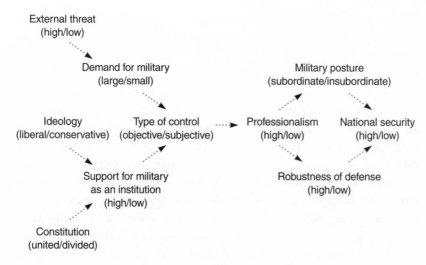

Figure 2. 1 Huntington's causal chain

for the foreseeable future, Huntington dictated a change in one of his other two explanatory variables: constitutional framework or ideological caste. Since Huntington further dismissed a constitutional change as unwieldy and unlikely (Huntington 1957, pp. 190–192), he was reduced by process of elimination to prescribing a change in the ideological variable—specifically, a shift from liberalism to conservatism.

Importantly, nowhere in *Soldier and the State* did Huntington suggest that Americans could simply become "liberal hawks," or liberals in everything but military policy—people who voted for an expansion of individual liberties *and* an expansion of the defense budget. On the contrary, Huntington considered liberalism to be quintessentially antimilitary. Liberalism had to go if the United States was to survive the Cold War challenge. According to Huntington's theory, the United States would have to become a conservative republic.

Huntington recognized that his prescription was harsh medicine. Huntington's way involved a rejection of much of what may be considered the *American* way. Huntington's way would mean the loss of individualism, replaced with a communalism that would subordinate the good of the individual to the good of society. It might even mean the loss of the "tiresome monotony and the incredible variety and discordance of small-town commercialism" (Huntington 1957, p. 465). The seamlessness of Huntington's view of the domestic and foreign components of liberalism, and thus the necessity of replacing the former to change the latter emerges in stark terms from his epilogue to *Soldier and the State*. In a section rarely quoted by political scientists, Huntington painted a disparaging portrait of Highland Falls, the Norman Rockwellian village to the south of the United States Military Academy at West Point. He contrasted it with the order and serenity of West Point itself and appealed for the triumph of the latter over the former. "West Point embodies the military ideal at its best; Highland Falls the American spirit at its most commonplace. West Point is a gray island in a many colored sea, a bit of Sparta in the midst of Babylon. Yet is it possible to deny that the military values—loyalty, duty, restraint, dedication—are the ones America most needs today? That the disciplined order of West Point has more to offer than the garish individualism of Main Street?" (p. 465).

In the end, Huntington defended this tough medicine as necessary to save the patient: "The requisite for military security is a shift in basic American values from liberalism to conservatism. Only an environment which is sympathetically conservative will permit American military leaders to combine the political power which society thrusts upon them with the military professionalism without which society cannot endure" (Huntington 1957, p. 464). In other words, Huntington's model of American civil-military relations made only two predictions: change or die.

Hence, the empirical puzzle: did the United States change or die? If Huntington's prescriptions were not followed and disastrous results did not ensue, how valid is Huntington's empirical model? In this chapter, I consider three possible answers. First, perhaps the United States did not prevail in the Cold War. Perhaps Huntington's prescription was not followed, yielding the unfavorable outcome his theory predicted. Second, perhaps the United States prevailed but for reasons that have nothing to do with civil-military relations. Huntington's theory could be wrong, irrelevant, or both. Third, and this was advanced by Huntington himself in a 1977 retrospective on *The Soldier and the State*, perhaps the United States essentially followed his advice (Goodpaster and Huntington 1977). Perhaps civilians rejected liberalism in favor of military conservativism, permitting the solution Huntington recommended.

As the rest of this chapter makes clear, none of these explanations fits the evidence well, and so I conclude that Huntington's model is incomplete. This conclusion necessarily begs a new theory of civil-military relations.

Did the United States Survive the Cold War and
Does It Matter for Civil-Military Relations Theory?

The first relatively trivial step is to show that the United States did in fact survive the Cold War. The conventional wisdom, of course, views this as obvious to the point of indisputable. Inevitably, revisionists have challenged the conventional wisdom, calling into question some of the more extravagant claims of victory.[1] But revisionists challenge only the spoils of victory and the costs of prevailing—whether too much was spent, or whether a less provocative policy would have secured accommodation earlier. No serious scholar questions that the United States survived more or less intact; certainly there is no doubt the United States prevailed on the terms Huntington laid out in *Soldier and the State*.

The second and more consequential step requires demonstrating that the favorable Cold War outcome matters for civil-military relations theory. Perhaps the United States prevailed in the Cold War for reasons that have nothing to do with Huntington's theory. His causal arguments could be correct, his prescriptions proper, but ultimately the entire issue could be moot because the Cold War was won on different grounds, perhaps because nuclear weapons provided security on the cheap or the Soviet threat was much less severe than Huntington feared. This explanation is logically possible, and since this book is not intended to be an exhaustive analysis of why the United States won the Cold War, it cannot be dismissed entirely. However, even if it is decided that the United States prevailed in the Cold War for reasons having little to do with Huntington's core theory, it is still worthwhile investigating whether the Cold War outcome supports or challenges Huntington's model.

The most plausible alternative explanation for U.S. success is that nuclear weapons provided a cheap way of guaranteeing security, thus creating a larger margin for civil-military error.[2] This does not, in fact, satisfactorily rescue Huntington's theory. Cold War budgets may seem small in retrospect, but only in comparison to an idealized maximum, for instance the idealized maximum associated with a Lasswellian garrison state. Likewise, despite the efforts of academic strategists, no U.S. government ever acted as if nuclear deterrence alone sufficed for national security. Indeed, Huntington cited the belief in the putatively cheap security offered by nuclear weapons as precisely the kind of liberal defense policy about which *he* worried and for which his theory of civil-military relations was supposed to correct (Huntington 1957, p. 394). Cold War military budgets as a percentage of GNP remained high, much higher than the United States had ever sustained for longer than it took to win a hot war. Thus, while the societal effort may not have reached the level about which Lasswell worried, it did exceed the level Huntington's theory would allow. Huntington's theory would demand a change in one of his explanatory variables to account for the level of defense effort achieved by the United States. In sum, there could be many reasons why the United States survived or won the Cold War, but any or all of those reasons would have to filter through Huntington's model of civil-military relations.

Was Huntington Correct about How Civil-Military Relations Played Out?

Huntington's prescription for surviving the Cold War was for civilians to reject liberalism and embrace the military's natural ideology of conservative realism. In his own retrospective written in 1977, Huntington noted the obvious fact that the United States had prevailed thus far. He went on to argue that this felicitous development was directly caused by the kind of ideological shift he had prescribed (Goodpaster and Huntington 1977, pp. 9–11). In his words: "The argument advanced in *The Soldier and the State* in 1957 was that, given the existing international situation, 'the requisite for military security' was a shift from liberalism to a 'sympathetically conservative' attitude toward the needs of military professionalism. To a surprising extent, that shift occurred" (p. 26).

Huntington marshaled a variety of evidence to support the claim that such a profound ideological shift had occurred. He cited the publication of his own book, which indicated a change in the intellectual climate, and the fact that "a large number of other books by scholars and journalists appeared that treated the military with a respect, and military needs with a consideration, most unusual in American history." Moreover, Huntington claimed the early Cold War elites "shared, by and large, an understanding and appreciation of the role of military force with respect to foreign policy matched only by that of the Federalists in the 1790s and the 'Neo-Hamiltonians' in the 1890s." Such an elite view was matched by parallel support among the mass public, at least through the mid-1960s (Goodpaster and Huntington 1977, p. 11). Huntington warned, however, that the Vietnam war and a related creeping antimilitarism, especially among elites, was threatening to undo the temporary triumph of conservative realism, replacing it with traditional liberalism, which would once again endanger U.S. security.

Indeed, even as he claimed that the requisite shift from liberalism to conservatism occurred during the 1950s and 1960s, he asserted as well that "in some measure, also, it has now been reversed. The immediate future [i.e., mid- to late 1970s] would thus appear to involve a combination of the liberal attitudes dominant before World War II (Phase I), but repressed during the Cold War (Phase II) with the security threats nonexistent in Phase I but predominant in Phase II. The dilemma that was partially resolved in the 1950s has returned" (Goodpaster and Huntington 1977, p. 26). The polling data he cited showed that the public strongly supported increased defense spending in 1957, when he warned of a "crisis of American civil-military relations," but that by 1971 the public strongly opposed an increase in defense spending.[3] Likewise, he suggested that the move to an all-volunteer military would reverse the Cold War trend toward a congruence in the personnel, function, and structure of the military establishment and civilian institutions (p. 25). Elsewhere in the same article, however, he observed that the ominous trends of the early 1970s were themselves beginning to reverse by 1973.[4] Although he acknowledged that it was too soon to tell whether the 1970s' turnabout would be temporary or indicative of future trends, he concluded his 1977 review on an optimistic note: "As the effects of the democratic surge, the Vietnam War, and the enthusiasm for détente fade into the past, the prevailing attitude of American society toward its military forces is likely to be one of modified or contingent toleration" (pp. 26–27).

Huntington thus proposed a complex and somewhat contradictory treatment of the changes in American values over time. For starters, by his own measures the ideological convergence on which his theory depended was stronger in 1957, when he gave his famous exhortation calling for the convergence, than in 1977, when he concluded that his prescriptions had been followed.[5] Many of the factors, like the emergence of a prodefense civilian elite and public support for high defense spending were considerably more pronounced in the mid-1950s when he warned about the dangers of liberalism, than they were in the 1970s when he said the problem had been largely solved.

Of greater concern, his evidence consisted largely of output measures, but his theory was a claim about input measures; the output was support for building sufficient armed forces, the input was the sway of liberalism in society, as measured by the degree of individualism in society. Huntington did not systematically evaluate each step in his causal chain (see Figure 2.1), and the evidence he did cite leans rather heavily on demonstrating the links between the later stages, particularly the link between popular support for the military and the provision of an adequate defense.[6]

In 1977, Huntington noted that on average over the previous two decades the amount of security provided by the military was high and the public support for a large military was also high. This observation, however, does not confirm an ideological shift, because Huntington explicitly conjoined domestic and national security components in his indictment of liberal ideology. To avoid a tautology, Huntington must measure a change in ideology independent of the military buildup, and he must demonstrate changes across the entire domain of liberal ideology. Moreover, any convergence must be a result of civilians moving toward the military and not vice versa. As I show below, reviewing the evidence in this way undermines Huntington's claim that his prescriptions were followed, and casts doubt on the thesis that the ebb and flow of liberal ideology coincided with the ebb and flow of the provision of national security.

Support for the military as an institution, as distinct from support for a large military establishment or support for a still larger military establishment in the form of defense budget increases, remained relatively high throughout the Cold War. Janowitz presented ambiguous data from a 1955 survey to suggest that a military officer's career had lower prestige than other professions, ranking seventh, behind public school teachers.[7] Tellingly, Janowitz found that the military's self-image included the presumption that civilian society did not respect military institutions. More systematic data, however, support the opposite conclusion: that the public generally held the military in high regard, even throughout the Vietnam War. Based on public opinion polls from 1964 to 1976, Segal and Blair found that respect for the military remained very high (between 70 and 75 on a 1–100 scale) throughout, including into the mid-1970s. At the same time, confidence in the people "in charge of the military" declined, along with a general decline in confidence in the leadership of other societal institutions, but even here confidence remained higher for the military than for other institutions (Segal and Blair 1976–77, pp. 10–11). A related study found that exposure to the generally negative media coverage of the military during the Vietnam War apparently had the perverse effect of *increasing* support for the military beyond what it otherwise would have been (Hofstetter and Moore 1979,

p. 261). Although it is more a measure of support than of respect, it is telling that from 1940 through 1967 support for universal military training (UMT) never fell below 60 percent, even or perhaps especially when the selective service draft was very unpopular. Intriguingly, respondents who supported UMT were as apt to justify their support in terms of the beneficial aspects of military service on the individual as they were the need for preparedness and national defense, suggesting that civilians held military service in high regard (Clotfelter 1969, p. 133–134). These results are matched by the findings of the Gallup public opinion polls, which asked from 1975 onward "how much confidence you, yourself, have in" the military as an institution. The percentage of respondents saying they had a "great deal" or "quite a lot" of confidence in the military never dropped below 50 percent (1981) and averaged 58 percent throughout (Gallup 1991, p. 100).

Furthermore, while the questions were not asked often enough to establish a firm trend, it is suggestive that the few times mass public opinion surveys asked about military influence or military culpability for failures, the responses were strongly supportive of the military against civilian leaders. In both a 1948 and a 1949 poll, almost twice as many respondents felt that military men did not have enough say, as opposed to too much say, "in deciding our policy with other countries." Similarly, in a 1951 survey 39 percent of the respondents mentioned General Eisenhower, General MacArthur, or another military person or institution in response to the question: "Of all men in public life, which ones do you yourself think are the best ones to handle our country's problems?" As for who was to blame for the lack of preparedness at Pearl Harbor, 44 percent blamed "political men in Washington" and only 21 percent blamed "errors of military men." And perhaps most interestingly, in a 1967 Harris poll the public clearly fixed blame for the lack of progress in the Vietnam War on Secretary of Defense McNamara, not General Westmoreland; the preference for Westmoreland over McNamara held true across all viewpoints on what to do in Vietnam, whether to pursue "total military victory," "fight to get negotiated peace," or "get out as quickly as possible" (Clotfelter 1969, pp. 126–132). Viewing these data as a whole, one analyst concluded that "the high-ranking military officer is not a despised alien in American society—not [in the late 1960s] and not in the World War II and post-war periods . . . his professional status is respectable, if not overwhelming" (ibid., p. 131).

These findings appear to contradict other polling data cited by Huntington that apparently showed a rise in antimilitarism in the early 1970s. The contradiction is easily reconciled. To be sure, as Huntington observed, there is evidence of antimilitarism, particularly among the elite (on which more below). But the evidence of antimilitarism among the mass public in the early 1970s is largely limited to a dramatic change in attitudes about the desirability of spending less on defense. The percentage favoring a decrease in defense spending hovered under 20 percent for the first two decades after the Korean War but then shot up to over 50 percent in 1969.[8] According to Russett, the mass public had been generally permissive of building an expensive defense establishment for the first two-plus decades of the Cold War but then "awoke" in the late 1960s and became stubbornly antimilitary (Russett 1974b, p. 76). Of course, what neither Huntington nor Russett could have known was that after a decade-long relative decline in defense spending during the 1970s, and in light of adverse developments in the international threat environment, the public would subsequently demand the Carter-Reagan defense buildup, begun in 1979.[9] Viewed in retrospect, public views on increasing or decreasing defense spending seem rather well correlated with the rise and fall of the efficacy of détente policies. Although détente ultimately failed, it did lower geopolitical tensions at the same time that the public was saying it was not necessary to increase defense spending. Huntington acknowledged that his threat variable declined coincident with declining force levels. He did not, however, conclude (as I do) that this provided a more compelling explanation for the force level declines than liberal antimilitarism (Goodpaster and Huntington 1977, p. 13). As Russett later argued, the changes in mass attitudes fit a rational-actor story of reasonable responses to changes in external events more closely than they fit a Huntingtonian account of an irresponsible liberal ideology hamstringing U.S. national security (Russett 1990, pp. 87–118).

More to the point, viewed in context with the other polling information about public respect for the military, cited above, attitudes about the need for increases or decreases in the defense budget are not reliable indicators of an underlying liberal hostility toward the military. To be sure, attitudes about the desirability of increases in defense spending are part of Huntington's equation for adequate national defense, but after several decades of support that resulted in a large national military establishment, it is not necessarily "antimilitary" to then support lower defense spending.[10] Huntington's real concern was whether a liberal society would support *enough* defense spending to prevail in the Cold War. Clearly, in retrospect, it did.

Evidence that American society supported enough military spending, however, is not evidence that Huntington's prescriptions were followed. Recall that Huntington viewed liberalism's views on national security as derivative of and nonseparable from liberalism's overall ideology. To confirm Huntington's theory, we would also need to see an accompanying shift to conservative values more generally. On the contrary, the evidence shows that American society as a whole almost certainly became even more individualistic and more antistatist than it was when Huntington warned of the dangers of liberalism in 1957.[11] The Cold War coincided with the flowering of the civil rights movement, the expansion of the New Deal social welfare system, and a dramatic enlargement in court-protected individual rights, all extraordinary extensions of classical liberalism's reach in American society.

While societal institutions as a whole became more liberal, the mass public's embrace of liberalism was more uneven, but in any case did not vary in a way consistent with Huntington's prescription for, and subsequent coding of, the Cold War. For starters, McCloskey and Zaller found a general trend toward greater tolerance, a key value in liberalism, in their evaluation of polling from the 1950s to the late 1970s. They also found enduring strong support for individualism, a key component of Huntington's definition of liberalism (McCloskey and Zaller 1984, pp. 41–42, 270–273). Mayer showed that American mass public opinion remained relatively stable in terms of the liberal-conservative dimension from 1960 to 1965; on some issues, notably racial equality and birth control, the public became more liberal, while on issues such as gun ownership or regulation the public became more conservative. From 1966 to 1973, however, Mayer found that the American public became considerably more liberal across a wide spectrum of issues. The mood swung back in a conservative direction between 1974 and 1980, although even then the public continued to become more liberal on issues dealing with racial equality and the role and status of women. Finally, Mayer documented a swing in the liberal direction between 1981 and 1988, a time when, by output measures at least, the United States almost certainly met Huntington's "requisite security" threshold (Mayer 1992, pp. 111–134).

Stimson traced a slightly different pattern in how liberal the public "mood" was over time. Relying more heavily on economic indicators of liberalism, specifically the role of government in the economy, Stimson identified five political eras: rising liberalism from 1956 to 1963, a dramatic swing to conservatism from 1963 to 1966, an equally dramatic swing back toward

liberalism from 1966 to 1972, a long and decisive move toward a conservative peak in 1980, and from 1980 to 1989 (when Stimson's data end), a
steady trend toward liberalism (Stimson 1991, pp. 62–65). Mayer's coding
fits somewhat better Huntington's 1977 reconsideration of his theory, and
perhaps the poor match with Stimson's data derives in part from Stimson's
narrow definition of liberalism in New Deal terms.

Both Mayer and Stimson, however, found a strong and relatively enduring embrace of liberalism throughout the Cold War. This finding is consistent with Huntington's 1957 warnings about American society but not with
his 1977 review of the evidence. Huntington is left in the curious position of
claiming that the high-water mark for the conservative values he prescribed
as necessary to avert a crisis in American civil-military relations preceded his
call for it.[12] And Huntington must also explain away the fact that for most of
the time—during the 1960s and 1970s—adequate defenses were sustained
despite a stubbornly ascendant liberal ideology.

Since Huntington's theory concerns the separate ideological profiles of civilian and military actors, he must also find an attitude convergence, with
civilians moving toward the military. The existence of a convergence should
be discernible in opinion polling of the civilian and military elite.[13] Huntington claimed that elite attitudes more or less tracked with the mass public,
although at each stage the elites would be more liberal than the general public. Hence, following the trends Huntington described in his 1977 retrospective, he must have seen civil and military elite opinion as divergent in the
immediate post–World War II era, converging in the late 1950s and mid-
1960s, diverging in the late 1960s and early 1970s, and then beginning to
converge in the mid-1970s.

Unfortunately, we do not have elite opinion polls covering both civilian
and military attitudes for the entire Cold War period. What data we do have
are ambiguous. Survey results generally support the existence of distinctly
military and civilian viewpoints (Bachman, Blair, and Segal 1977; Bachman,
Sigelman, and Diamond 1987). One suggestive study comparing the foreign
policy viewpoints of veterans and nonveterans in 1973 concluded that the
content of attitudes was quite convergent but the *organization* of foreign
policy beliefs in fact diverged somewhat. For instance, while veterans and
nonveterans roughly agreed on what the military's role in society ought to
be, veterans linked that role to an underlying rationale for the application of
force in concrete situations, whereas nonveterans viewed the military in a
more abstract manner (Kirkpatrick and Regens 1978, p. 44). More impres-

sionistic studies suggested a dramatic rise in elite hostility to the military in the late 1960s and early 1970s.[14] Arthur Hadley saw a "Great Divorce" between the civilian and military elites, suggesting that the gap remained large throughout the 1960s: a "less-than-amicable separation of the military from the financial, business, political, and intellectual elites of this country, particularly from the last two" (Hadley 1986, p. 22). On the other hand, Morris Janowitz, writing in 1960, saw a convergence between the civilian and military spheres in the years following World War II. However, in his prologue to the 1971 second edition of *The Professional Soldier*, Janowitz argued that the convergence peaked sometime in the 1950s and the spheres diverged thereafter (Janowitz 1971, pp. x–xviii). Janowitz's perceived convergence was only partly concerned with elite opinion and had more to do with overlapping roles and functions—an arena that is more relevant to Huntington's identification of the proper method of control, on which more below.

A convergence might be found in the ebb and flow of elite antimilitarism, but the polling data are contaminated by a problem affecting mass opinion: opposition to an increase in defense spending does not really constitute antimilitarism. A better measure would be found in systematic elite polling on a wide variety of public policy issues. While no such database exists covering the entire period, there is one major poll comparing military and business elite opinion in 1973 (Russett and Hanson 1975). Moreover, systematic polling of the civilian and military elite began in 1976 and continued to be conducted every four years thereafter (Holsti 1996, pp. 83–85, 100). The 1973 and 1976 data permit a test of the closeness of civilian and military attitudes on a wide range of national security questions. The data support the idea that civil and military elites agree on some things but disagree on many other important issues. The 1973 and 1976 data are not a perfect test of Huntington's 1957 theory and his 1977 reevaluation. Indeed, since Huntington claimed in 1977 that a revival of liberalism in the early 1970s augured a return of the crisis conditions he warned about in the mid-1950s, Huntington would expect to see some gaps between the civilian and military responses in the 1973 and 1976 elite surveys; however, since he also claimed a revival of conservative values following 1973, the gaps should not be very large.

With no pre-1973 polling data available for comparisons, and with some fuzziness in how large a gap Huntington's theory and coding of the Cold War should allow, the data cannot by themselves settle the question of whether Huntington's prescriptions were followed. For instance, these findings do not dispose of the possibility that the gap in opinion was even greater in the late 1940s and, therefore, that some convergence over the Cold War occurred. Nevertheless, the data strongly suggest that civilian and military preferences remained distinct. In other words, the data seem to indicate that Huntington's 1957 description of the distribution of preferences remained more accurate than his 1977 description. Moreover, since the data continue through to the present, it is possible to plot an extension of Huntington's argument into the late Cold War period. Did the higher levels of security provided in the late Cold War correspond with a convergence of civil-military opinion, as Huntington's theory expected?

In brief, the 1973 polling data collected by Bruce Russett and Elizabeth Hanson do not support Huntington but do support the idea that civilian and military preferences remained divergent, especially on foreign policy matters.[15] On matters of domestic policy, Russett and Hanson found that military elites were more conservative than civilian elites in general, although the business subsector of civilian elites was somewhat closer to the military (Russett and Hanson 1975, pp. 74–76). Russett and Hanson also found that military elites were more conservative and hawkish than civilian elites on a variety of foreign policy issues, even when the civilian sample was restricted to business leaders.[16] Along some dimensions, the gap matched the ideal-type descriptions of the civilian and military mind outlined in *Soldier and the State*.[17] More military respondents than business respondents saw war as likely; more military respondents than business respondents saw ground combat as effective and were willing to contemplate its use in hypothetical situations; more business respondents saw trade as beneficial; more military respondents than business elites thought defense cuts were deleterious (pp. 77, 80–81). Interestingly, Russett and Hanson concluded that the business elites were more "burned" by Vietnam than were the military respondents, with a far higher percentage withdrawing their initial support for the war as events progressed and a higher percentage adopting a "never again" lesson from the war (pp. 87–96).

Russett and Hanson supplemented their opinion survey with a content analysis of editorials and articles from the military and business press. They found that the business press was hawkish but "markedly less so than [was] the military press"; the frequency of approval for any kind of intervention was 62 percent in the business press and 81 percent in the military press, and the frequency of approval for use of combat troops was 56 percent in the business press and 73 percent in the military press (Russett and Hanson 1975, pp. 186–190).

The civil-military divergence also appears in an extensive 1976 elite poll conducted by Ole Holsti and James Rosenau.[18] In terms of ideological and political self-identification, military respondents were almost twice as likely as civilians to self-identify as "somewhat conservative" and three times as likely as civilians to identify as "very conservative." As one would expect, the mirror opposite divergence arose in response to self-identification as "very liberal" or "somewhat liberal"; civilians were nearly five times more likely than the military to self-identify as very liberal and more than twice as likely to identify as somewhat liberal. Likewise, those in the military were more likely than civilians to self-identify as Republican, although the modal military response was independent, reflecting the lingering effects of the military tradition of maintaining a nominally nonpartisan stance. Although the 1976 survey asked only two domestic policy questions, the survey responses corresponded roughly to the profile that emerged from self-identification questions. Military officers were less likely than civilians to give the "liberal" response to the question of whether racial integration was moving fast enough. Likewise, military officers were far more likely to favor the "conservative" goal of fighting inflation rather than the "liberal" goal of fighting unemployment or giving equal emphasis to both, while civilians were more evenly distributed across the three options.

The attitude divergence is paralleled by dissimilar responses to substantive policy questions.[19] For instance, the poll documented a statistically significant gap between civilian and military attitudes on the proper goals in the Vietnam War: asked about their opinion early on during U.S. involvement, 79 percent of those in the military claimed they favored victory rather than withdrawal, compared with only 43 percent of civilians; as to their opinion later in the conflict, 44 percent of the military respondents claimed to still favor victory while only 16 percent of the civilians did so. The poll likewise documented differences in attitudes toward the way force should be used. For instance, virtually all of the military respondents (95 percent) agreed somewhat or strongly with the statement that "necessary force should be applied in a short period of time rather than through a policy of graduated escalation," compared with only three-quarters of civilians; similarly, 68 percent of those in the military agreed somewhat or strongly with the statement that "rather than simply countering our opponent's thrusts, it is necessary to strike at the heart of the opponent's power," while only 40 percent of civilians agreed with such a view. Perhaps more strikingly, a noticeable majority of military respondents but less than a third of civilian respondents agreed somewhat or strongly that "when force is used, military rather than political goals should determine its application."

The gap is particularly pronounced on issues that will prove especially salient in the agency model of civil-military relations developed in subsequent chapters. Fully four-fifths of military respondents, compared with less than two-fifths of civilians, disagreed strongly or somewhat with the statement that "the conduct of American foreign affairs relies excessively on military advice"; a surprising one-third of civilians claimed to have "no opinion" on the question. Likewise, almost four in five military respondents, versus fewer than one in three civilian respondents, cited "insufficient attention was paid to advice from the military" as a very or moderately important factor in explaining the U.S. failure in Vietnam. The military respondents were far less willing than civilians to agree that "the press is more likely than the government to report the truth about the conduct of foreign policy"; 41 percent of those in the military agreed somewhat or strongly with that statement, while fully 64 percent of civilians did.

On some issues where traditional civil-military relations theory might expect to see divergence of opinion, such a gap did not appear or was not as great as might be expected. For instance, roughly the same percentage of military and civilian respondents agreed somewhat or strongly that the efficiency of military power was declining. Likewise, while those in the military were considerably more likely than civilians to agree strongly with the validity of the "domino theory," a roughly equivalent percentage of military and civilian respondents agreed somewhat. There was comparatively little difference between military and civilian attitudes on whether the democratic process placed serious restrictions on the ability of the United States to wield power effectively, a question that loomed large in Huntington's idealized antithesis of the conservative military versus the liberal civilian approach to military affairs (Huntington 1957, pp. 70, and 148–157).

The civil-military divergence found in 1976 persisted, with some flux, through the end of the Cold War. Appendix 2.1 at the end of this chapter details the findings from the 1976, 1980, 1984, and 1988 Foreign Policy Leadership Project surveys on key questions of interest, and Appendix 2.2 represents the civil-military gap graphically. I will discuss only a few items here.[20]

Table 2.1   Ideological self-identification, 1976–1988

Ideology	1976	1980	1984	1988
% Very liberal				
Military	2	0	1	0
Civilian	12	7	8	9
% Somewhat liberal				
Military	14	4	7	4
Civilian	30	27	28	29
% Moderate				
Military	23	24	17	20
Civilian	28	27	29	27
% Somewhat conservative				
Military	49	58	59	60
Civilian	26	31	29	27
% Very conservative				
Military	12	14	17	16
Civilian	4	7	6	8

Source: Data from Holsti 1997.
Note: Percentages may not sum to 100 due to rounding.

In general, the results support the idea that the gap in civilian and military preferences more or less endured throughout the Cold War. As Tables 2.1 and 2.2 show, the basic conservative-liberal gap persisted and even intensified through to the end of the Cold War.

In terms of ideological orientation, the twelve years from 1976 to 1988 show a sharp increase in the number of military respondents who self-identified as "somewhat conservative," while those who considered themselves "very liberal" and "somewhat liberal" all but disappear. At the same time, the civilian elite in the population grew only slightly more conservative and less liberal. The trend is even more marked in terms of partisan identification. The military became a stout partisan Republican bastion, thinning dramatically the ranks of those identified as "independent" and also reducing somewhat the numbers identified as Democrat. Again, the surveys show a much smaller movement away from "independent" to "Republican" for civilian respondents. The gap that appears in self-identification questions also shows up in attitudes to policy questions. The modal response for civilians is strictly liberal (liberal on both social *and* economic issues). At the same time,

Table 2.2   Party self-identification, 1976–1988

Party	1976	1980	1984	1988
% Republican				
Military	33	46	53	59
Civilian	25	27	30	29
% Democrat				
Military	12	10	12	9
Civilian	42	37	40	41
% Independent				
Military	46	40	29	27
Civilian	31	28	27	28
% Other & None				
Military	9	4	6	5
Civilian	0	1	3	3

Source: Data from Holsti 1997.

Note: Percentages may not sum to 100 due to rounding.

the modal response for military respondents is strictly conservative. Of the remaining two categories, "populist" (conservative on social issues but liberal on economic issues) and "libertarian" (liberal on social issues but conservative on economic issues), both civilians and the military were more likely to be populist than libertarian.

On substantive foreign and defense policy issues, the data presented in Appendixes 2.1 and 2.2 show the persistence of a gap, although there were interesting movements in certain military attitudes. The military embrace of force "applied in a short period rather than through a policy of graduated escalation" relaxed slightly from 1976 to 1988, whereas civilian attitudes remained essentially constant. Military distrust of the press intensified during the 1980s; the percentage agreeing with the statement that the "press is more likely than the government to report the truth about the conduct of foreign policy" was at an all-time high in 1976 (41 percent) and dropped in subsequent Cold War polls, to 35 percent, 16 percent, and 16 percent. Likewise, military fear that the American people lacked sufficient patience for successful foreign policy intensified dramatically; only 39 percent agreed strongly with this pessimistic view in 1975, whereas 60 percent did in 1984. At the same time, the military became more willing to consider "improving the standard of living in less-developed countries" a very important goal, while "maintaining a balance of power among nations" declined in importance for to military respondents.

Some of the "lessons of Vietnam" hardened over time: military elites were increasingly willing to blame American failure on domestic dissidents, or on reporting by the mass media, which turned the American public against the war; military attitudes about the blame to be allocated to Congress, however, were slightly more forgiving, going from 65 percent to 54 percent and back to 68 percent in the three polls from 1976 to 1984. Interestingly, military respondents were slightly more willing in 1976 than in 1984 to blame the Vietnam outcome on "insufficient attention" paid to "advice from the military"; attitudes about the importance of this factor spiked in 1980 with fully 83 percent citing it as important.

Perhaps the most anomalous movement concerned responses to the statement, "When force is used, military rather than political goals should determine its application." The 1976 poll showed 59 percent of the military agreeing, compared with only 30 percent of civilians. Curiously, in 1980 the percentage of military elites agreeing somewhat or strongly with this statement dropped precipitously to 33 percent, while the percentage of civilian elites agreeing increased slightly to 31 percent; at the same time, the percentage of military disagreeing strongly jumped sharply from 14 percent to 45 percent. In 1984, the responses moved back somewhat closer toward levels set in 1976: 38 percent of military elites agreed, compared with 30 percent of civilians elites. By 1988, attitudes had so shifted that only 18 percent of military respondents agreed, while again 30 percent of civilians agreed. In other words, by the end of the Cold War the military had become even less supportive than civilians of the idea that military rather than political goals should determine the application of force. This surprising movement, however, may simply reflect a growing sensitivity to an ambiguity inherent in the question's wording rather than a substantive change in attitudes. If the statement is taken to be asking whether military considerations should dominate *tactical* questions about the application of force, then the shift in military opinion is striking, for one would expect the military to always favor military considerations. The more immediate the memory of the Vietnam War and the famous political restrictions on bombing targets, the more likely military respondents would be to interpret the question thus.[21] The statement can, however, be taken as asking the standard Clausewitzean question of whether military operations should have clear political strategic objectives. In 1988, hard on the heels of the so-called Weinberger doctrine, which enshrined this principal as a criterion for the use of force, this latter interpretation may have been more salient, in which case the military response is not so surprising.[22]

Did Civilian Control Play Out as Huntington Predicted?

In short, the extensive opinion polling data show that while there was movement in the gap between civilian and military preferences, the movement was not consistent with a Huntingtonian explanation for the Cold War outcome. The divergence in civilian and military preferences, which Huntington identified as troubling in 1957, endured throughout the Cold War, thus casting doubt on Huntington's later claim that his prescription for a convergence had been adopted.

Tellingly, the record is equally mixed on whether American society adopted the form of objective control identified as necessary by Huntington.[23] The choice of control measures is a crucial intermediate step in Huntington's causal chain, but it played a far more prominent role in his 1957 explication of the theory than it did in the 1977 evaluation. Without using the terms, and without discussing the apparent contradiction, Huntington concluded in 1977 that institutional indicators for objective control varied inversely with the ideological determinants.[24] The institutional indicator for objective control was an absence of fusionism; the absence would be marked by a low level of congruence between civilian and military society, measured as "the extent of their similarity or difference in terms of the personnel, function, structure and other salient characteristics" (Goodpaster and Huntington 1977, p. 22). As before, the ideological determinants referred to the nature of the prevailing ideology of civilian society, whether liberal or conservative. Huntington concluded that the ideological variables were favorable in the 1950s and early 1960s, became unfavorable in the late 1960s and early 1970s, and then became favorable again in the mid-1970s. According to Huntington, however, the institutional indicators varied in an asynchronous way: there was an unhealthy overlap in functions in the late 1950s and 1960s but the traditional (Huntingtonian) division of labor was reaffirmed in the 1970s (Goodpaster and Huntington 1977, p. 24). This was at odds, moreover, with his 1957 observation that fusionism was waning in the American civil-military system (Huntington 1957, p. 459).

Huntington's 1977 treatment of the overlap of functions did, however, match Janowitz's arguments about civil-military convergence. Janowitz saw the convergence most of all in the civilianization of the military, in which the functional specialty of the military, the management of violence, lost its distinctiveness and the military increasingly adopted organizational and managerial tools from the civilian world of business and commerce. The convergence was also evident in the militarization of civilian society occasioned by the socialization of risk and especially the spread of the mass army via the draft institutions into civilian social structures (Janowitz 1971, pp. x–xviii). Janowitz laid greater stress on the movement of the military toward the civilian, but Huntington's theory demanded, and his evaluation of Cold War experience apparently confirmed, a movement of the civilian toward the military.

Other contemporaneous observers coded the period differently, but again not in a way that would preserve Huntington's explanation of the period. One observer wrote in 1973 with regret, "objective control has now lost any relevance it might once have had."[25] Another study showed a steady increase in the politicization of the professional education of military officers (Abercrombie and Alcala 1973). Certainly in critical issue areas like nuclear command and control, civilians showed a much greater willingness to assert control, "meddle" in the details, and otherwise violate the tenets of Huntingtonian objective control (Feaver 1992).

The extent to which the conditions of objective control were met will be dealt with in further detail in Chapter 5, where I argue that civilians did, in fact, monitor the military more intrusively during the Cold War than Huntington's ideal allowed. The difficulty of measuring objective control precisely—a task that Huntington never took up when he introduced the concept—probably precludes a judgment that would be beyond debate. Nevertheless, according to many of the indicators Huntington cited as critical, civilians did not adopt the objective control mechanism he claimed was the crucial causal mechanism between the explanatory variable of ideology and the dependent variable of adequate national security.

Conclusion

In sum, the evidence is not compelling that the United States prevailed in the Cold War because of a rejection of traditional American liberal values in favor of an embrace of the military's conservative ethic, which then allowed for objective control. Although Huntington claimed this happened in his 1977 reconsideration of *The Soldier and the State*, he did not evaluate enough of his model to prove the case. If one focuses on the beginning and intermediate stages in Huntington's causal model rather than on the later output variables, the match between what happened and what Huntington's theory requires is not very good. Civilian society did not become more conservative and civilians did not adopt objective control measures. The lack of fit strongly suggests that Huntington's theory does not adequately capture American civil-military relations. Another theory is needed.

APPENDIX 2.1: Data on Civil-Military Opinion Gaps during the Late Cold War

Table 2.3 summarizes survey data comparing civilian and military elite attitudes from 1976 to 1992. All data are from the Foreign Policy Leadership Project, as described in Holsti 1996. I am grateful to Ole Holsti for making the raw data available for secondary analyses.

Note that in 1984 the possible answers for three questions were shifted from "not important," "somewhat important," "very important" to "not at all important," "slightly important," "somewhat important." Answers for these three questions in 1984 are shown in Table 2.4.

"Intensity" is a simple measure of the variance of the sample across responses for a particular question and gives some sense of how intensely respondents felt about the question. The number summarizes whether most respondents tended toward the middle categories (agreeing or disagreeing only somewhat) or toward the extreme values (agreeing or disagreeing strongly) for a particular question. The formula is:

$$\frac{(\text{no. strongly agree} + \text{no. strongly disagree})}{(\text{no. agree somewhat} + \text{no. with no opinion} + \text{no. disagree somewhat})}$$

Thus, the higher the number on the intensity index, the more respondents were giving the extreme (agree or disagree strongly) response relative to the moderate response. Where there is no "no opinion" option for the response, the formula simply drops it, leaving only the agree somewhat and disagree somewhat counts in the denominator.

Table 2.3 Military/civilian elite survey data, 1976–1992

Question	Response	1976		1980		1984		1988		1992	
		Mil	Civ	Mil	Civ	Mil	Civ	Mil	Civ	Mil	Civ
Whether or not to pursue complete military victory in Vietnam—when the war first became an issue (0 = favor withdrawal; 1 = between; 2 = favor victory)	% Favor victory	79	43	72	52	76	43	79	41	81	45
	Intensity	5.3	2.3	6.8	3.0	5.2	2.3	5.02	2.4	6.2	2.5
Whether or not to pursue complete military victory in Vietnam—toward the end of U.S. involvement (0 = favor withdrawal; 1 = between; 2 = favor victory)	% Favor victory	44	16	39	24	48	18	48	19	30	18
	Intensity	2.6	4.2	1.7	4.2	2.6	4.2	2.0	4.3	2.57	4.0
U.S. policy on hostages in Iran (0 = immediately use force; 1 = favor bargaining; 2 = no bargain, no force; 3 = no bargain, use force; 4 = not sure)	% force (0 or 3)	—	—	64	34	—	—	—	—	—	—
	Intensity	—	—	.45	.208	—	—	—	—	—	—
If foreign interventions are undertaken, the necessary force should be applied in a short period of time rather than through a policy of graduated escalation[a]	% Agree (3 or 4)	94	73	95	76	96	75	91	75	93	77
	Intensity	2.7	.92	5.7	1.1	3.3	.82	2.0	.88	3.5	1.1
Rather than simply countering our opponent's thrusts, it is necessary to strike at the heart of the opponent's power[a]	% Agree (3 or 4)	68	40	70	43	68	35	66	40	91	57
	Intensity	.8	.8	.7	.7	.6	.7	.5	.7	1.4	.7

Table 2.3 (continued)

Question	Response	1976 Mil	1976 Civ	1980 Mil	1980 Civ	1984 Mil	1984 Civ	1988 Mil	1988 Civ	1992 Mil	1992 Civ
The efficiency of military power in foreign affairs is declining[a]	% Agree (3 or 4)	60	62	60	63	44	64	51	63	46	60
	Intensity	.45	.35	.72	.49	.41	.39	.33	.37	.47	.37
When force is used, military rather than political goals should determine its application[a]	% Agree (3 or 4)	59	30	33	31	38	30	18	29	29	34
	Intensity	.72	1.08	1.50	1.04	1.22	.92	1.63	.92	1.86	.96
The United States fighting "with a no-win approach" was a factor in its inability to achieve its goals in Vietnam[b]	% Very important	75	37	79	47	69	42	—	—	—	—
	Intensity	3.17	1.44	4.0	1.78	2.85	1.56	—	—	—	—
The "use of American air power was restricted" was a factor in its inability to achieve its goals in Vietnam[b]	% Very important	56	27	61	31	43	23	—	—	—	—
	Intensity	1.63	1.13	2.12	1.22	1.04	1.04	—	—	—	—
In retrospect, how would you assess American effort in Vietnam War? (0 = justified success; 1 = justified failure; 2 = unjustified success; 3 = unjustified failure; 4 = not sure)	% Failure (1 or 3)	—	—	91	90	—	—	—	—	—	—
	Intensity	—	—	.008	.001	—	—	—	—	—	—
Kindly estimate the impact on American prestige abroad of the Vietnam War (0 = helped prestige significantly; 1 = helped prestige some; 2 = not affected prestige; 3 = hurt prestige some; 4 = hurt prestige significantly)	% Harmful (3 or 4)	85	70	95	96	—	—	—	—	—	—
	Intensity	.85	.61	2.12	2.85	—	—	—	—	—	—

Table 2.3 (continued)

Question	Response	1976 Mil	1976 Civ	1980 Mil	1980 Civ	1984 Mil	1984 Civ	1988 Mil	1988 Civ	1992 Mil	1992 Civ
Recent events in Afghanistan are a direct result of a decline in U.S. influence in the aftermath of the Vietnam War[a]	% Agree (3 or 4)	—	—	67	53	—	—	—	—	—	—
	Intensity	—	—	.45	.61	—	—	—	—	—	—
Limited war cannot be conducted successfully because of constraints imposed by the American political system[a]	% Agree (3 or 4)	75	59	74	60	68	60	74	66	49	44
	Intensity	.67	.47	.50	.35	.43	.35	.45	.41	.41	.35
The consequences of Vietnam are likely to continue shaping U.S. foreign policy despite recent events in Iran and Afghanistan[a]	% Agree (3 or 4)	—	—	76	83	91	86	—	—	—	—
	Intensity	—	—	.32	.43	.27	.30	—	—	—	—
The memory of Vietnam will prevent the U.S. from using force even when vital American interests abroad are threatened[a]	% Agree (3 or 4)	43	46	45	43	67	55	—	—	—	—
	Intensity	.56	.45	.59	.45	.47	.43	—	—	—	—
The lessons of Vietnam have been superseded by events since the U.S. withdrawal from Southeast Asia in 1975[a]	% Agree (3 or 4)	—	—	51	54	38	51	—	—	—	—
	Intensity	—	—	.25	.30	.28	.23	—	—	—	—
"Pressures from domestic dissidents cast[ing] doubt on America's commitments" was a factor in its inability to achieve its goals in Vietnam[a]	% Agree (3 or 4)	75	68	82	71	84	68	—	—	—	—
	Intensity	.67	.72	.72	.79	1.13	.78	—	—	—	—

Table 2.3 (continued)

Question	Response	1976		1980		1984		1988		1992	
		Mil	Civ	Mil	Civ	Mil	Civ	Mil	Civ	Mil	Civ
"Reporting by the mass media turned the public against the war" was a factor in U.S. inability to achieve its goals in Vietnam[b]	% Important (3 or 4)	82	73	87	72	87	68	—	—	—	—
	Intensity	.82	.69	1.44	.69	2.1	.75	—	—	—	—
"Congressional involvement hampered the executive in the conduct of the war" was a factor in U.S. inability to achieve its goals in Vietnam[b]	% Important (3 or 4)	65	42	54	40	68	43	—	—	—	—
	Intensity	.75	.64	.67	.69	.54	.67	—	—	—	—
The conduct of American foreign affairs relies excessively on military advice[a]	% Disagree (0 or 1)	83	38	94	51	86	39	83	37	83	38
	Intensity	.75	.15	3.76	.54	1.44	.59	.92	.61	.72	.52
"Insufficient attention was paid to advice from the military" was a factor in U.S. inability to achieve its goals in Vietnam[b]	% Important (3 or 4)	78	32	83	44	72	37	—	—	—	—
	Intensity	.92	1.13	1.44	1.38	.79	1.13	—	—	—	—
There is considerable validity in the domino theory[a]	% Agree (3 or 4)	87	62	79	61	77	54	71	45	51	53
	Intensity	.75	.59	.47	.64	.47	.67	.23	.67	.27	.47
Effective foreign policy is impossible when the Executive and the Congress are unable to cooperate[a]	% Agree (3 or 4)	88	76	81	81	88	78	86	80	76	63
	Intensity	1.33	.69	1.00	.82	.89	.67	.85	.73	.49	.35

Table 2.3 (continued)

Question	Response	1976		1980		1984		1988		1992	
		Mil	Civ	Mil	Civ	Mil	Civ	Mil	Civ	Mil	Civ
The press is more likely than the government to report the truth about the conduct of foreign policy[a]	% Disagree (0 or 1)	55	33	59	41	83	42	84	35	75	36
	Intensity	.64	.75	.49	.56	1.50	.72	1.08	.82	.61	.67
The freedom to dissent at home inhibits the effective conduct of American foreign policy[a]	% Agree (3 or 4)	36	26	39	26	44	26	—	—	—	—
	Intensity	.69	1.38	.69	1.38	.92	1.56	—	—	—	—
The U.S. should maintain its military commitment to South Korea[a]	% Agree (3 or 4)	—	—	97	71	96	74	96	69	90	59
	Intensity	—	—	3.00	.64	2.70	.56	1.56	.47	.69	.33
Generally speaking, do you think that racial integration is going too fast, not fast enough, or about right? (0 = not fast enough; 1 = about right; 2 = too fast)	% Not fast enough	24	38	17	41	—	—	—	—	—	—
	Intensity	.64	1.08	.33	1.04	—	—	—	—	—	—
The American people lack the patience for foreign policy undertakings that offer little prospect of success in the short run[a]	% Agree (3 or 4)	84	74	90	74	97	80	—	—	—	—
	Intensity	.75	.54	.92	.52	1.56	.56	—	—	—	—
A nation will pay a heavy price if it honors alliance commitments only selectively[a]	% Agree (3 or 4)	91	76	93	80	93	81	—	—	—	—
	Intensity	1.38	.54	1.50	.79	1.00	.61	—	—	—	—

Table 2.3   (continued)

Question	Response	1976 Mil	1976 Civ	1980 Mil	1980 Civ	1984 Mil	1984 Civ	1988 Mil	1988 Civ	1992 Mil	1992 Civ
U.S. defense budget should be: (0 = increased while increasing taxes; 1 = increased while cutting domestic spending; 2 = kept same level; 3 = reduced while increasing domestic spending; 4 = reduced while cutting taxes)	% Increased (0 or 1)	—	—	94	57	17	6	—	—	—	—
	Intensity	—	—	.28	.32	.54	1.17	—	—	—	—
US defense budget should be reduced in order to increase the federal education budget[a]	% Agree (3 or 4)	—	—	—	—	—	—	13	65	14	79
	Intensity	—	—	—	—	—	—	1.3	.88	.44	.99
Helping to improve the standard of living in lesser developed countries[c,d]	% Very important	17	45	27	45	—	—	34	52	15	45
	Intensity	.49	1.08	.52	1.08	—	—	.86	1.22	.25	.96
Promoting and defending our own security[c]	% Very important	97	82	100	89	99	83	—	—	—	—
	Intensity	32	5.25	—	9.00	99	4.88	—	—	—	—
Maintaining a balance of power among nations[c,d]	% Very important	53	45	67	56	—	—	45	31	26	18
	Intensity	1.56	1.22	2.12	1.50	—	—	.92	.85	1.08	1.70
Promoting and defending human rights in other countries[c,d]	% Very important	—	—	8	29	—	—	16	32	14	40
	Intensity	—	—	.82	1.08	—	—	.33	.69	.30	.89

Table 2.3 (continued)

Question	Response	1976		1980		1984		1988		1992	
		Mil	Civ	Mil	Civ	Mil	Civ	Mil	Civ	Mil	Civ
Rate the job that the United States is now doing with respect to promoting and defending our own security (0 = poor; 1 = fair; 2 = pretty good; 3 = excellent)	% Favorable (2 or 3)	49	73	41	45	89	78	—	—	—	—
	Intensity	.41	.49	.41	.35	.56	.35	—	—	—	—
Intensity of party identification (0 = strong Republican; 1 = not very strong Republican; 2 = not very strong Democrat; 3 = strong Democrat; 4 = don't know)	% Strong Republican	48	20	32	20	—	—	—	—	—	—
	% Strong Democrat	5	35	2	26	—	—	—	—	—	—
Party affiliation (0 = Republican; 1 = Democrat; 2 = Independent; 3 = no preference; 4 = other)	% Republican	33	25	46	28	56	29	62	30	65	30
	% Democrat	12	42	10	40	13	43	9	42	6	43
(Independents closer to: 0 = Republican; 1 = neither; 2 = Democrat)	% Neither	33	30	15	24	—	—	—	—	—	—

a. This question used the following response option format: 0 = disagree strongly; 1 = disagree somewhat; 2 = no opinion; 3 = agree somewhat; 4 = agree strongly.

b. This question used the following response option format: 0 = not important; 1 = slightly important; 2 = not sure; 3 = moderately important; 4 = very important.

c. This question used the following response option format: 0 = not important; 1 = somewhat important; 2 = very important.

d. The response options changed for this question in 1984. The answers for 1984 only are presented in Table 2.4.

Table 2.4   Responses in 1984 to modified questions

Question	% responding "not at all important"		% responding "slightly important"		% responding "somewhat important"	
	Mil	Civ	Mil	Civ	Mil	Civ
Helping to improve the standard of living in less developed countries	5	4	44	51	51	45
Maintaining a balance of power among nations	5	45	44	37	51	18
Promoting and defending human rights in other countries	9	9	75	59	16	32

APPENDIX 2.2: Cold War Civil-Military Gaps Presented Graphically

Figures 2.2 through 2.15 illustrate the differences of opinion between civilian and military elites during the Cold War in several areas: political ideology and partisanship (Figures 2.2 and 2.3); social policy (Figures 2.4 and 2.5); foreign policy goals (Figures 2.6 through 2.8); and the use of force (Figures 2.9 through 2.15). The figures present in graphical form some of the data presented in Appendix 2.1. For question wording, the reader is encouraged to consult Table 2.3. While each question represents a slightly different dynamic, an overall pattern emerges consistent with the interpretation presented in the text: that the gap between civilians and the military remained and did *not* close as required by Huntington's interpretation of the Cold War experience.

Each figure represents the difference in means between the response of civilian elites and the response of military elites in the Foreign Policy Leadership Project's quadrennial surveys. The wider the shaded area, the wider the gap in preferences.

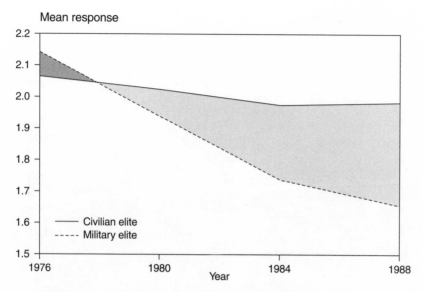

Figure 2.2 Cold War civil-military gap on party identification

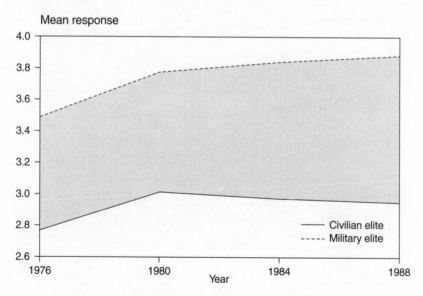

Figure 2.3 Cold War civil-military gap on political ideology

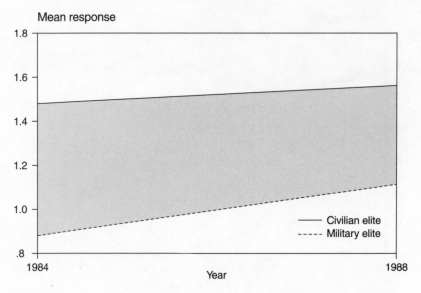

Figure 2.4 Cold War civil-military gap on racial integration by busing

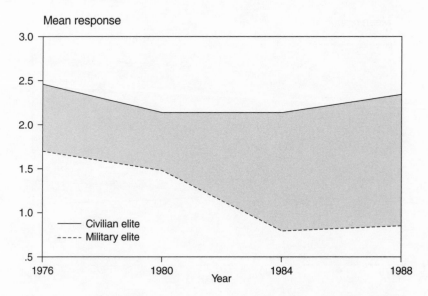

Figure 2.5 Cold War civil-military gap on truth of press over government

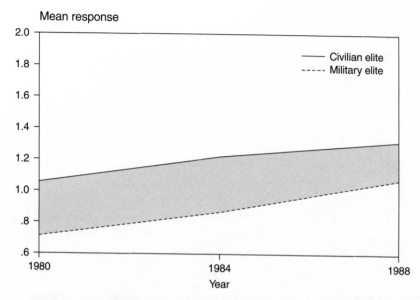

Figure 2.6 Cold War civil-military gap on importance of human rights

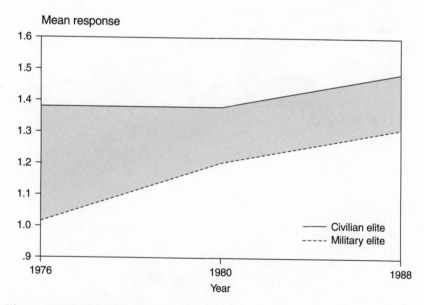

Figure 2.7 Cold War civil-military gap on improving standard of living of less developed countries

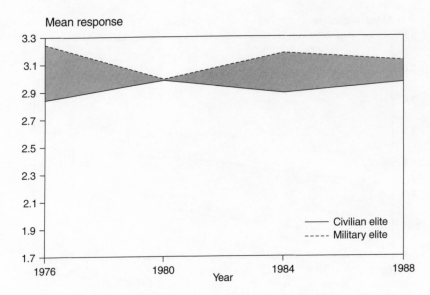

Figure 2.8 Cold War civil-military gap on congressional-executive disagreement

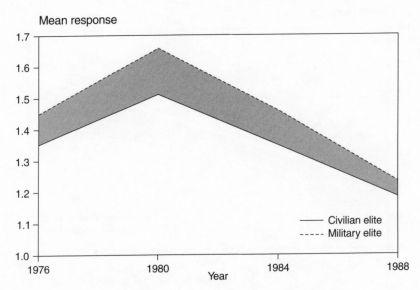

Figure 2.9 Cold War civil-military gap on importance of balance of power

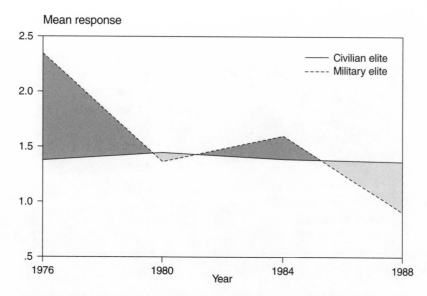

Figure 2.10 Cold War civil-military gap on military goals determining force

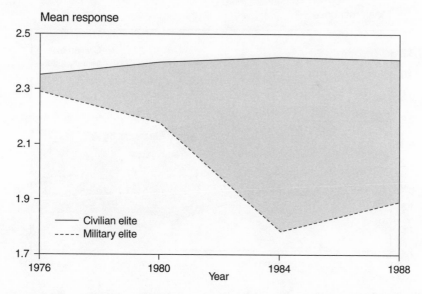

Figure 2.11 Cold War civil-military gap on efficiency of military power declining

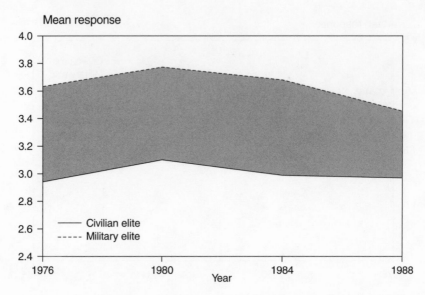

Figure 2.12   Cold War civil-military gap on intervention should be short

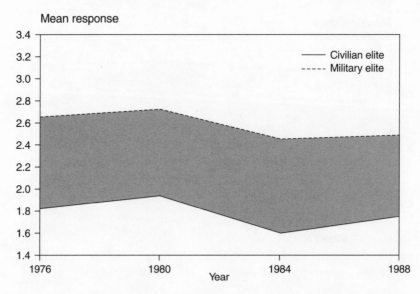

Figure 2.13   Cold War civil-military gap on striking at heart of opponent's power

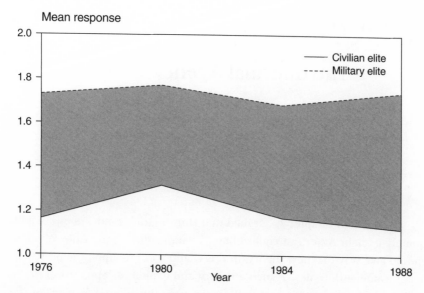

Figure 2.14 Cold War civil-military gap on pursuing victory in Vietnam (early stages)

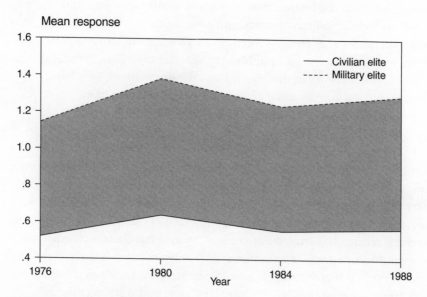

Figure 2.15 Cold War civil-military gap on pursuing victory in Vietnam (late stages)

CHAPTER 3

The Informal Agency Theory

In Chapter 2, I argued that Huntington's model does not adequately explain American civil-military relations during the Cold War and should give way to a new theory. In this chapter, I draw upon the principal-agent framework to derive such a theory and explore its application to the civil-military problematique. I will discuss here the general features of the principal-agent framework and apply them to civil-military relations—how civilian and military actors have divergent preferences and private information relevant to the relationship; how these conditions complicate the way civilians and the military interact, and advance the possibility that the military will not work as civilians intend; how civilians can mitigate these problems with monitoring and punishment mechanisms. The informal discussion of agency theory in this chapter lays the groundwork for Chapter 4, in which I build a simple formal game of civil-military interaction.

Civil-Military Relations as Principal-Agent Relations

Civilians invent the military, contracting with it to protect society from enemies,[1] but then civilians find it necessary to assure themselves that the military will behave as intended. Relations between civilians and the military are, in their most basic form, a strategic interaction carried out within a hierarchical setting. It is strategic interaction because the choices civilians make are contingent on their expectations of what the military is likely to do, and vice versa. It is hierarchical (at least in democracies) because civilians enjoy the privileged position; civilians have legitimate authority over the military, whatever their de facto ability to control the military may be.

These two features—strategic interaction and hierarchy—are the distinctive features of the principal-agent framework, an approach developed by economists to analyze problems of agency, where one person has delegated authority to someone else to act on his behalf (Alchian and Demsetz 1972, Niskanen 1971, Ross 1973, Bendor 1988). The employer (principal) would like to hire a diligent worker (agent), and, once hired, would like to be certain that the employee is doing what he is supposed to be doing (working) and not doing something else (shirking). The employee, of course, would like to be hired and so has an incentive to appear more diligent during the interview than he really is; this fact complicates the employer's efforts to pick the sort of employee who will want to work hard, a phenomenon referred to as the adverse selection problem. Once hired, moreover, the employee has an incentive to do as little work as he can get away with, all the while sending information back to the employer that suggests he is performing at an acceptable level; this fact complicates the employer's efforts to keep tabs on the employee and is called the moral hazard problem. The principal-agent approach, then, analyzes how the principal can shape the relationship so as to ensure that his employees are carrying out his wishes in the face of the adverse selection and moral hazard problems that attend any agency situation.

The most fruitful political applications of principal-agency have been in examinations of the way Congress or the president, or both, interact with the governmental bureaucracy.[2] The principal-agent framework has been used to explore whether the act of delegating policy implementation and, in some cases, policymaking power to bureaus and agencies is tantamount to an abdication of political control. I consider the basic concept of principal-agency as a "framework" rather than a "theory," since it is not a system of statements of cause and effect. But the framework can be adapted to yield a theory, which I do in this chapter and the next. To distinguish my application from the broader literature, I call my theory "agency theory."

The primary claim of the principal-agent literature is that delegation need not be an abdication of responsibility.[3] Debate continues as to whether Congress or the president is the most influential in exercising political control, but the general consensus is that political control of the bureaucracy is greater than the problems of delegation would indicate. Politicians have remained dominant in policymaking even in arenas where they have apparently delegated responsibility to strong bureaucracies, as in the case of environmental regulation. The reason, the principal-agent framework suggests, is that principals are able to exert control in nonobvious ways, for instance by building incentives for good behavior into the contract or by establishing third-party monitoring mechanisms that keep tabs on the agent for the principal. Even the absence of the more visible manifestations of oversight—intrusive audits and close monitoring of the agent's day-to-day behavior—does not mean the absence of control.

While most political science applications of the framework suggest the dominance of the principal (Congress) vis-à-vis the agent (bureaus), the conclusion that the principal solves all the problems of agency is not a necessary outcome of the model. Indeed, the framework lends itself to analyses of both the problems of agency and the possibilities for control.[4]

There are two prominent strands of analysis within this literature. One argues that agents work when monitored and shirk when not monitored, and so the solution to problems of agency lies in devising the optimal monitoring scheme, using intrusive and nonintrusive means (Kiewet and McCubbins 1991; McNollgast 1987, 1989, 1990a, and 1990b; McCubbins and Schwartz 1984). Another strand argues that monitoring is inherently inefficient and that optimal compliance comes from improving the quality of the agent and bringing the agent's preferences more closely in line with those of the principal (Brehm and Gates 1997).

My own application of the principal-agent framework seeks to blend elements of both strands, incorporating considerations of how agents are monitored and also the extent to which the preferences of principals and agents converge. I also add a further consideration that is surprisingly absent from existing principal-agent treatments: how agents behavior is a function of their expectation that they will be punished if their failure to work is discovered; traditional principal-agent treatments assume punishment is automatic but, as I argue below, that assumption must be relaxed when analyzing civil-military relations. My agency theory, then, draws on, modifies, and contributes back to the general principal-agent literature.

There have been relatively few applications of this framework to civil-military relations. Deborah Avant (1993 and 1994) was the first to use it, borrowing insights from the principal-agent framework to explain different propensities for innovation across British and American military organizations. Risa Brooks (2000) also uses the framework to compare how different patterns of civil-military relations produce different grand strategies. Amy Zegart (1999) uses it to explore the design of national security agencies at the start of the Cold War. And Sharon Weiner (1997) likewise uses it to explore the motivations behind the Goldwater-Nichols reforms. None of these analyses attempts to derive a general theory of civil-military relations, the project in view here, but they demonstrate the general utility of the approach; where appropriate, I note below how agency theory differs from these other analyses and why.[5]

In the civil-military context, the civilian principal contracts with the military agent to develop the ability to use force in defense of the civilian's interests.[6] Once the contract is established, the civilian principal seeks to ensure that the military agent does what civilians want while minimizing the dangers associated with a delegation of power.

The process might resemble the following stylized narrative.[7] Civilians recognize the need for instruments of violence, so they establish the military institution and contract with it the mission of using force on society's behalf. The contract is ritualized in the officer's oath of allegiance and reinscribed through a myriad of cultural symbols, such as the privileged place assigned to the military in celebrations of national holidays. The responsibility of the civilian does not end with this delegation of the protection mission.[8] Civilians must decide what ancillary mechanisms they will establish to make sure that the delegation is not abused. These mechanisms have associated costs, however, making the monitoring decision tricky. Civilians could delegate authority with one hand but then institute such restrictive controls with the other as to effectively, if unintentionally, undo the delegation; conversely, the monitoring could be so lax that the military agent is essentially free to act as it wishes. The optimal mix of monitoring mechanisms is the one that minimizes the incentives and opportunity for the agent to flout the principal's wishes, at the least cost to the principal and while preserving the efficiencies of specialization that come with delegation.

The military may share the civilians' desire not to lose on the battlefield, but it would also prefer not to be subject to interference (which it might deem "meddlesome") by civilian authorities. Moreover, as we shall see, it may not share identical preferences with the civilians on all policy questions and so may seek to manipulate the relationship so as to prevail in policy disputes. In short, the military has the ability and sometimes also the incentive to respond strategically to civilian delegation and control decisions—in the jargon of principal-agency, to shirk rather than to work. (I realize the terms *work* and *shirk* carry problematic connotations in the civil-military context. As I explain at length below, the terms as I use them have a specific meaning and I use them only because all other synonyms are equally if not more ill-suited.) But civilians retain the ability to punish shirking if they discover that it is going on. Thus, the military decision whether to work or shirk is shaped by how negatively those in the military view what civilians are asking them to do (how strongly, in other words, they would prefer to do it their way) and their expectation of the likelihood and severity of any punishment that might come their way should they shirk.

The process is iterative over time. As the external environment changes, for instance as threats to the state emerge or disappear, the civilians must revisit the problematique and make changes in the monitoring profile as needed. Of course, it is rather idealized to imagine civilians revisiting the civil-military problematique and deciding anew the question of delegation on every single security issue. In practice, the costs of reinventing the wheel probably make bureaucratic inertia (continuing the current pattern) attractive.[9] Civilians still have the option, however, of changing the relationship on any issue; that they often choose not to simply underscores how they are sensitive to costs, as the agency model captures.

In sum, civil-military relations is a game of strategic interaction. The "players" are civilian leaders and military agents.[10] Each makes "moves" based on its own preferences for outcomes and its expectations of how the other side is likely to act. The game is influenced by exogenous factors, for instance the intensity of the external threat facing the state made up of the players. The game is also influenced by uncertainties. The civilians cannot be sure that the military will do what they want; the military agents cannot be sure that the civilians will catch and punish them if they misbehave.

This rationalist approach to civil-military relations has its limitations. Some may find it off-putting to imagine the military choosing whether to obey or not based on crass calculations of self-interest. Indeed, most members of the military have a substantial moral commitment to what they do, and thus are motivated by more than resources or bureaucratic autonomy. The principal-agent approach does not rule out such nonmaterial incentives. On the contrary, the model establishes a rationalist baseline against which to measure the influence of these other considerations. It is, I would argue, only a point of departure, but a necessary one that has been undeveloped in the existing civil-military literature.

Divergent Preferences and the Work-Shirk Dimension

Like any agency relationship, the civilian delegation to the military could degrade into any number of suboptimal arrangements. The worst and most obvious are the central concerns of the civil-military problematique: collapse on the battlefield or military overthrow of the regime. Other less dramatic but nevertheless unsavory options are possible. The military could attempt to drag civilian leaders into an unwanted war, which, even if successful, would impose costs they might otherwise choose not to pay. The military could on a sustained basis extract higher resources from society than are really necessary. The military could successfully resist civilian dictates, perhaps by claiming that the action commanded is impossible (or too costly) or simply by failing to carry out the order. In this analysis, I focus attention on one set of conduct that I call shirking, when the military does not work as civilians direct.[11] This set is of particular interest for democratic civil-military relations because, by definition, civilian preferences must prevail over military preferences in a democracy.

The colloquial meanings of work and shirk are not particularly helpful, and the reason points to an important limitation of economic models in political analysis. The problem in civil-military relations is not a lazy military— or at least this is not the only nor the most important problem. While individual military officers might be lazy or shiftless, the general problem is more complex than simply keeping the military industrious.[12] In economic relationships, the principal and the agent have a different set of incentives regarding the basic work assigned to the agent: the principal wants lots of work for little pay, and the agent wants lots of pay for little work. In economic settings, it is not implausible to imagine that an agent would produce no work if he could get away with it. In the civil-military setting, this rarely makes sense. It is more reasonable to posit that both the civilian principals and the military agents want the same thing: security for the state. They can, however, disagree on how to provide that security, in general and especially in particular settings.

Areas of disagreement wax and wane—the preferences of civilians and the military can diverge and converge. As explained in greater detail below, one way civilians can shape military behavior is to seek a convergence in views by promoting military agents who hold preferences more similar to those of civilian principals. But there is a limit to how far convergence can go; perfect overlap is not feasible. For starters, military communities have strong identities that mark them as "different" from those of civilians, and this is deliberately cultivated and signified through uniforms, oaths of office, rituals, and so on; there is, in other words, some irreducible difference between military and civilian, and this will naturally extend to different perspectives. Moreover, the civil-military difference is compounded by the different role each plays, one as principal, the other as agent; there is a *de minimis* difference in perspective that attends agency, hiring someone else to do something for you. The empirical record bears out this fact: there are undoubtedly instances when civilian and military preferences greatly converged in the United States, but these instances have been limited in time and space and the preferences have not overlapped perfectly throughout the period under study. In sum, the agency problem of working and shirking arises because of civilian-military disagreement over means, if not ends, which itself arises from inherent differences in the roles played by civilians and the military.

Working is doing things the way civilians want, and shirking is doing things the way those in the military want. Shirking, in my use, has an explicit civil-military context. Shirking is part of a broader range of deviant behavior in which a soldier might engage—for instance, looting, going to sleep on duty, showing insubordination to an officer, mistreating prisoners of war, or failing to clean one's weapon (Bryant 1979). Of course, the civilian wants the military to obey all laws—not to rape, murder, steal, and so on. Such crimes as these rarely engage the civil-military relationship per se, although they can develop a civil-military connection, as the so-called "sex crimes" that preoccupied public attention in the spring of 1997 demonstrated.

Sometimes the behavior is readily categorized: a coup, General LaVelle's unauthorized bombing during the Vietnam War, and the My Lai massacre would all be clear cases in which civilian will was flouted. Other behavior, however, is far more difficult to pin down: is the military shirking when military estimates of what a given mission will cost are higher than civilian estimates? Or when the military-dominated review of service roles and missions returned the "finding" that there were no savings to be gained by consolidating the services, even though the civilians who asked for the review clearly thought there would be? (See Gordon 1992a, Schmitt 1993e.) The agency framework could consider these kinds of conduct to be shirking, even though they are obviously more ambiguous and less drastic than a coup.

Working, in the broadest sense of the word, means doing something to the principal's satisfaction. Shirking means not doing it to the principal's satisfaction. Since there is always the possibility of unforeseen circumstances beyond the control of either principal or agent that can stymie the agent's work, most principal-agent treatments narrow the meaning of work and shirk further: working involves a good faith effort to represent the principal's interests, or put another way, working is the ideal conduct that the agent would perform *if* the principal had full knowledge of what the agent could do and was in fact doing.

The issues at stake in civil-military relations, however, introduce a complexity that is missing from economistic applications of agency. Working, and hence its opposite, shirking, are multidimensional because civilian desiderata are themselves multidimensional. Recall the problematique discussed in the first chapter. Civilians want protection from external enemies *and* want to remain in political control over their destiny. The first goal may be called *functional* and the second may be termed *relational*. The agent may act in ways contrary to either the functional or the relational goal. Both inimical activities must be considered shirking.

Both the functional and the relational goal may be further disaggregated into tasks. The functional goal includes the following:

1. whether the military is doing what civilians asked it to do, to include instances when civilians have expressed a preference on both the "what" and the "how" of any given action;[13]
2. whether the military is working to the fullest extent of its duty to do what the civilians asked it to do;[14]
3. whether the military is competent (measured by some reasonableness standard) to do what civilians asked it to do.

The relational goal can be broken down into the following:

1. whether the civilian is the one who is making key policy decisions (i.e., no de facto or de jure coup) and whether those decisions are substantive rather than nominal;
2. whether the civilian is the one who decides which decisions civilians should make and which decisions can be left to the military;[15]
3. whether the military is avoiding any behavior that undermines civilian supremacy in the long run even if it is fulfilling civilian functional orders.

The functional component to shirking may be more obvious, but the relational component is at least as important and often more difficult to secure. For instance, the military may appear to obey civilian orders (it does everything the civilian asks it to), but that is only because the military is so powerful that the range of issues on which civilians can in fact ask it to do something is very constrained. If civilians are not able to set the boundaries for which decisions they choose to delegate to the military, then the relational goal is not met and the military is, de facto, shirking. As Welch (1976, p. 317) observed: "Perhaps the best measure of the strength and extent of civilian control of the military is governmental ability to alter the armed forces' responsibilities."

When the answers to all the functional and relational component questions are positive, then the military is working. When the answers are negative, then the military is shirking. Obviously, the responses can be mixed, yielding a gradation of working and shirking. At the extreme end of shirking is the traditional civil-military concern of a coup. At the extreme end of working is some ideal-type military that does everything the civilian has contracted with it to do, vigorously and without subversion.

The military's advisory role further complicates the concept of shirking in the civil-military context. Working does not imply that the military immediately and mutely executes every harebrained scheme that issues from the mouth of any civilian policymaker. Part of the military obligation is to advise civilians on the military implications of proposed courses of action. As Chapters 5, 6, and 7 will demonstrate, there is an exceedingly blurry line between advising against a course of action and resisting civilian efforts to pursue that course of action. Sometimes negative advice can rise to the level of shirking, especially if the advice is exaggerated. As one traditional treatment of civil-military relations put it, there is a difference between offering advice and "insisting that it is absolutely necessary to pursue a certain course of action if disaster is to be avoided"—where the latter might reach the level of shirking (Sapin and Snyder 1954, p. 55). Nevertheless, shirking is not synonymous with "persuading a civilian policymaker to change his mind." Thus, evaluating whether shirking has occurred is not as simple as discovering whether military advice was followed. Rather, it involves judgments about the integrity of the military advice itself as well as judgments about the conditions under which civilians changed their minds. Were military advisors exaggerating (or minimizing) the costs of a course of action so as to tie the hands of the policymaker? Did the policymaker abandon a course of action because military resistance was too strong, or because he was truly persuaded that it was unwise?

Just as civilian preferences are multidimensional, so too are the preferences of the military agent. A weakness in early applications of the principal-agent framework to political problems is that they overemphasized the perspective of the principal (Hamilton and Schroeder 1994, Moe 1987,

Spence no date). A simple-minded translation of the economic principal-agent relationship to the political realm misses an important aspect of the agent's motivations. Whereas economic agents may generally prefer shirking to working, political agents are likely to be motivated (at least in part) by a substantive interest in the policy itself. In short, there is a reason why an agent ends up working for the Department of Defense rather than the Department of Health and Human Services, and this has important implications for how the agent reacts to the principal (Brehm and Gates 1997). Specifically, the military agent is assumed to have three sets of preferences: over policy outcomes, over how his behavior is interpreted, and over how the relationship is monitored.

First, unlike an economic agent who might not care how many widgets he produces, the military agent cares about policy and has a general idea about what should be done.[16] The military agent would like to be told to pursue the policy he wants to pursue. While what the military agent wants will vary from situation to situation, the traditional civil-military relations literature has identified several standard features. The military agent is willing to risk life, but would prefer not to die needlessly (Huntington 1957, pp. 68–69).[17] The military agent would prefer to deal with threats from a position of advantage, controlling the tempo and the scope of the conflict. This translates into a general preference for offensive operations and even preventive operations, dealing with problems before they become unmanageable (Posen 1984, pp. 47–49; Sagan 1994, pp. 75–76). Moreover, the foregoing logic also suggests that the military agent would be more likely to inflate threats and inflate requirements for meeting those threats so there would be less chance of being taken by surprise (Allison 1971).

Related to policy preferences, but nevertheless distinct, is the second military preference, what might be called a general military preference for honor, or a desire for respect.[18] This is not to be confused with glory, or a desire for distinction, which connotes the militarism caricature. Rather, honor here captures the Aristotelian idea of getting credit for doing what is right, where right is acknowledged by others and defined according to some generalized conception of the good (*Nichomachean Ethics,* Book IV, No. 3). The desire for honor derives partly from the basic human desire for legitimacy—the desire to gain peer approval. It is worth noting that even the most heinous scoundrels in history sought to justify their actions, however lamely and self-servingly. Military men and women, like all men and women, partly seek the approbation of others, especially peers. Honor has always played a central role in military life.[19] Honor permeates the famous concept of small-group cohesion, the factor that makes human beings willing to risk their lives (Holmes 1985, pp. 290–315). In the civil-military relationship, the military preference for honor can be used to reinscribe the principle of civilian control; the military subordinates itself to civilians because, in a democracy, such subordination is recognized to be right and it would dishonorable to do otherwise (Janowitz 1971, 439–440). In democracies, civilian governments are presumed to be legitimate, and this general presumption is shared even by the military. Thus the preference for honor can work to mute the impulse to shirk for military agents, even when other factors (as discussed below) indicate they should. Traditional civil-military relations theory relies extensively on honor (also called the "ethic of subordination" and "professionalism") to explain civilian control. It can be incorporated in a principal-agent framework, but it is recognized as just one of the factors shaping the military's preferences.

The third basic military preference concerns the monitoring relationship. Regardless of what the military agent is asked to do, he would like to do it with the minimum of civilian interference and oversight. As in traditional organization theory, the military agent prizes autonomy—policy autonomy, the ability to decide what to do, and implementation autonomy, the ability to decide how to do it (Betts 1991, pp. 5–15; Posen 1984, pp. 52–54; Lebow 1987, pp. 76–79; Bouchard 1991, p. 30).

These three sets of preferences set up the possibility that the military might do what it wants instead of what the civilian wants—in other words, that it might shirk instead of work. If the military shirks, of course, it is evidence that the agency relationship has broken down, at least in that instance. It is important to note, however, that pure working does not necessarily mean that the outcomes of military action will please the civilian. This is because the functional goal itself, security, involves another actor not in the principal-agent relationship: the enemy. The functional goal of security can be broken down into tasks—develop a military capable of winning two medium-size regional conflicts nearly simultaneously, integrate women into combat roles, invade Haiti, and so on—but faithfully fulfilling those tasks may or may not provide ultimate security for the country. Indeed, some of the things the civilian wants done may in fact work contrary to the overall goal of providing security for the state. Moreover, in fulfilling the principal's functional directions, things can go wrong simply due to Murphy's Law or Clausewitzean "friction." Thus, working and shirking are not synonymous with winning and losing on the battlefield. Battlefield victory is a result of a two-sided interaction. One side can "work" and still lose if the other side has superior forces, or if the objective is ill-conceived. Likewise, one side can "shirk" and still win if the other side is even less competent, or if the task the civilian wanted done (the work) was in fact not appropriate for the security goal.

The security goal can even be met under suboptimal circumstances that would displease the civilian if he had perfect information. First, consider the case when the protection afforded by the military is costing more than it needs to cost. Here the civilian achieves the functional goal but overpays for it. A less costly military capability would suffice. Second, consider the case when the protection afforded by the military is sufficient but involves running undesirable risks. Here the civilian achieves the functional goal, but just barely and while skirting near disasters that a different policy mix might avoid more comfortably. Knowing how much is really enough, even with twenty-twenty hindsight, is so intractable as to make this line of inquiry less fruitful than focusing on other, more readily ascertainable instances of shirking. Even if the action is not displeasing to the civilian ex post, it still counts as shirking if it involves the military's taking a deliberate action that violates standing orders.[20]

The foregoing suggests that civilians and the military can share the goal of national security (and in the U.S. case, one can even stipulate this as largely true), but also that *civilians and the military are both imperfect judges of what is needed for national security.* The principal-agent problem arises when there is disagreement over what is needed or appropriate for national security, whether or not one side is "correct" about what is in fact needed.

In a democracy, civilians have the right to be wrong. Civilian political leaders have the right to ask for things in the national security realm that are ultimately not conducive to good national security. The military should advise against such policies, but the military should not prevent those policies from being implemented. While this view is a necessary and logical conclusion of the premises of democratic theory, it is nonetheless controversial. Many observers, especially military observers, may be more sympathetic to S. L. A. Marshall's view, as articulated in *Men against Fire:* "our Army should never be put under the necessity of humoring and yielding irretrievable ground to the inevitable minority of malcontents or of permitting governing principles to be influenced by voices from the lunatic fringe, even those which have been elected to Congress" (Marshall 1947, p. 165). Marshall's view may be appropriate if he is talking about *minority* positions within the civilian principal, but he misunderstands the military role if he advocates that the military ignore foolish "voices" that represent a governing civilian position. If the politicians are in fact wrong, then they are shirking in the deeper voter-as-ruler principal-agent relationship, and the voter-as-principal is obliged to punish the politician-as-agent by voting him or her out of office. It is arguable whether the military is in fact better able to judge the true national security needs of the polity; but even if true, in a democracy the military is not the one assigned to ensure that civilian politicians are not shirking.

This can be represented graphically as three points in a three-dimensional space, where each dimension represents a critical component of national security policy (for example, force structure, grand strategy, and operational plan). One point represents the policy mix that would produce true optimal security; this is what the civilian and the military ultimately want. Another point represents the civilian principal's desired policy mix, which is the civilian's best estimation of what is needed for security; this is what the civilian asks for. The third point represents the military agent's desired policy mix; this is what the military asks for. The work-shirk continuum concerns only the nearness of behavior to the civilian or military desired point, and does not directly address whether the output approximates theoretically optimal security.[21]

Even if the distances between the civilian, the military, and the true point are trivially small, however, the principal-agent problem still arises because of the relational imperative. Civilians still have to be calling the shots, and military behavior has to be consistent with civilian supremacy. Shirking can arise even if the military is doing what the civilians have asked for, and even if what the civilians have asked for will produce what the civilians want. Even under these happy conditions, it still matters whether the civilians are the ones who make key policy decisions (no de facto or de jure coup), whether the civilians are the ones who decide which choices civilians should make and which can be left to the military, and whether the military is behaving in a way that supports civilian supremacy in the long run. If the answers to any of those questions are negative, then the military is shirking, even though what it wants is not significantly different from what civilians want.

Shirking can even arise in advance of civilian directives, if the military acts in such a way as to tie the hands of its civilian leaders. Perhaps the most important example of this kind of shirking came in the context of the U.S. Army's response to its experience in Vietnam. Senior army leaders believed that one of the lessons of Vietnam was that the army should never be deployed without the full support of the American public.[22] Furthermore, the leadership believed that such support would come only if the civilian political leaders spent the political capital necessary to mobilize public opinion—and, finally, that civilian leaders would spend such political capital only if they were unable to deploy military forces any other way. In other words, the army believed that civilian leaders should not be given the opportunity to deploy combat troops on what appeared to be a "costless" mission; civilian leaders should commit to paying political costs, and those costs should be frontloaded. The army hardwired this lesson into its force structure, deliberately shifting to the reserve component key support functions, so that the army could not be deployed without mobilizing the reserves—precisely the politically costly move President Johnson had refused to take in the early phases of the Vietnam War. As one interviewer posed the question to a senior army general: "Was part of the thinking in integrating the reserves so deeply into the active force structure that we were making it very difficult, if not impossible, for the President to deploy any significant force without calling up the reserves?" The general replied, "That's it, with malice aforethought" (Sorley 1992, pp. 363–364). The issue is not whether the army was correct in interpreting the Vietnam War, nor even whether it is wise for the president to mobilize public support for a combat operation before committing U.S. troops to such an operation. The army may be correct on the substance, but the effort to tie the hands of the president constituted a usurpation of the civilian leadership's role in deciding when and how to use force.[23] Then Secretary of Defense Schlesinger claimed that the army was not being insubordinate, but contradicted his own assessment by observing that "the military sought to fix the incentives so that the civilians would act appropriately" (Sorley 1992, p. 364). This is, of course, precisely the principal's function in a classic principal-agent relationship, and it is certainly not the role of the military-agent.

An important exception is the case in which the civilian principal, like Odysseus, asks the military agent to tie his hands in some way so that the civilian can get what he knows he ultimately wants and not what he will *say* he wants under some limited circumstances. A classic example is the Base Realignment and Closure Commission (BRAC) established by the U.S. Congress to identify which military bases to close in the post–Cold War

drawdown. Congress knew that political considerations would make selecting bases impossible on a case-by-case basis, so it tied its own hands and delegated the selection authority to a separate commission. When the BRAC
posted the list of closures, the individual members could and did protest vigorously and seek desperate measures to undo the BRAC, even as Odysseus
tore at his chains, but in context received the outcome for which they had
contracted.

To sum up, shirking and working are multidimensional concepts, consist-
ing of both functional and relational components and reflecting the multidimensional and possibly divergent preferences of the civilian principal and
the military agent. The agent is said to work perfectly when it does what it
has contracted with the principal to do, how the principal has asked it to,
with due diligence and skill, and in such a way as to reinforce the principal's
superior role in making the decisions and drawing the lines of any delegation. The military agent is said to shirk when, whether through laziness, in-
solence, or preventable incompetence, it deviates from its agreement with
the civilians in order to pursue different preferences, for instance by not
doing what the civilians have requested, or not in the way the civilians
wanted, or in such a way as to undermine the ability of the civilians to make
future decisions.

In practical terms, military shirking in the U.S. context is rarely open insubordination and has never risen to the point of a coup. But shirking is possible even if the military never carries out a coup, and when it happens,
shirking by the U.S. military usually takes one of three forms: (1) efforts to
determine the outcome of a policy calculus by giving inflated estimates of
what a military operation would cost; (2) efforts to determine the outcome
of a policy calculus with "end runs," unauthorized public protest, leaks, or
appeals to other political actors; (3) efforts to undermine a policy through
bureaucratic foot-dragging and "slow rolling" so that the undesired policy
will never be implemented.

Information Asymmetries in Civil-Military Relations

Principal-agent relationships involve information asymmetries. Both sides
share common information; in the civil-military context, they know who
the domestic players are, the size of the defense budget, the general identity
and nature of their enemies. They also share a common history and political
memory. But each has private information that is discerned only dimly by

the other. The military agent's status as an expert on the management of violence confers significant informational advantages over civilians in areas like tactics and logistics. Of course, the extent to which the military agent's expertise exceeds that of the civilian principal, even in the arcana of operational art, varies with the backgrounds and résumés of the individuals involved; it is not uncommon for civilians on the staff of the Office of the Secretary of Defense to have more technical expertise than their military counterparts (Gibson and Snider 1997). But on average the military agent will have devoted more time (and more recently) to developing this technical expertise than will have his civilian political principal. Likewise, crucial aspects of military behavior and even military predilections may be unknown to civilians. For instance, the civilians cannot know for certain whether the military is inclined to shirk, nor can they know if the spirit of their orders is being carried out. Moreover, as the operation of the military moves closer to combat, civilians are at an even greater informational disadvantage. It is hard enough to monitor the activities of the military when it is bivouacked near the capital. When it is deployed on a distant battlefield in the fog of war, communications difficulties could render monitoring impossible for even the most attentive civilian leader.[24]

Likewise, some information is private to the principal. For instance, only the principal knows exactly how he judges various risks and how these judgments translate into preferences over outcomes. While the civilian principal may convey this information to the military agent in the form of orders, it is also possible that exogenous changes in nature—the outcome of military operations, the arrival of new threats and national challengers, and so on—will cause a shift in the preferences of the principal. The anticipated effect of these changes will certainly be hidden from the military agent, and may even be hidden from the principal himself. In other words, there is sufficient information hidden from the military agent to warrant fear of a "stab in the back" from civilian leaders; will civilian leaders abandon the military when things go sour, the quintessential fear that constitutes the "Vietnam syndrome" among senior military officers? In general, however, information asymmetries favor the military agent.

The special concern at the heart of the civil-military relationship—controlling the use of deadly force—introduces further peculiar twists into the standard principal-agent scenario. The first and most obvious distinctive feature is that the stakes are much higher. If an elected representative comes a cropper, the damage to the polity (even with the highest elected office) is bounded. Lousy political agents can commit many sins of omission and commission, but they are hard-pressed to bring down the republic. Failure to get the military agency problem right can result in one of two grave disasters: the military agent may turn on society and rob it of its political freedom, or the military agent may fail on the battlefield and leave the polity vulnerable to conquest by external enemies. In almost all cases, human lives will be lost in the process. Thus the cost of failure, the price of trial and error, borders on the prohibitive. Of course, the fate of the republic does not hang on every military issue and there are many mundane matters in which the stakes seem small. In general, however, the consequences of failure are profound and this will cast a shadow over the actors' decisionmaking.

It is also plausible that the basic information asymmetry problem inherent in any principal-agent relationship is particularly acute in the civil-military relationship. Traditional theory emphasizes the unique expertise of the military officer: the management of violence. Certainly civilians can gain expertise on a wide variety of defense policy issues, but civilians, by definition, leave combat to the military, and combat is the distinctive mark of military expertise.[25] Like many other complex policy issues, questions about technical competence and specialized knowledge exacerbate the basic informational challenges facing civilian principals.

Another distinctive feature is that the military is perhaps the only profession that never really gets a chance to practice. To be sure, the military can train and rehearse, but the essence of combat—wielding force against a determined enemy—cannot be simulated reliably. The unreliability of performance indicators is a common problem in principal-agent relationships, but the military condition adds an additional layer of uncertainty. Neither side, neither civilian nor military, can be sure about the military's type, at least with respect to performance on the battlefield. In conventional analyses, the expert agent generally understands the consequences of his actions even if the political principal may not. The military expert can claim that his expertise narrows somewhat the uncertainty boundary, but he still will not know for certain whether he will fail catastrophically in battle (Rogers 1940, p. 283). The military agent *will* have private knowledge about his inclinations to shirk, and will certainly know whether his day-to-day activities track with the performance indicators established by the civilian principal—neither of which the principal will know with certainty—but neither the military nor the civilians will know for sure what all this means for the ultimate purpose of the military: the probability that the military can protect society when challenged in a war.[26]

The information problem is further exacerbated by the secrecy restrictions that accompany military actions. A common obstacle in principal-agent relationships is the tendency of the agent to withhold information that reflects unfavorably on the behavior of the agent. The information classification system vastly eases the task of an agent who wishes to keep inconvenient information from being disseminated. While in theory the civilian principal may be entitled to know everything, in practice the costs of that are great in any principal-agent relationship. Those costs become prohibitive when secrecy laws, with strict punishments for the release of classified information, reinforce the agent's natural tendencies. Secrecy laws enjoy legitimacy because they are thought to contribute to the general protection of society. By association, this confers at least a certain amount of legitimacy on military efforts to keep principal civilians in the dark. Moreover, since so many of the principal-agent control mechanisms are essentially efforts to open the agent's hidden behavior to public scrutiny and thereby to alert the principal to improper agency, they are much less appropriate in contexts where even the principal agrees that the agent's behavior *ought* to avoid general public scrutiny (Lindsay 1994a, p. 283). Without this mechanism, however, it becomes easier for the agent to abuse the system, as was evidenced by Oliver North's off-budget covert operations.

Still another distinctive feature is the problem of competence. In its original microeconomic formulation, the principal was assumed to be as expert as the agent in all matters; the agent is hired merely to ease the work burden on the principal. A senior manager in a business has presumably worked his way up, learning the ropes of the junior positions, and hires workers merely for the sake of efficiency. Political science applications have tended to emphasize the difference in expertise between the principal and the agent, where the former may not be technically competent to do the things asked of the agent. Democratic theory further blurs the issue with the notion of political competence discussed earlier—the agent is not competent to judge risks even if he has special, even unique, technical competence (Dahl 1985). The special case of civil-military relations adds one further wrinkle: the military agent is asked to put his life on the line to protect the civilian. By virtue of his willingness to sacrifice, the military agent may be thought of as possessing a special moral competence, balancing somewhat the political competence of the civilian principal. This belief in moral competence serves to muddy the lines of authority between civilian and military, particularly when the civilian is directing the military to put itself in harm's way. The de jure hierarchy may be unchanged, but the moral ambiguity of the relationship bolsters the hand of a military agent should he choose to resist civilian direction.

The relative moral competence of civilians and the military ebbs and flows both with the qualifications of idiosyncratic civilian leaders and with changes in the modal career paths of civilians. Thus, civilians like Dwight Eisenhower and Bob Dole, who served in the military, would bring a larger measure of moral competence than would civilians like Bill Clinton and Newt Gingrich, both of whom went to extraordinary lengths to avoid military service. One of the most intriguing trends in U.S. civil-military relations has been, first, the rise of military civilians during the Cold War—as civilian political leaders shared a military experience in World War II, Korea, Vietnam, or at least in peacetime service—and now the rise of purely civilian civilians (Bianco and Markham 2001, Gibson and Snider 1997, Feaver and Gelpi forthcoming).

In combination, these novel features have a profound effect on the principal-agent relationship. Because the stakes are so high, the civilians have an incentive to revisit and tinker with agreements and conditions they may have found acceptable before. Because the military cannot claim exclusive knowledge about at least one specific value at stake—the probability of success on the battlefield—the civilian has grounds to justify this meddling. Because of classification restrictions, the military has an extra advantage in withholding information, thereby frustrating civilian oversight and control. Because the military is prepared to do something that the civilian is not required to do, the military has a formidable moral arsenal with which to fight unwanted civilian interference. In short, the expectation is that this principal-agent relationship should be particularly characterized by distrust and friction, and any equilibria of delegation and control are unlikely to endure, giving way instead to new arrangements as costs and benefits shift.

Adverse Selection and Moral Hazard in Civil-Military Relations

The interaction of divergent preferences and informational asymmetries produces two problems: adverse selection and moral hazard. Adverse selection refers to the moment of hiring in the employer metaphor. Has the employer hired someone who is naturally a hard worker or has he been deceived by the interview and hired a lout? Just how closely aligned are the preferences of the agent and the principal? The adverse selection problem means, in the first instance, that the employer cannot know for certain about the true preferences and capabilities of the applicant. But adverse selection is more than mere uncertainty about the applicant. It also refers to the fact that the very act of hiring creates perverse incentives for the agent to misrepresent himself, which thereby increases the chances that the principal will hire a lout: it is hard to verify the true type, and the lout has a great incentive to appear even more attractive than a good worker.[27] Indeed, because the employer offers a wage that is pegged to attract someone with the statistically average set of qualifications needed for the job, the job will be especially attractive to louts, who will know that the offered wages are higher than their own true worth; considerably more diligent employees are likely to find any given job less appealing because they know that the average wage understates their true value. More generally, adverse selection can extend beyond the hiring phase to include all those situations in which the agent presents himself, or some proposal, to the principal for approval or decision. For instance, it means that because of their informational advantage over superiors, subordinates tend to propose policies that benefit their own interests rather than the interests of the superiors.

In a civil-military context, the adverse selection problem shows up in the accession of personnel into the military, in the promotion of individuals up the chain of command, and in the ongoing give and take of military policy. First, it is at least plausible that the peculiar mission of the military—to kill people and blow things up—attracts a special kind of person, one who may make the principal-agent relationship particularly problematic. It is reasonable to expect that the demanding mission would attract people with a sense of adventure, a tolerance for hardship, a commitment to order and discipline, and so on. It is possible, however, that these same qualities (or others correlated with them) accentuate the difference between civilians and the military and so lead the military to be especially distrustful of civilian leadership. One of the major concerns of traditional civil-military relations theory was precisely the great divergence of viewpoint between what Huntington called the liberal civilian ideology and the military mind (Huntington 1957, pp. 59–79). This does not mean that all military officers think alike. As we shall see, manipulating differences of opinion *within* the military is an im-

portant method of civilian control. Adverse selection could suggest that the
civilians are liable to pick either people who are poor warriors (perhaps because they pick people like themselves) or good warriors who are likely to
resent their authority. The decision to "hire" the military is revisited at regular intervals in decisions to promote or to fire certain individuals. Of course,
as personnel proceed through the ranks the uncertainty should ease somewhat, since civilians gain more and more information on which to base such
decisions.

Adverse selection also crops up in the uncertainty civilian leaders have in
evaluating proposals originating from military organizations. Is this budget
request necessary to accomplish the mission, or is it padded to serve the military organization's interests? Again, because the military has an information advantage it can advance artfully drawn proposals that appear to meet
civilian needs but in reality are tailored to its own interests. In the extreme,
adverse selection might lead civilians to adopt policies they think will increase the military's ability to protect society but that in fact will increase the
ability or even the propensity of the military to undermine society.

Moral hazard refers to the behavior of the employee once hired. Like adverse selection, moral hazard refers at a general level to the problem that
principals cannot completely observe the true behavior of the agent and so
cannot be certain whether the agent is working or shirking. It has an additional specialized meaning based on the perverse incentives in the agency
relationship.[28] Employees have an incentive to shirk rather than work; if
you can get paid for doing less, why do more? The principal, of course, tries
to minimize shirking because it is inefficient. The best way to minimize
moral hazard is to reward (or punish) the agent based on whether he is
working (or shirking). If the behavior of the agent is hard to monitor, however, how does the principal know whether the agent is really working or
shirking? In many principal-agent relationships the behavior of the agent is
hard to observe. In these cases, performance is usually measured by proxies
that substitute, with some loss of validity, for the true goal (in an academic
setting, however, number of publications substitutes for scholarly contribution to one's field). Once established, however, the workers have an incentive to optimize on the indicator rather than on the true behavior desired.
The gap between the indicator or rule and the desired behavior can be so
great that devious subordinates can bring organizations grinding to a halt
simply by strictly observing the official rules. Indeed, "work-to-rule" is an

effective form of workers' revolt in large complex bureaucracies like post offices and police forces.

Moral hazard pervades the civil-military relationship. How do we know that the military is doing what it is supposed to be doing? How do we know that the military is serving the interests of the country and not parochial interests, either of individual officers or of some larger group (such as a service or branch)? The problem is especially acute because the real goal of the military, being ready to protect society from its enemies, is not directly observable most of the time. In its stead, we can observe what the military is doing in terms of training, buying weapons, and so on. But how can civilians ensure that the peacetime behavior they are able to monitor correctly indicates that the military will perform as directed during wartime? Moreover, if in the meantime the military is rewarded based on a set of indicators that only imperfectly measure the true desired output, the military has a strong incentive to optimize on those indicators, not on the true output.

Mechanisms for Civilian Oversight of the Military

A central premise of political applications of the principal-agent framework is that despite all of the foregoing problems, political control does not end with the delegation decision. Civilians still have means available with which to direct the military and thereby mitigate the adverse selection and moral hazard problems inherent in delegation. In essence, control or monitoring mechanisms are ways of overcoming the information problems discussed above, perhaps by getting the agent to reveal information or perhaps by adjusting the incentives of the agent so that the principal can "know" that the agent wants what the principal wants.[29] The difficulty of observing battlefield operations does not in and of itself preclude close monitoring. The principal-agent framework cues us to look for operational control measures in nonoperational contexts. For instance, control over budget and doctrine could be surrogates for control over the performance of the military on the battlefield—an arena the principal cannot directly oversee. By shaping budget or doctrine in a certain way, the principal can know something about the likely activity of the agent, even without directly observing him.

Consider the most obvious form of monitoring: restricting the scope of delegation to the military. Some degree of agency is inevitable in modern civil-military relations. Not everyone can go to the battlefield to fight. But in theory any amount of delegation short of that basic distinction is possible. Force management can be broken down into three broad categories: strategy, structure, and operations. These broad categories can be further broken down into still smaller discrete steps. Consider the hypothetical case of a single use of force, say the decision to bomb a Serbian artillery site outside Sarajevo. This might consist of: the decision to flip the switch that drops the bomb; the decision to use a manned aircraft to deliver the ordnance; the decision to target that particular artillery piece; the decision to target an artillery site; the decision to use force against the Serbs; the decision to establish an artillery exclusion zone; the decision to defend the Muslim enclave at Sarajevo; the decision to get involved in the former Yugoslavia; the decision to commit to security and stability in Central Europe; the decision to commit to NATO; the decision that Europe is a vital national interest; and, finally, the decision to be engaged in world affairs rather than isolationist. One could imagine another parallel or interwoven series of decisions that would walk back from the ordnance and aircraft, through the pilot's training regimen, through the aircraft production, to line items in the defense budget.

Civilians could devise the strategy, deduce operations and battle plans therefrom, specify tactics to achieve those aims, outline logistics and equipment needed to accomplish all this, and direct the provisioning of the forces—in essence giving complete marching orders to the military. At the other extreme, civilians could simply tell the military, "Deliver us from our enemies," and let the military decide all the rest. The former would be tremendously costly—not to mention risky, if the civilians are incompetent. In the extreme, overmeddling could so jeopardize the lives of the military, or the fate of the mission, that the military would turn in revolt. Overdelegation would be the least burdensome and would avoid a de jure coup, but it would amount to a de facto coup: the military would be deciding policy and making decisions that by rights belong to the civilian political masters. This is precisely the fear of Kohn (1994) and Weigley (1993) with respect to the post–Cold War United States. Overdelegation requires the greatest trust in the military and leaves civilians vulnerable to the agency problems discussed above.

The military can be monitored, therefore, by restricting the scope of delegation.[30] At least insofar as military operations go, this type of monitoring takes the form of rules of engagement, standing orders, mission orders, and contingency plans. Rules of engagement, in principal-agent terms, are reporting requirements concerning the use of force. By restricting military autonomy and proscribing certain behavior, rules of engagement require that the military inform civilian principals about battlefield operations whenever developments indicate (to battlefield commanders) that the rules need to be changed. Rules of engagement, then, are both a leash on the military and an information source for senior leaders, civilian and military. So long as the military operators do not "pull" on the leash, the senior commanders know that the pace of the military operation is less than the bounds set by the rules. The more restrictive the criteria, the more closely senior commanders can monitor the military operation (Sagan 1991). Similar dynamics obtain with standing orders, mission orders, and contingency plans, all of which are forms of detailed guidance on how operations are to be carried out (Bouchard 1991, pp. 32–34).

While all monitoring mechanisms can be more or less restrictively implemented, some are inherently less intrusive on military autonomy. The least intrusive forms of monitoring concern the designing of the contract that establishes the principal-agency relationship in the first place. Most economic applications stress controlling the agent through contracts that give agents an economic incentive to perform in ways that the principal wants; giving an agent a financial interest in the firm's residual—that is, profit sharing—is a classic example. Political scientists have had difficulties applying this solution to political situations of agency because there is no obvious "profit" to be distributed.[31] Profit sharing is straightforward when the organization's basic output is easily measured (number of widgets) and the main goal of the principal is greater efficiency (more widgets at less cost). In political applications, the output (policy) itself can be in dispute or only imprecisely measured, and economic efficiency (more policy at less cost) is not the only desideratum. Political actors are sensitive to costs, however, and so a potential political analog is something called "slack," the difference between the actual budget appropriation and the minimum cost of providing the service. Slack can be used to buy things that the agent (bureaucrat) wants, like new equipment, perquisites, and so on, but does not actually need to provide the service (Moe 1984, p. 763). In this way, the agent has an incentive to be efficient in providing the desired service, since he can spend the slack on things he values. Giving bureaus a fixed amount and allowing them to allocate it as desired is the most common use of slack in political organizations. The problem with using slack as a control mechanism is twofold. It requires that the principal consistently overpay for the service. And more important, slack does not solve the problem of ensuring that the policy output in fact accords with the principal's desires and is not simply coming in at a lower cost.

The principal-agent perspective suggests that contractual incentives should be at the heart of the control relationship between civilians and the military. In the absence of an obvious profit to be shared, however, and given the limitations of slack as a surrogate, what are plausible incentives? Part of the problem of incentives is addressed through screening mechanisms (discussed below) that serve to populate the military with people who share, so much as possible, civilian preferences over outcomes. There are also historical examples of crass versions of profit sharing as a means of ensuring civilian control: the Romans, for instance, essentially bribed the capital garrison to keep it out of politics.[32] Wages and benefits, and the implied sanction of withholding them, may be modern equivalents.

A particularly intriguing incentive, however, can be found in traditional organization theory's premise that organizations (agents) prize autonomy. Autonomy is slack without a monetary denomination. Since monitoring mechanisms vary in their degree of intrusiveness, and assuming that the military prefers less intrusive means, civilians have a powerful incentive with which to influence military behavior: offer to use less intrusive means to monitor military agents. Indeed, this is how traditional civil-military relations theory treats autonomy. It is the centerpiece of Huntington's ideal-type objective control and is even supported by fierce critics like S. E. Finer (Feaver 1993, 1996a; Clausewitz 1976, pp. 605–606; Brodie 1973, p. 494; Huntington 1957, pp. 83–85; Smith 1951, pp. 50–51; Finer 1962, pp. 39–56, especially 47–56, and 141–144; Betts 1991, p. 10; and Hendrickson 1988, p. 11). Claude Welch describes it as a *"noli-me-tangere"* approach: civilians promise autonomy to the military in matters of lesser import as an incentive for military acceptance of the ethic of subordination (Welch 1976, pp. 33 and 318).

A slightly more intrusive form of monitoring involves using screening and selection mechanisms to ensure that only the right sort of agent enters into the contractual relationship. This directly addresses the adverse selection problem, but it may be thought of as a relatively unintrusive information-gathering device. The way to make sure you have not hired a lout is to identify the characteristics of people who are *not* louts and then hire only them. Once you "know" the type of agent you have, you should be able to predict his behavior with greater confidence. Education requirements, skill tests, and problem-solving exercises all represent attempts by employers to screen undesirables out of the candidate pool. Importantly, all traditional civil-military relations theories emphasize screening mechanisms of one sort or another, and the professional military education system is devoted to this kind of screening and socialization (Masland and Radway 1957).

Accession policy, determining who can join the military and how, is the military version of a screening and selection mechanism. Of course, the military uses elaborate physical, emotional, and mental tests to weed out poorly qualified applicants; this directly addresses the civil-military problematique by ensuring that the military will have the physical capacity to defend the country as needed. Accession policy can also mitigate civil-military problems by selecting or promoting personnel who will share civilian preferences. For instance, one of the primary arguments in favor of conscription is that it helps leaven the military mind-set with a steady supply of nonmilitary personnel, citizen-soldiers whose primary sense of identity and loyalty will be with civilian society. And by law in the United States, civilians have a fair amount of influence over the makeup of the officer corps. Congress votes on all officer promotions, and the more senior and influential the promotion, the more carefully the applicant is screened by Congress. Likewise, the president and his civilian staff often personally select the officers to be promoted to the most senior and sensitive posts, and in this way they shape the collective preferences of the officer corps. Changes of administration can result in changes in the degree of convergence between the officers appointed by a previous administration and the incoming civilian leaders (Whitworth and Watson 2001).

Compared with agency relationships in the other sectors of the bureaucracy, however, civilian principals have less discretion in using screening and selection to choose military agents. The president has virtually no limits on his selection of civilian foreign policy advisors, but he is limited to a finite number of senior military officers when he picks his most trusted military advisors. Of course, the president need not follow strict seniority precedence, and every president has exercised at least some latitude in promoting military advisors whom the president believes will be more in harmony with his administration's policies (Halperin 1972, p. 310). Janowitz found that the lower the rank of the military officers, the more frustrated they were with civilian viewpoints, and this suggests that promotion and selection procedures winnow out people who do not like civilian control, or at least that the views of those who get through the process are shaped by the organization (Janowitz 1971, p. 368; Schoenberg 1971).

The ability to shape viewpoints leads to yet another way that screening can serve to monitor delegation: through organizational culture. Organizational culture serves to provide mutual conceptions of behavior, allowing actors in a political game to have shared expectations of what the other will do.[33] Brehm and Gates found that these cultural factors, which they variously called "cohesion," "solidarity," and "professionalism," had great explanatory power in determining when subordinates would work or shirk (Brehm and Gates 1992a, 1993). In the civil-military context, an organizational norm that stresses obedience gives both civilians and the military a common expectation that the military will be subordinate. In this one respect, the principal-agent framework shares a finding of traditional civil-military relations theory: that a common culture of subordination—Huntington's "professionalism," Welch's "cult of obedience," Smith's "norm of civilian control," Hendrickson's "ethic"—is a crucial component civilian control (Huntington 1957, pp. 70–78; Welch 1976, p. 33; Smith 1951, p. 5; Hendrickson 1988, p. 26).

Beyond selection and screening mechanisms, the next most intrusive form of monitoring involves the use of third parties to watch the agent and report on key outputs, called fire alarms (McCubbins and Schwartz 1984). A third party who has a vested interest in the actions of the agent—for example, an interest group or affected constituents—can set off an "alarm" to alert the principal whenever the agent misbehaves. Thus the Sierra Club watches the Environmental Protection Agency, the American Association of Retired People watches the Department of Health and Human Services, and so on. The interest group environment is different in the military sphere, where there are fewer mass public organizations independent of the government, but there are many defense-oriented think tanks that investigate and report on the activity and adequacy of the defense establishment. It is also possible to think of conscription-based accession policies as playing something of a fire-alarm function: draftees, as resident civilians whose primary identity and loyalty is with civilian society, may be expected to sound the alarm if things are going awry.[34]

The most prominent fire alarm on defense policy is the news media. The media act as independent third agents, self-appointed public watchdogs. Anecdotal evidence suggests that the media play an important role even for senior policymakers who have a wealth of internal sources of information. Reading the Early Bird clipping service, a daily compilation of all Department of Defense–related articles in the major newspapers, is usually a top priority for senior policymakers; within the Pentagon, the joke is, "If it isn't in the Early Bird, it didn't happen."

Interservice rivalry operates as another, slightly more intrusive fire alarm. Traditional civil-military relations theory has long recognized that the separateness of the American military services can bolster civilian control. In monitoring military behavior, a sister service may not face the same information asymmetries as would a civilian overseer. Civilian intervention can be triggered when one service complains about another either to the secretary of defense or to Congress. Civilian principals, lacking at least some relevant military expertise, cannot be sure that any particular military advice is sound. Having separate military services available to "sound off" and provide alternative military opinions is a guard against this.[35] This function was explicitly recognized in the congressional debates around the military unification movement immediately after World War II. Defenders of the status quo (strong separate services) touted the importance of alternative military voices. While the National Security Act of 1947 did centralize the military establishment in one Department of Defense, it preserved at least the framework of ongoing service rivalry in the separate service departments, each headed by a civilian service secretary, so as to make sure that alternative voices were heard.[36]

Interservice rivalry can also be thought of as an institutional check. Institutional checks are related to fire alarms, but the principal-agent literature usually treats them as distinct. An institutional check is a separate agent, established by the principal and empowered with a veto to block action of the other agent. The function of a simple fire alarm is to alert the principal, who will then intervene to punish or adjust behavior as needed. The function of an institutional check is more assertive—to block, either legally or in some cases physically, any behavior that might be considered untoward. Institutional checks play a key role in civil-military relations. They are integral to what Huntington calls "subjective control," and they have proven important in preserving military subordination to political authorities in ethnically divided states (Huntington 1957, p. 82; Frazer 1994; Horowitz 1985; Belkin 1998). In the U.S. case, the classic institutional check for the use of force is the Constitution's division of military decisionmaking authority between the executive and the legislative branch; here, the framers of the Constitution treated the electorate as the principal and government as the agent. By extension, the presence of senior civilian officials in the Department of Defense, over which Congress, through the Senate confirmation process, has some control, is also an institutional check. Likewise, the civilian staffs of congressional committees are another important institutional check, since they can block the activity of the executive branch. The framers clearly intended institutional checks to be the bulwark of civilian control over the armed forces; the purpose of a separate militia (now the National Guard) was to be a last line of defense against the regular standing army, should it prove bent on a usurpation of control.

The role of the militia and the National Guard has declined more than the framers would have expected, however, and to a certain extent interservice rivalry can be thought of as a replacement check. To the extent that the existence of separate services makes carrying out a coup that much more difficult, the services can be treated as separate sub-veto groups. At least in the U.S. case, however, interservice rivalry has played a more important role as an information gathering device for civilian principals, so I treat it as a traditional fire alarm rather than as an institutional check. The fire alarm function of interservice rivalry feeds back into institutional checks in an interesting way. Congress has historically been the most interested in preserving interservice rivalry, because the information asymmetries hit Congress especially hard. Congress wants to make sure that independent service chiefs will be able to come to Capitol Hill and disagree with each other, and especially with the administration, when necessary (Scroggs 1996).

Congress's institutional interest in interservice rivalry makes the push for the 1986 Goldwater-Nichols' reforms especially interesting from a principal-agent perspective (Weiner 1997). One of the main goals of Goldwater-Nichols was to weaken interservice rivalry by strengthening the ability of the Joint Chiefs of Staff (JCS) to provide a joint military viewpoint. In so doing, Congress was putting a muzzle on the interservice rivalry fire alarm. There are several reasons why it may have done this. First, Congress may not have thought the reforms would entirely silence interservice disagreements. Indeed, the reforms explicitly preserved the service end-run option to Congress, so the muzzle was not so restrictive as it may at first glance seem. Second, interservice rivalry had proven a less-than-ideal fire alarm from Congress's viewpoint. The service chiefs had learned to logroll among themselves without making real strategic trade-offs. Then they would present a united front to Congress and the president, and this would force civilians either to spend too much on the military function or make ill-informed cuts (Hoopes 1954, p. 228). Third, perhaps Congress viewed the newly strengthened Joint Staff as creating yet another fire alarm, rather than dampening existing ones. The Joint Staff would watch the services closely and could provide a strong warning if the services colluded or shirked in untoward ways.

The foregoing suggests that principals are sensitive to the costs of fire alarms, and these costs extend beyond the intrinsic costs emphasized in the literature: the likelihood that the fire alarm will lie or will be unable to accurately report on what the agent is doing (Lupia and McCubbins 1994). The civil-military story points also to extrinsic costs. For instance, interservice rivalry may provide useful and valid information to civilian principals but only at a cost, such as potentially needless duplication and interoperability problems. Likewise, the media can be a useful fire alarm when it reports on peacetime abuses involving hazing or sexual harassment. But in wartime, the media may not be the kind of fire alarm on which civilians will want to rely because, in keeping with the metaphor, both firefighters and arsonists can learn from a fire alarm; if the media report that the military has not adequately defended a certain sector, this is useful information for the principal but it is also useful information for the enemy. Hence the ubiquity of media restrictions during military operations (Smith 1992, Bennett and Paletz 1994).

Public fire alarms like the news media also have another cost deriving from the fact that the civilian policymaking principal is himself an agent of a still more ultimate principal, the voter. A fire alarm that alerts the policymaking principal that something is awry also alerts the voter that something has gone wrong on the policymaker's watch. For this reason, the policymaker has an incentive to prefer a monitoring mechanism that produces reliable information *privately*, or at least in a way that can be shielded from the voter.[37]

Institutional checks also have associated costs. Institutional checks work best when the interests of two agents are in conflict, either because they face different contract incentives (one is paid for cutting costs, the other for boosting production); otherwise, the two agents could collude and the principal would be back facing the moral hazard problem. Moreover, for an institutional check to be effective, each must have something akin to the power of a veto over the other. For these reasons, interservice rivalry is not a formidable institutional check. The services all are tasked with the same thing—providing security—and the services do not really have a veto over each other, except at the most rudimentary and theoretical level of being able to counterbalance each other in any military takeover attempt. Institutional checks can be effective, but there are high costs associated therewith: they make it harder for the agent to do bad things, but they also make it harder for the agent to do good things.[38] Civilian principals have from time to time created new institutional checks in the evolution of American civil-military relations, but only when the stakes are particularly great. The most obvious example was the establishment of the Atomic Energy Commission to assist civilian control over nuclear weapons (Feaver 1992).

The next most intrusive form of monitoring has been dubbed "police patrol" monitoring (McCubbins and Schwartz 1984). This involves regular investigations of the agent by the principal—fishing expeditions, if you will, where the quarry is general information on what the agent is doing. Police patrols include regularized audits and intrusive reporting requirements designed to turn up evidence of agent wrongdoing and, through regularized inspection, to deter moral hazard. Public investigative hearings and specific mandated reports are staples of congressional oversight and represent one of the more visible avenues of political control. Similar mechanisms operate within the executive branch to facilitate hierarchical control and some, like the Planning, Programming, and Budgeting System in the Department of Defense, directly concern security issues. Congressional investigations have at times featured prominently in the history of American civil-military relations, particularly the Committee on the Conduct of the War during the Civil War and the Senate Permanent Investigations Subcommittee under Senator Joseph McCarthy. Likewise, reports and audits are ubiquitous in the politics of the defense budget.

In the civil-military context, an important indicator of police patrol monitoring is the size of the civilian secretariat of the Office of the Secretary of Defense and the service secretariats. These are extensions of the executive branch principals, the patrol officers, who are in place to monitor closely and directly the activities of their military counterparts. Accordingly, large numbers of civilian officials are evidence of a police patrol monitoring mechanism.

Inspectors general are a hybrid of police patrol and fire alarm monitoring. On the one hand, they are internal to the organization and have full audit authority; on the other hand, an inspector general's investigation is not a regularized audit but is usually triggered by some precipitating factor, like a leak.

Other examples of police patrol monitoring in the civil-military sphere are the activities of the various governmental investigative agencies, the Congressional Budget Office, the General Accounting Office, and the Office of Technical Assessment. While they bolster the strength of Congress vis-à-vis the executive branch, and so may be thought of as part of an institutional check, they function to increase access to military information by the civilian principals as a whole. The annual reports to Congress are likewise examples of police patrol monitoring; while their nominal audience is Congress, the reports are first reviewed by civilians in the executive branch, and the act of writing and reviewing them produces valuable information for monitoring the activity of the military establishment. In a different context, communications links from national command authorities to operational commanders constitute tangible monitoring and auditing channels. Also, as discussed above, restrictive rules of engagement that narrow the scope of delegated authority are examples of police patrol monitoring. Like traditional principal-agent oversight mechanisms, these measures are costly in terms of civilian attention (not to mention dollars) but can mitigate somewhat the informational asymmetries in the civil-military relationship.

At the most intrusive end of the oversight spectrum would be a decision to revisit the original decision to delegate authority to the military agent in the first place. Civilian principals have the option of redrawing the boundary, crossing over into the military zone to make or implement a decision on a particular issue or set of issues. For instance, President Johnson delegated responsibility to General Westmoreland to conduct the Vietnam War, and civilians oversaw that delegation through a prescribed set of reporting requirements, rules of engagement, and so on. Despite this arrangement, from time to time the president and his senior civilian advisors intervened in the war not only to tinker with the monitoring system but also to make operational decisions themselves. Interventions such as the celebrated practice of selecting bombing targets from the basement of the White House had the effect of directly narrowing the freedom of action of the military agent and so constitute an especially intrusive form of oversight.

Table 3.1 summarizes the various oversight mechanisms just discussed.

Of course, civilians would not rely on just one or two mechanisms but rather would use a mix. Moreover, the mix would be in most instances cumulative. Thus, if civilians sought to monitor the military more intrusively, they might bolster the civilian complement within the Office of the Secretary of Defense (add police patrolmen) without shutting down defense-oriented think tanks (preserving existing fire alarms). Similarly, a move toward less intrusive monitoring would be indicated not so much by the establish-

Table 3.1   Summary of oversight mechanisms in ascending order of
intrusiveness

Monitoring mechanism from principal-agent literature	Civil-military analog
Contract incentives	Offer by civilians to use less intrusive monitoring in exchange for obedience
Screening and selection	Skill requirements for entrance into military Loyalty oaths Other accession instruments Professionalism
Fire alarms	The news media Defense-oriented think tanks Interservice rivalry
Institutional checks	Militia system and National Guard Interservice rivalry (sometimes) Civilian staffs in Congress Atomic Energy Commission Confirmable civilian secretariat
Police patrols	Planning, Programming, and Budgeting System and the budget process Civilian secretariat and Office of Secretary of Defense Restrictive rules of engagement Restrictive standing or mission orders Limits on delegated authority Audits and investigations Inspectors General Congressional Budget Office, General Accounting Office, Office of Technical Assessment
Revising delegation decision	Intervening in a military operation to make a decision that was hitherto in the scope of delegated authority (e.g., picking bombing targets from the White House)

ment of new fire alarms as by a reduction in the more intrusive forms of monitoring. *Ceteris paribus,* the addition of a fire alarm without any other compensating action, would increase the degree of intrusiveness by adding sets of eyes to the monitoring mission.

Civilian Punishment of the Military

While attention to monitoring mechanisms is a hallmark of the principal-agent literature, punishment mechanisms are often only implicit. It is assumed that the only problem is detecting whether shirking is going on; once detected, punishment is automatic, or at least unproblematic. To the extent that the literature does consider postmonitoring issues, it is usually in the context of the reward incentives built into the original contract. The agent works in order to receive the rewards, and if the agent shirks, and this is detected, the withholding of rewards constitutes a form of punishment. Proactive punishments, materially reducing the agent's utility beyond the withholding of a reward may be only summarily mentioned (Kiewet and McCubbins 1991, p. 29; Lupia and McCubbins 1994, pp. 104–105; Milgrom and Roberts 1988, p. 157; McNollgast 1987, p. 252; and McNollgast 1989, p. 439).

A few treatments make punishment more explicit and have it play a more central role in ensuring compliance. For instance, Bianco and Bates's analysis of iterated games found that the leader's ability to set punishments was critical to the initiation and sustainment of cooperation (Bianco and Bates 1990, Pollack 1997). Similarly, principal-agent games between an electorate and a leader turn on the ability of the electorate to vote out of office, or punish even more severely, leaders who fail them (Goemans 2000, Downs and Rocke 1995, Bueno de Mesquita and Siverson 1995). Lindsay compared congressional oversight of domestic and foreign policy and concluded that the difficulty Congress had in punishing foreign policy actors was a primary factor in explaining the diminished congressional control in that arena (Lindsay 1994a, pp. 283 and 298).

One important application of the principal-agent framework, however, has explicitly challenged the role of punishment. John Brehm and Scott Gates claim that credible threats of punishment from supervisors are inefficient means of gaining compliance.[39] They argue that compliance is far more efficiently gained when agents share the preferences of the principal. Principal-agent models have generally assumed widely divergent preferences—principals want agents to work, and agents want only to shirk—and Brehm and Gates dismiss this as an unproven assumption "cloaked in theological robes" (Brehm and Gates 1997, p. 20). I accept part of their critique; as explained above, in civil-military applications of the principal-agent framework one must incorporate a richer spectrum of military agent preferences, including the possibility that the preference gap will be narrow under certain circumstances. But to show that agency problems are diminished when principals and agents share preferences is to show that people who agree with each other tend to cooperate. Downs and Rocke strongly criticize this view and argue that the cooperation one gets in this way tends to be shallow (Downs and Rocke 1995). *Some* divergence of preferences some of the time is inevitable and so the moral hazard problem is not completely avoidable.[40] If there is moral hazard, there is at least the potential for punishment, a consequence of particular interest in the civil-military context.

Punishment has received an uneven treatment in the civil-military relations literature as well. On the one hand, the military has been distinctive as an organization with a high reliance on coercion to enforce discipline—as in the famed Churchillian trinity of the British Navy: "rum, sodomy, and the lash." Likewise, harsh punishments for battle cowardice *pour encourager les autres* was long an accepted means of forging an effective fighting force. Thus the role of coercion, at least insofar as it concerned obedience *within* the military organization, has always been a part of the military organization (Bryant 1979, pp. 34–35). Military sociology has for years debated whether rigid enforcement of rules, often with extreme physical coercion, is more effective in enforcing unit obedience than softer forms of manipulation, persuasion, and group consensus (Janowitz 1971, pp. 38–53; Henderson 1985, pp. 9–26).

On the other hand, punishment is rarely discussed in the theoretical literature on civil-military relations as a relevant tool in enforcing discipline *across* the civil-military divide. Punishment is not emphasized in the theoretical literature partly because the military uniquely controls coercive power. If the civilian tries to punish the military, what is to stop the military from resisting by force? One of the distinctives of the civil-military relationship is the fact that the subordinate is almost always more powerful than the superior. This is always true in the most basic sense of brute force. It can even be true for more intangible measures of power. The military may have tremendous political power because it is an important consumer block in a market economy. Likewise, the military can enjoy a prestige that confers political power quite apart from any consideration of physical coercion. Given the overall power differential, an exclusive focus on punishment would seem misguided. Yet, as I will argue below, civilians *can* punish the military, and sometimes they do.

The relative inattention to punishment may also be explained by the orientation of the theoretical literature on which most of the civil-military relations literature draws. Both the Huntingtonian and Janowitzean schools essentially accept the neoclassical critique of classical organization theory.[41] The classical organization theory of Frederick Taylor and Max Weber saw coercion and material incentives as an essential element of any bureaucracy. The neoclassical work of Carl Friedrich, Chester Barnard, and Herbert Simon was a reaction against the material and coercive basis of organizational behavior and emphasized instead the role of professionalism, cooperation, and bounded rationality. Huntington adopted the neoclassical emphasis on professional norms as the determinant of behavior, and Janowitz likewise embraced socialization to codes of behavior as the key to military obedience.[42] The empirical foundation of the neoclassical rejection of coercion and punishment is not unassailable, however. A limitation of all the studies that show coercive power is relatively ineffective is that they measure compliance based on self-reports.[43] The most accurate summary of existing empirical data, then, would be: respondents who perceive that their superiors are relying on professional norms and persuasion rather than coercion to induce compliance are more likely to report that they comply with their superiors' orders.[44] This is an important finding, but it makes something less than a compelling case that coercion either plays no role or ought to play no role.

Therefore, I explicitly consider the role punishment plays in U.S. civil-military relations. In so doing, however, I sidestep a problem that arises in some civil-military settings but not in most instances of principal-agent relations: whether civilian principals *can* punish the military agents. There are numerous examples of coups triggered by a civilian decision to punish some part of the military for an earlier disobedience. Such a coup effectively neutralizes any ability to punish. At some level this problem is simply assumed away by the principal-agent framework. As discussed above, agency theory is only applicable in those settings where the military conceives of itself as the agent of the civilian; crucial to that conception is a recognition of the civilian's right to sanction, and hence an explicit commitment to submit to sanctions. Such an assumption is reasonable in the U.S. case. There is ample evidence that American civilians are able to punish the military, if they so choose. Civilians have the ability to fire even hugely popular military officers, as Truman's dismissal of MacArthur makes clear. Many senior military officers have been sacked before and since for a wide range of offenses that can be grouped collectively under the heading of shirking. But it bears emphasis that the power to punish rests on a normative foundation—that is, the willingness of the military to be punished—and this normative foundation is thus a prerequisite for democratic civil-military relations. It exists in the United States and other advanced democracies but not necessarily in all countries. As discussed in the concluding chapter, this may limit the applicability of the agency model to other countries.

In democracies, therefore, civilians *can* punish the military. Nevertheless, *whether* civilians will use their ability to punish is uncertain—MacArthur evidently did not think it was guaranteed that Truman would punish him. The principal-agent literature acknowledges that punishment is a costly action by the principal and is by no means assured in every instance of agent shirking. The primary finding from the literature is that when there are multiple principals, a shirking agent can play one off the other and thus reduce the likelihood of being punished (McNollgast 1989, p. 439). In the U.S. civil-military context, the ability of the military to play Congress against the president and vice versa is an obvious analog (Avant 1994, p. 14).

Thus, in addition to the uncertainty over whether the behavior will be discovered, there is uncertainty over how the alleged shirking behavior will be interpreted by the civilian principal. Most principal-agent applications assume that the behavior is hidden or unobservable, but that the character of the behavior would, if known, be unambiguous (Downs and Rocke 1995). In most instances, this is a reasonable assumption. In the civil-military context, however, it is plausible that the nature of the behavior itself is ambiguous, subject to different interpretations by different civilian principals. What is excessive force in combat? How much candor can senior military display in their testimony before Congress when they disagree with administration policy? Some activities might be obvious—collecting war booty, for example—but the norms governing the acceptability of the behavior may change (Schmitt 1992a). Civilian principals have the right and the ability to set the boundary of appropriate behavior and to interpret ambiguous behavior as they see fit. Obviously, information about what really happened, as well as information about any extenuating circumstances, will partly influence the perception of the behavior as shirking or not. But it will also depend on other factors, including calculations of costs not unlike those that I argue govern monitoring and shirking decisions: the salience of the issue, the popularity of the offending military agent, and so on.

If civilians decide to punish the military, they can select from an almost infinitely wide range of punishment tools, which may be grouped into five broad categories. The first involves imposing the kind of monitoring arrangements the military dislikes. As noted above, the military has a strong preference for nonintrusive monitoring. If in response to some outbreak of shirking the civilians impose an intrusive monitoring regime, it constitutes something of a punishment, albeit not a draconian one. Of course, it is difficult analytically to distinguish this kind of punishment from the prior decision to monitor. Such monitoring is often experienced as punishment by the military agent—consider, for instance, the heightened public scrutiny of the way the military has integrated women since the U.S. Navy's Tailhook crisis—but its intended function may fit better under the heading of monitoring than sanctioning.

The second set of punishment mechanisms involves cutting budgets and reducing the perquisites enjoyed by the military. In the civil-military context, this is most often seen as a by-product of a standoff between the congressional and executive branches. In such cases, Congress may make compensating cuts in appropriations or temporarily hold up promotions in order to force some compliance with a policy that the executive branch is resisting. I do not know of instances when this was used as a punishment of the military by the civilian executive branch, but it would seem plausible.

The third set of punishments, and by far the most prevalent, involves variations on forced detachment from the military—the military equivalent of firing. The military is distinctive as a profession with both an up-or-out career path and a very generous prize for those who stay in a "full" term, historically twenty years. The rewards for "making it to retirement" are substantial—a guaranteed pension equivalent to roughly 50 percent of one's last base pay, payable immediately—and they are won after just twenty years of service. Moreover, the rewards climb exponentially with seniority. The longer one serves, the greater the preretirement baseline salary and also the greater the percentage of that baseline salary one receives as retirement pay. The fully vested retired military officer can be as young as forty-one (a fully vested enlisted person can be under forty), young enough to start a second career while collecting military retirement pay. And there is also a vast array of other amenities, like subsidized shopping services and subsidized medical care. There is more than a little irony in the fact that the military that prevailed against world communism is also the American institution that most closely approximates the idealized benefits of a socialist society. But these rewards accrue only to someone who makes it to retirement, that is, someone who successfully earns each successive promotion and so is not discharged before twenty years are served. In theory, the up-or-out trigger is meant to ensure that underperformers do not last long enough to win the benefits. Retirement pay thus works as a carrot to entice the better soldiers and sailors to remain in the military rather than seek more immediately lucrative careers in civilian society, and also as a stick to enforce compliance, lest one is prematurely discharged from the service and thus denied a plum benefit.

The retirement benefit can be manipulated as punishment in several ways. Most obviously, a deviant officer can be discharged from the military for cause. If the officer has not yet served twenty years, he or she loses the most important service benefit, retirement pay. A slight variation on this involves failing to promote an officer. Officers serve with a time-limited commission. They become eligible for promotion by accession-year cohorts, according to a strict and linear time-in-service calculation. A promotion board of more senior officers, using guidance approved by the senior civilian leadership in each of the services, decides which officers in a cohort will be promoted and which will not. Generally, candidates not selected for promotion the first time they are eligible have one more chance at the promotion. "Twice passed-over" candidates must leave the service when they are ordered to do so. During the Cold War, a steady influx of junior officers pushed out those who had not been promoted to higher ranks. Not promoting an officer can thus be equivalent to firing that officer.[45] Competition for promotion intensifies the more senior the officers get; consequently, the more sensitive those officers become to having adverse information in their personnel record.

Another variation involves the ability to retire an officer at a lower rank than the highest one he achieved. This can be done directly by the service secretary, as an explicit punishment for behavior that otherwise did not rise to the level requiring a formal discharge. It can also be done indirectly via a rule that requires officers to serve a certain length of time at a rank before that rank can be the basis for retirement pay calculations. If they retire before they have served long enough to claim that rank for retirement purposes, in effect they retire below grade. This is of particular significance for the highest ranking officers, admirals in the navy and generals in the other three services, because these ranks are tied to specific billets and assignment to those billets may be for a shorter term than is required to guarantee the retirement privileges of the rank associated with that billet. If they lose the billet (for example, commander of the Seventh Fleet) before the requisite two years and are not assigned to another billet requiring the same rank, they will have to retire at a lower grade, with correspondingly lower pay.

The final variation is the more well known system of discharges. There are three administrative discharges: the honorable discharge (under which all privileges are maintained), the general discharge (an intermediate discharge reflecting some minor disciplinary infraction, under which certain benefits may be maintained), and the general discharge under other than honorable conditions (a more severe dismissal, usually given in lieu of a court-martial, under which most benefits are lost). And there are two punitive discharges that carry the stigma of a felony conviction, that can be issued only by a court-martial, and that deny virtually all benefits: a bad conduct discharge (which can be issued by a special court-martial) and, the most severe of all, a dishonorable discharge (which requires a general court-martial).

The fourth set of punishments involves the complex system of military justice as specified under the Uniform Code of Military Justice (UCMJ). This can involve the separation of the service member from the military, but it need not. The UCMJ has provisions for capital punishment, imprisonment, or simply the military equivalent of fines and community service. The UCMJ and its historical antecedent, the Articles of War, have not primarily been instruments of civilian control, although the military judicial system has relevance for military subordination. The UCMJ has first and foremost functioned as an instrument for maintaining command discipline *within* the military—that is, as a tool for senior military commanders to use in controlling the behavior of their military subordinates (Lurie 1992). Nevertheless, to the extent that civilian leaders determine which behaviors are proscribed by law and which areas are left to commanders' discretion, and to the extent that senior military officers take their cues about exercising this discretion from civilian leaders, the military justice system can be considered a part of the civilian monitoring and punishment edifice.

The fifth set of punishments involves extralegal civilian action taken against specific military personnel. This is a miscellaneous category of actions ranging in severity from private oral rebukes all the way to the infamous Stalinist purges against the Soviet military in the 1930s in which thousands of officers were shot for suspected disloyalty to the Soviet regime. An intermediate form might be a situation in which the military advisor is publicly reprimanded or denied access to the civilian leader because that leader has lost confidence in him. What distinguishes this as a means of punishment is that it is a direct expression of civilian supremacy and is usually directly tied to the kinds of shirking behavior of interest to civilian principals.

One might argue that the domain of civil-military relations offers yet a sixth form of punishment that does not appear in domestic principal-agent settings: war. War, of course, inflicts hardships on the military, including the possibility of the ultimate sanction, loss of life, and one might consider war as a form of punishment. If war performance is itself a function of civil-military relations, then battlefield defeat could be a form of punishment experienced by the military (and, less directly, by the civilians as well) for adopting suboptimal civil-military arrangements. Intriguingly, Cohen (2001) argues that, contrary to a cherished military view, war performance improves with vigorous civilian involvement in the details of the war (what the agency theory considers to be intrusive civilian monitoring). In this sense, military shirking or resistance to intrusive monitoring might increase the risk of battlefield collapse and thus constitute a punishment of sorts. War is rare enough that it probably does not form a primary punishment vehicle anyway, and it certainly does not preclude a role for the more mundane forms of punishment discussed above and summarized in Table 3.2.

Table 3.2   Military punishments available to the civilian principal

General category	Examples
Restrictive monitoring	Audits Mandatory remedial training (as in sexual harassment training)
Material disincentives: current	Budget cuts Restricting liberty
Material disincentives: future	Discharge prior to earning benefit Retirement below grade Loss of retirement privileges Other-than-honorable discharges
Military justice system	Nonjudicial punishment Courts-martial
Extralegal action	Verbal rebukes Purges

Conclusion

The civil-military relationship is at its heart an agency relationship, and so the principal-agent framework developed in microeconomics and already used in various political applications can be profitably extended to the study of civilian control of the military. The civilian principal establishes a military agent to provide the security function for the state, but then must take pains to ensure that the military agent continues to do the civilian's bidding. Given the adverse selection and moral hazard problems endemic in any agency relationship, but particularly acute in the civil-military context, civilian oversight of the military is crucial. Fortunately, civilians have available a wide variety of oversight mechanisms, each involving a different degree of intrusiveness and therefore each posing a different set of costs on the actors. The oversight regime is supported by a sanction regime, which provides civilians with options for punishing the military when it shirks, that is, deviates from the course of action prescribed by civilians. This basic story is analyzed in a formal game in the next chapter.

CHAPTER 4

A Formal Agency Model of
Civil-Military Relations

In Chapter 3, I used the principal-agent framework to identify the fundamental building blocks of a new theory of civil-military relations, agency theory. In this chapter, I use basic tools of formal analysis to build a game that permits analysis of the strategic interactions central to civil-military relations. The game's multiple equilibria solutions underscore that there is not a single resolution to the civil-military problematique. On the contrary, many different outcomes are possible. Analyzing the equilibria allows us to identify the factors that determine which outcome is likely under which conditions.

Civil-military outcomes—whether civilians monitor intrusively and whether the military works or shirks—are more observable than the strategic calculations that produce those outcomes. As will be demonstrated in subsequent chapters, the model permits a "reverse engineering" of the civil-military relationship: taking an observed civil-military outcome and predicting the values of certain key variables, some of which have been slighted in previous examinations of American civil-military relations. In subsequent chapters, the model's expectations will guide the empirical exploration of important phases of American civil-military experience since World War II. I begin here by identifying the assumptions on which the model rests and then describing the civil-military interactions reflected in the game. I analyze the game for equilibria and examine the parameters that the model identifies as important in governing the civil-military relationship. I conclude by briefly discussing how this approach constitutes an advance over existing applications of the principal-agent framework.

Assumptions

My formal analysis of civil-military relations rests on several assumptions. First, I assume that the players operate according to some minimal standards of rationality, in particular as subjective, expected-utility maximizers. This does not assume away the influence of political psychologic factors, most of which can be incorporated as cost factors in each player's decision calculus. Rather it simply assumes that players are aware of costs and benefits arising from their actions, that they can rank order outcomes according to some subjective estimate of the benefits minus the costs, and that they make some reasonable (albeit imperfect) effort to adopt courses of action that they believe will (so far as possible) produce outcomes in which the benefits exceed the costs, or at least exceed the payoffs from alternative courses of action. The rationalist explanation is the logical place to begin theorizing, even if there is reason to believe that other explanations may also be relevant, for instance an ideational one based on the construction of the military and civilian identities. Without a rationalist baseline explanation it is difficult to compare alternative explanations (Goldstein and Keohane 1993, Fearon 1995).

Second, and more restrictively, I assume that the players conceive of themselves as either principals or agents. This assumption is more controversial in the civil-military context. After all, isn't civil-military relations interesting precisely because the putative agents, the military, sometimes choose to reject the superior-subordinate relationship? At first glance, this provision appears to assume away the coup problem that preoccupies much of the civil-military relations literature. As we shall see, however, the principal-agent framework does not assume agent obedience; on the contrary, it expects a certain amount of conflict and disobedience, even, perhaps, to the point of a coup. It does assume, however, that the players share a common conception of the relationship in which the civilian is supposed to be superior to the military, even if this is not in fact the case, or even if the de facto distribution of power would permit it not to be so. Such an assumption is entirely reasonable in the American case, the focus of this study, and is generalizable to other democracies. This assumption is also becoming more valid even for traditionally coup-prone military dictatorships as the consolidation of the third wave of democratization continues. Because my focus is on the United States, I bracket an important problem that emerges in a comparative context: when the military sees itself as the agent of the disembodied state or society rather than of the government/regime and so does not view the government as even being in a position to delegate (and *not* to delegate) authority. While the question, Who is the military an agent of? is largely settled in the U.S. context, it remains a major issue for comparative civil-military relations, of course. The theory I develop here would have to be modified to incorporate this problem for comparative studies.

Third, as a point of departure I assume only two players, a civilian principal and a military agent. This assumption is off-putting to traditional civil-military scholars because, as we know, there are in fact multiple principals (the president, Congress, the secretary of defense, and so on) and multiple agents (four services, the quasi-autonomous Joint Staff, more or less independent combatant commands, the National Guard, and so on). The assumption is not required by the principal-agent framework; indeed, Deborah Avant's principal-agent analysis of American civil-military relations makes the divided principal the centerpiece of her theory. Following Huntington, Avant argues that systems like the United States that divide civilian control between the executive and legislative branch will inevitably have less-responsive military agents than parliamentary systems like Great Britain that provide for a unified civilian principal (Avant 1994). Even with the American divided-principal system, Avant allows for some gradation of division: when Congress and the president agree on basic foreign policy objectives the military will be more responsive than when there is prominent disagreement—hence, what seemed like military insubordination in the 1990s, Avant argues, was merely the natural military reaction to disagreements between Congress and President Clinton over peace operations (Avant 1996–97). This is an appropriate if limited deduction from the principal-agent framework, but I did not make it central to the development of my original version of the agency model because my more parsimonious formulation allowed for a richer range of insights (the role of monitoring mechanisms, the range of punishments, the strategic interaction between players, etc.) and made the model more tractable for analysis.

Even analyses (such as Avant's) that do incorporate more players make simplifying assumptions for the sake of tractability. For instance, Avant distinguishes between two civilian players (the president and the Congress) but in fact the range of relevant civilian players is virtually unlimited. The legislative branch is an amalgam of numerous actors who have important roles to play in the day-to-day management of civil-military relations: the authorizing and appropriating committees (and subcommittees); the chairs and ranking members of the committees and subcommittees and the various majority and minority leaders on the floor; other individual members of Congress with special or episodic interest in military matters; the staffs, including divisions between committee and personal staffs. Then the executive branch can be chopped up into numerous bits: the individual members of the National Security Council; the staff of the National Security Council (who themselves cluster into regional and functional offices that often compete with each other, albeit out of the public eye); the staff in the Office of the Secretary of Defense, an amalgam of numerous offices and bureaus; the service secretaries and their staffs; and so on. And if the civilian principal is to be divided, why not incorporate the obvious divisions within the military agent: the services, the branches within the services, the complex relationship between the Joint Staff and the individual service staffs, the various regional and functional combatant commands, and so on. Every theory of civil-military relations must make some simplifications to make sense of this welter of players, and I know of no analysis (whether theoretically or historically oriented) that is not vulnerable to the charge that the actual practice of civil-military relations is more complicated than the analysis reflects. Thus, as a point of departure, the original limitation of agency theory (a single principal and a single agent) is as good a place to draw the line as any. And, moreover, it is not that far removed from Huntington's simplifying assumptions. While Huntington did analyze congressional-executive relations and discuss the role of the National Guard (and, to a lesser extent, interservice rivalry), his preferred policy of objective control assumed that the civilian branch could be made to act as a more or less unified principal vis-à-vis an equivalently unified officer corps (Huntington 1957). As will be discussed below, moreover, the agency model captures at least some of the complexity of divided principals and agents by varying expectations of punishment as a function of how united or divided the principals and agents are.

The Game: What the Players Do and Why

The game begins with the civilians deciding how to monitor the military. Traditional civil-military relations theory has treated this as a normative question—how *ought* civilians monitor—hence Huntington's embrace of the Clausewitzean distinction: civilians handle policy (politics), the military handles operations.[1] To understand how civilians *will* monitor as opposed to how they *ought* to monitor, it is necessary to have some theory of civilian motivation. Most principal-agent treatments assume that principals are cost sensitive, and I adopt the same rationalist point of departure.[2]

Traditional treatments assume that political principals are primarily electorally motivated, and then measure cost in terms of whether the activity diverts from reelection efforts. It is not that political principals are lazy but rather that time spent doing the work that could be done by agents is time not spent out on the campaign trail. This, however, probably understates costs in the civil-military context (and, indeed, in foreign policy generally). If political principals were *only* electorally motivated—if they had no other interest in policy, neither for reasons selfish (historical legacy) nor noble (a belief in using political power for good)—they would probably not devote much time to civil-military relations at all, since its direct electoral impact is marginal.[3] That political principals *do* concern themselves, however, does not make them cost insensitive or even electorally unmotivated. Rather, it suggests using a richer understanding of costs, to include both *electoral costs* (time and effort) and what may be called *policy costs:* the disutility they attach to a divergence between their preferred policy and the actual policy outcome.

Both sets of costs affect the monitoring decision. It is bothersome to monitor an agent very closely. As anyone who has ever employed a helper knows, if the helper requires too much monitoring, one might as well do the job oneself. Of course, different arrangements make the same level of intrusive monitoring more or less costly. For instance, e-mail and voice mail can reduce the time required to monitor a research assistant closely; instead of requiring both parties to be available at the same time (if not the same place) for a status report, these technologies allow for frequent reporting at comparatively lower cost. Thus, the first set of costs may be thought of as some reflection of the intrinsic time and effort required to conduct the monitoring. In the civil-military context, these costs are directly affected by changes in communications technology. As the command and control system modernizes, previously impossible mechanisms of control—for instance, precisely moving ships in order to send a complicated diplomatic signal of resolve and restraint—become possible.

The policy costs of monitoring derive from the expertise and competence considerations discussed above. While the civilian is politically competent to make decisions and dictate how those decisions are carried out—and, moreover, under democratic theory has a right to be wrong—the different level of technical competence suggests that civilian interference may degrade the performance of the military agent. Even if the civilian is not actively directing the military into foolish behaviors, micromanagement may so interfere with the conduct of a mission as to produce similarly negative results. Concern about these costs motivated Huntington's normative prescription for civilians not to monitor intrusively, to recognize what he referred to as "autonomous military professionalism" (Huntington 1957, p. 83). He feared that excessive interference would undermine military professionalism and, consequently, the military's ability to adequately do its job of defending the state. These policy costs presumably vary with the extent to which the issue in question hinges on military expertise. Micromanaging an assault on a defended beach may have more pernicious side effects than micromanaging an auction among bidders hoping to establish fast-food franchises on military bases. In other words, for matters touching most closely on military expertise, civilians will have more confidence that the military will produce better policy and less confidence that they can do it—and the costs of intrusive monitoring should, *ceteris paribus*, be higher (Feaver 1992, Bawn 1995).

Changes in these monitoring costs are thus expected to change the outcome of the civil-military game. But it should be emphasized that changes in the monitoring costs are themselves largely exogenous to the civil-military game. For instance, monitoring costs vary with changes in technology—the gradual march to cheaper and faster communications networks. Obviously there are many factors that affect the evolution of communications technology, and while civil-military concerns may have some small role to play,[4] they are probably not central and it would be impossible to model all of them. Likewise, the policy costs of monitoring vary with the external threat, which agency theory treats as exogenous; thus the end of the Cold War might have resulted in a radically different threat condition, which could have resulted in a radically different cost of monitoring. Agency theory treats the end of the Cold War as exogenous, although it is at least possible that different configurations of civil-military relations over time contributed to the end of the Cold War. If that is so, agency theory, at least in its introductory form, cannot account for it.

Treating the changes in monitoring costs as exogenous does not mean pretending that they are irrelevant to civil-military relations. On the contrary, it means agency theory shows how changes in the costs of monitoring affect civil-military relations but does not show how changes in civil-military relations might affect the costs of monitoring. Like any other analytical approach, agency theory must identify things it is trying to explain and bracket off things it is not trying to explain.

Once the civilian has chosen his mix of monitoring and control mechanisms, it is the military's turn to act. The military chooses between working *(W)* and shirking *(S)*, between doing what the civilian wants exactly and implementing the civilian's orders as the military would prefer to implement them.[5] At least two considerations go into the military's choice. First, the difference between *W* and *S*, between what the civilian is asking and what the military would like to do anyway, will affect the propensity to shirk; other things equal, the smaller the difference, the less incentive the military has to shirk—in the extreme, if the civilian asks the military to do something it already wants to do, then the concept of shirking does not really apply. The difference between *W* and *S* is exogenous, a function of other factors outside the agency model, such as the nature of the external threat; again, "outside the model" does not mean irrelevant to civil-military relations but rather "something that is best thought of as affecting civil-military relations rather than being affected by civil-military relations." The second consideration is endogenous to the game: specifically, how the civilian principal responds to shirking.

After the military has moved, nature has a move: will the shirking be caught or not? Not all shirking will be detected; indeed, this is the essence of the agency problem. The probability of being caught is a function of the monitoring system; the more intrusive the civilian monitors, the greater the likelihood that military shirking will be detected. If shirking *is* detected, the civilian has a move: whether or not to punish *(p)* the military agent. As noted in the previous chapter, punishment is not a foregone conclusion, for the civilian may lack the political power or will to punish a popular military figure who shirks. The probability of punishment, then, is an exogenous factor that will vary with changes in the makeup of the civilian and military actors. For instance, the combination of a popular president and an unpopular general will result in a different probability of punishment than the combination of an unpopular president and a popular general. Likewise, unified agents might be harder to punish than divided agents; conversely, unified principals may be more likely to punish than divided principals.[6]

The Civil-Military Game in Formal Terms

The foregoing can be represented in the following simple game. Suppose there are two players, Civ and Mil. The game begins with Civ deciding how to monitor the delegation given to Mil. Once the monitoring is set, Mil decides whether to shirk or not, followed by Civ's response either to punish or not. In such a game, there are six possible outcomes. I will use uppercase letters to denote the payoffs to civilians and lowercase to denote payoffs to the military. Note, therefore, that $S2$, the civilian payoff of military shirking if Civ does not punish is entirely different from $s2$, the military payoff of shirking with intrusive monitoring.

Players:

Civ (decides how to monitor and then punishes or not)
Mil (decides whether to work or shirk)

Game sequence:

1. Civ decides whether to monitor intrusively or not (police patrol versus fire alarm)
2. Mil decides whether to work or shirk
3. Nature decides whether shirking is detected
4. Civ punishes or not

Lexicon:

W: Work done as the civilian principal wanted it
S: Work done as the military agent wanted it (shirking)
$C1$: Civilian costs of monitoring (time/effort costs and the policy costs of inexpert meddling)
$S1$: The civilian payoff of military shirking if civilian punishes
$S2$: The civilian payoff of military shirking if civilian does not punish
p: Costs to military of punishment (makes shirking less valuable to the military)
$w1$: The military payoff of working with unintrusive monitoring
$w2$: The military payoff of working with intrusive monitoring
$s1$: The military payoff of shirking with unintrusive monitoring
$s2$: The military payoff of shirking with intrusive monitoring.
a: The probability of detecting shirking if there is unintrusive monitoring
b: The probability of detecting shirking if there is intrusive monitoring
g: The probability of punishing shirking

Outcomes:

$O1$: Civ monitors intrusively; Mil works $[W - C1, w2]$
$O2$: Civ monitors intrusively; Mil shirks; Civ punishes $[S1 - C1, s2 - p]$

O3: Civ monitors intrusively; Mil shirks; Civ does not punish [$S2 - C1$, $s2$]

O4: Civ does not monitor intrusively; Mil works [W, $w1$]

O5: Civ does not monitor intrusively; Mil shirks; Civ punishes [$S1$, $s1 - p$]

O6: Civ does not monitor intrusively; Mil shirks; Civ does not punish [$S2$, $s1$]

Restrictions:

$b > a$, the probability that shirking will be detected is greater if the civilian monitors intrusively

$C1 > 0$, there is some finite cost to monitoring

$p > 0$, the military perceives some finite cost to punishing

Assumptions:

g, the probability of punishing shirking, if shirking is detected, is exogenously determined. This parameter is a function of factors external to the model, such as the relative popularity or political strength of civilian and military leaders, or the individual style of a civilian principal.

$s1 > s2$, and $w1 > w2$, the military payoff of shirking (or working) with no monitoring is greater than the military payoff of shirking (or working) with monitoring, independent of any punishment. This expresses, in formal terms, the common claim of organization theory that military organizations do not like intrusive monitoring.

How will Civ and Mil rank their preferences over these six outcomes? The ranking for Civ is straightforward, based on the notion of the civilian as sensitive to costs. Civ would prefer to have the work done with the least amount of delegation and monitoring costs. If Civ is going to invest the time and effort to monitor, Civ would prefer to detect any shirking and, consequently, to punish it if detected. (As discussed earlier, Civ's decision to punish detected shirking is not automatic. The model would capture the various factors that make punishing less likely in low values for g). Thus Civ would first prefer the work outcomes W and $W - C1$, in descending order of cost. Civ's preference ranking for the four shirking outcomes reflects the desire to punish shirking and the desire not to have to spend the effort to monitor intrusively: $S1$, $S1 - C1$, $S2$, and $S2 - C1$.

As discussed in the previous chapter, the agent's orientation means that Mil has a rank ordering of preferences different from Civ's. Indeed if they had the same preferences, many of the agency problems would virtually disappear; there would still be a relational component to the principal-agent interaction, however, because in a democracy the responsible civilian officials must ultimately retain authority. Consequently, Mil would prefer to do things its own way, especially if it did not get punished for it, and Mil always prefers less-intrusive monitoring; thus Mil's first two preferences are $s1$ and $s2$. The rest of the ordering is debatable. Punishment is a negative value in that it reduces the utility of the shirking outcome from the point of view of Mil; if Mil is going to shirk, it does not want to get punished. But whether or not this reduces the value of shirking below the value of working depends on Mil's cardinal values, the three parameters working *(w)*, shirking *(s)*, and punishment *(p)*, and it is not feasible to measure the cardinal values with any confidence. In societies where the military has reason to believe that p is always negligible—for instance, in Guatemala for most of its history—there is nothing to reduce the shirking outcome relative to the working outcome. In such a case, the military may rank all forms of shirking ahead of working. However, given the empirical domain of my study (the American democracy), it seems more plausible to assume that the military prefers working to shirking with punishment. Thus, the remaining ranking is: $w1, w2, s1 - p, s2 - p$. Although Huntington obviously does not frame his argument this way, setting the military preference in this way is at least partially consistent with his theory. He dismisses the shirking possibility entirely in the case of a professional military (thus he would challenge a ranking that put shirking without punishment ahead of working), but by extension his logic must also place working ahead of shirking with punishment. Thus, the ranking I use is essentially Huntington's, but with the additional twist that a professional military might shirk if it thought it could get away with it. Table 4.1 summarizes the preference order.

Figure 4.1 depicts the expanded game. Before analyzing the game for equilibria conditions, it is possible to group together the branches under the shirking node. Given the uncertainty over whether shirking will be detected and whether it will be punished if detected, the payoff for shirking can be viewed as the expected value of shirking without getting punished minus the expected value of shirking and getting punished. Through basic algebraic steps, this simplifies the game into the one depicted in Figure 4.2.

It is now possible to analyze the game for equilibria, for instance to see the conditions under which we would expect Mil to work or shirk.[7] By the rationalist assumption, Mil will work when it expects a better payoff from that

Table 4.1 Preferences of the players

Ranking	Civ	Mil
1	W	$s1$
2	$W-C1$	$s2$
3	$S1$	$w1$
4	$S1-C1$	$w2$
5	$S2$	$s1-p$
6	$S2-C1$	$s2-p$

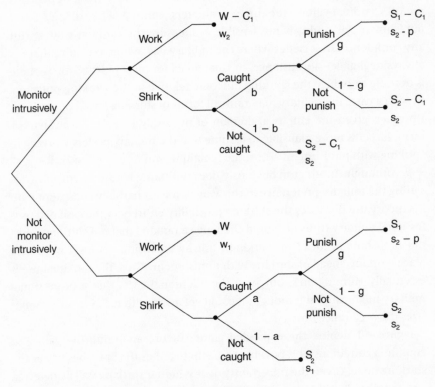

Figure 4.1 Expanded civil-military game

course of action. If Mil finds itself in a world of intrusive monitoring, the payoff from working will be greater than the payoff from shirking if the following inequality is true:

$$w2 > s2 - bgp$$

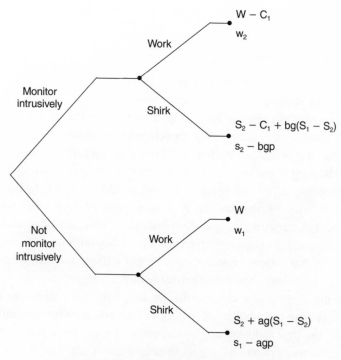

Figure 4.2 Reduced civil-military game

If Mil finds itself in a world of no intrusive monitoring, the payoff from working will be greater than the payoff from shirking if the following inequality is true:

$$w1 > s1 - agp$$

By assumption we know that Mil prefers shirking to working, $s2 > w2$ and $s1 > w1$. Thus Mil will work only if the punishment is great enough to reduce the net gain of shirking below that of working. If the punishment (p) is too light, Mil may shirk regardless of how likely it believes it is that the punishment will be levied against it (that is, how great a, b, and g are); intuitively, even if an agent is certain it will receive punishment, this may not be an effective deterrent if the punishment is trivial. The probability parameters are distributed between 0 and 1, while the punishment parameter is effectively without a maximum. Thus, it is possible to identify $p(\text{min})$, the minimum punishment necessary to affect the agent's decision. This parameter, $p(\text{min})$, is a function of the gap between s and w, the difference between

Mil's subjective value for shirking and Mil's subjective value for working; specifically,

$$p(\text{min}) = s - w$$

When the punishment involves pain less than the value Mil sees from shirking—when $p < p(\text{min})$—then the likelihood of receiving such punishment does not matter anymore. When p is greater than $p(\text{min})$, then the probability of receiving punishment can decisively influence Mil's calculation.

If traditional organization theory's claim that the military dislikes intrusive monitoring is not true, then the payoffs for the game would be different: specifically, $s2$ would equal $s1$ and $w2$ would equal $w1$. In this special case, other things being equal, the decision to work or shirk depends only on the probability of getting caught. And since the probability of getting caught with monitoring (b) is greater than the probability without monitoring (a), then the military agent would always be more likely to shirk under nonintrusive monitoring than under intrusive monitoring.

Since monitoring is a continuum, ranging from very intrusive to very unintrusive, the probabilities of getting caught are likewise continuous. At the limit, the probability of getting caught under nonintrusive monitoring can approach the probability of getting caught under intrusive monitoring $(a$ can approach $b)$, for instance if the issue area is such that intrusive monitoring is not very reliable or nonintrusive monitoring (like relying on a media fire alarm) *is* very reliable, or both. In such a case, the difference in the net payoff of working versus shirking under intrusive monitoring and under no intrusive monitoring may disappear altogether.

Civ's best choice, whether or not to monitor intrusively, depends on how Civ assesses four possible agent responses: that Mil always works, that Mil always shirks, that Mil works if monitored but shirks if not monitored, and, finally, that Mil shirks if monitored and works if not monitored. Table 4.2 describes the conditions under which each of these four responses holds.

What would be Civ's best response in each of these cases? The easiest case is if Mil always works. The conditions for such a Mil strategy are straightforward: Mil will pursue such a strategy in a world where its intrinsic payoff from shirking is small relative to working (its policy preference is not that different from that of Civ's) or it has a relatively high expectation of punishment if it shirks, or both. In such a world, Civ is comparing payoffs W and $W - C1$, the payoffs for monitoring unintrusively and monitoring intrusively, respectively. So long as there is some cost to monitoring ($C1 > 0$), then given

Table 4.2   Military responses and their associated conditions

Responses	Payoff conditions under which Mil would have such a response
Always work	$w1 > s1 - agp$ and $w2 > s2 - bgp$
Always shirk	$w1 < s1 - agp$ and $w2 < s2 - bgp$
Work if monitored intrusively, shirk if not monitored intrusively	$w2 > s2 - bgp$ and $w1 < s1 - agp$
Shirk if monitored intrusively, work if not monitored intrusively	$w2 < s2 - bgp$ and $w1 > s1 - agp$

a cost-sensitive Civ, Civ will most prefer W, the payoff for not monitoring intrusively. If Mil always works, Civ's best choice is not to monitor intrusively—in other words, Civ never monitors intrusively.

Note that this set of results essentially replicates Huntington's prescription. Huntington recommends objective control, encapsulated here as "nonintrusive monitoring," as the best way for civilians to get their most favored outcome, W. Huntington is correct provided that the conditions are met; that is, provided that the difference in policy preferences is small or the military has a high expectation for punishment. As we will explore in greater detail in Chapter 5, Huntington's claim that professional militaries will obey civilians and thus allow civilians to adopt objective control is, in terms of the model, a claim about the preference rankings of professional militaries; since Huntington's story contains no punishment, there is no other leverage point at which Huntington affects the game. Thus, his claim about professionalism is a claim that professional militaries will share civilian preferences, so civilians need not monitor intrusively. If the military is guaranteed to work, then the civilian would clearly prefer not to monitor intrusively, since of necessity W is greater than $W - C1$ (although as monitoring costs approach zero the civilian would become increasingly indifferent between intrusive and nonintrusive monitoring, even if the military was guaranteed to work). Hence, Huntington's normative claim: if you can be sure the military will do what you want, you need not closely monitor the military. Stated in this way, of course, it skirts on the edge of a tautology. To achieve this convergence, he recommends that *civilians change their preferences to match the military's*—this is how the model would operationalize his recommendation that American civilian society eschew its traditional liberalism and embrace the conservatism of the military ethic. In the limit, however, if civilians and the military share preference rankings, then the concept of working and shirking loses much of its meaning. There is not much of a principal-agent problem when preference rankings are identical.

Thus Huntington's account is true, but not helpful. The civil-military challenge is to get work outcomes when civilian and military preferences diverge. If they diverge, then there must be some other factor at work—the punishment expectation has to be that factor, and that factor is partly endogenous to the reliability of the monitoring system in place.

Turning to the case in which Mil always shirks, Civ makes the following comparison:

$$S2 + ag(S1 - S2) \text{ versus}$$
$$S2 - C1 + bg(S1 - S2)$$

This is the case when Mil's expected payoff to shirking always exceeds its expected payoff to working, because its policy preferences sharply diverge from those of Civ or because it has a low expectation of receiving serious punishment. Civ's best choice is to monitor intrusively when:

$$S2 - C1 + bg(S1 - S2) > S2 + ag(S1 - S2)$$

Grouping terms together simplifies the inequality somewhat:

$$bg(S1 - S2) > ag(S1 - S2) + C1$$

Now by assumption, the probability of being caught if there is no intrusive monitoring is less than the probability of being caught if there is intrusive monitoring, that is $a < b$. Thus, $bg(S1 - S2)$ will always be greater than $ag(S1 - S2)$. If, however, the costs of monitoring are very great ($C1$ is very large), then the inequality is less likely to be true. How great must $C1$ be for Civ to decide not to monitor intrusively? By solving the inequality for $C1$, we get the following:

$$C1 < bg(S1 - S2) - ag(S1 - S2), \text{ or,}$$
$$C1 < (bg - ag)(S1 - S2)$$

The inequality says that the costs of monitoring must be very large to get Civ not to monitor intrusively if one or both of the following conditions are true:

first, if b is much bigger than a, meaning that the reliability boost from intrusive monitoring is very high; second, if $S1$ is much bigger than $S2$, meaning that Civ's value from shirking with punishment is much higher than Civ's value from letting shirking go unpunished. In plain English, in the case where Mil always shirks, then Civ will monitor intrusively if the costs of monitoring are not great, or if monitoring intrusively will significantly increase the chance of detecting shirking, or if Civ is very concerned not to let some shirking go unpunished.

In the third case, Mil will work if monitored and will shirk if not monitored. In this case, Civ compares $W - C1$ and $S2 + ag(S1 - S2)$. Civ will monitor if:

$$W - C1 > S2 + ag(S1 - S2)$$

Grouping the terms in another way yields the following equivalent expression, which captures the factors as a function of the gap between civilian and military preferences:

$$W - S2 > C1 + ag(S1 - S2)$$

When the Civ payoff from working, less any payoff Civ would receive from shirking, is greater than the costs of monitoring plus the expected value of the shirking with punishment minus the shirking without punishment, then we would expect Civ to monitor intrusively. Solving for $C1$ tells us how low the costs of monitoring have to be to satisfy this condition:

$$C1 < W - S2 - ag(S1 - S2)$$

As explained in Appendix 4.1, this condition is more easily maintained than the condition in the previous case (in which Mil always shirks). If Mil is pursuing a strategy of working if monitored intrusively and shirking if not monitored intrusively, then Civ will monitor intrusively even if the costs of monitoring are relatively high, high enough to cause Civ to abandon intrusive monitoring in the case where Mil always shirks.

Finally, Civ considers the case in which Mil will shirk if monitored and work if not monitored. This is a counterintuitive case, a fact reflected in the special combination of Mil payoff conditions necessary for this case to obtain. For Mil to pursue such a strategy, it would have to be true that Mil prefers working when there is no monitoring and shirking when there is monitoring. In formal terms, it must be simultaneously true that $w2 < s2 - bgp$ and that $w1 > s1 - agp$. As explained in Appendix 4.2, so long as the impact of intrusive monitoring degrades Mil's estimation of the value of shirking the same as it degrades Mil's estimation of the value of working (so long as $s1 - s2 = w1 - w2$), then this inequality cannot hold. Therefore, we do not need to consider this case.

Conclusion

The model thus captures observable patterns of civil-military relations—combinations of civilian choices regarding intrusive monitoring and military choices regarding working and shirking—as a function of other potentially observable factors: the costs of monitoring, the probabilities of being punished, and so on. The agency model, moreover, is making a causal argument in these cases, that specific outcomes are observed because certain equilibrium conditions rather than others are also met in each case: for example, civilians are choosing more intrusive monitoring because the costs of monitoring are low or because the expectations of shirking are high, and the military is choosing to work because its preferences are converging with those of civilians or because the likelihood of getting punished is high. Of course, such answers beg further questions—why are costs of monitoring low, and why are expectations of punishment high? Agency theory raises these questions but it ultimately does not answer them. Perhaps this is a limitation of agency theory, but similar limitations apply to all other theories as well. And, uniquely, agency theory tells us why we should care about such questions, which do not arise from analyses based on traditional civil-military relations theory.

The algebraic expressions generated by the formal model may seem too complicated and overly reliant on intersubjective comparisons to yield definitive insights. How can we tell whether the costs of intrusive monitoring are less than the value of working minus the value of shirking, and so on? As we shall see in subsequent chapters, if we have reason to expect systematic changes in some of these parameters, we should be able to assess the likelihood that these inequalities will hold, and hence the likelihood that civilians will monitor intrusively or that the military will shirk. Moreover, like all social science, agency theory can do no more than make a probabilistic claim—that given certain values for the equilibrium conditions, we expect that one set of outcomes is more likely than another set of outcomes. The idiosyncrasies of willful human agents mean that we do not live in a deterministic social universe—game theory, for all its ambitions for greater precision, does not pretend otherwise.

Despite the potentially off-putting jargon of the formal method, the agency model is actually quite simple and the results may even seem intuitive. As the probability of detecting or the probability of punishing goes down, the military agent is more likely to shirk. The probability of catching wrongdoing is a function of the type of monitoring done. And so on. A more complicated model, perhaps modified along lines discussed in the concluding chapter, might yield a larger array of counterintuitive hypotheses.

As a point of departure for the first-cut empirical investigations of the next several chapters, however, even these intuitive results represent an advance over traditional civil-military relations theory. What is striking about agency theory is that factors that emerge as so obviously central from the deductive logic of the model—the costs of monitoring, the expectations of punishment, the strategic calculus of the actors—are nevertheless essentially absent in traditional civil-military relations theory. Within the confines of traditional Huntingtonian or Janowitzean theory, one does not end up with hypotheses about the military's expectations of being punished. Beginning from the deductive base of agency theory, such hypotheses are inescapable.

While agency theory represents a dramatically different way of thinking about civil-military relations, it does not require us to reject all the insights of traditional civil-military relations theory. On the contrary, the agency model subsumes much of what traditional theory already argues. For instance, the model shows how Huntington's arguments about the optimal form of delegation can be true under certain conditions, some of which Huntington recognized and some of which he did not explicitly identify.

The monopoly on the legitimate use of force is what distinguishes government from other institutions. Understanding how this monopoly is delegated and controlled is therefore central to the enterprise of political science. My model provides what is lacking in traditional civil-military relations theory: the microfoundations, that is, how the structure of choices and incentives facing the relevant actors shapes their relations. Modeling these choices and incentives makes the step-by-step logic of the argument more explicit, and this allows the logic to be more readily tested and either supported or undermined by empirical evidence (the task for Chapters 5 and 6). It also paves the way to exploring what political scientists call the "causal mechanism," the logic whereby observed correlations are understood to be causally related.

Agency theory draws upon insights gleaned from the study of other domestic institutions, but is tailored to the political challenges peculiar to the civil-military problematique. The model seeks to explain changes in patterns of civil-military relations over time and in response to at least potentially observable features of particular civil-military relationships. The model uses standard insights from principal-agent analysis to identify a wide range of control mechanisms available to principals. The model goes beyond many previous applications of principal-agency, however, in offering hypotheses for how principals might choose to monitor that delegation, in light of the agents' incentives to shirk.

The model developed here is already an advance over prevailing treatments of civil-military relations. It recognizes that the civil-military relationship is characterized by strategic political interaction, even in cases (as in the United States) where the most basic question of "who is in charge" seems settled. It treats civilian control not as a once-and-done choice between Weberian ideal types but rather as an ongoing decision about how to monitor the delegation of responsibility to the military. It reflects the fact that civilians and military leaders confront the problems of agency on a day-to-day basis. Therefore this model is particularly well suited to illuminating changes over time.

It is also an important theoretical advance over existing principal-agent analyses and not simply an application of established theories to a new empirical domain. By endogenizing the monitoring decision, it specifically raises the question of how principals select from among an array of options for mitigating the problems of agency. The bulk of the existing political principal-agent literature is devoted to challenging the proposition that delegation amounts to abdication. In comparison, with a few exceptions (Bawn 1995; Brehm and Gates 1992a, 1992b; Hamilton and Schroeder 1994; Lupia and McCubbins 1994; and Spence no date), remarkably little attention is paid to the determinants of the principal's choice. Likewise, by treating the probability of punishment as a variable (albeit an exogenous variable), agency theory shows how shirking can arise even in situations where the agent's behavior is likely to be exposed. Finally, the model also extends principal-agent analysis beyond most existing political applications by treating the agent as a strategic actor rather than a passive player simply acted on by a wiser principal.

APPENDIX 4.1

In this appendix I show that the conditions under which the civilian (Civ) would monitor intrusively are less restrictive if the military (Mil) is pursuing a strategy of working if monitored and shirking if not monitored than if Mil is pursuing a strategy of always shirking.

If Mil is always shirking, then Civ will monitor intrusively if the costs of monitoring meet the following condition:

$$C1 < (bg - ag)(S1 - S2) \qquad\qquad inequality\ 1$$

If Mil is working if monitored intrusively and shirking if not monitored intrusively, Civ will monitor intrusively if the costs of monitoring (which I will call here $C1*$) meet the following condition:

$$C1* < W - S2 - ag(S1 - S2) \qquad\qquad inequality\ 2$$

By assumption, we also know that $S1 < W$, because Civ's payoff from Mil's working is higher than Civ's payoff from Mil's shirking with punishment. And for the same reason, $S2 < S1$. Furthermore, because bg is a probability, it must lie between 0 and 1. Therefore the following expression must also be true:

$$[S2 + bg(S1 - S2)] \leq S1 < W$$

If we substitute the leftmost expression from this inequality for W in another expression, we would reduce that expression. Thus,

$$W - S2 - ag(S1 - S2) > [S2 + bg(S1 - S2)] - S2 - ag(S1 - S2)$$

The right side of this inequality can be simplified algebraically to yield the following:

$$W - S2 - ag(S1 - S2) > (bg - ag)(S1 - S2)$$

The righthand expression is the same one appearing in inequality 1 and the lefthand expression is the same one appearing in inequality 2. Therefore, substituting for the costs of monitoring, we see that:

$$C1* > C1$$

APPENDIX 4.2

In this appendix I show that the fourth notional military strategy does not hold in equilibrium. Consider the fourth Mil strategy, to shirk if monitored intrusively and work if not monitored intrusively. This is the best Mil strategy when the following two inequalities hold: $w2 < s2 - bgp$ and $w1 > s1 -$

agp. Given the assumptions and restrictions of the model, and given a reasonable additional inference, these conditions cannot be met simultaneously.

By restriction $b > a$, the probability of being caught is greater with intrusive monitoring than with no intrusive monitoring. Therefore, $bgp > agp$. By assumption, $w1 > w2$ and $s1 > s2$; consistent with traditional organization theory, Mil intrinsically does not like intrusive monitoring, thus if Mil is going to work, Mil prefers working without intrusive monitoring, and the same holds for shirking. It also seems plausible that the *amount* of this Mil preference for no intrusive monitoring is the same whether Mil is considering working or shirking; when Mil thinks about the four options, namely the intrusive monitoring versus no intrusive monitoring possibilities for both working and shirking, Mil prefers the no-intrusive-monitoring outcome by the same amount, regardless of whether it will work or shirk. In formal terms, this would be: $s1 - s2 = w1 - w2$. This expression is equivalent to: $w2 - s2 = w1 - s1$.

Given this auxiliary assumption, it is possible to show algebraically that the inequality conditions cannot hold:

$w1 > s1 - agp$ and $w2 < s2 - bgp$; thus,

$w1 - s1 + agp > 0$ and $w2 - s2 + bgp < 0$; thus,

$w1 - s1 + agp > w2 - s2 + bgp$;

since $w1 - s1 = w2 - s2$, we can substitute and get

$w1 - s1 + agp > w1 - s1 + bgp$; or,

$agp > bgp$

But by assumption $bgp > agp$, therefore the inequality conditions cannot hold. Q.E.D.

Note that this is true only because we have made the reasonable assumption that traditional theory's claim that organizations do not like intrusion will produce the same amount of intrinsic disutility whether Mil contemplates working or shirking. If this assumption is not true and, on the contrary, the presence of intrusive monitoring changes the relative intrinsic utility difference between shirking versus working, then Mil might indeed consider working if not monitored and shirking if monitored. In such a case, Civ would have to consider this fourth military strategy, producing a fourth set of conditions, as follows.

Civ compares $S2 + bg(S1 - S2) - C1$ with W. In this case, Civ will monitor intrusively if the following inequality holds:

$$W < S2 + bg(S1 - S2) - C1$$

Regrouping the terms yields:

$$W - S2 < bg(S1 - S2) - C1$$

Given the ordinal payoff structure Civ, $W - S2$ is always greater than $S1 - S2$. Also, bg is always less than or equal to 1; $C1$ is always at least greater than 0. Therefore, this inequality never holds and in this instance the model yields a trivial result: if Mil shirks if monitored intrusively and works if not monitored intrusively, it never makes sense for Civ to monitor intrusively.

CHAPTER 5

An Agency Theory Solution
to the Cold War Puzzle

As argued in Chapter 2, Huntington's theory does not account well for American civil-military relations during the Cold War. In this chapter, I use the agency theory developed in Chapters 3 and 4 to reconsider Cold War civil-military relations. Consistent with agency theory, the available evidence suggests that the Cold War fit a rough equilibrium outcome of civilian intrusive monitoring coupled with military working. Civil-military relations landed at this equilibrium because the costs of monitoring were relatively low and the expectations of punishment were relatively high. Agency theory's contribution is not explaining *why* the costs of monitoring were low or expectations of punishment were high, but rather *how* those factors then affected civil-military relations in the United States.

The chapter proceeds as follows. I subsume Huntington's theory into my theory by mapping his prescription onto the various monitoring and working outcomes postulated by the agency model. I next evaluate the Cold War as a whole to identify which of the outcomes best fits the available evidence. This will tell us what happened, but it will not directly say why it happened. The agency model allows us to take something relatively easy to observe (with the benefit of hindsight), namely civil-military outcomes, and use those observations to make inferences about less-observable microstrategic processes. In other words, given an observed outcome, the model can be used to generate predictions about the likely values of the parameters governing the equilibria. We can then weigh the evidence to see if these parameters do indeed seem to hold the values expected by the model. This process, which I am calling "reverse engineering," is nothing more than basic social science: making predictions based on hypotheses about causal relationships. If agency theory is superior, then within the limitations of measuring complex social phenomena we should expect the historical record to support more of the observable implications of agency theory's logic than is the case for Huntington's theory. I generate these hypotheses and test their empirical validity by weighing the evidence for the Cold War as a whole, by considering counterinstances, and by examining more closely one important subcase, the Vietnam War.

Agency theory thus provides an explanation for U.S. civil-military relations at several levels of analysis. It accounts for the most general pattern observed at the aggregate level that treats the entire U.S. Cold War experience as a single case. It also provides a systematic account for at least some of the variation seen within that case—that is, the instances when U.S. civil-military relations diverged from the overall pattern. And it can guide a closer examination of the important subcase of Vietnam.

Can Agency Theory Subsume Huntington's Theory?

Although the evidence does not support Huntington's claim about the convergence of civil and military preferences, this does not in and of itself invalidate all of his underlying logic. Indeed, the agency model shows that both of Huntington's postulated outcomes—his nightmare scenario and his prescription—are merely special cases of a more general theory of civil-military relations. The agency model can therefore resolve the Cold War puzzle by suggesting alternative explanations for what happened and why.

Agency theory provides for four general patterns of civil-military relations: military working with nonintrusive monitoring by civilians, military working with intrusive monitoring by civilians, military shirking with nonintrusive monitoring by civilians, and military shirking with intrusive monitoring by civilians. The outcome of working with nonintrusive monitoring corresponds to Huntington's prescription: give the military autonomy, and the military will do what civilians have asked them to do.[1] Likewise, the working with intrusive monitoring outcome corresponds to Huntington's nightmare scenario of a systematic violation of the autonomy the military needs to be professional—in other words, intrusive monitoring by civilians (subjective control). Huntington acknowledges that such methods might ensure that civilians get what they asked for (W, working), but he goes on to warn that it would not be what civilians really want, namely adequate protection from external enemies. This is because there are considerable costs associated with such monitoring; in terms of the agency model, this is a claim that $C1$ is very large, thus the civilian's net payoff, $W - C1$, is very small.

The two shirking outcomes do not map very well to Huntington's theory, in part because Huntington does not consider military disobedience to be a serious concern in the American case. For instance, Huntington claims that during World War II U.S. civil-military relations were pathological and the U.S. military enjoyed too much political power. Even then, however, Huntington claims that the U.S. military essentially did exactly what civilians wanted it to do (Huntington 1957, p. 315). Nevertheless it is not too much of a stretch to consider the shirking and no monitoring outcome as a form of Lasswell's garrison state: maximum delegation of all civilian functions to the military and minimal safeguards on how the military exercises these responsibilities, with the result that military considerations dominate the political process. The fourth outcome, shirking and intrusive monitoring, would be characterized by relatively high civil-military friction. Table 5.1 summarizes the four outcomes and the corresponding identifier from traditional civil-military relations theory.

The agency model also confirms the deductive logic of Huntington's prescription. If civilian and military preferences converge, as Huntington recommends, there is a greater likelihood of ending up at the nonintrusive monitoring and working outcome. The convergence of civilian and military preferences can be represented as a narrowing of the gap between W and S and so the expression $W - S$ gets smaller. When this happens, as Chapter 4 showed, the equilibrium conditions for strategy pairs that would produce the no-intrusive-monitoring-and-working outcome become easier to sustain, precisely what Huntington's informal theory expects.[2] Note, however, that the agency model is agnostic on any significance attaching to the direc-

Table 5.1 Agency model payoffs and traditional theory

	Military works	Military shirks
Civilian monitors intrusively	Agency payoff: $W - C1$ Huntington's "crisis"	Agency payoff: $S2 - C1 + bg(S1 - S2)$ Extreme civil-military friction
Civilian does not monitor intrusively	Agency payoff: W Huntington's prescription	Agency payoff: $S2 + ag(S1 - S2)$ Lasswell's "garrison state"

tion of the movement. For instance, it matters not whether the civilian conception of work moves closer to the military ideal point or vice versa. For Huntington, of course, this was crucial. Civil-military relations would be at their best if the civilian preference moved toward the military; conversely, relations would be pathological if the military preference moved toward the civilian, as happened, Huntington claims, in World War II (Huntington 1957, p. 315).

Thus, the agency model is able to incorporate a significant portion (though not all) of Huntington's argument. It confirms that Huntington's theory is logically consistent on how civil-military relations might have played out during the Cold War. Had civilian and military preferences converged as Huntington prescribed, it would have led to a greater expectation that civilians could eschew intrusive monitoring without running too great a risk of military shirking. However, as discussed in Chapter 2, the evidence that civilian and military preferences converged in the way Huntington's theory requires is not particularly persuasive. Of course, the gap was not static. Changes in the external threat, the shift to the all-volunteer force, and the ability of presidents to selectively promote senior officers all allowed for convergences and divergences over time. But the preference gap did *not* make a sustained movement in the direction dictated by Huntington's theory. In other words, Huntington could have been right about what happened to civil-military relations in the Cold War, but the evidence appears to show that he was not.

Which Agency Theory Outcome Best Describes Cold War Civil-Military Relations?

The questions remain, what happened to U.S. civil-military relations during the Cold War, and why? Put another way, which cell of Table 5.1 best represents the U.S. Cold War experience, and why did the United States end up in that cell?

The answers will vary by issue area and time period. For instance, civilians monitored nuclear policy more intrusively than nonnuclear policy, and even with nuclear policy the intrusiveness varied over time (Feaver 1992). Likewise, the military "worked" in some areas more consistently than in others. For the purposes of demonstrating the plausibility and utility of the agency approach to civil-military relations, a broader-gauge evaluation focusing on one crucial policy component is preferred. I will focus on the use of force, bracketing for future research other policy domains of budgeting, personnel policy, arms procurement, and so on. Viewing the entire Cold War period as a whole, which characterization of civilian intrusiveness and military working best represents the historical record in the area of use of force?

Did Civilians Monitor Intrusively?

It is very difficult to precisely measure intrusive civilian monitoring of the military. Given data and measurement limitations, the best we can do is look for broad comparisons with previous eras and examine plausible surrogates for the underlying concept. Under those restraints, compared with the kinds of civilian oversight characteristic of the pre–World War II military establishment, it seems clear that civilians monitored intrusively during the Cold War.

Prior to World War II, civilians simply lacked the infrastructure to monitor the military intrusively. Within the executive branch, responsibility was distributed to the War and Navy Departments, which had only very small civilian staffs. The White House staff was similarly tiny; indeed the Executive Office of the President and the six agencies of central management, including the Bureau of the Budget (the predecessor to the Office of Management and the Budget) and the Office of Personnel Management were established only in 1939 (Kernell and Popkin 1986, p. 88). During the Cold War, the monitoring capacity increased substantially. For instance, there were but 165 budgeted and detailed staff of the White House in 1935; the number climbed to nearly 632 in 1970 before dropping to around 361 in 1978 (ibid). While only a portion of this staff was responsible for coordinating national security policy (and therefore "monitoring" the military), the aggregate growth reflects an increased capacity to oversee and direct activity from the White House. Similarly, interagency mechanisms for oversight, for instance the National Security Council, were not established until 1947. A similar enhanced capacity for monitoring intrusively was developed within the relevant cabinet offices. Innovations introduced by Secretary of Defense McNamara, particularly the Planning, Programming, and Budgeting System (PPBS) likewise represented a qualitative increase in the capacity of civilians to oversee military policy, compared with what was available before the Cold War.

The mechanisms for civilian oversight that did exist prior to the Cold War were generally less robust than their Cold War counterparts (Smith 1951, pp. 63–64). Victor Metcalf, the Secretary of the Navy under President Theodore Roosevelt, described his position in dismissive terms: "My duties consist of waiting for the Chief of the Bureau of Navigation to come in with a paper, put it down before me with his finger on a dotted line and say to me, 'Sign your name here.' It is all any Secretary of the Navy does'" (Rogers 1940, p. 289). Paul Appleby's evaluation of prewar secretarial oversight suggests that Metcalf's experience was representative: "The War and Navy departments have done more than all other organizations to popularize the 'staff' idea—and more to destroy it above the military level. Neither department has much truly general staff in any other than military terms. Neither has any real general staff in departmental or secretarial terms" (Appleby 1948, p. 72).

In contrast, summary assessments of civil-military relations during the Cold War hold that civilians monitored the military far more intrusively, although the intrusiveness varied across administrations (Ingram 1968, O'Meara 1978, Barrett 1983, Feaver 1992). O'Meara claims that monitoring became generally more intrusive over the course of the Cold War, and that unspecified conservative administrations were less intrusive than liberal ones (O'Meara 1978, p. 88). By all accounts, including his own, Secretary of Defense McNamara represented at least one of the high-water marks in civilian intrusive monitoring, although the conventional wisdom likewise holds that civilian monitoring was less intrusive during the Reagan era.[3]

These summary assessments are supported by some basic measures of civilian capacity for intrusive monitoring. The measures are admittedly crude, but they represent the best attempts so far to operationalize this difficult concept within the limits of the data available.[4] As a first cut, the staff of the Office of the Secretary of Defense (OSD) might be considered the "police patrolmen" of intrusive civilian monitoring. Figure 5.1 shows that in the first few years following creation of the Department of Defense in 1947, the Office of the Secretary of Defense's staff increased dramatically, to nearly 2,500 employees. Declining somewhat after the Korean War, the number of staff grew strongly upward through the late 1960s to more than 3,000. Declines in the 1970s returned staff size to the lower levels of the late 1950s (around 1,700 employees).[5] Beginning in the late 1970s, the OSD staff size grew steadily until the end of the Cold War.[6]

Of course, the absolute size of the OSD staff is the crudest of measures. The intrusiveness of civilian monitoring is best thought of as a relative concept; a more informative measure would compare the OSD staff with the

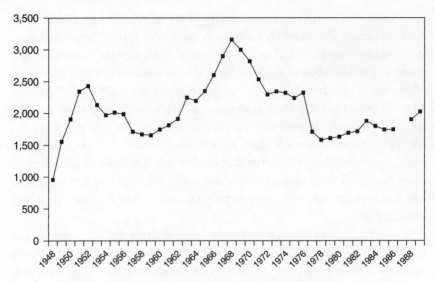

Figure 5.1   OSD personnel, 1948–1989

size of the military establishment it must monitor to get a sense of how proportionate civilian capacity is to the task. There are several ways to measure the proportionality of civilian monitoring, and it is not clear which way is superior. Figure 5.2 gives the ratio comparing civilian staff to two plausible indicators of the monitoring task: the overall size of the armed forces and the overall size of the defense budget outlays.[7]

The ratio based on troop strength took a quick jump down when the military end-strength surged to meet the Korean War mobilization. From that point on there was a slow and steady increase in intrusiveness until the mid-1970s. The shift toward nonintrusiveness from 1975 to 1977 may be partly due to changes in the way the OSD staff size was reported, rather than from a change in the underlying level of monitoring; around this time, staff and functions were shifted out of the OSD to newly established agencies. From the mid-1970s through to the mid-1980s, the ratio based on budget figures shows a gradual trend toward less-intrusive monitoring, whereas the ratio on troop strength oscillates slightly around the level set in 1976. As will be discussed in the next chapter, the ratios change as we head into the end of the Cold War and post–Cold War period. The ratio on budget outlays follows a remarkably similar pattern (for the years reported), giving us somewhat

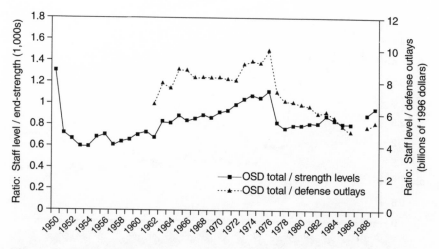

Figure 5.2 OSD staff levels relative to military strength levels (1950–1989) and relative to total defense outlays (1962–1989)

more confidence that these rough indicators are tapping into the same underlying concept.

A somewhat different picture emerges if the size of the military institution to be monitored—the military denominator—is represented by the personnel in the office of the Joint Chiefs of Staff, as seen in Figure 5.3. The JCS staff deserves special scrutiny because it is the part of the military institution responsible for fusing a "military qua military" viewpoint, rather than "military qua service" one and thus plays a special role in civil-military relations. Moreover, the JCS staff is almost entirely a Pentagon headquarters operation, with extensive interactions on a day-to-day basis with civilian counterparts in the policymaking process. Especially after the Goldwater-Nichols reforms of 1986, the JCS staff emerged as the critical military institution supporting the principal military voice in civil-military relations, the chairman of the Joint Chiefs of Staff. Figure 5.3 compares the size of the OSD staff to the size of the JCS staff during the Cold War. This figure suggests more intrusive monitoring during the 1950s, when the JCS staff was tiny (indeed, limited by statute to 210 personnel), than in later years when changes in the size of the OSD staff and the size of the JCS staff moved more or less in tandem. Nevertheless, the defense reforms of 1958, which lifted the statutory restrictions on the size of the JCS staff, marked a turning point. The Cold

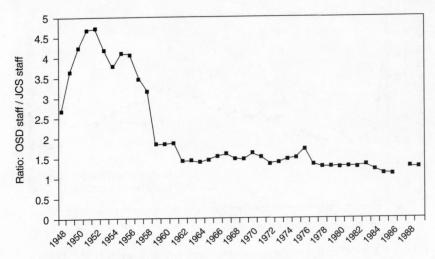

Figure 5.3 OSD staff levels relative to JCS staff levels, 1948–1989

War picture from the early 1960s on tells a simpler story that seems consistent with the picture that emerges from the other figures: overall intrusiveness with a very slight decline from the mid-1970s to the mid-1980s, reaching a Cold War low around the time of the 1986 Goldwater-Nichols reforms.

The intrusiveness of civilian monitoring during the Cold War was also significantly augmented by the activities of Congress. From an agency theory perspective, at least in the initial formulation presented here, there is no reason to distinguish between legislative or executive branch monitoring. The crucial function of monitoring is changing the military agent's expectations about the likelihood that shirking will be exposed. For that function, it does not matter whether the shirking is exposed through a congressional investigative hearing or through the efforts of a civilian auditor in the Office of the Secretary of Defense. Thus, to measure the intrusiveness of monitoring at any given period, it is appropriate to combine the activities of all the branches of government—indeed, the activities of nongovernmental monitors as well.

Congressional oversight of the military had been rather spotty prior to World War II. There were spasms of intensive micromanagement especially during wartime, most famously with the Committee on the Conduct of the War during the Civil War; but the general pattern was one of substantial delegation (Smith 1951, pp. 169–193). During the early years of the Cold War, the increased intrusiveness of civilian oversight was reflected largely within the executive branch, although Kolodziej argues that congressional oversight during this period was also more vigorous than is popularly thought (Kolodziej 1966, p. viii). By all accounts, however, congressional oversight increased most dramatically after the Vietnam War. Blechman details a dramatic increase in congressional activity on the defense budget. The portion of the defense budget requiring authorizing legislation, one measure of congressional micromanagement, climbed from 0 percent in 1962 to essentially 100 percent by 1983 (Blechman 1990, p. 31). Likewise, the number of studies and reports required of the Defense Department by Congress, the number of other mandated actions, and the number of programs adjusted (from the original budget proposed by the president) all increased dramatically from 1970 through to the end of the Cold War (ibid., p. 41). The annual measures of congressional requests for information from the Department of Defense—hundreds of hearings, many hundreds of witnesses, thousands of hours of testimony, and tens of thousands of written inquiries and telephone inquiries—all show extensive oversight.[8]

The general assessment of intrusive monitoring is somewhat at odds with Bouchard's analysis of naval operations in four key Cold War crises, which concludes that civilian control generally fit the category of nonintrusive monitoring.[9] Significantly, Bouchard finds uneven use of the kinds of mechanisms of indirect control that the principal-agent framework emphasizes. Eisenhower and Kennedy did make extensive use of detailed rules of engagement, carefully prescribed contingency plans, special mission orders, and the like, but Johnson and Nixon did not (Bouchard 1991, pp. 64, 101, 141, 165). However, the navy is always the least intrusively monitored of military forces because connectivity is much harder to maintain, and this was especially true before satellite communications were widely deployed. Moreover, it is not clear what is the basis of comparison for Bouchard's qualitative assessment. It appears to be in comparison with some ideal type of direct positive control under which civilian leaders monitor movements in real time and the on-scene commander must request permission before doing anything.[10] As Bouchard himself notes, civilian leaders attempted to monitor naval action more closely than they had historically, and the advance, albeit slow, of communications technology facilitated this effort. For instance, Bouchard notes that on-scene commanders complained about the deluge of requests for information from senior commanders that tied up scarce communications channels. Likewise, in every case Bouchard studies, the White House gave strict and precise instructions on the geographical limits of where the navy could operate during the crisis (Bouchard 1991, pp. 72–73, 76, 128, 136, 141, 163, and 185). On balance, it seems reasonable to interpret Bouchard's data somewhat differently than he did and to conclude that there was relatively intrusive monitoring even in these cases.

Did the Military Work or Shirk?

There is no systematic measure of whether the military worked or shirked during the Cold War, and given the long time frame and wide variety of tasks assigned, it would not be profitable to compile a single index. But it is possible to come to a summary judgment of similar scope to Huntington's original theory. Recall that working and shirking involve more than a determination of whether the United States prevailed in the Cold War (that is, whether the civilian desired outcome of gaining security was achieved). Obviously, the United States prevailed in the Cold War and the desired security was achieved. In and of itself, this fact does not decide the work/shirk question. Rather, it is necessary to break work down into its constituent elements and then identify how the military and the civilian might disagree on each of these elements. Whether the military worked or not depends on whether it met all the civilian desiderata; were civilian functional preferences followed, and were they followed in such a way as to meet the relational goals as well?

Numerous incidents throughout the long Cold War rise to the level of shirking, according to this definition. The most famous example, and arguably the pivotal experience in modern American civil-military relations, was General Douglas MacArthur's challenge to President Harry Truman in the Korean War (Spanier 1959; Donovan 1982; Millis, Mansfield, and Stein 1958, pp. 259–332; Brodie 1973, pp. 81–91; and Flint 1991, pp. 223–267). The dispute consisted of a series of disagreements between General MacArthur, who wanted a freer hand to pursue tactical opportunities and, if necessary, to expand the war, and President Truman along with his stateside military advisors, who were concerned to limit the war and greatly wished to avoid escalation. General MacArthur's views were shared by Truman's Republican critics in Congress and by numerous public opinion polls. Bolstered by this support and convinced of his own superior ability to form military policy (particularly given that he was on the scene in Korea and the civilian leaders were sitting in Washington), General MacArthur persisted in resisting President Truman's expressed desire for how the war should be prosecuted. The controversy climaxed with MacArthur's decision to hold a press conference in which he damaged prospects for peace negotiations by issuing a humiliating ultimatum to the enemy, going against an express order from Truman to clear any policy announcements in advance with the State Department.

For this disobedience, along with his publicly expressed doubts about administration policy in the Far East, Truman removed him from his command and ordered him to retire from the army. MacArthur returned home to a hero's welcome from the American public and especially from the opposition party in Congress, which gave him a bully pulpit to outline his views. MacArthur defended his behavior as justified by the officer's oath, which was to defend the Constitution, not to obey the commander in chief; he argued, "I find in existence a new and heretofore unknown and dangerous concept that the members of our armed forces owe primary allegiance or loyalty to those who temporarily exercise the authority of the Executive Branch of Government rather than to the country and its Constitution which they are sworn to defend" (Taylor 1952, p. 354; as cited in Finer 1962, p. 23). MacArthur's justification, of course, violates the basic premise of civilian control and constitutional authority. The Supreme Court has the responsibility for reviewing the constitutionality of executive action, while the electorate and Congress have the responsibility for reviewing the suitability in policy terms of executive decisions. MacArthur usurped authority that was not his in order to pursue a policy directly contrary to what his civilian superior desired. In short, he shirked.

After MacArthur, perhaps the most important shirker was General Curtis LeMay of the air force, who was commander in chief of Strategic Air Command and later air force chief of staff. LeMay's subversion of civilian authority concerned his views on nuclear war, views that fortunately were never put to the ultimate test. By his own words, LeMay intended to shirk if civilian orders on nuclear operations were not to his liking. In one account, when told that his proposed launch-on-warning policy was "not national policy," LeMay reportedly replied, "I don't care. It's my policy. It's what I am going to do" (Kaplan 1983, p. 134; see also Rosenberg 1981–82, p. 13; and Herken 1985, pp. 96–98). Elsewhere, LeMay showed a similar lack of scruples about the policy in the late 1940s of keeping weapons under civilian custody:

I remember sending somebody out—I don't know whether it was Monty or somebody else—to have a talk with this guy with the key [to gain access to the nuclear stockpile]. I felt that under certain conditions—say we woke up some morning and there wasn't any Washington or something—I was going to take the bombs. I got no static from this man. I never had to do it or anything, but we had an understanding . . . If I were on my own and half the country was destroyed and I could get no orders and so forth, I wasn't going to sit there fat, dumb, and happy and do nothing . . . I was going to take some action at least to get ready to do something. Lacking orders and lacking the assumption that I was going to get some in the near future, I would take some action on my own. (Kohn and Harahan 1988, pp. 83–85; see also Herring 1994, p. 29)

LeMay may have been simply the personification of a deeper problem afflicting the entire nuclear edifice: what might be called "latent shirking." Based on the extraordinarily rich empirical investigation into the details of nuclear operations now available, it seems clear that civilian leaders would have been greatly surprised by the lack of responsiveness that would have attended an order to use nuclear weapons (Bracken 1983; Blair 1985, 1993; Carter, Steinbruner, and Zraket 1987; Feaver 1992; Lebow 1988; Nolan 1989; Rosenberg 1986; Sagan 1989, 1993). Some of this would have been due to a certain naïveté on the part of civilian leaders, as in President Reagan's apparent belief that missiles could be recalled. But enough of the blame could be laid appropriately at the door of the military itself for it to deserve the label of shirking, particularly the efforts of Strategic Air Command to resist meaningful civilian control over any operational details.

Perhaps the most ambiguous area to evaluate concerns efforts by the military to influence the policy process by going over the heads of its direct civilian superiors, as it were, and appealing directly to the American people. Such an effort was central to MacArthur's insubordination, but it has been practiced in more nuanced forms ever since. For instance, conservative elements of the military led by army Chief of Staff Matthew Ridgway were instrumental in mobilizing opposition to President Eisenhower's New Look policy of fiscal moderation on defense spending and its complementary nuclear strategy of massive retaliation with the so-called "alert" seminars and "freedom forums."[11] While the public activities were not organized by the services in a formal conspiratorial campaign, they were nonetheless the fruits of an intentional behind-the-scenes bureaucratic maneuver to undermine the massive retaliation strategy, which one historian considered to be organized insubordination:

Between the autumn of 1953 and the summer of 1955, the United States Army took it upon itself to mount an explicit challenge to civilian control. Through a determined effort aimed at overturning the national security policies promulgated by President Dwight D. Eisenhower . . . Army leaders sought to restrict the ability of senior civilian leaders to determine basic national strategy. (Bacevich 1997, p. 307)

Ridgway's machinations to undermine Eisenhower's strategy have been variously disparaged as petty interservice rivalry and a misguided effort to salvage military professionalism by carving out a role for the army; however characterized, it involved the full gambit of shirking, including foot-dragging obstruction within the administration, repeated attempts to revisit decisions that were made by the president, calculated leaks to the media, speeches and articles to public audiences, and even a carefully crafted subversive rewrite of the army doctrine so as to make it incompatible with the undesired national military strategy (ibid., pp. 318–329).

In certain circumstances, the end run to Congress, in which a service attempts to mobilize sympathetic members of Congress to reinstate a treasured program or policy that was dropped as part of the executive policymaking process, can reach the level of shirking. Eisenhower referred to this as legalized insubordination.[12] Of course, there is nothing wrong per se with explaining public policy to the general public. Huntington (1961b), for instance, describes this activity without making a judgment as to whether it undermines civilian control. Moreover, the military has a constitutional obligation to keep Congress informed about defense policy matters. Whether or not a public relations effort qualifies as shirking depends on whether it is an attempt to undermine or overturn civilian decisions, and on this point the record is too murky for confident assessments but probably favors a conservative evaluation. Evidence abounds of military efforts to influence public debates; evidence of military efforts to subvert civilian decisions in this way is considerably more scarce, although the army's efforts to overturn the New Look strategy probably qualifies (Clotfelter 1973, pp. 94–147; Bacevich 1997).

Despite these famous (or infamous) examples, the overall record seems to support a view of military working throughout the Cold War. Michael Desch presents a list of some thirty-five prominent civil-military disputes and concludes that the military unambiguously shirked in only two cases, President Carter's effort to withdraw U.S. forces from Korea in 1977 and President

Reagan's efforts in 1982 to institute a nuclear doctrine aimed at fighting a protracted nuclear war.[13] Similarly, Lawrence Korb judges that for most of the Cold War the military had very little impact on the size of the defense budget and that civilian political leaders got their way on most budget issues (Korb 1976, p. 131). Allan Millett, reviewing the first thirty years of the Cold War, concludes that "one cannot assert that military organizational preferences or the advice of senior military officers have dominated foreign policy decisions" (Millett 1979, p. 38).

A Closer Look at the Cold War Use of Force

This general assessment is supported by a closer look at one crucial issue area, the use of force. A rough measure of shirking can be derived by evaluating Cold War deliberations to use force in terms of three questions:

1. Whose preferences prevailed in the initial decision to initiate the use of force?
2. Whose preferences prevailed in decisions over *how* to use force?
3. Did military operations diverge from what civilian leaders wanted?

Answering these questions across the sweep of Cold War history necessarily involves simplifications and aggregations that are appropriate for the broadgauge scale of the agency model but that blur the rich detail of any particular case. Identifying a "civilian" or a "military" preference is something of a procrustean exercise.[14] If one digs in the record deep enough, one can always find a uniformed official advancing a view that would seem better characterized as the civilian-preferred policy in that instance and one can always find a nonuniformed official at some level siding with the military. Similar problems arise in evaluating the implementation of decisions. Nevertheless, since the purpose here is to make a summary judgment of the Cold War case as a whole, quibbles about the details of particular cases and nuances in coding are less of a concern.

The distinction between a "whether" and a "how" decision on the use of force is blurred in practice, as is the distinction between a "how" decision and the actual conduct of the operation. In agency theory, however, the distinctions are warranted. It makes sense to distinguish a *decision* on a policy, which sets the principal's directive, from the *implementation* of the policy, which incorporates the agent's ultimate execution of the directive. "Whether" decisions are the easiest to monitor; even inattentive civilian leaders are likely to know whether the U.S. military has carried out an order to use or not to use force in a crisis. "How" decisions are somewhat more difficult to monitor—was force applied gradually to allow for diplomatic maneuvering or massively from the outset? In some cases, however, a "how" decision on intrawar escalation can be so transparent that in monitoring terms it approximates a "whether" decision; thus, in Table 5.2 below, I will treat as a "whether" decision both the initial policymaking on whether to get involved in Vietnam from 1961 to 1963 and the post-Tonkin escalation decision (which otherwise might be considered simply a decision on "how to wage the intervention already decided"). Operational decisions are the hardest for the principal to monitor and so form a qualitatively different category of military activity.

Table 5.2 addresses the question of whether military shirking occurred in Cold War crises over the initial decision to use force, as distinct from follow-on considerations about how to use force or the actual employment thereof.[15] The first column identifies the case. The second column reports whether there was substantial civil-military disagreement over the decision to use force (as distinct from the follow-on decision on how to use force). I code conflict as present if the sources identified one of the members of the Joint Chiefs of Staff or the relevant theater commander as advising either a more aggressive or less aggressive posture than the prevailing civilian viewpoint. This somewhat overstates the intensity of civil-military disagreement, because in all but six of the cases at least some members of the JCS sided with the dominant civilian view. Any bias that results from this coding will be discussed below. The third column explains whether the military preferences diverged in the direction of being more or less aggressive than the dominant civilian preference. The fourth column identifies whether the military worked or shirked; that is, whether the military used illicit or unauthorized means to champion its preferences. The fifth column briefly details the decision taken.

In most cases, civilian preferences prevailed in Cold War decisions to use force. Military preferences prevailed in only six of the twenty-nine cases analyzed. Significantly, in each of the cases where military preferences prevailed, the military successfully resisted a civilian desire to use force. In no case did the military intervene in the face of a civilian order not to. Military shirking on the initial decision to use force during the Cold War, therefore, took only the form of defaulting to the status quo of not acting. While this still counts as shirking, it is arguably a less disconcerting form of shirking

Table 5.2 Working and shirking on the decision whether to use force, 1945–1989

Case	Conflict	Nature of military opposition	Working vs. shirking	Decision described
Berlin 1948	Yes	Theater commander more aggressive	Work	Airlift
Korea 1950	Yes	Theater commander more aggressive, JCS possibly less aggressive	Work	Korean War
Indochina 1954	Yes	Army, CNO, and marines less aggressive	Shirk[a]	No intervention despite initial civilian desire for it
Taiwan Straits 1954	Yes	CNO more aggressive, army less aggressive	Work	Naval presence authorized
Taiwan Straits 1958	Yes	CNO more aggressive	Work	Naval presence and Quemoy resupplied
Berlin 1958	Yes	Theater commander more aggressive	Work	No action
Lebanon 1958	No	—	Work	Marines land unopposed
Laos 1961	Yes	JCS resists civilian calls for limited intervention	Shirk[b]	No use of force
Laos 1962	Yes	JCS resists civilian calls for limited intervention	Work	5,000 U.S. Marines to Thailand
Cuba 1961	No	—	Work	Bay of Pigs invasion
Berlin 1961	No	—	Work	Reinforcement of Berlin but no use of force

Table 5.2 (continued)

Vietnam 1961–63	Yes	Air Force more aggressive	Work	Increased military aid and advisors
Cuba 1962	Yes	JCS unanimously more aggressive	Work	Quarantine and no air strikes
Vietnam 1964 (Tonkin)	Yes	JCS chairman, CNO, air force, marines, and CINCPAC (but not MACV) more aggressive	Work	Limited bombing in retaliation for Tonkin
Dominican Republic 1965	No	—	Work	Invasion
Pueblo 1968	Yes	CNO and theater commander more aggressive	Work	Naval presence but no retaliation
EC-121, North Korea 1969	Yes	Army, air force, and theater commander less aggressive	Shirk[c]	Naval presence but no retaliation despite initial civilian preference for action
Jordan 1970	Yes	JCS chairman and army less aggressive	Shirk[d]	No use of force
Cambodia 1970	No	—	Work	Invasion
Yom Kippur War 1973	No	—	Work	U.S. resupplies Israel and goes on nuclear alert
Mayaguez 1975	No	—	Work	Rescue operation launched
Iran 1980	No	—	Work	Desert One rescue operation attempted

Table 5.2 (continued)

Case				
Nicaragua 1983	Yes	JCS chairman, army, and theater commander less aggressive	Shirk[e]	Advisors to El Salvador but no invasion to topple Sandinistas
Lebanon 1982–83	Yes	JCS less aggressive	Work	U.S. troops join multinational force
Lebanon 1983	Yes	JCS less aggressive	Shirk[f]	Minimal retaliation and total withdrawal
Grenada 1983	Yes	JCS less aggressive	Work	Invasion
Libya 1986	No	—	Work	Bombing raid conducted against Libya in retaliation for terrorist acts
Persian Gulf 1987	No	—	Work	Reflagging to protect Kuwaiti tankers
Panama 1989	No	—	Work	Invasion

CNO = chief naval officer; JCS = Joint Chiefs of Staff; CINCPA = commander in chief of the Pacific; MACV = Military Assistance Command, Vietnam.

a. The case is controversial since it is difficult to know how enthusiastically Eisenhower supported the use of force to rescue the French at Dien Bien Phu. Nevertheless, the army under Gen. Ridgway generated pessimistic reports arguing how a difficult ground effort would be necessary to save the French. It cut against Eisenhower's expressed determination not to lose Indochina to the communists. Also, during the consideration of Operation Vulture to grant the French air support, Ridgway tried to stop discussions among the Joint Chiefs by challenging Adm. Radford's authority to hold the meeting without the president's explicit approval. This maneuvering could be interpreted as bureaucratic obfuscation—a mild form of shirking. Gacek 1994, pp. 102–109; George and Smoke 1974.

Table 5.2   (continued)

b. The JCS provided Kennedy with only severe military options for Laos in April 1961, including estimates as high as 140,000 troops. A limited occupation plan involving 11,000 American troops was rejected as insufficient, and the JCS insisted that Kennedy had to be prepared to use nuclear weapons if China intervened. Gacek 1994, pp. 167–172.

c. Authorized by the secretary of defense, but contrary to the intentions of either Kissinger (NSA) or Nixon, all spy flights were cancelled after the EC-121 shoot-down. Kissinger, who wanted the United States to respond aggressively to the crisis, protested in vain for four weeks before they were reinstated. Isaacson 1992, pp. 180–182.

d. This case is controversial, but Secretary of Defense Laird, with the support of the JCS, was consistently less aggressive than Nixon during the crisis. Quandt writes, "There was little desire, particularly on the part of the military, to intervene directly in the fighting." Blechman and Kaplan 1978, p. 278. This lack of enthusiasm coincides with advice that "substantial ground forces needed to enter Jordan and to rescue the hostages were not available on short notice" (ibid.). It is difficult to say for sure whether the military was engaging in obfuscation; Kissinger was also fighting to avoid the use of U.S. ground troops, so military shirking was not necessary to change Nixon's course. Still, Defense Secretary Laird's announcement that he saw "no need for U.S. intervention" on September 19, the very day that Nixon raised the alert status of West German units and the 82nd Airborne, seems oddly out of step (ibid., p. 276).

e. See Petraeus 1987, p. 216, on the military's reluctance to update contingency plans for Central American intervention lest civilians be more inclined to choose direct use of force in situations like Nicaragua, 1983. Another source, however, suggests that President Reagan himself was never really serious about pursuing direct U.S. intervention in Central America. Cannon 1991, pp. 355–388.

f. After a suicide truck bombing killed 258 marines in Lebanon, senior civilians wanted strong retaliation. However, Secretary of Defense Weinberger, with the cooperation of the military, blocked U.S. participation alongside the French, who had also lost soldiers, in retaliatory raids against Syria. In January 1984 a military commission report sponsored by Weinberger provoked a furious reaction in Congress against continued involvement in Lebanon, and withdrawal soon followed. Petraeus 1987, pp. 193–194.

than if the military initiated action without civilian authorization. With a few notable exceptions, then, the military worked during the Cold War insofar as the initial decision to use force was concerned.

Several caveats deserve mention. First, the coding here obscures the role that persuasion plays in changing preferences over the course of a crisis. Even in the cases where the military could be said to have shirked, there is no documented case of the military refusing to use force when expressly ordered to do so. Rather, military shirking took the form of vigorous opposition before civilian principals rendered a final decision, opposition that was sufficient to deflect what otherwise would have been the civilian-preferred policy. Since under any theory of civil-military relations the military has an obligation to give advice, it might seem unfair to accuse it of shirking when its advice is simply efficacious. To guard against this, the military advisory role was considered pernicious only if one of three conditions obtained: (1) the advice consisted of estimates that the military shaded or inflated so as to misstate the true anticipated costs of a course of action; (2) the military did not respect a civilian decision to overrule its advice and publicly or privately continued to seek to prevent civilians from taking the civilian-desired course of action; or (3) the advice was accompanied by bureaucratic foot-dragging and "slow rolling" that collectively shifted the policy off the civilian-preferred course. For instance, military advisors in the Reagan administration may well have inflated their estimates of what was needed for a possible invasion of Libya so as to make military action seem prohibitively expensive.[16] In the Central American case during the early Reagan administration, it appears that the army deliberately refused to develop contingency plans for military intervention so as to reduce civilian options and compel the president to decide against military action (Petraeus 1987, p. 247).

Since all policymaking in a bureaucratic system like ours involves some element of these shirking indicators, ultimately the coding comes down to a judgment call that naturally invites quibbles. I have tried to allow for vigorous predecision debate, and to identify shirking only where the civilian side was clearly cognizant of countervailing military advice but remained firm (as in Laos 1961 and Nicaragua 1983) and where one of the other shirking indicators—inflated estimates, end runs, or slow rolling—was present; military action was not counted as shirking when civilians readily changed their minds when presented with a negative military appraisal, as was arguably the case in the Taiwan Straits crisis of 1954.[17] Yet the possibility of overcounting shirking cannot be dismissed, because in virtually all cases, the civil-military debates in question preceded a presidential decision. Thus, the "civilian" preference represented the viewpoints of senior civilian policy-makers, but not *the* civilian principal. The military could well posit that it is not shirking to oppose a proposal from the secretary of state, only one from the commander in chief. Allowing shirking to include stubborn policy debating among senior advisors may overstate somewhat the extent to which the military prevailed against, as opposed to persuaded, its civilian superiors.

This potential for overcounting shirking is balanced by a different bias that has the potential for skewing the conclusion in the opposite direction. The coding rule of identifying a civil-military conflict whenever at least one member of the JCS provides dissenting advice inflates somewhat the number of civil-military disputes, thereby also inflating the number of times the military "worked" even when it disagreed. This has the possible effect of overstating the conclusion that the military in general worked during the Cold War. There were only six cases in which the military viewpoint was unanimously opposed to the civilian: Laos 1961 (and even there the military was divided between the chief naval officer [CNO], who advocated more aggressive measures, and the rest, who advocated staying out of Laos), Cuba 1962, Jordan 1970, Nicaragua 1983, Lebanon 1982–83, and Grenada 1983. Not coincidentally, three of these also appear on the list of cases coded as military shirking: Laos 1961, Jordan 1970, and Nicaragua 1983. The three cases coded as working despite unanimous military opposition may be less consequential than they appear. The military mounted stiff opposition only in the Cuban missile crisis and the Lebanon 1982–83 cases; military opposition in Grenada was mild in comparison. At the same time, shirking even though the military was divided was very rare; only the decision not to intervene conventionally on behalf of the French in Indochina in 1954 and the decision not to retaliate against North Korea in 1969 for downing the EC-121 would be examples of when elements of a divided Joint Chiefs of Staff prevailed over civilian preferences.[18] Put another way, military preferences were more likely to prevail over civilian preferences in the initial decision to use force the more they approximated a unanimous military viewpoint. Since the military was rarely unanimous in its viewpoint, this undercuts slightly the general inference that military shirking, rather than military unanimity, was itself rare.

A similar picture emerges from analysis of decisions on *how* to intervene. The implementation decision is in fact a compilation of thousands of smaller decisions. There is far more room for negotiation and compromise by which civilian preferences might be sacrificed in favor of a military's preferred course of action. In general, civilians gave military advice greater weight on "how" than they gave on "whether" questions. One analyst reviewing the Cold War history concluded that the U.S. military had been remarkably successful in resisting the use of force under terms the military did not approve (Johnson 1996). The two most prominent exceptions, Vietnam (on which more below) and Lebanon 1982–83, were notable in that they both were deemed failures and consequently they both hardened military resolve to resist any further assignments along those lines. Although he did not use the term *shirking*, Johnson did described the Cold War military services as being in "control of their own destinies" and the military in general as "usurping its traditional role of subservience to civilian authority" (Johnson 1996, pp. 38, 36).

This rather pessimistic assessment of civilian strength in policymaking on how to use force does not show up in the data presented in Table 5.3.[19] The first column identifies the case; note that the major wars, Korea and Vietnam, are broken into subsidiary cases. The second column reports the employment issue potentially in dispute, given a decision to use force. The third column reports whether there was civil-military disagreement. I code conflict as present if the sources indicate at least one of the members of the Joint Chiefs of Staff or the relevant theater commander as advising either a more aggressive or less aggressive posture than the prevailing civilian viewpoint. In almost every case there was at least some disagreement. The fourth column explains whether the military preferences diverged in the direction of being more or less aggressive than the dominant civilian preference. The fifth column identifies whether the military worked or shirked. The sixth column briefly details the decision taken.

The data suggest that the military worked most of the time. In only four cases did the military thwart civilian preferences: the Korea 1950 case of approaching the Yalu, the Korea 1950–51 case of advocating publicly expanding the war to China, the 1975 decision to mount the *Mayaguez* rescue operation without a B-52 retaliatory raid, and the decision in 1983 to invade Grenada with a very large force. In the latter two cases, one could make the argument that the military simply successfully persuaded civilian leaders as to the wisdom of the military-preferred approach. Even the Korean cases are ambiguous; MacArthur's effort to expand the war to China was clearly shirking, for he was fired because of it, but MacArthur was adamant that his directives from both the JCS and the civilian authority granted him the

Table 5.3 Working and shirking on the decision how to use force, 1945–1989

Case	Issue	Conflict	Nature of military opposition	Working vs. shirking	Decision described
Berlin 1948	How to supply Berlin	Yes	Theater commander more aggressive	Work	Airlift, no ground troops deployed
Korea 1950	Inchon landing	Yes	Theater commander more aggressive	Work	Inchon offensive
Korea 1950	Crossing 38th parallel	Yes	Theater commander more aggressive	Work	Truman and UN persuaded
Korea 1950	Approach to the Yalu	Yes	Theater commander more aggressive	Shirk[a]	UN forces approach Yalu
Korea 1950–51	Expanding war to China	Yes	Theater commander more aggressive	Shirk[b]	War limited to Korea, MacArthur punished
Korea 1951–53	Limits on conflict	Yes	Theater commander more aggressive	Work	War limited to Korea, ongoing cease-fire negotiations
Taiwan Straits 1954	How to deploy	Yes	CNO more aggressive, army less aggressive	Work	Naval presence only
Taiwan Straits 1958	How to deploy	Yes	CNO more aggressive	Work	Naval presence, resupplying of Quemoy only
Lebanon 1958	Extent of occupation	Yes	JCS more aggressive	Work	Occupation limited to Beirut

Table 5.3   (continued)

Cuba 1961	Air and naval support to rebels	Yes	JCS more aggressive	Work	No support provided
Vietnam 1961–63	Counterinsurgency doctrine	Yes	Air force more aggressive	Work	Counterinsurgency implemented
Cuba 1962	Bombing vs. quarantine	Yes	JCS more aggressive	Work	Quarantine but no bombing
Vietnam 1964	Tonkin retaliation	Yes	JCS chairman, CNO, air force, marines more aggressive	Work	Limited bombing
Dominican Republic 1965	Size of invasion	Yes	Theater commander more aggressive	Work	Limited invasion
Vietnam 1965	Ground combat units in Vietnam	Yes	JCS and theater commander more aggressive	Work	Reserves not called up, ground war limited to South Vietnam
Vietnam 1965	Bombing North Vietnam	Yes	JCS and theater commander more aggressive	Work	Limited bombing of North Vietnam
Vietnam 1966–67	Bombing and ground limits	Yes	JCS and theater commander more aggressive	Work	Limits remain in place
Tet 1968	Escalate or deescalate	Yes	JCS and theater commander more aggressive	Work	Bombing slowed, negotiations continued, no reserve call-up

Table 5.3 (continued)

Vietnam 1968–72	Decrease U.S. ground role	Yes	JCS and theater commander more aggressive	Work	U.S. ground role decreases, heavy bombing, negotiations
Cambodia 1970	Size of incursion, bombing	Yes	JCS and theater commander more aggressive	Work	Limited incursion
Mayaguez 1975	B-52 retaliation	Yes	JCS less aggressive	Shirk[c]	No retaliation after rescue
Iran 1980	Rescue attempt	No	—	Work	Rescue attempt
Lebananon 1982–83	Size and scope of presence	Yes	JCS more aggressive	Work	U.S. troops remain static near airport
Grenada 1983	Size of invasion	Yes	JCS more aggressive	Shirk[d]	Overwhelming force used and Cubans on island engaged
Libya 1986	Bombing	No	—	Work	Single bombing raid
Persian Gulf 1987	Reflagging Kuwaiti tankers	No	—	Work	Kuwaiti tankers reflagged and protected with escorts
Panama 1989	How to invade	No	—	Work	Overwhelming force used

a. Although neither civilian authorities nor the JCS ever countermanded MacArthur's orders as he pushed UN troops closer to the Yalu, the intent of their directives to MacArthur had been to keep American troops away from the Chinese border with North Korea. MacArthur lifted all restraining lines without consulting his superiors. Though the Far East commander never violated the letter of his directives on the Yalu, the chiefs later testified that he had used the distance from Washington and the brisk tempo of the military advance to resist civilian control. Spanier 1959, p. 129.

Table 5.3   (continued)

b. See discussion in text. Also Kaufman 1986, p. 159; James 1985, p. 595.

c. This is a close call. Petraeus (1987, pp. 150–152) reports that acting chairman of the Joint Chiefs David Jones was reluctant to offer options and that he advised that it would be impossible to retaliate on Secretary of State Kissinger's timetable. Petraeus judges that, once Jones did produce the options, they were not offered in an obviously biased way against Kissinger's position. Nevertheless, the delay may have been instrumental in pushing President Ford to shift from his original inclination to strike Cambodia with B-52 bombers.

d. Gacek (1994, p. 259) reports that while the military could not avoid sending troops to Grenada, once the decision was made to invade, commanders managed to avoid civilian oversight. To the extent that civilians wanted to know more about military plans before they were implemented, officers managed to secure their own preferences without having to persuade civilian superiors.

tactical flexibility to approach the Yalu with UN forces (MacArthur 1964, p. 392). MacArthur may have a point. The main argument against him with respect to the Yalu offensive is that he violated the intent if not the letter of his directions without consulting his superiors beforehand, possibly because he suspected (rightly) that his superiors were likely to object.

Significantly, there appear to be many instances in which the military worked even though it unanimously opposed the civilian employment decisions. Six of these cases involve the Vietnam War, which will be discussed in greater detail later in the chapter. Most of the remaining seven can be rationalized with idiosyncratic explanations—for instance, the limits placed on the Dominican invasion clearly reflected Vietnam War considerations, while the free hand in Grenada probably reflected civilian sensitivities over the recent bombing of the marine barracks in Beirut. Others stand out as prominent counterexamples that subsequently strengthened the hand of the military (for example, the civilian-imposed restrictions in Lebanon).

The surprisingly strong finding of military working may also be partially an artifact of several conservative biases in coding. A case is not coded as shirking unless civilians vigorously pressed for specific alternative strategies and failed. In most cases, civilians were forced to select from options presented by the military. Civilians may have preferred a more restricted use of force than the one ultimately employed, but they did not press the matter, perhaps in tacit exchange for military compliance on the overall decision to intervene (Petraeus 1987, pp. 249–253). Also the decision whether to use force is binary, while the decision how to use force is a continuum. If civilians and the military disagree on whether to use force, it is relatively easy to see which side prevailed. The nature of a "how" decision is much harder to characterize and so it is much harder to ascertain whose preferences prevailed. I adopted a conservative coding rule, namely that shirking occurs only if civilians advance a specific plan and are unable to force the military to accept that plan; this probably understates the frequency with which military preferences prevail. Caveats notwithstanding, the data on decisions about how to use force reinforce the assessment that the military worked during the Cold War.

Finally, turning to the question of whose preferences prevailed at the operational level, the evidence is open to conflicting interpretations. Operations, as I use the term, refer to the actual implementation of the whether and how policy decisions. Because of the limitations of the historical record, there is not sufficient information on military behavior at the operational level to construct a table that would reliably detect the rate of shirking across all cases, as was done for the whether and how policy decisions. The best that can be done is to review the anecdotal evidence.

It is axiomatic in bureaucratic politics that the implementation of policy can change the content of a policy decision. Some scholars suggest that shirking was relatively endemic at the operational level. Citing examples like the U.S. Navy forcing Soviet submarines to the surface during the Cuban missile crisis and General John Lavelle's unauthorized bombing raids of North Vietnam in 1971 and 1972, Posen comes to the following conclusion: "In peacetime, civilians are seldom exposed to the intricacies of military planning, and, in wartime, when civilian intervention in the details of military policy is much more likely, soldiers often interpret policymakers' injunctions in ways that allow them maximum operational discretion. There are many historical examples which demonstrate military evasion of civilian control over military operations" (Posen 1982, pp. 31–32). The higher expectation of shirking arises because the operational issues are closest to military expertise and so the military would most intensely resent civilian operational directives that conflict with military preferences (Lebow 1988, pp. 41–45).

Despite this expectation, examples of unambiguous operational shirking of the sort MacArthur engaged in are surprisingly rare, although there are numerous accounts of behavior that could be interpreted as shirking. Given that primary-source research on military operations has not been as extensive as it has for debates on whether and how to intervene, it is possible that future research will uncover enough shirking to require a revision of the assessment presented here.

Bouchard's detailed examination of the naval role in four major Cold War crises comes to an ambivalent judgment on the question of military shirking. Bouchard codes for the extent to which tactical naval operations became "decoupled" from the political strategy being pursued by senior civilian leaders. "Decoupled operations" is not synonymous with shirking and Bouchard is at pains to distinguish deliberate unauthorized acts by the military from those cases in which the blame can be laid on civilians—for instance because their decisionmaking ability was impaired in a crisis—or on the complexity of the situation itself—for instance because the tactical interaction happened too fast for political decisionmakers to catch up. Shirking, as I use it, excludes situations directly attributable to the fog of war but includes all other instances of decoupled military activity. Thus shirking includes "constructive unauthorized action," even though, as Bouchard argues: "Not all unauthorized deliberate actions are harmful to crisis management efforts. An on-scene military commander with an appreciation of the political objectives being pursued by national leaders could well decide to ignore orders that are inappropriate for the local situation and pursue a course of action that better supports crisis management efforts" (Bouchard 1991, pp. 25–43, quote on p. 27). Civilians have the right to be wrong and, as explained in Chapter 3, the working and shirking continuum is not synonymous with wise and foolish action.

On the one hand, Bouchard finds only modest levels of behavior that constituted shirking, and he dismisses even those as largely due to the fog of war. In the 1958 Taiwan crisis he notes that on-scene commanders sent destroyers to defend the offshore islands in advance of presidential orders to do so and likewise continued to convoy resupply ships for a day after they had been ordered to suspend operations; but he dismisses these incidents as due to ambiguous orders and communications problems in the context of a fast-changing tactical situation. In the 1973 Middle East crisis, he finds that the Sixth Fleet took steps to attack Soviet ships preemptively—steps that the Soviet trailing ships could detect—even though the White House had clearly tried to position the fleet so as to show resolve *without* aggressive intent; Bouchard likewise dismisses this as largely due to communication failures and impairment of the political leadership that resulted in the issuance of tactically inappropriate orders (Bouchard 1991, pp. 177–178). He finds no serious instances of shirking involving naval forces in the 1967 Middle East crisis nor in the Cuban missile crisis.

On the other hand, Bouchard may set the threshold for shirking too high. His primary interest is whether inadvertent war could arise out of unauthorized actions, and since none of the crises escalated to general war, it is not surprising that he also finds no decoupled behavior of that magnitude. He dismisses some incidents of decoupling as trivial because they were neither countermanded nor punished by civilian authorities. For instance, during the 1967 crisis, U.S. naval forces engaged in game of "chicken" with trailing Soviet ships, a provocative action that Bouchard agrees was inconsistent with President Johnson's political strategy of minimizing tensions with the Soviet Union; however, since it was not punished, Bouchard does not view the matter as very serious (Bouchard 1991, pp. 154–155). Moreover, given his analytical focus, he is willing to excuse a range of behavior that might be called "benign shirking": deliberate, unauthorized actions that, with hindsight, Bouchard credits as being constructive. For instance, he cites approvingly CNO Anderson's insubordinate behavior toward Secretary of Defense McNamara, saying Anderson "took the lead in preventing what he perceived to be unreasonable civilian interference in naval operations" (Bouchard 1991, p. 135). Perhaps, but Anderson was surely shirking.

The Cuban missile crisis deserves special attention, not least because it is surely the most thoroughly researched Cold War case. Bouchard's generally sanguine assessment of naval operations during the crisis is at odds with the traditional interpretation that the military chafed greatly under extraordinarily tight civilian command (Blight and Welch 1995, pp. 825–829). For instance, Lebow's interpretation of the Cuban missile crisis damns the military with faint praise. He says that civil-military conflict was unavoidable and the numerous instances of military intransigence were likewise understandable because "leopards do not change their spots." Indeed, he credits the military leaders for the extent to which, "when pushed, they departed from routine and improvised procedures that responded to presidential directives and needs." But on the whole, Lebow's judgment seems to be that the military shirked, albeit understandably so from the point of view of organization theory (Lebow 1987, p. 79). This is also the assessment offered by the two books most influential in shaping the conventional wisdom on the Cuban missile crisis, Allison's *Essence of Decision* (1971) and Kennedy's *Thirteen Days* (1971).

Bouchard is at pains to debunk certain myths of military shirking during the Cuban missile crisis. For instance, he rebuts Allison's claim that standard operating procedures caused the navy to defy civilian orders to move the quarantine line closer to Cuba (Allison 1971, pp. 129–130). Given their close monitoring of the quarantine and in particular of the ships' locations as reported in the navy's Pentagon command center, Bouchard reasons, civilians would have known that the ships remained at the 500-nautical-mile arc; any covert shirking was impossible. Moreover, Bouchard argues that President Kennedy merely *suggested,* vice *ordered,* that the quarantine line be moved and that the president concurred with his military advisors, who cautioned against this plan for fear of the threat to the ships from land-based aircraft (Bouchard 1991, pp. 111–112). He also gives a decidedly less melodramatic account of the famous incident in which CNO Anderson confronted Secretary of Defense McNamara on the conduct of the quarantine (Allison 1971, p. 131; Bouchard 1991, pp. 255, n. 127). Given his extensive exploitation of previously unavailable material, Bouchard's analysis is a useful corrective to Robert Kennedy's self-serving account of a military barely kept from running amok by heroic civilian leadership (Kennedy 1971, p. 97).

At the same time, there is ample evidence that some low-level operations deviated from civilian expectations, if not from explicit orders. For instance, Blight and Welch claim that the famous incident in which Cuban air defenses shot down the American U-2 spy plane should not have happened; military adherence to standard operating procedures resulted in continued routine flights of U-2s over Cuba despite the manifest civilian preference to minimize provocation during the crisis. Blight and Welch blame civilians for failing to anticipate this problem, but the gap between military behavior and civilian preference was nevertheless sizable (Blight and Welch 1995, p. 831). Sagan also documents numerous episodes that he claims raise serious questions about the safety and reliability of the nuclear forces during the crisis.[20] While Sagan is not analyzing the affair in terms of a civil-military agency model—and no incident resulted in a bona fide nuclear accident—his findings are suggestive of a certain degree of military shirking. The first incident concerns the attempt by Commander in Chief of Strategic Air Command (CINCSAC) General Power and Chief of Staff General LeMay of the air force to pressure civilian leaders to change safety rules so as to permit immediate deployment of a new nuclear bomb just then entering the stockpile. The civilian assistant to the secretary of defense for atomic energy, Dr. Gerald Johnson, resisted the effort but noted afterward that he had had no guarantee that the air force would respect his ruling. Sagan concludes, "We may therefore never know who really won the dispute" (Sagan 1993, pp. 72–73). In another episode, SAC officers conducted a previously scheduled test launch of an Atlas intercontinental ballistic missile (ICBM) from Vandenberg Air Force Base, even as they were converting other test silos at Vandenberg to a combat function. Civilian authorities were not aware of the launch, which Sagan argues was contrary to the civilians' overall desire to restrict nuclear operations during the crisis (Sagan 1993, p. 78–80). More seriously, Sagan claims that safety rules designed to prevent an unauthorized launch were deliberately not followed in at least one instance during the crisis. SAC commanders rushed several Minuteman I missiles onto alert status at the Malmstrom Air Force Base even though only one launch control center (LCC) was operational, in defiance of the two-man rule on launch procedures. Malmstrom commanders apparently also colocated launch panels and positive control materials with the single LCC, thus violating backup rules designed to inhibit an unauthorized launch when conditions prohibited observance of the two-man rule.[21] In another case, the Air Defense Command ordered all nuclear air defense weapons to be alerted, even though it lacked authority to do so at that time under the prevailing alert procedures. Moreover, at least one subordinate commander further violated safety rules in implementing this order (Sagan 1993, pp. 95–98).

Some of the shirking might be coded as intramilitary shirking. For instance, when Supreme Allied Commander, Europe (SACEUR) Norstad tried to dampen the alert status of NATO forces under his command, he was undercut at least temporarily by orders passed directly through service channels (Sagan 1993, pp. 103–104). Other problems could be traced not to military shirking but to civilian inattention to important details, as in the case where the Executive Committee of the NSC placed extraordinary limits on the operations of NATO missiles in Turkey but failed to place similar limits on the nuclear-armed quick-reaction alert, or QRA (ibid., pp. 108–111). This latter inattention is particularly surprising because civilian leaders were well aware of the peculiar risks of unauthorized use posed by the QRA aircraft—indeed, the QRA risks had been the impetus behind the Kennedy administration's earlier decision to buttress civilian control of nuclear weapons with coded locks called permissive action links (PALs) (Feaver 1992, pp. 172–198).

Beyond the evidence from the Cuban missile crisis, it is worth noting that Bouchard's optimistic findings are at odds with Joseph Sestak's earlier analysis of the Seventh Fleet operations in the Western Pacific during the Cold War. Sestak finds "with disturbing regularity" that "the operational force posture of the Seventh Fleet was often at odds with mandated policy or, at the least, with what policymakers expected it to be" (Sestak 1984, p. 1). Some of the shirking Sestak documents was directed at senior military commanders rather than at senior political leaders; for instance, the Seventh Fleet was at pains to ensure that it could operate independently of any non-navy theater commander (ibid., pp. 41–62). But in other cases, the shirking was in response to civilian policy. Sestak alleges that the Seventh Fleet resisted President Eisenhower's massive retaliation policy and deliberately emphasized conventional-only operations, at one point during the 1954 Indochina crisis even failing to have a nuclear-capable carrier within range of Dienbienphu, although it was aware that President Eisenhower was contemplating a use of nuclear weapons (ibid, pp. 10–24). Arleigh Burke also apparently countermanded orders from President Eisenhower to deploy "all-attack carriers"—carriers without fighters to provide air defense for the carrier battle group—and permitted his subordinate commanders to ignore geographical restrictions on where they could sail if those restrictions were dictated by the nuclear-oriented Single Integrated Operational Plan (SIOP) (ibid., pp. 24–33). Moreover, the Seventh Fleet often changed its alert status and deployment patterns without higher authorization, or at least without explicit authorization from above the chief of naval operations in the chain of command (ibid., pp. 63–72).

The evidence from crisis and peacetime operations thus supports a mixed assessment of working and shirking. The record is certainly not one of perfect obedience, even allowing for the normal friction of complex organizations. In some cases, as with MacArthur in Korea, the behavior clearly crossed the line and was unambiguously detected and punished as such. In other cases, the alleged behavior may have crossed the line but the available evidence is too sketchy to draw a firm conclusion.[22]

Yet despite these tantalizing traces of problems, with some notable exceptions, especially in the navy, the empirical record does not support a picture of a renegade military resolutely thumbing its nose at civilian leaders. Although it is hardly dispositive, the military's own self-assessment is more favorable. It is rare for military officers to admit on the record that civilian orders were disregarded, or, as General LeMay did, that they fully intended to disregard civilian orders if they considered it necessary. Interestingly, however, at least one military officer worried about the reliability of General Power, the SAC commander during the Cuban missile crisis. One of General Power's subordinate commanders, General Horace Wade, later recalled in an oral history, "I used to worry about General Power. I used to worry that General Power was not stable. I used to worry about the fact that he had control over so many weapons and weapon systems and could, under certain conditions, launch the force" (Sagan 1993, p. 150). But quotes like this are noteworthy precisely because they are rare. Evidence of operational shirking is most plentiful in the nuclear realm, but even there it must be acknowledged that military obedience was almost certainly the rule. To a very great extent, then, civilians got the military to do what civilian leaders asked them to do.

Aggregating across the three areas—decisions whether, decisions how, and the actual operations—leads to a general summary conclusion that, on balance during the Cold War, the military worked, especially regarding the issue of greatest importance to civil-military relations, the exercise of its monopoly on the use of force. This generally positive conclusion does not excuse the military for the instances of shirking that did transpire, but the conventional wisdom probably is correct: the United States during the Cold War enjoyed a remarkable degree of military obedience. Broad summary judgments like this obscure some of the variation uncovered, the rare instances of shirking in an otherwise general picture of working. A benefit of a microfoundational theory like agency theory is that it should be able to account for the phenomena observed at both the aggregate and the disaggregate levels of analysis; in the section that follows I evaluate hypotheses drawn from both levels of analysis. However, the broader level is appropriate for a first-cut test of agency theory. And at this summary level the assessment is that the military worked.

Why Did the United States Reach the Instrusive-Monitoring-with-Working Outcome?

The agency model developed in Chapters 3 and 4 translates this empirical finding about the Cold War configuration of working and intrusive monitoring into hypotheses about the values of other parameters in the civil-military relationship. Agency theory says that working with intrusive monitoring is the outcome when civilians and the military act in certain ways, which they are more likely to do under certain circumstances, called the equilibrium conditions. Thus, the theory "retrodicts" that if we see intrusive monitoring with working, it is likely that these other equilibrium conditions also obtain, as summarized in Table 5.4.

On balance, American civil-military relations during the Cold War belong in the "intrusive monitoring and working" cell. According to the agency model, this would be the outcome when civilians monitor intrusively and the military adopts a strategy of working when monitored intrusively and shirking when not monitored intrusively. The conditions associated with this equilibrium (listed in column three of the table) suggest that this outcome is more likely when some or all of the following circumstances are true: the costs of monitoring intrusively ($C1$) are low relative to the stakes as civilians see them ($W - S2$); the expectation that civilians would catch and punish shirking in the absence of intrusive monitoring *(ag)* is low or civilians perceive little difference between punishing shirking and letting shirking go unpunished ($S1 - S2$); the military expectation of punishment under the intrusive monitoring regime *(bgp)* is large enough to compensate for the

Table 5.4 Equilibrium conditions associated with monitoring/working outcomes

Monitoring and working outcome	Strategy pairs that would produce this outcome	Equilibrium conditions associated with strategy pair
Monitoring intrusively/working	Civilians monitor intrusively and the military works if monitored but shirks if not monitored	$C1 < W - S2 - ag(S1 - S2)$ and $w2 > s2 - bgp$ and $w1 < s1 - agp$
Monitoring intrusively/shirking	Civilians monitor intrusively and military always shirks	$C1 < (bg - ag)(S1 - S2)$ and $w1 < s1 - agp$ and $w2 < s2 - bgp$
Monitoring unintrusively/working	Civilians do not monitor intrusively and the military always works	$C1 > 0$ and $w1 > s1 - agp$ and $w2 > s2 - bgp$
Monitoring unintrusively/shirking	(1) Civilians do not monitor intrusively and the military always shirks	(1) $C1 > (bg - ag)(S1 - S2)$ and $w1 < s1 - agp$ and $w2 < s2 - bgp$
	(2) Civilians do not monitor intrusively and the military works if monitored but shirks if not monitored	(2) $C1 > W - S2 - ag(S1 - S2)$ and $w2 > s2 - bgp$ and $w1 < s1 - agp$

Table 5.4   (continued)

Lexicon:

W: Work done as the civilian principal wanted it

S: Work done as the military agent wanted it (shirking)

C1: Civilian costs of monitoring (time/effort costs and the policy costs of inexpert meddling)

S1: The civilian payoff of military shirking if civilian punishes

S2: The civilian payoff of military shirking if civilian does not punish

p: Costs to military of punishment (makes shirking less valuable to the military)

w1: The military payoff of working with nonintrusive monitoring

w2: The military payoff of working with intrusive monitoring

s1: The military payoff of shirking with nonintrusive monitoring

s2: The military payoff of shirking with intrusive monitoring.

a: The probability of detecting shirking with nonintrusive monitoring

b: The probability of detecting shirking with intrusive monitoring

g: The probability of punishing shirking

"benefit" the military would derive from shirking ($s2 - w2$); the expectation of punishment under the unintrusive monitoring regime *(agp)* is not high enough to compensate for the benefit the military would derive from shirking ($s1 - w1$).

These circumstances, furthermore, imply the following about the real-world values of certain key parameters during the Cold War: the gap between what civilians wanted *(W)* and what the military wanted *(S2)* was high; the costs of monitoring were low; the reliability of nonintrusive monitoring regimes (fire alarms) was relatively low; the military expected to be punished when it was caught shirking under an intrusive monitoring regime; the military was less concerned that it would be punished under a nonintrusive monitoring regime. The last two conditions further suggest that the values of g, the expectation that shirking would be punished if detected, and p, the pain of the punishment, were relatively great, but that the ability to detect shirking varied significantly across monitoring regimes. If the real-world values of these parameters match their hypothesized value (high or low), then agency theory is supported; if they do not, our confidence in agency theory is undermined.

Chapter 2 has dealt in depth with the question of whether the gap between civilian and military preferences narrowed during the course of the Cold War, concluding that for the most part the gap remained wide, as expected by agency theory. I evaluate the remaining hypotheses in three ways so as to explore as many observable implications of the theory as possible, given reasonable research constraints. First, I treat the entire Cold War as a single case and, weighing the evidence accordingly, come to a judgment about the overall values of the parameters. Second, I examine cases in which the military shirked—that is, where the coding diverges from the general assessment given for the Cold War as a whole—to see if there were corresponding changes in the equilibria parameters. Third, I consider more closely one subcase, the Vietnam War, to see whether agency theory expectations hold in that instance. Vietnam is a particularly interesting case not only because of its substantive importance but also because it fits the pattern of intrusive-monitoring with the military working that was true for the Cold War as a whole, even though several of the parameters hold extreme values—it was a high-stakes issue and military and civilian preferences strongly diverged. Thus, the agency model would expect to see similarly pronounced values for the other parameters in order to produce the equilibrium outcome.

Evidence from the Cold War in General

Were the Costs of Intrusive Monitoring Relatively Low?

The evidence about monitoring costs during the Cold War is generally supportive of the agency model, though not conclusively so. The agency model identifies two kinds of monitoring costs that the civilians considered: (1) electoral costs, which include considerations of time, effort, and feasibility, and (2) policy costs, which refer to the likelihood that civilian monitoring would degrade into harmful meddling.

The Cold War saw an important change in the electoral costs of civilian monitoring. Compared with pre–Cold War periods, there was a higher direct electoral payoff for politicians focusing on military issues (Russett 1990, pp. 88–92). The American electorate recognized that military issues mattered in a way that they perhaps did not prior to the Cold War, and they punished and rewarded politicians accordingly. For instance, with the exception of the 1973 to 1980 détente period, national security issues were regularly cited by the public as among the most important problems facing the nation (Russett 1990, p. 90). One analysis of Cold War presidential elections finds that the electorate's perception of differences between candidates on foreign affairs and defense policy issues were "consequential" (Aldrich, Sullivan, and Borgida 1989, p. 135). Although the electoral connection was weaker for members of Congress, even congressional civilian principals found ample incentives to invest time and energy in national security issues (Lindsay 1994b, pp. 33–52). This suggests that civilian principals during the Cold War were less inclined to see monitoring the military as a waste of time or a distraction from other more electorally fruitful activities. Note that this consensus on the *importance* of foreign policy did not translate into a public consensus on *what* that foreign policy should be; still less did it constitute a consensus in favor of the conservatism that Huntington prescribed. Rather it simply meant that the costs to civilian principals for paying attention to military affairs was lower than it had been in a previous era.

Just as monitoring seemed less costly in electoral terms during the Cold War, it also became more feasible across a wider range of military activity. For peacetime military activities, the Planning, Programming, and Budgeting System established by Secretary of Defense McNamara in the 1960s institutionalized a form of intrusive monitoring that gave civilians far greater access to information than had been available previously (Enthoven and

Smith 1971, Yarmolinsky 1971) Once established, intrusive monitoring regimes made intrusive monitoring that much easier in the next round. For instance, the growth of congressional staffs with oversight responsibilities in national security affairs was itself a manifestation of intrusive monitoring. But, once established, the ready availability of a large expert staff lowered the costs of engaging in intrusive monitoring on the next issue.

Advances in communications technology likewise lowered the costs of monitoring force deployments and military operations in the field. The telecommunications revolution, foreshadowed by novel applications fielded in World War II, marked the most significant advance in command and control technology since the advent of the telegraph enabled President Lincoln to monitor Civil War battles (Weigley 1993, p. 38; Allard 1990, pp. 60–61, 108–111, 138–147). For instance, Bouchard details how communications technology allowed for more intrusive monitoring during the Cuban missile crisis than was possible in the 1958 Taiwan Straits crisis (Bouchard 1991, pp. 62–68 and 93–108). To be sure, civilians rarely exploited the new communications capabilities to their fullest. During the Cuban missile crisis, President Kennedy had the ability to speak directly to the commanders of the naval vessels patrolling the quarantine line. He did not do so, although he probably listened to reports coming in from those ships (Bouchard 1991, p. 96). However, at the time of the Pueblo crisis in 1968, President Johnson exploited the capability to speak directly with the on-scene commanding officer aboard the aircraft carrier *Enterprise,* although Johnson apparently did not give "rudder orders"—precise directions for moving ships and positioning escort vessels (Sestak 1984, p. 72). By the time of the 1975 *Mayaguez* crisis, central commanders (in this case, the JCS) were giving rudder orders. The general pattern, then, was for intrusive monitoring to increase as advances in communications technology facilitated it; while civilians may not have taken advantage of the most intrusive capability the first time it became available, they did so gradually in something like a stepwise fashion. This is part of a more general trend in which advances in military technology have permitted greater independence and initiative at lower tactical and operational levels, which has in turn necessitated the growth of centralized staffs to coordinate and control this increased activity (Irvine 1938; Van Creveld 1985, 1989). Civilian leaders became accustomed to a level of monitoring that would have been stifling in a previous technological regime. Insofar as military operations went, the intrusiveness of civilian monitoring was largely a function of what was permitted by prevailing communications technology; as improvements in technology permitted greater intrusiveness, *ceteris paribus,* civilian principals took advantage of the new capacity (Sestak 1984, pp. 71–72; Bouchard 1991, pp. 217–220; Van Creveld 1985, pp. 232–260). To be sure, President Reagan's apparent willingness not to micro-manage the invasion of Grenada provides an interesting counterexample and suggests that presidential style plays a role as well (Weinberger 1990, p. 120).

The agency model also directs attention to the policy costs of monitoring. Traditional treatments of civil-military relations hold that the costs of civil-ian micromanagement are severe.[23] Because civilians are inexpert, their in-terventions are likely to be counterproductive; because military operations are so complex, intrusive monitoring by civilians is likely to be a dangerous distraction. While the model is not dispositive on this question, it does raise the intriguing hypothesis that the policy costs are lower than popularly be-lieved. To my knowledge, no one has done a systematic test of the hypothe-sis that civilian intrusive monitoring incurs high policy costs. There have been, however, at least some scholars advancing the view that civilian intru-siveness is not as pathological as popularly thought.[24] And, obviously, civil-ian principals who decide to monitor intrusively evidently agree, at least at that moment, with Woodrow Wilson, who claimed that his war was so un-precedented that it could and should be run by "amateurs" (Rogers 1940, p. 291).

There is one further reason for suspecting that the policy costs of civilian monitoring were lower in the Cold War than in previous periods in Ameri-can history. The Cold War saw the flowering, for the first time, of a civilian-based expertise in strategy and national security (Lyons 1961, pp. 56–60). Nuclear strategy and unconventional war theory were essentially civilian-invented disciplines that the military eventually imported. Thus, perhaps the gap between civilian and military expertise was less than traditional the-ory would expect. If democratic theory posits that civilians have a right to be wrong, the agency model interpretation of the Cold War suggests that civil-ians may have been wrong less often than one would expect.

On balance, then, there is sufficient evidence to support the first agency theory hypothesis: the costs of monitoring intrusively were relatively low.

Were Nonintrusive Monitoring Mechanisms Relatively Unreliable?

The second condition implied by the agency model concerns the reliability of nonintrusive monitoring, and here the evidence is more mixed. Recall from Table 5.4 that the parameter reflecting the reliability of nonintrusive monitoring (a) shows up in all the inequalities governing this equilibrium, and it influences civil-military relations along two distinct causal pathways. First, it affects civilian calculations about the necessity of monitoring intrusively. The intuition is simple: if nonintrusive monitoring is sufficiently reliable, civilians will rely on that, especially if the stakes $(W - S2)$ are low and the costs of monitoring are high. The fact that civilians did monitor intrusively suggests civilians were unwilling to rely on fire alarms like the media and nongovernmental experts to monitor military behavior. The second pathway concerns military calculations about whether to work or shirk. Again, the intuition is plain: when nonintrusive monitoring has a low probability of detecting shirking, the military can maximize its utility by working when it is intrusively monitored and shirking when it is not monitored intrusively. Since we have already determined that on balance civilians monitored intrusively and the military worked during the Cold War, the agency model leads us also to expect that neither civilians nor the military considered the nonintrusive monitoring regimes to be very reliable.

The evidence for this hypothesis is inconclusive. The availability of nonintrusive monitoring during the Cold War was high by historical standards, although there are reasons why civilian and military actors may have doubted its reliability. As explained in Chapter 3, a nonintrusive monitoring regime involves the extensive use of indirect mechanisms of civilian oversight: contract designs, screening and selection mechanisms, and fire alarms that monitor the military and then alert the civilian principals when they detect shirking. These categories include such measures as offers by civilians to use less intrusive monitoring in exchange for obedience, skill requirements for entrance into military service, loyalty oaths and other accession instruments, the ethic of professionalism, the news media, defense-oriented think tanks, and even interservice rivalry. All of these measures were used during the Cold War. Some, like the activity of third-party fire alarms, clearly flourished; others, like accession policies and the ethic of professionalism, at least were points of emphasis during the Cold War.

The civil-military fire-alarm network came into its own during the Cold War. A vigorous national security media and an extensive system of nongovernmental watchdog organizations grew up from a baseline of almost zero to become a quite sizable presence in the policymaking process. Prior to 1945, there were only a handful of organizations focusing on foreign and defense policy matters. The short list would be headed by the Council on Foreign Relations, the Navy League, and a few service-oriented journals like

the *Proceedings of the Naval Institute*. By the mid-1970s, the list of organizations focusing on military and foreign affairs had ballooned to include doz-
ens of journals and a wide spectrum of organizations. By the end of the Cold
War, the number of interest groups lobbying the federal government on defense and foreign policy issues was estimated at more than 900, and this
does not even include the sizable military-expert community in academia
(Zegart 1999, p. 239). Compared with virtually any other country of interest, the United States has enjoyed the most robust of "fire alarm" communities, with a vigorous, attentive, and relatively free press regularly reporting
on the doings of the military and forcing the pace of civilian oversight.
Moreover, the Foreign Policy Leadership Project's public opinion surveys
found that the civilian elite placed a remarkably high degree of trust in the
reporting of the press, at least in comparison with reporting by the government itself.[25] Thus, there is at least some reason for believing that civilian
leaders would trust these third-party organizations to serve as fire-alarm
monitors of military behavior.

At the same time, this large watchdog community was balanced during
the Cold War by an extraordinary growth in governmental secrecy. The effect of security classification was to move a large portion of defense affairs
out of the public eye. To some extent, the reliability of these independent
and quasi-independent monitoring systems was also undercut by the simultaneous rise of an aggressive public relations operation by the official defense establishment (Clotfelter 1973, pp. 134–141). In a sense, then, the efforts of the fire-alarm community to detect and report on shirking may have
been countered at least somewhat by the ability of the military establishment to withhold and shape information, which had the effect of hiding
shirking and otherwise coloring perceptions about military behavior. Thus,
compared with the higher probability that shirking would be uncovered
with direct intrusive monitoring, the nonintrusive monitoring regime may
have been less reliable than one would otherwise suspect based on a crude
comparison with the pre–Cold War era. Moreover, although the national security "fire alarm" community grew substantially over the Cold War, its
size may not be that large, relative to the task assigned to it and relative
to other issue arenas. For instance, the domestic policy community of fire
alarms dwarfs that in the security policy arena—more than 8,000 versus
more than 900—and one could therefore infer that the national security
watchdogs are relatively less important than their domestic counterparts
(Zegart 1996, pp. 36–37). Arguably, then, civilian policymakers, accustomed

to the information-rich domestic policy environment, might not have been willing to rely on the much more rarified nongovernmental security policy community.

The contractual and screening mechanisms associated with a nonintrusive monitoring regime were likewise a prominent part of Cold War civil-military relations, but the empirical record does not rule out the possibility that they were insufficiently reliable to substitute for direct intrusive monitoring. Military sociologists have documented that the United States military over the course of the Cold War shifted from what is called the institutional model to an occupational model of military service (Moskos 1977, Segal 1986, Moskos and Wood 1988). The institutional model is the traditional paradigm of military service, in which effort is valued on normative grounds and members are motivated by intangible incentives like honor and duty to country. The occupational model resembles employment in the civilian marketplace, where prestige is based on levels of compensation and members are motivated by tangible incentives like pay and benefits. The shift to an occupational orientation predated the abandonment of the draft, but the move to an all-volunteer force inevitably accelerated the trend. The shift would at first appear to indicate that contractual mechanisms became more effective over the Cold War as a means of nonintrusive civilian monitoring. But, as I argue below, the increasingly prominent role of contract incentives may have done more to raise the profile of punishment than to substitute for intrusive monitoring systems. Moreover, the shift, which most military sociologists decry as destructive of military effectiveness, may have worked to undermine the other leg of the nonintrusive monitoring chair: traditional professionalism. The institutional model is, more or less, the Huntington ideal of military professionalism. Occupational impulses, whether in the form of increased emphasis on pay or an elevation of the individual over the group, erode the institutional identification that Huntington claims is an integral part of military professionalism's ethic of subordination. Thus, the increased emphasis on certain forms of nonintrusive monitoring may have had the perverse effect of undermining the effectiveness of other mechanisms in regulating the shirking phenomenon.

There is no question that rivalry between the four military services during the Cold War served the monitoring function expected by the general agency model. What is less clear is whether it was sufficiently capable to be a substitute for, rather than a complement to, other more intrusive forms of monitoring. There is at least some reason to believe that interservice rivalry became a less reliable monitoring system as the Cold War ran on. Korb observes that by the 1960s and 1970s, the JCS had worked out a system of log-rolling that reduced the number of "split-decisions" among the chiefs (Korb 1976, p. 24). Indeed, by the mid-1980s there was widespread dissatisfaction with the functioning of the JCS, in particular with the quality of advice that the service-dominated system provided (Barrett 1983, pp. 82–85). This dissatisfaction led to the Goldwater-Nichols reforms, which had the effect of greatly strengthening the operation of the Joint Staff at the expense of the individual services. Thus, the perceived usefulness of interservice rivalry declined over the course of the Cold War. This decline may indeed have influenced the reliability of this relatively nonintrusive monitoring mechanism, as indicated by the agency model.

On balance, the historical record is not conclusive on whether nonintrusive monitoring mechanisms were relatively unreliable during the Cold War. However, the agency model itself is not determinative on the question. It is possible, for instance, that civilian intrusive monitoring was dictated entirely by a relatively low cost of monitoring despite a high "true" value for the reliability of fire alarms. It is also possible that civilian monitoring would have been even more intrusive but for the presence of a fairly robust nonintrusive monitoring system. Given the ambiguity of the available evidence, it is probable that different dynamics were at work for different issue areas and different time periods. Future research could be directed at unpacking this relationship with more detailed analysis.

Were Expectations of Punishment High?

Agency theory diverges most dramatically from other theoretical treatments of U.S. civil-military relations in the prominence it gives to civilian punishment, the final set of equilibria conditions. The model suggests three things about expectations of punishment during the Cold War: (1) that the military had a relatively high expectation that shirking would be punished if detected, (2) that the military expected such punishment to be relatively severe, and (3) that the ability to detect shirking varied significantly across monitoring regimes. I already discussed the third condition above, but the first two deserve closer scrutiny. On these, the evidence from the Cold War as a whole is remarkably supportive. There is no direct evidence of the values of these parameters—survey polls did not, for instance, ask questions about expectations of punishment. Nevertheless, the record seems to suggest that the military had reason to have a high expectation of punishment.

The agency model suggests, for instance, that the Truman-MacArthur controversy played a larger role in shaping Cold War civil-military relations than Huntington's traditional narrative allows. Despite the examples of Lincoln, Truman, and others, punishment plays a curiously muted function in traditional theory on American civil-military relations. Military disobedience does not feature prominently in *Soldier and the State;* civilian punishment of military figures even less so. Surprisingly, given the proximity of the event, Huntington touches only lightly on the Truman-MacArthur controversy.[26] In a brief section discussing the possible conflict between military obedience and political wisdom, Huntington compares MacArthur with the generals who resisted Hitler during the 1930s, chastising both sets: "Both the German officers who joined the resistance to Hitler and General MacArthur forgot that it is not the function of military officers to decide questions of war and peace" (Huntington 1957, p. 77). Huntington analyzes in great detail the etymology and evolution of MacArthur's attitudes toward the abolition of war, noting with disapproval that by 1956 MacArthur had articulated a liberal position that even Henry Wallace could endorse. Huntington appears to argue that it was the liberal roots of MacArthur's attitudes to war that laid the justification for his insubordination (Huntington 1957, pp. 367–373). Huntington scrutinizes rather less closely Truman's decision to relieve MacArthur, and does not discuss the impact this decision likely had on American civil-military relations (Huntington 1957, pp. 383, 385, 386, 390).

In writings separate from his theory of civil-military relations, however, Huntington does evaluate the MacArthur controversy, and his observations there differ in important ways from the view implied by *Soldier and the State* (Brzezinski and Huntington 1964, pp. 331–365). For instance, Huntington notes that MacArthur's actions were shaped by a low expectation that he would be punished, because Truman was so politically weak:

> The President's appreciation of his political weakness was one reason he had not relieved MacArthur in August or December 1950. The longer he delayed, however, the more precarious his position became . . . Truman reluctantly took what seemed to be his last chance to get rid of MacArthur. In the light of these circumstances, the amazing thing is that Truman was able to act at all. (Brzezinski and Huntington 1964, p. 363)

Huntington concludes that Truman was finally able to act, despite his weakness, because of the presence of military leaders within the Truman administration, causing Huntington to give a surprising endorsement of subjective control: "In the American system . . . top-ranking officers such as Marshall,

Bradley, and Eisenhower could become thoroughly involved in politics without threatening civilian control. Indeed, just the reverse was true: their very participation helped in the assertion of civilian control" (Brzezinski and Huntington 1964, pp. 364). Finally, Huntington observes that the firing of MacArthur served to cement future military subordination: "Many of Mac-Arthur's subordinate commanders shared his strategic views. Yet they stayed on at their posts, not because it was impossible for the Truman Administration to dismiss them but because it was unnecessary to do so. If MacArthur could be fired, anyone else could also" (Brzezinski and Huntington 1964, pp. 360–361). This explanation of the MacArthur crisis is hard to square with Huntington's theory of civil-military relations, but it fits the agency model remarkably well.

Indeed, this is precisely the way the agency model would interpret the MacArthur incident: Truman's dramatic firing of General MacArthur proved crucial in shaping military expectations of punishment throughout the Cold War. Truman's action is especially noteworthy because public opinion overwhelmingly backed the general over the president and because MacArthur was also strongly supported by the opposition Republican Party, which was putting increasing pressure on Truman from Congress on a large number of issues (Clotfelter 1973, p. 124). Arguably, these factors gave General MacArthur ample reason to expect that President Truman would not punish him. General MacArthur makes no direct mention in his memoirs of his expectations regarding the likely response of President Truman to his actions in Korea, except to claim that he was never insubordinate and so never considered his actions worthy of punishment. But it is suggestive that a recurring theme in his discussion of Korea is the indecisiveness and vacillation of the civilian leadership at that time. Perhaps MacArthur's low estimation of President Truman's resolve vis-à-vis the Chinese translated into an equally low estimation of Truman's resolve vis-à-vis MacArthur (MacArthur 1964, pp. 327–392).

In any case, President Truman's decision to relieve General MacArthur was dramatic and, I would argue, became the dominant metaphor for Cold War civil-military relations. MacArthur's disagreement with Truman, and vice versa, was a quarrel over the proper way to use force in the nuclear age—whether all or nothing, as the dominant military viewpoint held, or whether with politically set limits, as civilian strategists argued. The military's frustration with the civilian-directed limitations on the use of force in Korea gave rise to a "Never Again Club" of military strategists determined not to repeat the error of fighting under self-imposed limitations. This debate framed deliberations over virtually every subsequent military operation, whether Dienbienphu in 1954, Laos in 1961, or Vietnam throughout. The argument resurfaced in the debate between Secretary of State Shultz and Secretary of Defense Weinberger over Lebanon and Central American policy in the Reagan administration, and the military position became enshrined in the so-called Weinberger-Powell doctrine that emerged the apparent rhetorical victor by the Cold War's end (Gacek 1994). If the Truman-MacArthur debate cast such a long shadow over the use-of-force policy, it is equally plausible that the original resolution of that debate—the reassertion of civilian supremacy and, depending on one's point of view, the reassertion of the civilian's right to be wrong—likewise cast a long shadow over Cold War experience. The willingness of one of the most unpopular presidents to fire one of the most popular generals thus established a high floor on the military's expectation that shirking would be punished if detected, an expectation that the agency model suggests played an important role in shaping civil-military interactions for the next several decades.

The MacArthur example was reinforced when army chief of staff General Ridgway's campaign to undermine President Eisenhower's New Look strategy also ended in punishment. Though expected to grant Ridgway a second two-year term as chief of staff, the Eisenhower administration changed its mind and effectively fired the general.[27] The expectation was further reinforced by President Kennedy's decision not to give his controversial CNO, Admiral George Anderson, his customary second tour (Wicker 1963). Anderson earned the ire of Secretary of Defense McNamara during the Cuban missile crisis when he actively resisted what he considered to be unwarranted civilian interference by the secretary of defense in military operations. The punishment was muted somewhat by Anderson's subsequent consolation appointment as ambassador to Portugal and by the president's decision personally to award him a second Distinguished Service Medal. But the public frame given to the event, and likely the one internalized by senior military officers, was that civilian superiors can win civil-military contests (Raymond 1963, No author 1963).

There is still another reason why the military expectation of punishment if shirking was detected might have been relatively high, at least for the first twenty-five plus years of the Cold War: congressional deference to the executive branch. The principal-agent framework draws attention to how unified agents can exploit divided principals, playing one boss off the other in an effort to avoid punishment. Traditional theory of American civil-military relations emphasizes precisely this problem, which Huntington has called the "structural constant" laid out in the Constitution (Huntington 1957, pp. 163–192) The constitutional framers' desire to prevent abuses of power by an overstrong civilian executive led them deliberately to divide authority for military affairs between the executive and legislative branches. The checks and balances within the civilian government created openings for an opportunistic military to resist civilian control and, in the words of Huntington, "a perpetual invitation, if not an irresistible force, drawing military leaders into political conflicts" (Huntington 1957, p. 177). Avant's principal-agent analysis of American civil-military relations relies on precisely this divided principal problem to argue that American civilian leaders had a greater difficulty in enforcing military compliance during the Vietnam War than did civilian leaders in the British parliamentary (unified principal) system in the Boer War (Avant 1994). To be sure, the consensus should not be exaggerated; there are numerous examples of congressional-executive struggles over defense policy throughout the Cold War period. The struggle occurred both at the macro level of grand strategy—for example, in debates over Eisenhower's New Look strategy, Vietnam, and arms control—and at the micro level of individual defense procurement programs and petty funding issues. At the same time, in comparison with the pre- and post–Cold War periods, and in comparison with domestic policy issues during the Cold War itself, congressional-executive relations on national security matters were characterized by more interbranch cooperation and consensus. As one survey of the congressional role in defense policy observed, "from the early 1950s until the mid-1970s, the list of who mattered in the realm of foreign and defense policy stopped with the president and the national security bureaucracy" (Ripley and Lindsay 1993, p. 4). Moreover, as Kolodziej (1966) documents, Congress had very little ability to prevail against the executive for much of the Cold War period. Vietnam shattered whatever consensus existed, and the conventional wisdom traces the "resurgence" of Congress and the decline of the imperial president to the Vietnam catalyst (Sundquist 1981, Ripley and Lindsay 1993, Lindsay 1994b). In terms of the agency model, however, the bipartisan consensus, so long as it lasted, served to unify the civilian principal vis-à-vis the military agent. In other words, Huntington's structural "constant" was to some extent made a variable by the willingness of Congress to defer to executive prerogatives in military affairs. The partial unification of civilian leadership would affect the agency model outcome through the parameter of the military expectation of punishment, reducing the willingness of one civilian principal to shield a shirking military agent from discipline at the hands of another civilian principal and so increasing the likelihood that shirking would be punished if detected.

This effect was strengthened by the persistence of interservice rivalry within the military establishment. Just as a divided principal weakens the civilian branch vis-à-vis the military, so a divided agent weakens the military vis-à-vis the civilian. Until the Goldwater-Nichols reforms of 1986, the individual services held the upper hand over the Joint Staff and the military remained divided on many issues. The Goldwater-Nichols reforms greatly strengthened the Joint Staff and especially the chairman of the JCS, at the expense of service prerogatives.[28] The agency perspective would therefore expect significant changes in the relative civil-military strength and a concomitant change in the military expectation of punishment as the Goldwater-Nichols reforms took root.[29] For most of the Cold War, however, the combination of a relatively unified civilian principal and a relatively divided military agent would produce a correspondingly high expectation that shirking would be punished, if detected.

Finally, when punishments did enter the formal procedures of the courts-martial system, the military officer accused could be fairly certain he would be convicted. The conviction rates remained high throughout the Cold War, down from a World War II high of 99 percent to a still impressive 92 percent in 1984. Since the absolute number of courts-martial declined dramatically over the same period (from 1,426 in 1947 to 63 in 1984), these high rates probably reflect a selection effect, as commanders pursued courts-martial only in the cases where they were fairly certain that the conviction would hold (Hicks 1991, p. 65–68; Jacobs 1978, p. 397). The decline in the rate of courts-martial correlated with the rate at which convictions were appealed to the Court of Military Appeals, although not with the rate at which convictions were overturned. Thus, even though the convictions often stuck, commanders appeared to be less willing to risk the chance that their judgment would be second-guessed by higher authorities and opted instead for the more certain, though less harsh, nonjudicial punishment at their disposal (Hicks 1994, p. 126).

There was, in fact, an important change in the modality of the punishments, which in the agency model would reflect a change in the "p" value, the disutility associated with the punishment received. Janowitz traces how professional military authority moved from a reliance on coercion to a reliance on persuasion, reflecting (and in some cases prefiguring) a similar transformation within civilian organizations. The reasons offered for the transformation vary—whether it came about out of a growing expectation of comfort as standards of living improved or as a requirement imposed by advances in military technology that gave the advantage to the combat force that can best exploit initiatives (Janowitz 1971, p. 40). The trend was accelerated by the reform movement after World War II and the effort to correct the perceived abuses of coercion during the war, reforms that were codified in the Uniform Code of Military Justice.[30]

While there have been notable exceptions,[31] the trend continued and is reflected in the reduction in the number of formal courts-martial, the reduction in the severity of punishments handed out for military infractions, and the growing reliance on positive incentives rather than punishments to maintain unit cohesion (Janowitz 1971; Radine 1977; Jacobs 1978; Hicks 1991, 1994). Whereas in the past deviant behavior might have been punished with incarceration or even capital punishment, increasingly over the Cold War the military simply relied on "expulsion from what had become a lucrative and sought-after occupation" to punish soldiers who shirked; as noted earlier, this trend shows up in a dramatic drop in the per capita frequency of courts-martial and a corresponding increase in administrative nonjudicial punishment (Hicks 1994). The data show that from a high in 1948, the number of courts-martial per 10,000 soldiers per year steadily dropped, even during the Vietnam War and during the malaise of the 1970s. The drop predated the switch to the all-volunteer force and simply reflected a growing reluctance on the part of commanding officers to opt for a formal punishment process that increasingly incorporated civilian norms about due process and the rights of the accused. The shift was precipitated in part by the gradual extension of civil rights protection into the courts-martial system, which made courts-martial far more uncertain from the point of view of a commander seeking to discipline subordinates (Hicks 1991, pp. 4–5, 26). Thus, the certainty of punishment remained high even if the severity of the punishment declined somewhat.

The data on courts-martial appear to contradict the agency expectation that the pain of the expected punishment remained severe, but this may be more than counterbalanced by the concurrent rise in occupational rewards and incentives. The replacement of the draft with the all-volunteer force compelled the military to compete for recruits in the marketplace, and so pay and benefits increased (Hicks 1991, p. 71). Arguably, as compensation and other benefits increased, the value for individual officers of staying in the military also increased and thus the sanction of being denied those benefits increased as well. In this way, the threat of being thrown out of the military—and in most cases of military shirking, forced departure from the service is the dominant form of punishment—may have been a sufficiently severe replacement for the more traditional physical forms of punishment. The threat of expulsion and the end of a career may have proved sufficiently severe to meet the expectations of the agency model.

Evidence from Divergent Cases

Our confidence in agency theory's utility is further bolstered by cases in which the civil-military relationship deviated from the general trend. The agency model predicts that when the outcome deviates from the general working and monitoring pattern in particular instances, there should be analogous changes in the associated conditions. For example, the agency model would expect that instances of shirking would be associated with one of several factors: (1) a particularly large gap between what civilians ask the military to do and what the military wants to do ($w1 - s1$, and $w2 - s2$); (2) unusually low values for the expectation of punishment; or (3) the absence of intrusive monitoring, which would itself be associated with particularly high costs of monitoring in that instance.

Arguably the first condition helps explain the instances of shirking identified earlier in the review of Cold War uses of force. As shown in Table 5.2, military shirking on the decision whether to use force during the Cold War was correlated with the unanimity of the military actors. Military shirking was less likely when there were sharp divisions between the services and at least some key military actors agreed with civilians, but was more likely if the military presented a unified position to the president. The unanimity of opinion can represent the intensity of the military preference, capturing the idea that what civilians were contemplating in that instance was sharply at odds with the military preference.

Alternatively, these same data can be interpreted as reflecting the second condition, a change in the expectation of punishment. When military advisors present a unified viewpoint on a decision to use force, their bureaucratic position is considerably stronger than when the services are sharply divided on the appropriate course to take. In these cases, civilian leaders would find it harder to overrule military counsel, and the military could expect that some shirking would go unpunished, thus adjusting downward the g parameter as the model's second condition would predict.

These explanations do not appear to hold for the decision how to use force, however. According to Table 5.3, unanimity here may have been less consequential. The two Korean shirking cases involved a theater commander who exploited his local autonomy against the D.C.-based JCS and civilian principals. The other two cases coded as shirking (*Mayaguez* 1975 and Grenada 1983) did involve a unified JCS, but there were many other cases coded as working in which an apparently unified military simply acquiesced to civilian policy preferences on how to use force. However, the coding problems at this level limit the confidence we can place in any inferences about the irrelevance of unanimity in decisions about how to use force. For instance, the ability of the military to control option formation and to take back at the operational level what it has conceded at the policy level suggests that a unanimous military may have found more opportunities to shirk than were detected in the available historical record.

The relatively few instances of shirking on the decision how to use force do suggest one pattern that is consistent with the agency model. Each of these decisions—in the approach to the Yalu in Korea, the question of expanding the Korean War to China, the *Mayaguez* retaliation, and the Grenada invasion—was made against the backdrop of an evident failure in the previous civilian-directed policy. Truman bowed to MacArthur only after defeat in Korea seemed imminent and after the Inchon success appeared to confirm MacArthur's superior understanding of the war. President Ford's decision to defer to the military and not authorize greater retaliation against Cambodia for seizing the *Mayaguez* came after the utter failure of U.S. policy in Southeast Asia. President Reagan deferred to the military (even *allowed* the military to shirk?) in the conduct of the Grenada operation, perhaps because it came so soon after the 241 marines died in the Beirut bombing, a tragedy that the military could blame on a flawed civilian policy on Lebanon. In other words, shirking came on the heels of apparently decisive evidence that the policy costs of recent civilian meddling were exorbitant. When the policy costs of monitoring are higher, or perceived to be, civilians have a greater incentive not to monitor intrusively and the military has a greater opportunity to have its preferences prevail. The other cases in which military operations ended in a disaster—the Bay of Pigs, the Iranian hostage rescue attempt, and, of course, the various operations that comprise the Vietnam War—may be exceptions that underscore the rule. The first two were failures after the fact, and so the military did not have an opportunity to parlay the policy costs of monitoring into political advantage over decisionmaking. They were also very short, small-scale operations, in each case the first time force was used in that particular administration; as such, they received closer scrutiny by civilian leaders than they might have otherwise. The Vietnam cases cannot be explained away so easily, and I address them below.

Finally, the hypothesis that shirking should be associated with the absence of intrusive monitoring, which would itself be associated with particularly high monitoring costs in that instance, finds support in the impression one gets from the record: shirking on the more easily monitored whether and how decisions was rare relative to the more difficult to monitor operational level. The hypothesis also is congruent with Sestak's finding from the history of the Seventh Fleet. Shirking by the fleet was facilitated by its geographical remoteness from Washington, which was only belatedly overcome by advances in communications technology (Sestak 1984, pp. 102–103). Sestak also argues that shirking was greater when the theater commander was from the same service as the military officer. In terms of the agency model, this would translate into a reduction in the reliability of the fire alarm monitoring mechanism, a function interservice rivalry otherwise fulfills (Sestak 1984, pp. 106–107). The agency model also would imply that there is more military shirking to be discovered in areas where civilian monitoring was less intrusive. Empirical scholarship on nuclear operations in the late 1980s uncovered hitherto unnoticed cases in which de facto military practice diverged from declaratory doctrine, thus forcing a revision in the dominant view about how well military behavior was integrated with grand strategy. In a similar fashion, the agency perspective would expect that future empirical research will uncover shirking in those areas where civilian monitoring was lax and where nonintrusive monitoring mechanisms were likely to be ineffective.

The agency model, with some exceptions, is thus able to provide an explanation for at least some systematic variation within the Cold War case. For reasons of scope and length, the treatment here is necessarily brief, and a priority for future research would be to extend this analysis further.

A Case in Point: The Vietnam War

The Vietnam War was a pivotal experience in modern U.S. civil-military relations and so it is instructive to single out that traumatic period for special attention, to see how the expectations of the agency model hold. It is of particular interest for evaluating the agency model's interpretation of the Cold War as a whole, because the Vietnam War is a case of military working even in the presence of a sharp disagreements between civilians and the military. Given scope constraints and the immense literature that the Vietnam War spawned, the analysis presented here is necessarily abridged. The evidence does, however, support agency theory's interpretation of the Cold War as a whole.

The agency perspective begins with the premise that civilians have the right to be wrong. Civilian principals have the right to ask military agents to do something that ultimately proves costly, foolhardy, and even disastrous. Military agents have an obligation to advise honestly about the consequences of proposed courses of action, but in the final analysis they must obey even dumb orders. Therefore, the agency perspective does not concern itself principally with evaluations of whether the United States should or should not have intervened in Vietnam, an important but separate question that has occupied the bulk of Vietnam scholarship and polemics. Instead, the agency perspective is concerned first and foremost with whether and why military agents acted as directed by civilian principals. Secondarily, the agency perspective is concerned with how patterns of civil-military relations affected the course of the war.

The literature on Vietnam is as varied as any in the security studies field, reflecting the deep and emotional divisions that the war produced within America society as a whole. Nevertheless, a consensus has emerged on several points of interest to civil-military relations. First, it is generally conceded that the military did not press the war on reluctant civilian leaders but rather the reverse (Clotfelter 1973, p. 228; Palmer 1978; Summers 1982; McMaster 1997). Even Buzzanco (1996), who offers an otherwise fairly orthodox leftist interpretation of the war, concedes this point. At the most basic level of generality, then, the Vietnam War can be coded as an instance in which the military obeyed an order to fight.

It is also generally conceded that civilians monitored intrusively by micromanaging operations, although as I argue below there is a dispute over the costs of that monitoring (Palmer 1978, Summers 1982, Rosen 1982, Petraeus 1987, Davidson 1987, Herring 1994, Buzzanco 1996, Pape 1996, Record 1996–97, Cerami 1996–97, McMaster 1997). Examples of intrusive monitoring abound, the most famous being Johnson's boast of personally selecting bombing targets (Kearns 1976, pp. 330–331). General Westmoreland complained that civilian efforts were made to tailor the forces sent to

Vietnam in order to send nuanced signals to the North Vietnamese, without regard to the military mission the new reinforcements were meant to meet (Westmoreland 1976, pp. 119–125, 161). It is also generally conceded that the intrusive monitoring of the war relaxed somewhat under the Nixon administration (Record 1996–97).

As to whether the military shirked beyond the initial decision to get involved in Vietnam, opinions vary. The claim by several analysts that the army refused to develop a counterinsurgency doctrine integrated with the grand strategy articulated by President Kennedy is tantamount to a claim that the military shirked in Vietnam (Krepinevich 1986, Komer 1986, Avant 1994). Buzzanco also accuses the military of shirking, but in a devious way. He claims that the military consistently made proposals it knew the White House would reject—the "Washington Monument strategy" discussed in Chapter 3—in the hopes that civilians would reject the proposals and thus enable the military to claim that its hands had been tied (Buzzanco 1996, p. 345). Buzzanco argues that the military's primary concern was not to win the war in Vietnam, nor even to deliver an outcome that civilians could accept as a success, but rather simply "to avoid blame for failure in Vietnam" (Buzzanco 1996, p. 349). Buzzanco does not present a "smoking gun" in the form of evidence that the military deliberately asked for things it knew it would not receive, but he does argue persuasively that the military must have been aware that its requests would continue to be rejected.[32]

In a war as long and as divisive as Vietnam, of course, one can find instances in which senior military officers engaged in behavior that would constitute shirking. Perhaps the most famous of these would be the military's testimony before Congress in 1967. For the first time, the military chiefs gave open testimony in support of an expanded bombing policy that had been rejected by President Johnson. Certainly the Johnson administration viewed the military testimony with great alarm and devoted extraordinary energy in an effort to rebut the testimony while papering over the civil-military disagreement. In response, the military chiefs contemplated resigning en masse (Perry 1989, pp. 162–166; Herring 1994, pp. 54–57; Buzzanco 1996, pp. 300–309). But the chiefs did not resign and in fact publicly denied they had considered doing so. While the incident ended without a significant change in the course or conduct of the war, it did increase military influence within the Johnson administration from that point on (Herring 1994, p. 57). Another controversial example is General Lavelle's alleged decision to relax the rules of engagement in order to bomb previously off-limits targets in North Vietnam in late 1971. Contemporaneous news accounts allege that Lavelle, who was responsible for all air force combat flights in Southeast Asia, authorized the bombing, which continued over a three-month period and were reported to superior headquarters as "protective reaction" strikes. The bombing apparently sabotaged Kissinger's secret negotiations with North Vietnam. Lavelle was relieved of his command and was forced to retire below rank, but he avoided a court-martial, and a congressional investigation largely exonerated him. There remains a dispute as to whether Lavelle operated under his own authority or whether he had the tacit approval of more senior military officers;[33] either way, it was shirking by the military.

Gelb and Betts note that the military may also have deliberately falsified battlefield reports in order to present a more optimistic version of their tactical virtuosity.[34] A still more curious example is the so-called JCS spy ring inside the White House in the first Nixon administration. Out of frustration at being cut out of the loop of National Security Advisor Henry Kissinger's back-channel peace negotiations, the JCS allegedly instructed one of the enlisted navy message clerks at the White House to steal and copy documents from Kissinger and send them to Admiral Moorer, then chairman of the Joint Chiefs of Staff. When Nixon and Kissinger learned of this obvious insubordination, they did not publicly rebuke the military for fear that it would damage the military's reputation; they, however, did use the information to make the military "more compliant" in other areas, notably in support for the SALT I treaty.[35]

At the same time, the conventional wisdom among the post-Vietnam military is that senior officers did not shirk enough, particularly in the early days of the war. The military did not resolutely resist pressure from the Kennedy and Johnson administrations to intervene (Palmer 1984, p. 46; McMaster 1997; Summers 1982, especially pp. 71–84; and Davidson 1987). Janowitz likewise suggests that the appropriate military response in the early days of the Vietnam war would have been to resign in protest; he accuses the military of being "'overprofessionalized'—more prepared to follow orders than to exercise independent professional skill and judgment."[36] According to this view, the goals pursued by Presidents Kennedy and Johnson were fundamentally flawed. The chiefs were foolishly and unjustifiably loyal to President Johnson in carrying out his orders and forgot their higher oath of allegiance to the Constitution which, according to this view, obligated them to seek to work with Congress to thwart the administration's policies.[37] Even Buzzanco, who otherwise sees a fairly high level of military defiance in the war, draws attention to a prominent example of military subordination: the chiefs' decision not to carry out their August 1967 plan to resign in protest of Johnson's handling of the Vietnam war.[38]

Viewed in context, I am persuaded that the military did not shirk as much as one might have expected, given the extraordinary demands raised by the Vietnam War. I am not persuaded, however, that the military *should* have shirked more to defend the country from foolish civilian leaders. Such a view is reminiscent of MacArthur's discredited arguments presented during the Korean War controversy and has no place in a mature democracy. Nevertheless, it is striking that Vietnam-era military leaders did not disobey or subvert civilian leaders as much as some modern analysts wish they had. In terms of the agency model, civilians monitored intrusively and the military apparently worked during the Vietnam War. Why, and to what result?

One explanation suggested by agency theory is that the famously intrusive monitoring increased military expectations of punishment by increasing the likelihood that military shirking would be detected (raises the probability term b). Moreover, it is surely significant that the traditional fire alarms of American civilian control, the media, enjoyed greater influence in the Vietnam War than in previous wars (thus raising probability term a). Note that the most prominent example of military shirking, General Lavelle's unauthorized bombing of North Vietnam, came *after* the Nixon administration relaxed some of the restrictive monitoring system established by Johnson and McNamara to oversee air operations (Betts 1991, p. 49).

Intriguingly, there is direct evidence supporting the agency interpretation that military expectations of punishment were high. In particular, the Vietnam case appears to underscore the importance of the MacArthur example, which the agency interpretation of the Cold War as a whole also emphasizes. McMaster cites the Truman-MacArthur experience as salient in warning the chiefs about "overstepping the bounds of civilian control" (McMaster 1997, p. 330). Similarly, Rosen claims, "In the back of everyone's mind in the 1960s was the memory of General Douglas MacArthur's insubordination in Korea" (Rosen 1982, p. 100). President Johnson obliquely warned senior military officers of the same by invoking the MacArthur image in an exchange with General Westmoreland in February 1966: "General, I have a lot riding on you . . . I hope you don't pull a MacArthur on me" (Westmoreland

1976, p. 159). Herring lays special weight on Johnson's "rigid standards of loyalty" and on his "terror of a military revolt," which led him to do "everything in his power to avert it."[39]

Another factor suggested by the agency model concerns the ability of civilian principals to narrow the gap between the military payoff for working *(w)* and the military payoff for shirking *(s)*. While civilian and military preferences on Vietnam per se widely diverged, civilian principals may have been able to narrow the overall gap by offering the military other desiderata. Interservice rivalry and the preoccupation of senior military officers with advancing their own service interests gave civilian principals the opportunity to offer service "side payments" in the form of an expansion in the size of the Marine Corps or control over particularly desirable billets that inflated the value of working (Herring 1994, pp. 39–40; McMaster 1997, p. 330). The gap was also narrowed by the ability of civilian leaders to promote senior military officers who concurred with the civilian viewpoint, or at least did not disagree so strongly.[40]

The agency interpretation of the Vietnam War also raises questions about the costs of intrusive monitoring in Vietnam. The conventional wisdom is that intrusive monitoring proved very costly (Herring 1994, p. 45). For instance, Rosen says that a failure to delegate, which flowed from the civilian failure to trust the military for fear of another MacArthur episode, was directly responsible for the military's failure to innovate tactically and thereby come up with a way to win the war in Vietnam (Rosen 1982, pp. 111–112; Davidson 1987). Indeed, even at the time, the general public thought this was the case. In a 1967 Harris Poll, 65 percent agreed and only 10 percent disagreed with the statement, "In Vietnam, the military has been handicapped by civilians who won't let them go all out." Moreover, 52 percent agreed that "In wartime, civilian government leaders should let the military take over running the war."[41] Also, it is suggestive that at least one North Vietnamese military official cited the civilian-imposed restraints on bombing as critical in vitiating the airpower advantage the United States enjoyed throughout the conflict (McGarvey 1969, p. 156).

Nevertheless, civilian micromanagement may not have been as costly as popularly thought, or at least may not have been as detrimental as the military's own decision to pursue an attrition strategy prior to 1968. A recent review of the literature concludes that while civilians did impose "significant, and in some cases tactically absurd, restrictions on the use of force . . . What remains disputable is whether those restrictions thwarted a decisive military victory" (Record 1996–97, p. 58). Other analysts agree (Clark et al. 1987, pp. 322 and 330). Even the classic advocate of the military conventional wisdom concedes, "Our problem was not so much political interference as it was a lack of a coherent military strategy" (Summers 1982, p. 143). In a similar vein, Cohen (1984, pp. 344–346) argues that micromanagement in the form of restraints on the use of force are inevitable in small wars, and military resistance to it is unrealistic and counterproductive. Moreover, the most famous example of intrusive monitoring—restrictions on bombing targets—was simply not as costly in policy effectiveness as the conventional wisdom believes.[42]

From the point of view of civil-military relations, Vietnam's most enduring legacy is the "lessons" the military learned from the experience. While criticism of the military performance in Vietnam by the military abounds, virtually all of such criticism takes the form of chastising the military for not resisting civilian mismanagement more vigorously or for "abdicating" to civilian leaders too much responsibility for determining strategy and tactics in the war. In other words, the dominant military lesson from Vietnam is that there was too much civilian control during the war, not too little. Even the military's insistence on the need for public support before embarking on a risky operation, or the need for clear goals (exit criteria, in modern parlance), are in fact veiled criticisms of the way civilians ran the Vietnam War. The military "learned" that civilians cannot "stick it out" over the long haul, that civilian interference produces disasters and ties the military's hands, and that civilians do not understand the proper use of force (Taylor and Petraeus 1987, pp. 253–254; Petraeus 1987; Clark et al. 1987, pp. 322 and 330; Lovell 1987; Gacek 1994). Without debating the merits of the lesson, it is striking the extent to which the Vietnam experience "taught" the military to doubt the wisdom of submitting to civilian control.

In sum, the agency model is sympathetic to the interpretations of Vietnam that lay blame for the war not so much on intrusive monitoring (micromanagement) or military shirking as on a flawed strategic goal. The goal civilians pursued, the substance of "working," was to preserve South Vietnam without conquering North Vietnam—in other words, an avoidance of defeat rather than a quest for victory. This was quite clearly what civilian leaders wanted, and they refused to pay for anything more. Such a goal was inappropriate and perhaps unachievable, given three strategic realities: an enemy that was implacably bent on total conquest of the south; an enemy allied with the Soviet Union, which was willing to resupply the north until victory was achieved; and an ally that was hopelessly corrupt and so unable to mount a sustained defense (unlike South Korea). But it was the policy the civilians asked for and, by and large, it was the policy the military delivered.[43] So far as civil-military relations go, civilians have a right to be wrong. This time they were.

Conclusion

Chapter 2 argued that civil-military relations in the United States during the Cold War did not meet the prescriptions of Huntington's theory. The crucial gap between civilians and the military did not narrow as Huntington prescribed, and the result was that civilians monitored intrusively.

In this chapter, I used agency theory to explain what did in fact transpire. While acknowledging the difficulty of coding the key concepts, nevertheless the weight of the evidence supports the conclusion that civil-military relations during the Cold War fit the pattern of intrusive civilian monitoring and military working. Agency theory predicts that this outcome will obtain when there is a wide gap between civilian and military preferences, when the costs of monitoring intrusively are fairly low, when the reliability of unintrusive monitoring is fairly low, and when military expectations of being punished for shirking are fairly high.

By and large, the evidence from the Cold War as a whole and from divergent cases supports these hypotheses. Polling data (presented in Chapter 2) show that the preference gap did not narrow substantially. Costs of monitoring intrusively were fairly low because the high stakes of the Cold War meant there was an electoral payoff for civilian representatives who emphasized national security matters. The growth of secrecy and compartmentalization within the national security establishment and the perverse side effects of service rivalry may have undermined the reliability of fire alarms, although these nonintrusive monitoring mechanisms did gain in prominence as time went on. The early dramatic example of an unpopular president (Truman) punishing a popular military hero (MacArthur) for shirking likely shaped the expectations of future actors in the civil-military game. Punishment was present in the day-to-day workings of civil-military relations, even if it is largely absent from the prevailing theories of civil-military relations.

No doubt quibbles over how to code and interpret complex concepts like shirking or expectations of punishment may persuade some readers that this is not a conclusive test of the agency model. Nevertheless, the evidence presented here should increase our confidence in the ability of this theory to illuminate the civil-military relationship. In the next chapter, I use the agency model to interpret the changes in American civil-military relations brought about by the end of the Cold War.

CHAPTER 6

Explaining the Post–Cold War "Crisis," 1990–2000

Even a casual reader of the newspaper would be struck by the prominence given civil-military relations since the end of the Cold War.[1] The range of issues is broad: sexual harassment concerns within the military, charges of military insubordination at the highest levels, concerns about the moral authority of the commander in chief, questions over who should shape the roles and missions of the post–Cold War force, and so on. The sustained intensity with which the drama has played out on the public stage is perhaps unprecedented.

In this chapter, I use the agency model to interpret post–Cold War civil-military relations. I argue that the concerns expressed about the health of American civil-military relations reflect the unease associated with a move from the Cold War equilibrium of working with intrusive monitoring to a new equilibrium that has to a great extent involved both shirking and continued intrusive monitoring. I show that this result occurred because the factors most commonly cited as central to explaining the pattern of relations—the end of the Cold War, the prominence of operations other than war, the tenure of a commander in chief with unusual personal baggage—conspired to give particular values to the parameters that govern the civilian decision to monitor intrusively and the military decision to shirk.

I begin by briefly reviewing the literature on the post–Cold War "crisis" in civil-military relations. I distinguish among the many attempts to describe the phenomenon, showing that while analysts focus on different aspects of the crisis, there is nevertheless an emerging consensus that relations during the Cold War were markedly different from those after. I next discuss the agency model explanation, taking the observed pattern of behavior as a point of departure and using the agency model to deduce hypotheses about the likely values of key parameters such as the expectations of punishment, the costs of monitoring, and so on, and along the way I evaluate the evidence for and against these hypotheses generally. I conclude by briefly evaluating the advantages of the agency explanation over other existing accounts.

A Discordant Relationship

Two famous anecdotes, both from the early days of the first Clinton administration, serve to frame post–Cold War civil-military relations in the United States. Soon after the inauguration of the first president elected after the collapse of the Soviet Union, Lieutenant General Barry McCaffrey, then JCS liaison to the White House, had reason to visit the White House compound. While there, he greeted a young Clinton staffer who allegedly replied, "I don't talk to the military." McCaffrey presumably related the incident back at the Pentagon, for the story quickly spread throughout the Beltway community as apparent confirmation that the new commander in chief—who once wrote that he loathed the military—was surrounding himself with advisors who were "viscerally antimilitary." The White House, which was already reeling from the backlash against the president's proposal to lift the ban on gays serving openly in the military, quickly scrambled to undo the public relations damage of the petty snub. In a highly choreographed move, the president invited General McCaffrey to jog with him at a summit meeting, and the distinguished military officer agreed, thus graciously conferring absolution on his commander in chief (No author 1993c, McCaffery 1993, Martin 1993). Ironically, McCaffrey became a favorite of the president and was given the high-profile job of drug czar later on in the first term (Zoroya 1996).

In the second anecdote, the snub went in the other direction. In May 1993, Major General Harold N. Campbell, deputy chief of staff for plans and programs at Air Force Materiel Command at Wright Patterson Air Force Base, rose to give some after-dinner remarks at an air force awards banquet in the Netherlands. For reasons that have never been fully explained, General Campbell reportedly referred to President Clinton as a "gay-loving," "pot-smoking," "draft-dodging," and "skirt chasing" commander in chief. The public attack on the president's character by a senior uniformed officer was without modern precedent, and the story quickly became front page news. Initially, the White House seemed skittish in dealing with this gross violation of military protocol; one senior staff member (thought to be George

Stephanopoulos) complained, "What should we do? Fire someone with a Silver Star?" After a few anxious days, however, the air force chain of command rallied and General Campbell resigned in disgrace (Lancaster 1993a, 1993b; Schmitt 1993a, 1993c).

The anecdotes remained popular throughout Clinton's two terms and were revived regularly in media accounts because they appeared to be representative of a general problem. Simply put, civil-military relations have been exceptionally discordant since the end of the Cold War, reaching and perhaps surpassing the levels experienced during the Vietnam War trauma. The discord has not escaped public notice and comment—indeed, the literature discussing and dissecting post–Cold War U.S. civil-military relations is large and growing.

What Is the Problem?

Shortly after the end of the Cold War, and well before President Clinton's much-discussed problems with the military became manifest, a number of scholars and analysts began to express concern about the health and direction of civil-military relations. The alarms were somewhat ironic, because the peaceful end of the Cold War and the triumphant victory of the coalition forces in the 1990–91 Gulf War seemed to augur nothing but good things for the future of the national security establishment. The Gulf War in particular represented a high point in U.S. civil-military relations. Civilian respect for the military was at record levels (Rosenstiel 1991). The military seemed to be able and willing to do anything civilians asked it to do, and the relationship between the commander in chief, President Bush, and his senior military officers could hardly have been more cordial.

Nevertheless, some observers found things to worry about. One of the early alarms was raised by an air force lawyer, Colonel Charles Dunlap, who wrote an engaging essay describing how military policies in the late 1980s and early 1990s, many of them civilian-inspired, laid the seeds for a military coup in the year 2012.[2] Dunlap's concern was that the military was becoming too competent and pliant; civilians were asking the military to do things that it could but probably should not do—patrol for drugs, help wayward youths in the inner city, feed the world's starving masses. In Dunlap's fictional account, the military emerged as the only public institution that "worked" anymore, and so the military expanded to fill a vacuum of competence at the governmental level. Every additional task expanded the military's influence and reach in society, while at the same time distracting the military's focus from the priority concern of preparing to fight large-scale conventional wars. A false sense of omni-competence bred hubris, and hubris bred ultimate defeat in a war and a collapse of the social order. Into the breach stepped a thoroughly politicized American military, producing the first American military coup. Dunlap published several variations on this theme, but each contained the same core argument: the military was being asked to do too many things and was developing a politicized officer corps that would be unable to prevail in conventional military missions but would be willing and able to usurp control of the government (Dunlap 1994, 1996).

Another alarm was raised shortly thereafter by one of America's most distinguished military historians, Russell Weigley (Weigley 1993). Although his article was published during the spring of Clinton's military discontent, Weigley's focus was actually on civil-military problems in the earlier Bush administration. Weigley's target was General Colin Powell, the popular and charismatic chairman of the Joint Chiefs of Staff, and Powell's role in arguing against the use of force to stop the war in Bosnia. Weigley reviewed the relations between presidents and their senior generals back to Lincoln's famous struggle with McClellan and concluded that no senior military officer had ever resisted civilian proposals as consistently, systematically, and successfully as had General Powell. Weigley's article echoed Kurt Campbell's (1991) prescient analysis of Colin Powell's growing prominence, but where Campbell speculated on possible problems, Weigley concluded unreservedly that power relations were out of balance.[3] Although Weigley and Dunlap identified different aspects in the civil-military relationship as problematic, the nuanced differences were lost on most observers, who grouped them together as part of a larger "something is wrong" view.

The general sense that something was wrong with U.S. civil-military relations crystallized with the election of President Clinton and especially the military's reaction to Clinton's efforts to lift the ban on gays serving openly in the military. As will be discussed in greater detail below, Clinton came into the White House with considerable civil-military baggage, and his early missteps compounded this problem. President Clinton's troubled relations with the military was the theme in scores of newspaper articles, editorials, and television shows. Every presidential encounter with the military, especially every ceremonial event, was interpreted through the lens of Clinton's problems with the military and provided an opportunity for journalists and pundits to rehearse the litany of grievances, anecdotes, and even myths that surrounded the president (No author 1993f, Jonas and Frank 1993). Every military issue the Clinton administration faced in the first several years seemed to call forth a spate of editorials on the president's precarious position vis-à-vis the military, whether it was the fiftieth anniversary of D-Day (Alter 1994; Komarow 1994; Ricks and Birnbaum 1994; Apple 1994; Devroy 1994; Dowd 1994a, 1994b; Drozdiak 1994; No author 1994a, 1994c; Rabinowitz 1994) or the contretemps concerning the deployment of forces to Haiti in October 1994 (Devroy and Smith 1994, Barnes 1994a). The contempt reached the point of absurdity when military officers began complaining about the limpness of the presidential salute (Matthews 1993). Even more absurd, perhaps, was the awkwardness of the president's most senior staff concerning the delicate problem of "who would beard Clinton and give him a lesson" on how to give a smart military hand salute (Halberstam 2001a, p. 230). The drumbeat of negative incidents rarely let up, and President Clinton's first year in office closed with the spectacle of one secretary of defense forced out of office over charges of ineptness while his designated successor, a former navy admiral, informed the world that before he had agreed to become secretary of defense he had felt the need to reach a comfort level, "to be very comfortable," with Clinton's role as the commander in chief (Wines 1993, Engelberg 1993).

Clinton's problems with the military overshadowed the earlier alarms and confirmed the sense that the military was "out of control," as put in the title of an article by another military historian, Richard H. Kohn (1994). The central thesis of this view was that under Colin Powell's leadership the military, and especially the Joint Staff, had become so powerful—while at the same time the civilian sectors of the national security establishment, under a weak and vacillating president and a disorganized and disheveled Secretary of Defense Les Aspin, had become so weak—that the military was essentially dictating policy to its civilian masters. The thesis was endorsed by a variety of observers across the political spectrum and was confirmed in countless editorials and news analyses in the leading public organs (Luttwak 1994; No author 1995a; Johnson 1996; Powell et al. 1994; Korb 1996a; Bacevich 1993, 1994–95; Lane 1995; Cushman 1994; Johnson and Metz 1995; Lancaster 1993a; Holger and LeSueur 1994).

Of course, the view that something was wrong was not universally embraced.[4] Notably, Colin Powell took pains to rebut the "out of control" article and assured readers that every step he took was fully vetted and approved by his civilian supervisor, first Secretary of Defense Cheney and then Aspin (Powell et al. 1994, p. 23). Samuel Huntington also weighed in on the side of the optimists, asking, "Does a crisis exist in American civil-military relations?" and then answering his own question with a definitive, "the answer is no" (Powell et al. 1994, p. 27). But even here, the statements were less a rebuttal of the charge that something dramatic was happening and more a series of quibbles over the degree of exaggeration in the early analyses. For instance, Huntington's optimistic assessment of post–Cold War civil-military relations rested on a rather equivocal evaluation that "the short-term, immediate problems are not serious enough to be a crisis, and the highly serious underlying problems are too long-term to constitute one" (Powell et al. 1994, p. 27). Likewise, Kohn has been at pains to stress that an enterprising editor penned the hyperbolic "Out of Control" title and that his concerns were largely directed at what the then-new discordancy portended for the future (Powell et al. 1994, p. 29).

It is also debatable how novel the post–Cold War civil-military strife really is. Individual issues had obvious historical parallels. The military resistance to Clinton's proposal on gays in the military bore obvious similarities to the reluctance to integrate African Americans in the late 1940s. Public debates over the use of force recalled debates about Lebanon in the mid-1980s, not to mention MacArthur and the Korean War. The difficulty of reshaping the forces in light of deep reductions in defense spending paralleled the post-Vietnam and the post–World War II drawdowns, each of which engendered analogous controversies over how and how much to cut.[5] The concerns about military ruminations over the moral decay in American society were reminiscent of the brooding occasioned by the Vietnam War.[6] Even the disrespect afforded civilians in the Clinton administration recalled the epithets military officers hurled against Secretary McNamara and his civilian whiz kids.

But what is striking about this period is the coincidence of numerous strands of civil-military disputes. Any one of these disputes could be dismissed as par for the civil-military course in a democracy, but collectively they contribute to the sense that something important really had changed. Just what had changed (and why) is a matter of debate. Indeed one can discern some five different descriptions of the crisis, albeit representing potentially mutually reinforcing, or at least not contradictory, phenomena.[7]

The most extreme description of the crisis is the charge that the military had to some degree stopped submitting to civilian control.[8] This description is implied in the early crisis literature, but is most clearly specified by Desch (1999). Desch defines civilian control in terms of whether civilian policy preferences prevail over military preferences when the preferences diverge. Desch systematically evaluates some seventy-five civil-military disputes from 1936 until 1997 and claims that whereas civilian preferences prevailed in virtually every Cold War policy dispute (fifty-nine of sixty-three), military preferences have prevailed in seven or eight of the twelve post–Cold War policy disputes (see Table 6.2 presented later in this chapter).

A second, less extreme description of the crisis emphasizes the degree of military influence over policy (Stockton 1996). This version differs from the first only in degree and perhaps clarity. Desch's description requires military preferences clearly to prevail for relations to be considered problematic. The military-influence focus, in contrast, codes ambiguous cases as problematic if the military is seen to shape unduly civilian attitudes. The exemplar might be the decision to restore President Aristide to power in Haiti. Desch codes this as a success for civilian control because the invasion was finally launched in 1994, but a close reading of the dispute shows that military influence was substantial and helped delay forceful action for several years (Desch 1999, p. 31).

The most developed variant of this "undue influence" school relies on the tools of communication theory to highlight the dominance of military discourse over nonmilitary discourse. Cori Dauber argues that "civil-military relations are in a state of crisis today because the military has won the fight over whose argument standards trump whose" (Dauber 1998, p. 435). This approach springs from a core insight of argumentation theory: where policy certainty is impossible, "argument" (defined as debate over what is best) that produces consensus constitutes control over policy; in these cases, however, selection of the "standards of argument" (defined as the criteria that determine which argument is superior to another) often predetermine which argument is going to win, or at least privilege one side over the other. For instance, in courts of law, the presumption of innocence and the standard of "proof beyond a reasonable doubt" privilege the defense over the prosecution. In policy arguments, the standards of argument are divided into three spheres: private (as in personal taste or personal experience), technical (expertise in the Weberian sense), and public (as in conflicting conceptions of the public good). For Dauber, the civil-military crisis has taken the form of the military's preferred standards for evaluating argument, namely technical expertise, displacing public standards even in matters of general public policy on military matters. As a consequence, civilian officials are "persuaded" to defer to military preferences in the whole range of military policy questions. David Johnson reaches much the same conclusion, arguing that the military "paradigm" for how best to use force—a paradigm under which the military controls all operational decisions and in which military criteria shape political goals—dominates other paradigms and carries with it excessive military influence over policy (Johnson 1996).

Yet a third (and arguably less extreme) characterization of the crisis references the plethora of military scandals and shenanigans. This version differs somewhat from the others in that it focuses on the implementation level—how well the military abided by the terms of policies it had more or less agreed to execute. Even a cursory survey of press coverage from the last decade or so yields numerous examples of misbehavior that has called into question the integrity of the military institution. Certainly the most infamous example is the Tailhook scandal, which involved charges of sexual harassment and assault at a naval aviator convention (McMichael 1997, United States Department of Defense 1993). Each of the other services has its own illustration: the army's spate of sexual assaults by drill instructors at the Aberdeen proving ground; the air force's celebrated adultery and perjury case involving Kelly Flinn, its first female B-52 pilot; and the marines' scandal about widespread cheating on a crucial orienteering test at its officer training school (Graham 1996, Sciolino 1997, Scarborough 1996). Individually, each episode suggests a breakdown in the chain of command; collectively, the episodes suggest a military fundamentally out of step with society, if not engaged in a rear-guard action to undo controversial policy initiatives such as the further integration of women into the military. Even when the events are demonstrably unrelated or idiosyncratic, the journalistic conceit of recalling superficially similar episodes and rehearsing them at the end of the story gives the appearance of a systematic pattern (Rowan 1997).

A fourth depiction of the crisis focuses on the discordancy and rancor in the civil-military relationship, and especially on the apparent lack of respect each party has had for the other. On the military side, these problems are manifest in expressions of contempt that undermine the authority and dignity of the commander in chief. The problem is also evident among civilians who show insensitivity, if not outright hostility, toward the military as an institution. This is a more expansive description of the crisis and would include all events identified as insubordination, undue influence, or military scandal. But it would also encompass episodes in which civilian control could be said to have prevailed but just barely, and when civilian control prevailed but only by running roughshod over military customs and sensibilities. In this vein, I have elsewhere described the crisis as an undue level of friction in day-to-day relations between senior civilian and military leaders (Feaver 1996c). Likewise, Thomas Ricks has discussed the way boot camp apparently fosters contempt for civilian society in marine recruits and the way some elements of the military have discussed the need to "reform" a decadent civilian culture (Ricks 1997, Arthur 1996).

Examples are not hard to find. In addition to the two famous anecdotes cited at the beginning of the chapter, one could mention the ambivalent reception President Clinton received when he visited the sailors aboard the aircraft carrier *Theodore Roosevelt,* or the president's unfortunate address before veterans at the Vietnam War Memorial on 30 May 1993 (Richter 1993, Friedman 1993c). Public displays of disrespect for the commander in chief are an offense under the Uniformed Code of Military Justice (called an Article 88 offense). Yet disrespect for President Clinton was so ubiquitous that senior military authorities were obliged on several occasions to send official reminders to the troops about the nature of Article 88 (Kohn 2002). Of course, those reminders only underscored just how desperate President Clinton's position was, and while they may have toned down public displays of disrespect, they probably worsened the problem below the surface. Likewise, the official journal of the Marine Corps, the *Marine Corps Gazette,* published a remarkable series of articles written by active and retired military officers whose central thesis was that the next major war to engage the U.S. Armed Forces would be waged on American soil and would be triggered by an assault on traditional American Judeo-Christian culture led by the forces of political correctness and intolerant multiculturalism (Lind, Schmitt, and Wilson 1994; Wyly 1995). What all these examples have in common is that they suggest a gradual erosion in the mutual trust on which the civil-military relationship depends.[9]

Finally, some analysts focus attention not so much on military resistance to civilian direction as on what might be called oversubordination to civilian authority. In this version, the crisis is not an insubordinate military but rather an overly compliant military, willingly, even servilely cooperating with one harebrained civilian scheme after another—for instance, the alleged double standard that allows physically unfit women in combat roles. The crisis is not military predations on the civilian sphere but civilian predations on the military sphere. This version has the broadest appeal within the uniformed ranks, and among a vocal group of veterans (Webb 1997; Lynch 1997; Hillen 1998, 1999). This characterization of the crisis can also be seen in the extraordinary popularity given to H. R. McMaster's examination of the early years of the Vietnam War. McMaster reviews President Johnson's relations with his generals and concludes, without any apology or even awareness of the irony in his words, that the specific "dereliction of duty" perpetrated by the senior leadership of the military was to obey the orders of the commander in chief and secretary of defense.[10] McMaster's book was a bestseller among those at the Pentagon and was generally heralded as reflecting the military's cherished interpretation not only of the Vietnam War but of proper civil-military relations as well. Interestingly, McMaster himself never served in Vietnam, nor had most of his large coterie of admirers; rather, the reception *Dereliction of Duty* enjoyed is an indication that the army had institutionalized Vietnam's "lesson" and passed it along to subsequent generations of officers.

There is in the literature, then, a range of problems and behaviors that are considered indicators of a post–Cold War crisis in civil-military relations. The foregoing is summarized in Table 6.1.

Table 6.1   Alternative descriptions of the civil-military crisis

Crisis as. . . .	Exemplars
Military insubordination	Military vetos Clinton's gays-in-the-military policy
Excessive military influence	Military decides post–Cold War drawdown and participates in domestic policing actions
Excessive scandals, especially relating to the integration of women	Tailhook, Aberdeen sexual harassment scandal, Flinn adultery case, etc.
Military disrespect, friction in the relationship	President greeted with catcalls when he visits the troops
Military deference and embrace of political correctness	The alleged emergence of a double standard that allows physically unfit women in combat roles

Why Have Civil-Military Relations Changed?
The Agency Explanation

Virtually every description of the post–Cold War crisis in civil-military relations has involved at least an implicit explanation for why the problem
emerged. The existing explanations, however, are by and large ad hoc, by
which I mean that they fail to ground their story in a general theory of civil-
military relations. (At the end of this chapter, I assess several theoretically
grounded alternative explanations that, I argue, are useful but inferior to
the agency theory approach.) Most analysts confuse the debate by con-
flating descriptions of problems—for example, military insubordination—
with discussions of factors that might lead to problems—for example, civilian ignorance and unfamiliarity with military culture. The agency model's
great advantage over existing treatments, in fact, is that it is able to incorporate many of the insights of other observers by showing the causal logic
whereby these developments could be expected to have produced the observed pattern of civil-military relations.

The agency model explanation proposes a three-faceted description of the
troubled civil-military relationship that is manifest in increased friction and
public discordance: continued intrusive monitoring by civilians; shirking
along the functional dimension, where military preferences have prevailed
over civilian; and shirking along the relational dimension, where even when
civilian preferences appear to prevail, they do so with extraordinary military
grumbling, or because the military has exerted undo influence in constraining civilian preferences, or because civilians have had to bargain away other
prerogatives in such a way as to undermine civilian pride of place. The reason for these phenomena is that the underlying monitoring/working strategic calculation has changed, largely, I would argue, because of a continuing
preference gap between civilians and the military and a dramatic lowering
of military expectations of punishment. These factors, in turn, can be traced
to many of the deeper changes of the past decade, including the end of the
Cold War, changes in the relative power position of the military vis-à-vis civilians, and the exacerbating factor of President Clinton's personal baggage,
which he brought to the office of commander in chief. Other analysts have
likewise claimed that these exogenous changes were significant, but agency
theory's novel contribution is in tracing how they worked together to shape
civil-military relations.

As explained in Chapters 3 and 4, the agency model cues us to catalog different patterns of civil-military relations according to different mixes of monitoring and shirking. Under certain conditions, the civilians will monitor intrusively and, even with that intrusive monitoring, the military may shirk in some circumstances and work in others. Each of these monitoring/ working combinations reflects a game theoretic equilibrium: the rational best responses each side would make, given expectations of the other's behavior. While each of these equilibria represent "best" outcomes in a rational choice sense, they are not equivalent in a public policy sense. For instance, one would not expect the same amount of civil-military conflict in each mix of monitoring and working. Intrusive monitoring introduces conflict because the military, like all bureaucracies, prefers autonomy. Shirking likewise produces conflict. When shirking is punished, the conflict is obvious. Even when shirking is not punished, however, it can still introduce conflict because it deviates from the "perfect" civil-military relationship idealized in democratic theory. The agency model would lead us to expect that the highest level of civil-military conflict would be generated by the coincidence of intrusive monitoring and shirking.

Under what conditions is this high-conflict, intrusive-monitoring-plus-shirking state of affairs likely to obtain? Recall that each equilibrium is governed by associated inequalities expressed in such terms as the probability of punishment or the civilian's subjective utility from working. The more these inequalities hold in the real world, the more we would expect this path to be the one civilian and military actors take; the more these inequalities are violated in the real world, the less we would expect that associated equilibrium to be the one adopted. Thus the agency model predicts that when intrusive monitoring and shirking coincide, we will also find that the associated equilibrium conditions will hold, with strong values for at least some of the parameters related to those conditions. The conditions were summarized in Table 5.4 in Chapter 5.

The civilian has strong incentives to monitor intrusively and the military has strong incentives to shirk when the following three inequalities hold simultaneously:

1. $C1 < (bg - ag)(S1 - S2)$
2. $w1 < s1 - agp$
3. $w2 < s2 - bgp$

The first inequality holds when $C1$ is small, or when g is great, or when the difference between b and a is great, or when the difference between $S1$ and

*S*2 is great. In plain English, the first inequality holds when any of the following propositions are true: the costs of monitoring (*C*1) are low; the probability of punishment *(g)* is relatively high; intrusive monitoring is needed to detect shirking because the other means (for example, the press) are unreliable (*b* is much greater than *a*); or the civilian payoff of military shirking if the civilian punishes (*S*1) is much higher than the civilian payoff of military shirking if the civilian does not punish (*S*2). In other words, the civilian is likely to monitor intrusively when the costs of monitoring are perceived to be low or when the reliability of other control measures is perceived to be relatively low. Note that not all of these propositions have to hold at the same time, but if one of the propositions does not hold, it should be counterbalanced by extreme values in the other related parameters. For instance, for this equilibrium to be maintained, if the probability of punishment is in fact relatively low, we would expect the costs of monitoring also to be very low (or some extreme value for the reliability of nonintrusive monitoring, and so on).

The second two inequalities hold when *w*1 and *w*2 are small, or when *s*1 and *s*2 are great, or when *a, b, g,* or *p* is small. In plain English again, this refers to any of the following propositions: the military payoff of working with no monitoring (*w*1) and the military payoff of working with intrusive monitoring (*w*2) are both low; the probability that shirking will be detected (*a* and *b*) is low; the probability that shirking will be punished if detected *(g)* is low; the subjective costs to the military of punishment *(p)* are low. In other words, these inequalities simply reflect the idea that the military is more likely to shirk when the military's preference strongly diverges from the civilian's preference, the military has reason to believe that it is not likely to face punishment, or both.

In short, the agency model explanation for the headlines that have characterized post–Cold War civil-military relations in the United States is precisely that exogenous factors have conspired to move the relationship from a more felicitous equilibrium of intrusive monitoring and working to an equilibrium of intrusive monitoring and shirking. To show that this has in fact occurred, I will first demonstrate that the post–Cold War era has been marked by a mix of civilian intrusive monitoring and military shirking. I will also show that there are strong values for at least some of the parameters predicted by the agency model. While it is impossible to measure each of these parameters precisely, it is possible to gain rough approximations of whether the parameters are relatively high or low. Significantly, the post–

Cold War period seems to be characterized by extreme values in several parameters, especially those pertaining to the military decision to shirk.

Monitoring in the Post–Cold War Era

Several measures would indicate that civilian control was relatively intrusive, at least in the immediate post–Cold War period. Extending the figures presented in the previous chapter into the post–Cold War era shows a fairly consistent pattern of relatively intrusive monitoring.[11] Figure 6.1 shows the total size of the Office of the Secretary of Defense through 2000. The figure reveals that, contrary to what one might expect, the OSD did not shrink in size with the end of the Cold War.

The increasing size of the OSD staff, coupled with the post–Cold War drawdown in military end-strength and in the defense budget, meant that the *relative* intrusiveness of the monitoring was sharply increased. Indeed, as shown in Figure 6.2, the relative measure of intrusive monitoring peaked in the early post–Cold War years, reaching Vietnam-era levels in the case of the ratio involving defense outlays and reaching levels not seen at all after World War II in the case of the ratio involving military end-strength.

Likewise, as Figure 6.3 relates, the ratio of OSD staff to JCS staff moved in precisely the same direction, showing a marked increase in the intrusiveness

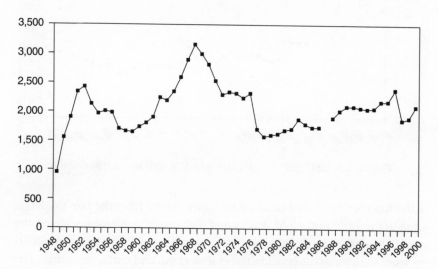

Figure 6.1 OSD personnel, 1948–2000

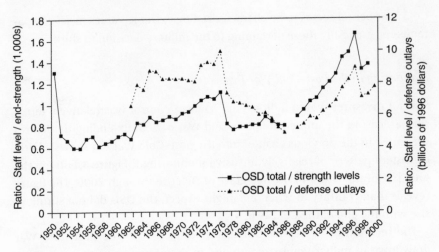

Figure 6.2 OSD staff levels relative to military strength levels (1950–1999) and relative to total defense outlays (1962–2000)

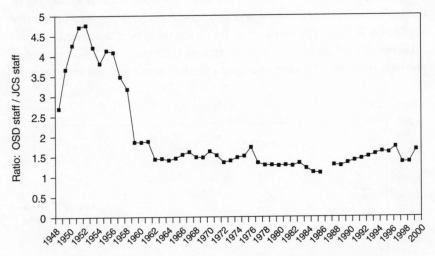

Figure 6.3 OSD staff levels relative to JCS staff levels, 1948–2000

of the monitoring as civil-military relations moved from the late Cold War years to the early post–Cold War period. Because of a different scale on the y-axis, the change in the JCS monitoring measure looks dramatically different from the swings observed in the end-strength and outlay measures. The difference is, in fact, notable—from 1986 to 1996 the end-strength and outlay ratios nearly doubled whereas the JCS measure increased by roughly half; nevertheless, in each case, the swings represented as big a change as that ratio captured in more than thirty years.

At the same time, the number of political appointees in the OSD (a particularly salient measure of intrusive monitoring), went from 193 in 1992 to 234 in 1996, a two-thirds increase over the figure at the height of the Reagan Cold War in 1984 (142).[12]

Taken collectively, if the personnel ratios are a valid measure of the capacity to monitor intrusively and therefore, to some extent, of the intrusiveness actually realized, then the post–Cold War period showed a sharp increase in intrusive civilian monitoring. This increase continued throughout President Clinton's first term in office and only abated somewhat with the second-term cuts in OSD staff.

Another indicator of intrusive monitoring is the number of requests for information that the civilian principals send to the military, for instance the number of formal requests sent by the White House, Congress, and the Department of State to the Department of Defense, and the responses DoD had to make, as detailed in Figure 6.4.[13]

At the height of the Reagan-era Cold War (1983–1985), the average yearly number of requests was 10,375, necessitating an average of 7,808 responses. At the end of the decade and with end of the Cold War (1989–1991), the numbers were 13,390 and 9,860, respectively. In the period covering the first few years of the Clinton administration (1992–1994) the numbers were off slightly (12,291 and 9,187), but they were still roughly a quarter again as much as during the height of the Reagan Cold War. Interestingly, the indicators of intrusive monitoring based on requests for information follow the same pattern established by the personnel ratios: increasing through 1996 and then declining somewhat in the second Clinton term. The number of requests for information sent to the Department of Defense from the White House, Congress, and the State Department dropped off markedly.

The data are not entirely unambiguous. For instance, during the first several years of Clinton's first term, many senior political posts in the Department of Defense went unfilled and the administration enjoyed the dubious distinction of having more mid- to senior-level vacancies than in any of the three previous administrations.[14] These numbers reflect a general slowness that characterized the Clinton administration's personnel policy. By 1 May 1994, 20.6 percent of the top 325 appointments were still unfilled and 41

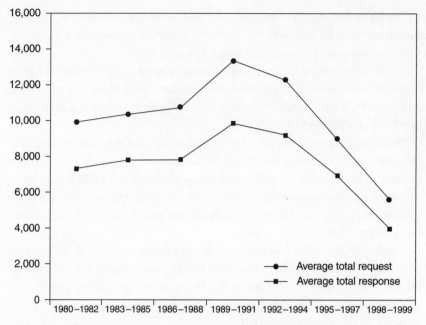

Figure 6.4 Total requests for information from White House, Congress, and State Department and responses from DoD (three-year average)

positions did not even have a nominee pending. This slowness was due to numerous factors, some of which reflected a general historical pattern: the growth in the number of potential appointments; Clinton's refusal (following a precedent established by Reagan and Bush) to delegate personnel decisions out of the White House to the various departments; and the ever-stiffer ethics restrictions that scared off many potential candidates and delayed the vetting process. Some other factors were unique to the Clinton administration: the administration's determination to meet ethnic, gender, and geographic diversity quotas, and the president's penchant for delaying decisions (Pfiffner 1996, pp. 168–172 and 191–196). While the unfilled positions cut against the net intrusiveness of the monitoring, I would argue that the greatest effect would be on the expectation of punishment, as I will discuss below.

Also under the Clinton administration, the makeup of the Office of the Secretary of Defense underwent a change that could undercut somewhat the sense of intrusive monitoring by civilians. While the number of political appointees in the OSD did increase dramatically under Clinton, this was matched by an increase in the number of uniformed military personnel within the OSD: from 2,322 in 1992 to 2,794 in 1996 (up from 2,016 in 1984). From one perspective, the increase in uniformed military personnel merely indicates an increase in the staff capacity of the OSD—thus indicating an increase in intrusive monitoring. From another perspective, however, the military presence on the OSD staff dilutes the "civilian" aspect of the OSD monitoring.

On balance, however, the evidence points to a coding judgment of relatively intrusive monitoring, especially for the earliest post–Cold War years—intrusive even by the standards of fifty years of Cold War, but certainly intrusive when compared with the immediate past experience of the relevant actors.

Why Was There Intrusive Monitoring?

The measures of intrusive monitoring are imperfect, and changes in them are due to many factors, some unrelated to any intentional adjustment to civilian monitoring. For instance, changes in the civilian-to-military ratio were driven first by the lumpy downsizing (cutting military personnel before matching those cuts on the civilian side), and then by the desire to introduce "best business practice" reforms, especially in the procurement side of DoD operations. Nevertheless, even if not deliberate, these factors influence de facto monitoring because they capture at a crude level the capacity of civilians to monitor military activities. Moreover, the agency model leads us to expect that the effect of these changes on the monitoring regime would be recognized by responsible principals—thus, other things being equal, we should see strong values in some of the parameters associated with the conditions governing the civilian decision to monitor intrusively: namely, $C1 < (bg - ag)(S1 - S2)$. Compared with the conditions associated with military shirking discussed below, the evidence here is at best ambiguous. For instance, there does not seem to be any reason to expect a significant change in the civilian payoff of military shirking if the civilian punishes ($S1$) relative to the civilian payoff of military shirking if civilian does not punish ($S2$). At the same time, the probability of punishing (g) has, if anything, moved in a direction opposite to the one implied by the first equilibrium condition; the probability has likely *not* increased but rather decreased in the post–Cold War era (on which more below).

As for the reliability of direct monitoring relative to relying on third parties like the media (*b* versus *a*), this is hard to assess with confidence. On the one hand, by the end of the Cold War there was a large and vigorous permanent watchdog community in the form of the national media and numerous independent defense-analytic groups like the Defense Budget Project, the Natural Resources Defense Council, defense intellectuals, and so on, that "monitored" the military establishment in myriad ways. Indeed, more than any other country, the United States should have some confidence in the ability of nongovernmental groups to report on military misbehavior. On the other hand, the sensational reports of sexual shenanigans first in connection with the navy's Tailhook Association and later within the army's training camp system do seem to indicate that problems could persist for a fairly long time before they would be discovered by these third-party monitoring mechanisms.

The remaining parameter, the costs of monitoring, is perhaps easier to assess. The costs of monitoring include the distraction of time and effort that could be profitably used in the service of other goals the civilian is pursuing. The costs of monitoring also include policy costs, referring to the disutility associated with micromanagement. It is plausible that changes in the external threat have a contradictory effect on these two components. When threat is high there is a large electoral payoff for devoting attention to defense policy; consequently, when the threat is low there is a premium on concentrating on domestic policy, hence candidate Clinton's oft-repeated promise in the first post–Cold War presidential campaign to focus like a laser beam on the economy.[15] Thus, the electoral costs of monitoring vary indirectly with external threat. At the same time, the policy costs of monitoring probably vary directly with threat. When the external threat is low, policy decisions appear less consequential and so policy costs are lower. What does it matter if civilian interference has disastrous side effects when there is no Soviet menace to capitalize on the error? Moreover, since at least some of the intrusive monitoring consists of institutional arrangements, for instance the presence of a large civilian bureaucracy dedicated to the monitoring function, it is reasonable to expect something of a lag in the effect with a decline in threat. By this logic, one could argue that the costs of monitoring intrusively were very low in the immediate aftermath of the end of the Cold War. The negative consequences of monitoring intrusively immediately decreased while availability of intrusive monitoring mechanisms, embodied in the large Cold War monitoring edifice, lingered.

Shirking in the Post–Cold War Era

Although the model is only modestly useful in illuminating the intrusive monitoring side of the post–Cold War civil-military picture, it is more helpful in elucidating the shirking side. Recall from Chapter 3 that shirking has both a functional and a relational component. The military is shirking if it does not do what civilians have asked it to do or if the military is nominally fulfilling functional orders but in such a way as to undermine civilian supremacy. The post–Cold War period has been marked by an unusual degree of both aspects of military shirking, and, as the agency model expects, this can be explained by the coincidence of strong values on the parameters governing the military's incentives to shirk.

Michael Desch has argued that shirking (he calls it military noncompliance) increased markedly in the post–Cold War era. (Desch 1999, pp. 22–38). Table 6.2 relates Desch's claims that military preferences prevailed over those of civilians in seven out of twelve significant issues of civil-military dispute; civilian preferences prevailed on four, and on one issue, the extent of restrictions placed on women in combat, the outcome was mixed.

One can quibble with the selection and coding of the cases. For starters, there are many cases of apparent shirking that Desch does not list, perhaps because they seem more reflective of the complexity of management than of an underlying civil-military conflict. For instance, a rather obvious case of shirking *not* on Desch's list would be when the air force learned that safety regulations were being systematically flouted and that this may have contributed to the April 1996 plane crash in Bosnia that claimed the life of Secretary of Commerce Ronald Brown. While this counts as shirking *within* the uniformed ranks, Desch is probably correct to leave it off the list, since the regulations in question were not the result of a civil-military debate and did not touch on a broader civil-military political concern (Bird 1996). Other cases that might count as shirking occurred after Desch's endpoint and not enough details have reached the public record to make firm judgments. For example, without more information it is hard to know what to make of Richard Kohn's claim that JCS officers (in conjunction with military officers on the National Security Council) tried to subvert President Clinton's desire to enunciate a "Clinton Doctrine" in 1999 by hastening the *National Security Strategy Report* into print before Clinton could head in a different direction; if true, this was shirking, but the details remain murky (Kohn 2002).

Table 6.2   Whose preferences prevailed in the post–Cold War era?

Date	Issue	Civilian	Mixed	Military
1990	Gulf War strategy (Bush = offensive; JCS/CENTCOM = defensive)	X		
1992	Bosnia (intervene or not)			X
1992–94	Gays in the military (Clinton = yes; JCS/Nunn = no)			X
1993	FY 1994 defense budget (Clinton/Aspin vs. Powell)	X		
1993–94	Change services' roles and missions (Clinton/Nunn = yes; JCS = no)			X
1993–94	"Win-hold-win" (Clinton/Aspin) vs. "win-win" (JCS)			X
1994	Invade Haiti (Clinton/Talbott = yes; Perry/JCS = no)	X		
1994	No restrictions on women (Clinton/West = yes; JCS = no)		X	
1996–97	Try Bosnian war criminals (Clinton/Albright = yes; Cohen/JCS = no)			X
1997	Flinn honorable discharge (Widnall = yes; Fogelman = no)			X
1997	Restrictions on land mines (Clinton/Gore = yes; JCS = no)			X
1997	Khobar Towers responsibility of air force commanding officer (Cohen = yes; Fogelman = no)	X		

Source: Adapted from Desch 1999, pp. 138–139.
JCS = Joint Chiefs of Staff; CENTCOM = Central Command.

Even in the cases Desch lists, the civil-military divisions were rarely as neat as the table implies. In no case did all civilians line up entirely on one side of the issue with the entire military establishment on the other side. Indeed, Avant (1994) argues that military shirking (my word, not hers) on use of force questions was a natural and even healthy military response to divisions between civilian principals in Congress and the executive branch. For this reason and as I explain below, I would recode the Bosnia case as "mixed" rather than clear shirking.

In some cases, an argument could be made that the outcome reflected a successful persuasion effort on the part of military advisors. For instance, it is conventional wisdom that the Clinton administration came into office wanting to adjust the roles and missions of the four services and thus the minimal changes that resulted seem to indicate that its preferences were stymied. One could argue, however, that civilian preferences were honored with the Aspin-led Bottom-Up Review and the subsequent creation of the independent Roles and Missions Commission. Although the final outcome of the Bottom-Up Review, the Roles and Missions Commission, and the Quadrennial Defense Review (QDR) matched rather closely the original Base Force concept developed by General Powell, this might be because the JCS position was more persuasive. Of course, it might also be because the JCS staff was more adept at managing the process of the various studies and because the Clinton administration lost its stomach for a showdown on radical defense restructuring after the imbroglio over gays in the military.[16] In this respect, it is striking that, according to one of the service chiefs, JCS chairman Shalikashvili explicitly (though privately) directed the senior military leadership, "In the QDR we want to work hard to try and maintain as close to the status quo as we can"—in other words, prejudging and resisting a civilian-led effort that was designed to be a comprehensive review of defense posture with an eye to making sweeping changes (Kohn 2001, p. 12).

At the same time, presenting issues as single-shot cases, as in Table 6.2, obscures important details and, possibly, opportunities for working and shirking. Desch treats Bosnia as only two decisions: the decision under Bush whether to intervene in 1992 and the decision in 1996–97 about bringing war criminals to trial. In fact, Bosnia was a bone of contention throughout the Clinton administration and (as I do in the next chapter) one can disaggregate the case into multiple decision points, some of which permit a judgment on military shirking. Similarly, Somalia does not even make Desch's list, although it is arguably the defining moment for Clinton civil-military relations, at least insofar as the use of force is concerned. Clearly, there is more going on in post–Cold War civil-military relations than can be captured in a simple summary table.

Even the paradigmatic case of military shirking, gays in the military, is open to interpretation. The conflict emerged when President Clinton, in one of his first acts in office, took the fateful first step toward removing the long-standing ban on gays serving openly in the military. On the day of his inauguration, aides to the president confirmed rumors that he would quickly keep his campaign promise on lifting the ban. Although candidate Clinton had publicly promised to do this on several occasions, the promise was not part of his regular stump speech (it was trotted out only for more liberal audiences) and it never received much attention during the campaign. Nevertheless, the issue resurfaced shortly after the election, and Colin Powell and the other chiefs of staff expressed their dismay and immediately launched an effort to persuade the president-in-waiting not to issue an executive order (Moss 1992, Hines 1992, Gellman 1992). As the inauguration drew near, Clinton's aides frantically sought some sort of postponement of the decision to avoid a showdown with defenders of the exclusion policy in Congress, including the leading Senate Democrat on defense, Senator Sam Nunn (Drew 1994, p. 44). Shortly after the inauguration, however, Clinton signaled that he was determined to go ahead with his plan to lift the ban, thus ushering in what was arguably the gravest predicament (after impeachment) Clinton faced as president (Korb 1996b, pp. 293–294).

On the day after the inauguration, the new secretary of defense, Les Aspin, informed the Joint Chiefs of Staff of President Clinton's determination to go ahead with his promise to lift the ban. They promptly requested a direct meeting with the president, which was held with great fanfare a few days later, on 25 January 1993. The meeting was described as rough and seemed to end in an impasse, with Clinton promising to press ahead and the chiefs withholding any firm promise of military support (Drew 1994, pp. 46–47). The military had powerful allies in Congress who were threatening to enact the existing ban into law by attaching it to the president's cherished family leave bill, and it was in response to this pressure that Clinton offered a compromise on 29 January 1993 (ibid., p. 47). He directed Aspin to take six months to develop an executive order that would lift the ban (Moss 1992, Hines 1992, Gellman 1992). Over the spring, congressional opposition hardened, and by 19 July 1993, when he announced the ultimate "honorable compromise" that would be known as "don't ask, don't tell," Clinton found that he lacked the political capital to make the changes in policy that he had promised. While the new policy did mandate that the military not actively investigate personnel in the absence of some credible information as to the individual's sexual orientation (that is, no "witch hunts"), thus including a concession of sorts to the Clinton effort to lift the ban altogether, it nevertheless rested on the same proposition as the previous policy, namely that open homosexuality was incompatible with military service (Korb 1996b, pp. 294–295).

In this case, congressional opposition was crucial to explaining the outcome of the gays in the military debacle, so the problem of a divided principal cannot be ignored. The case does not fit neatly into either of two classic principal-agent scenarios: an intransigent agent shirking in the face of unambiguous direction from the principal, or a passive agent whipsawed by a conflict between two competing principals. The military's principals, the commander in chief and the Congress, *were* divided and President Clinton's initiative was ultimately overturned in Congress. But Congress acted in concert with a strong lobbying effort on the part of the military that was generated to overturn the expressed preferences of the elected commander in chief. The military orchestrated much of the opposition by urging retired officers to speak up and by coordinating with congressional opponents of the president's plan; moreover, the military leaked word that there would be massive resignations in protest if the ban were lifted, further threatening the president's ability to set policy (Kohn 2002). From the president's perspective, the military was shirking, even if the White House would not admit to that on the record. Of course, General Powell would not accept the shirking label either; on the contrary, Powell argued that Secretary Aspin "exercised solid, unmistakable civilian control over the Armed Forces and me" (Powell et al. 1994, p. 23). But it cannot be denied that the final resolution, the "don't ask, don't tell" policy, was a reluctant compromise between all parties and was a far cry from the bold order originally announced by the White House.[17]

Regardless of the merits of the proposed reforms of the policy on gays in the military, the way the reforms were introduced and then managed was an example of what one former senior Clinton administration official described as the West Wing staff's "tin ear" on civil-military matters.[18] The significance of the issue extended far beyond the confines of civil-military relations or even defense policy more generally. The gay issue essentially defined the first 100 days of the Clinton administration and formed the backdrop for civil-military relations from that point on (Friedman 1993d; Hackworth 1993; Lancaster 1993a, 1993b, 1993c; No author 1993c, 1993f; Lancaster and Dewey 1993; Philpott 1993; Schmitt 1993e; Thomas 1993). The issue proved so contentious partly because it appeared to confirm a caricature of President Clinton—out of touch with the military and insensitive to its interests—and partly because it involved a radical insertion of civilian policymaking into a hitherto off-limits area of military prerogative, determining the kinds of behaviors the military could deem "prejudicial to good order and discipline and small-unit cohesion." But, as I will argue below, the agency theory framework leads us to expect that the gay issue had broader ramifications for civil-military relations, changing the way the military perceived and responded to its principal, the commander in chief, even in very different issue areas such as the use of force.

In sum, even allowing for the ambiguities inherent in coding difficult cases, the change from the Cold War period is striking. Shirking in some form was more prominent in the 1990s than it was in previous decades. The puzzle is not whether but why.

Why Shirking? An Enduring "Gap" and Changes in expectations of Punishment

The agency model suggests that shirking will increase when the military's incentives for shirking increase. According to the equilibrium conditions outlined in Table 5.4, the military's incentives to shirk increase when the following two inequalities hold: $w1 < s1 - agp$ and $w2 < s2 - bgp$. These two inequalities hold when either or both of the following two conditions are true: (1) that the gap between what the military would prefer to do and what civilians have asked it to do is great (when the difference between s and w is large); (2) when the expectation of punishment is small (when a, b, g, or p is small). In the post–Cold War era we have seen extreme values in both sets of parameters. The first set of parameters is captured by the so-called civil-military gap; the second set of parameters is captured by the so-called Clinton problem.

The civil-military gap refers to the divergence (or convergence) of the attitudes, values, perspectives, opinions, and personal background of members of the military compared with members of civilian society. Of course, there has always been a gap between the military and society, but some have argued that for a variety of reasons this gap is growing and, as a consequence, is contributing to the changes in civil-military relations.[19] The military itself has drawn attention to the apparently growing gap between civilian and military values, and some have even warned darkly about a role for the military in the country's culture wars (Lind, Schmitt, and Wilson 1994). By the end of the 1990s, the civil-military "crisis" literature had evolved into a debate over the existence and significance of the civil-military gap, a debate that was joined by the Triangle Institute for Security Studies (TISS) Project on the Gap between the Military and Civilian Society. In various TISS project publications, I explore the gap thesis in greater detail, but here I consider only how the gap might play out within the agency framework, specifically how changes in the gap change the incentives for the military to obey, other things being equal.[20]

The principal finding of the TISS Project on the Gap between the Military and Civilian Society is that there is not one civil-military gap but many, and that some have widened and others narrowed over the past generation. Because of the research design, the TISS study enabled direct comparisons of opinions and attitudes across three different groups—elite civilians, the general public, and the elite military (defined as up-and-coming officers in the midlevel ranks). It is therefore something of a simplification to synthesize from the extraordinary detail of the TISS study into the general judgment on "has the gap narrowed or not" demanded by the agency framework.

Of course, the civil-military opinion gaps have not all been yawning, and on some issues what is striking is the degree of consensus that emerges. For example, all respondents place a high priority on preventing nuclear proliferation and now put containing communism much lower on the agenda (Holsti 2001, Feaver and Kohn 2000a). Likewise, Deborah Avant and James Lebovic surveyed staff college-level officers (army, marine, and air force captains and majors, and navy lieutenants and lieutenant-commanders) in 1996 and 1997 and found a surprising degree of support for the new missions of humanitarian assistance, antiterrorism, and drug interdiction (Avant and Lebovic 2000). Significantly, officer support for these missions was positively correlated with whether the officers thought civilian leaders in Congress (and the general public) supported the new missions. Avant and Lebovic conclude that officers would be even more supportive of the new missions if they believed that civilian principals were united in their support for them—in other words, that the opinion gap on the appropriate uses of the military has narrowed and could narrow still further.

Nevertheless, the figures in the appendix to this chapter show that while some of the gaps explored in Chapter 2 narrowed, more of the gaps remained large and some even widened. On balance, the civil-military gap did not disappear with the end of the Cold War. The widest opinion gaps tend to be between the civilian elites and the military officers, precisely the groups most relevant to the agency framework because the civilian principals in the bureaucracy are drawn from the civilian elite and the military agents of greatest consequence emerge from the military elite.

Moreover, on one important dimension the civil-military gap widened markedly in the form of a growing identification of the officer corps with the Republican Party. Over the past generation, the percentage of up-and-coming officers who identify themselves as Independent (or as having no party affiliation) has gone from a plurality (46 percent) to a minority (27 percent), and the percentage that reports as Republican has nearly doubled (33 percent to 64 percent) (Holsti 1998–99, p. 11; 2001). By 1999, these officers were eight to one Republicans over Democrats, while elite civilians and the mass public were split about evenly between the parties.[21] The so-called republicanization traces its roots to many factors, not the least being the disappearance of the pro-defense wing of the Democratic Party after the Vietnam War and active courting of military voters by the Republican Party at least since the Reagan administration. The emergence of the all-volunteer force undoubtedly had an impact as well, as the military increasingly comprised a self-selected group of Americans. Importantly, this trend, which certainly predates the end of the Cold War, had the effect of sharply widening the civil-military gap in 1992 when the Democrats retook the White House. With the election of Clinton, coupled with the increasingly republicanized officer corps, overnight the political gap between the military and at least one crucial sector of the civilian political elite—the president and his political appointees—widened dramatically. From a principal-agent perspective, it is not surprising that Clinton clashed sharply with the military; on at least some dimensions, they brought sharply diverging perspectives to the civil-military relationship.

The opinion gap was exacerbated by what may be called an "experience gap," the gradual decline in the number of military veterans serving in the political elite (defined as the elected members of Congress and the cabinet). During the Cold War, military service was seen as an important qualification for national leadership and every president and vice president from Franklin Roosevelt to George Bush had served at least for a short while in the military or National Guard. More important, throughout the twentieth century the percentage of veterans in the political elite rose and fell in direct correlation with the percentage of veterans in the general public, but always with a veterans' bonus—more veterans in Congress than in the comparable cohort in the general population. Beginning in the mid-1970s, this veterans' bonus gradually eroded, and by 1994 there was actually a lower percentage of veterans in the House of Representatives than in the comparable cohort in the general public (Bianco and Markham 2001). This change was due, no doubt, to the shift to the all-volunteer force and the changes in party structure after Vietnam. The trend predated the end of the Cold War but was accelerated by it. As the Soviet threat receded, the country's political elite could focus on domestic priorities where military service no longer seemed relevant. From the agency perspective, the important issue is not *why* the experience gap emerged but simply that it did. Today, fewer members of the civilian political elite have experience interacting with military officers, let alone military experience of their own.

At the same time, the military establishment was going through the post–Cold War drawdown, reducing the opportunities for civil-military interaction that might narrow the gap. Whereas at the height of the Cold War in 1984 there were some 888 bases scattered across the fifty states, by 1998 that figure had been cut by more than 40 percent to 519, and the remaining bases were more concentrated in the South, as well as in California and Hawaii.[22] Likewise, the reductions in personnel translated into fewer people connected to the military through friendship or family.

This overall civil-military gap corresponds to a preference gap in the agency framework that increases incentives for the military to shirk. Importantly, the issues at stake in most of the post–Cold War civil-military debates are precisely the kinds of issues on which civilian and military preferences are most likely to diverge widely—that is, where the military payoff for working is very low and its payoff for shirking is very high. Whereas traditional explanations would highlight resource issues (size of budget, force structure, and so on), the agency model would expect the most contentious issues to be those having to do with the monitoring connection itself (operational control questions, constraints on the kinds of force to be used), because they represent a renegotiation of the basic terms of relationship. Resource issues have come into play with the post–Cold War downsizing—the roles and missions debate and fractious Quadrennial Review process are cases in point—but they have generated more partisan or intramilitary troubles than civil-military friction. On the contrary, the civil-military crisis arose over issues largely unrelated to budgets: the ban on gays serving openly in the military and the use and constraints on use of force in Somalia, Haiti, Bosnia, and Kosovo.

The second parameter singled out by the agency framework as crucial is the military agent's expectation of punishment. Arguably, this has also undergone significant changes since the end of the Cold War. The military had reason to believe that the probability of punishment (g) had dropped after the Cold War, declining still further with the arrival of the Clinton administration. This dramatic change is evident when one looks at the constituent elements that go into the military's expectation of punishment: the structural and personal factors that determine the relative strength of civilians vis-à-vis the military.

On the structural side, the most important development has been the cumulative effect of changes in the degree of military training and preparedness for involvement in political-military policymaking, a trend that can be traced to a reaction to the McNamara and Vietnam traumas but which was greatly accelerated by the 1986 Goldwater-Nichols reforms. As Christopher Gibson and Don Snider document, ever since Vietnam the military has steadily increased the level of training and experience its most promising officers receive in political-military affairs, as measured by advanced educational degrees and years of experience in job assignments that require extensive civil-military policymaking interactions.[23] Gibson and Snider argue that the military set out deliberately to improve the "potential to influence" ratio, which was decidedly in the favor of the civilian OSD staff under Secretary McNamara because of the depth of expertise and experience the McNamara team enjoyed. As a consequence, postgraduate degrees and experience in political-military billets were identified as important stepping stones to promotion, thus creating an incentive for the best officers to pursue them. This trend received a boost with the Goldwater-Nichols reforms, which were intended to strengthen the joint military staffs at the expense of the service military staffs, but which also had the unintended effect of strengthening the joint military staffs at the expense of the civilian staff in the Office of the Secretary of Defense. Because there has been no comparable effort directed at civilian staffs, Gibson and Snider find that the civilian staff in the OSD in the past decade had considerably less expertise, less experience, and therefore less "potential to influence," relative to the military staffs, than in previous eras.

While Gibson and Snider's conclusions are limited simply to the speculation that these more capable military representatives are better positioned to persuade in interagency deliberations, their findings would also apply to the feedback possibility of changing expectations of punishment. The weaker civilian staffs are more easily rolled in bureaucratic tussles and are less able to impose a price on the military when that happens. Especially during the early Clinton years, this structural factor was exacerbated by Clinton's failure to fill the senior civilian slots in the Department of Defense in a timely manner, thus contributing to a vacuum at the top of the chain of command.[24]

The relative strength of civilians and the military may also vary with the popularity of the officer in question. Early in George Bush's tenure, Secretary of Defense Cheney very prominently flexed the civilian's punishment prerogative by firing General Dugan (Woodward 1991, pp. 290–296). General Powell himself invoked the probability of punishment as evidence that he would not shirk during the Bush era, writing, "It was not lost on me that Mr. Cheney had shown he knew how to fire generals" (Powell et al. 1994, p. 23). But in the midst of the 1992 campaign, Bush's willingness to punish was demonstrably lower, at least insofar as the popular General Powell was concerned. Consider the example of General Powell's efforts to head off any political decision to use limited air strikes against the Serbs in 1992. As discussed in detail in Chapter 7, Powell's behavior might be coded as shirking under agency theory, but President Bush chose not to perceive the behavior as shirking, for an obvious reason: General Powell was very popular and Bush was in the middle of a desperate campaign for reelection.[25] Consequently, General Powell was not punished, at least not observably so.

Furthermore, the relative strength of civilians over the military is a function of the extent to which the president commits his political capital, which is manifest in the prominence given military and foreign policy issues in any administration. The administration's most powerful actor is, of course, the president himself. The more time he spends personally on an issue, the more the administration's position can prevail over intransigent bureaucratic actors, including military ones. The president is the final buck-stopper in the cumbersome interagency process run by the National Security Council (NSC) staff. This presidential authority can be delegated and enhanced by a powerful NSC staff, or it can be hoarded and diminished by a weak staff. Those on the NSC staff are meant to be the president's personal representatives on any given issue, standing somewhat apart from other political appointees in departments that may have other institutional interests to represent. Disputes are decided at lower levels by players who are able to anticipate what would happen if the president were actually to intervene personally on a particular issue and through the related ability of the NSC staff to threaten credibly exactly that outcome. In this light, one of the most significant changes from the Bush administration to the Clinton administration was the dramatically lower profile given national security issues by President Clinton (at least in his first term). It was widely understood in the government that national security was a lower-profile issue, and that the president's top national security staff had remarkably little access to the president (Halberstam 2001b, pp. 214–215, 241–247). The diminution of the president's role in this area inevitably weakened the hand of the civilians against the military and, by extension, contributed to a lower expectation of punishment, especially in Clinton's first term.

By far the largest factor affecting the probability of punishment in the post–Cold War era, however, was the complex of personal characteristics and conflicts collectively referred to as the "Clinton problem." President Clinton was the first commander in chief elected after the end of the Cold War, and he brought a unique personal history to the position. During the 1992 campaign, Republicans sought to make an issue of Bill Clinton's own efforts to avoid the draft during Vietnam (Putzel 1992, Taylor 1992, Kranish 1992), and what began as a campaign tactic may have unwittingly contributed to the problems plaguing relations between civilians and the military more generally.

Like many of his generation, Clinton opposed the Vietnam War, and also like many of his generation, he tried to avoid serving. His efforts to dodge the draft were rather run of the mill by the standards of the day. However, in comparison with President Bush's record as not only the victorious commander in chief of the Gulf War but also a bona fide war hero in his own right—he was a naval aviator in the Pacific in World War II, and his plane was shot down while trying to bomb Chichi Jima, an island in the South Pacific—Clinton's stature was all the more diminished. What would be a public relations challenge under the best of circumstances was compounded by four weaknesses. First, as governor of a small state running on a platform of domestic issues, Clinton had no record of competence in foreign policy and national security matters to compensate for his lack of personal experience in the military. Second, neither Clinton the candidate nor his campaign team ever gave a convincing account of how and why he never got drafted. On the contrary, the Clinton team sought to dissemble on his efforts to avoid the draft.[26] At the outset, they claimed he entered the draft after changing his mind about the ROTC program at the University of Arkansas but was never called up; in the face of mounting evidence to the contrary, they admitted that Clinton received an induction notice in April 1969 while at Oxford and then said that the draft board in Arkansas told him to ignore the notice because the date had already passed (Debenport 1992). Third, some of the evidence that emerged over the course of the campaign suggested that Clinton sought to avoid military service not simply out of cowardice or antiwar principle but out of a deeper dislike for the military as an institution (Greig 1992). In a particularly damning letter to Colonel Eugene Holmes, the army ROTC commander at the University of Arkansas, Clinton wrote that he was one of those who found themselves "loving this country, but loathing the military" (Mathis 1992b). Fourth, Clinton's political handlers, beyond the effort to dissemble on what really happened, were particularly heavy-handed in their attempts to neutralize the issue. They took the unusual step of assembling as many retired generals and admirals as they could find to offer a staged, public endorsement of their candidate's fitness to serve as president (May 1992, Mathis 1992a). Since the officers were retired, the action was not a direct assault on the long-standing military tradition of political neutrality, but the use of senior retired military officers to close off a debate about the candidate's fitness for office was unseemly and added to the image of a candidate who did not understand the military and was cynically willing to exploit it.

The draft-dodging issue did not prove decisive in the campaign, but it did leave president-elect Clinton at a decided disadvantage in relations with the military. Clinton's mendacity on the issue indicated moral cowardice to military officers, and Clinton arrived in office knowing that the military held this view (and knowing that the military knew that he knew). It greatly undermined Clinton's personal moral authority, which is an important ingredient in military expectations of how the commander in chief will function. This message was reinscribed in the many unavoidable ceremonial responsibilities of the commander in chief, and the events gave legs to the story of Clinton's strained relations with the military. Every speech for Veteran's Day, Memorial Day, Armed Services Day, every visit to a military base, even the juxtaposition of the president and the marines and airmen responsible for transporting the president—all became opportunities for the press to rehearse Clinton's equivocal standing on military matters. It is telling that President Clinton reportedly mused to friends during his last days in office that if he had a chance to live his life over again, he would have agreed to serve in Vietnam. His views on the morality of the war had not changed, he is reported to have said, but he now believed that his failure to serve had drastically curtailed his effectiveness as commander in chief.[27]

With such baggage, President Clinton would have been at a disadvantage in dealing with any military officer. But during the crucial early months of his tenure, Clinton had to deal not just with any military officer but with Colin Powell, one of the most popular figures in America. Powell's biography was something like a purified version of Clinton's own, with all the assets (an American morality tale of a poor kid making it to the top) and none

of the liabilities (Powell served in Vietnam and had none of the infidelity rumors or character flaws associated with the president). One observer described it this way: "Powell's greatest strength—his resume—was Clinton's
greatest weakness; both of them knew it, and they knew that the Congress
and the public at large knew it as well" (Halberstam 2001b, p. 238).

Given their relative positions, the political costs of punishing Powell were
prohibitive for the Clinton team, and this fact was widely appreciated by
people in and out of government at the time. The impossibility of punishing
Powell was the biggest downside President Clinton and his advisors saw to
the otherwise attractive idea of offering Powell the post of secretary of state;
bringing him aboard would have given them some insulation from external
critics, but at the price of hiring a subordinate who could have easily eclipsed
his superior (Halberstam 2001b, p. 300). Such a dramatic disadvantage at
the top ripples through the civil-military system, strengthening the hand of
lower-level military officers against lower-level civilian officials, and contributing to a generally lower expectation of punishment.

The administration's first foray into military policy, the abortive effort to
lift the ban on gays and lesbians serving openly in the military, seemed to
confirm the worst fears that the Clinton team just "did not get it" when it
came to military affairs. The administration viewed the issue of gays in the
military as more of a civil rights matter than a national security matter. Consequently, the point person in the White House for the policy was not Anthony Lake, the national security advisor, but George Stephanopoulos, then
the communications director but in function the president's closest political advisor (Halberstam 2001b, p. 205). General Powell and senior military
leaders were not consulted on whether or how to implement the new policy. They were simply informed, as if the matter were a minor issue or a
technical correction to existing policy. To the military, however, this matter
concerned "good order and discipline" and "unit cohesion," the touchstones
of combat effectiveness. The overwhelming majority of military personnel
opposed allowing gays to serve openly in the military, and their opinion was
grounded in traditional morality concerns as well as the fear that open homosexuals would create a sexually charged atmosphere, given the close
quarters of barracks and shipboard life—an atmosphere that might cost lives
by reducing troops' combat effectiveness (Miller and Williams 2001). President Clinton and his advisors, however, considered this viewpoint to be ab-
horrent—an atavistic "homophobia" grounded in ignorance and prejudice.
Clinton's team considered opposition to homosexuals' serving to be no more

morally legitimate than earlier racist concerns about integrating African Americans into the ranks. The debate thus quickly polarized the two camps, each viewing the other as pursuing not just an imprudent or improper policy but, at its root, a fundamentally immoral one.

When first the Congress and then public opinion sided with the military against President Clinton's proposal, the administration was forced to back down. Backing down in the face of such insubordination, however, only reinforced the perception that the president was not able to serve as commander in chief and could be rolled by the military. The gays in the military issue thus presented the administration with a lose-lose proposition. The proposal itself, both its substance and in the way it was handled, suggested that the administration was neither ready nor able to lead the military. Had the administration prevailed on the issue in the face of unanimous military opposition, the victory surely would have been Pyrrhic; the damage to the president's relations with the military would have been irreparable. Failing to prevail on the proposal, however, showed that the president was indeed vulnerable on military issues and that he was sufficiently uncertain about his mandate that he would back down in the face of determined opposition. The gays in the military issue thus started the administration out with the worst of both worlds, a Pyrrhic defeat. Whereas Clinton's political advisors first were attracted to the gay ban issue because it looked like an "easy" way to fulfill a campaign pledge and thus to establish the president as a political force to be reckoned with, in fact the issue did the opposite. Clinton's famed campaign war room thus gave the administration a grave self-inflicted wound; in the words of one journalist, "That it would make the Clinton team even more vulnerable to its critics and weaken him in his overall relationship with the military, an area where he was already on thin ice, was never fed into the equation" (Halberstam 2001b, p. 206). Or, as another observer has noted, the military became Clinton's "third rail," which he avoided as best he could; his choices of secretaries of defense indicated a wish to delegate his military responsibilities to congressional Democrats (Aspin), to the military-industrial complex (Inman and Perry), and finally to Republicans (Cohen). Each choice reflected a desire on the part of Clinton to avoid strong command over the military (Kohn 2002).

From an agency theory perspective, Clinton's failed challenge to the military greatly weakened his position, and contributed to greatly reduced expectations of punishment on the part of the military. From that point on, the administration proved exceptionally gun-shy on military matters. The

White House embarked on an ambitious charm offensive, seeking to woo the military and persuade the American people that the president did not, after all, loathe the people who served in the armed forces.[28] His press secretary, Michael McCurry, described the effort thus: "I can't think of any one thing the president has put more personal attention and caring into than his relationship with the military at all levels . . . He did it because he understood that he began with a significant deficit. He has tried to make a personal and human connection with his commanders and all the way down the chain" (McGrory 1998). The sustained wooing appeared to bear fruit in the form of more military soundbites expressing confidence in the president and fewer anti-Clinton soundbites parroting the critiques of partisan conservatives (Lancaster 1993d, Devroy 1994, McGrory 1998). The reduction in tension led some observers to speculate that the problem was more a spasm of discomfort than a cancer eating away at the body politic (Drozdiak 1994, Dobbs 1996, Pine 1996). Nevertheless, while the daily drumbeat of negative headlines did abate somewhat, episodes of civil-military conflict continued, and each new issue provided an opportunity for pundits to rehearse the past litany of problems.[29]

Below the level of such superficial soundings, the charm offensive had the effect of further undermining the authority of the president as commander in chief; like a divorced parent trying to get a child to support a custody arrangement, the White House effort to win the allegiance of those who were already obligated to obey only reversed the lines of de facto authority. Having been burned so badly on the gays in the military issue, the administration refused to spend scarce political capital on a range of other difficult policy fights, such as the so-called Bottom-Up Review of force posture and the effort to reinstate President Aristide in Haiti. In each case, the administration walked back from campaign promises and accepted policies that were more in line with military preferences. Likewise, the administration endured a seemingly never-ending procession of slights and insults from the military, most of the time without comment or public effort to reinforce discipline.

Although civil-military conflict was especially personal during the early years of Clinton's first term, by the time of the 1996 election the ad hominem vitriol had abated somewhat. President Clinton's convincing victory over yet another war hero, Senator Dole, seemed to put the matter of his personal qualifications to rest.[30] But the issue returned with a vengeance in Clinton's second term during the Lewinsky-impeachment travail. Revelations of President Clinton's misconduct prompted numerous unflattering comparisons to the double-standard that allowed the commander in chief to get off scot-free for behavior that would end the careers of his military subordinates (Graham 1998). Several serving officers gained notoriety by giving public voice to discontent that was presumably widespread in the ranks (Priest 1998). Even one veteran serving on the president's own White House staff (in the office of the drug czar) joined in the chorus, writing a very public op-ed in the *Wall Street Journal* that objected to the president's conducting liaisons with intern Monica Lewinsky while on the phone mobilizing support for the Bosnian peacekeeping mission (McDonough 1998). Concern was widespread that the president's political difficulties were influencing civil-military relations in yet another way, by inducing the president to authorize questionable uses of force as a distraction, mirroring the plot of the movie *Wag the Dog,* about a fictional president in similar political straits (Hersh 1998, Baker 1998).

By itself, of course, the "Clinton factor" cannot explain the whole story. Certainly Clinton's personal liabilities exacerbated civil-military conflict, but the first alarms about excessive military influence and even military insubordination concerned General Powell's behavior in the Bush administration, well before Clinton arrived on the national scene. Yet from the agency perspective, Clinton's personal liabilities surely loomed large, and agency theory provides a coherent way of showing how those liabilities affected day-to-day relations: by reducing the military's estimation of the probability of punishment. President Clinton's weakness rippled throughout his staff; one high Pentagon civilian is reported to have said, "[what] weighs heavily . . . every day . . . [is] the reluctance, indeed refusal, of the political appointees to disagree with the military on any matter, not just operational matters" (Kohn 2002). Or, as one reporter observed, Clinton "was intimidated more by the military than by any other political force he dealt with"; this view was supported by at least one former senior NSC official who confided to a reporter, "I don't think there was any doubt . . . that [Clinton] was out-and-out afraid of them" (Halbserstam 2001a, p. 230).

This weakness colored every major use of force during the Clinton administration and led to a situation in which the president appeared to be courting the military, not vice versa.[31] The weakness was displayed in its most stark form in the anecdote introduced at the beginning of the chapter: the spectacle of White House aides fretting over whether they dared punish a senior air force general who had publicly referred to the president as a "gay-loving, pot-smoking, draft-dodging, and womanizing" commander in chief.

The obvious hesitation the White House staff showed about punishing a senior officer for behavior that was egregious by any standard underscored just how low an expectation of punishment the military could reasonably hold during the Clinton years.

Of course, General Campbell was fired, and punishment has not been entirely absent in the post–Cold War era. As noted earlier, Secretary Cheney rather pointedly punished General Dugan, and Powell claimed the point was not lost on him. Arguably, Cheney's action only heightened the contrast between the Bush and Clinton administrations and thus, in agency theory terms, had a very temporary effect on military calculations. The best-known case of a general's "punishment" during the Clinton tenure was the rather shabby way General Clark was replaced as SACEUR after the Kosovo war, discussed in more detail in Chapter 7. On the one hand, Clark was clearly being punished for crossing swords with his masters, specifically General Shelton and Secretary of Defense Cohen. On the other hand, the way the punishment was meted out undercut whatever salutary or reputational effects civilians might have hoped the action would engender, conveying an impression of "score settling" rather than an assertion of civilian control. Arguably, protestations of noninvolvement by the White House, however sincere, simply underscored the overall picture of civilian weakness (Halberstam 2001b, pp. 478–480).

In the same way, military complaints about widespread and apparently capricious punishment levied in the wake of the Tailhook scandal may have had a perverse effect on expectations of punishment (Webb 1997). Precisely because the punishment was considered to be capricious, the military's ability to predict with confidence what behaviors will produce punishment and what will be excused was eroded. Relatively sudden changes in the civilian climate concerning political correctness, coupled with a dramatic change in the relative prestige of the president, made those instances of punishment somewhat unforeseeable.[32] Moreover, because the monitoring and punishment were so clearly and narrowly focused on the arena of sexual relations, consistent with the agency theory model its chief consequence was likewise narrowly focused: the pervasive political-correctness fear in the military about sexual relations. The result was a curious combination of concern for a "zero defect" military simultaneous with remarkable manifestations of public contempt for the commander in chief.

This is perhaps the best way to make sense of the Khobar Towers case and the subsequent early retirement of air force Chief of Staff Donald R. Fogleman. Fogleman asked for early retirement when he learned that Secretary of Defense Cohen intended to block the promotion of Brigadier General Terryl Schwalier. Schwalier had been local commander of the base that included the Khobar Towers, which a terrorist bomb had destroyed in 1996.[33] After several internal investigations exonerated Schwalier from culpability, Fogleman recommended that he be promoted. Secretary Cohen disagreed and blocked the promotion on the grounds that the commander must be held accountable for the welfare of his troops. Fogleman felt that punishing Schwalier, even though it had been determined that he had done everything that could be expected of a commander, "would have a chilling effect on commanders around the world who might then infer that protecting their forces outweighed accomplishing their missions" (Kohn 2001, p. 7).

Fogleman's request for early retirement was widely perceived as a resignation in protest, the "honorable" course of action for a senior commander who had, in his own words, "lost respect and confidence in the leadership that I was supposed to be following." Fogleman himself believed that he had struck a balance: not resigning *in protest*, with all the public denunciation that would involve, but nonetheless leaving in disgust because "the way the United States Air Force as an institution was treated, for purely political reasons, and the way an individual was treated . . . was fundamentally wrong."[34] In his words, "You really do have to get up and look at yourself in the mirror every day and ask, 'Do I feel honorable and clean'" (Kohn 2001, p. 19). Interestingly, Fogleman does admit that he used the threat of resignation to persuade air force secretary Sheila Widnall not to give an honorable discharge to Kelly Flinn, the celebrated first female B-52 bomber pilot who lied about her affair with the husband of a junior enlisted person in her chain of command (Kohn 2001, p. 18). The trigger for Fogleman's decision to retire was thus his conviction that civilian superiors were punishing military officers capriciously—being reluctant to punish the clearly guilty (Flinn) for political correctness reasons and then determined to punish the not guilty (Schwalier) on equally dubious political grounds. Because military officers generally interpreted and celebrated Fogleman's response as a rebuff of his civilian leaders, the entire affair contributed to the confused climate concerning expectations for punishment.

In sum, there were strong, almost extreme values for the parameters that would induce the military to shirk—a continued wide gap between the military and civilian actors, coupled with the political weakness and thus reluctance of the civilian principals to punish military misbehavior. Relative to the Cold War, the military had both motive and opportunity to thwart civilian preferences and could do so with relative impunity. To be sure, the result was not a coup or some other civil-military catastrophe; it was, rather, a decade's worth of fractious and troubled relations.

Alternative Explanations

There are two broad camps of alternative explanations for post–Cold War civil-military relations. In the first camp are many atheoretical ad hoc explanations that make compelling arguments for the importance of a few key factors. These are useful in highlighting certain aspects of the relationship—say, Clinton's idiosyncratic relationship with the military—but they are easily subsumed by agency theory as shown above. From a theoretical point of view, the more important alternative explanations are those explicitly grounded in a comprehensive theory of civil-military relations. In this latter camp, there are two that merit consideration here: Deborah Avant's argument that post–Cold War civil-military relations have largely been dictated by the lack of consensus across the executive and legislative branches of government; and Michael Desch's argument that post–Cold War civil-military relations have been a function of the confluence of a low external threat and a low internal threat.

Deborah Avant's argument is a particularly interesting alternative to agency theory developed here because it is also derived from the general insights of the principal-agent literature. Her primary argument is that the military agent is more likely to obey when the two civilian principals, Congress and the president, are in agreement (Avant 1994). When there are divisions across the principals, the military agent gets conflicting direction, has more room to play one side off the other, and as a consequence is more free to resist the direction of one of the principals. She develops this argument via an analysis of the new institutionalist literature exploring congressional oversight of the bureaucracy, but it is consistent with Huntington's earlier "old institutionalist" analysis of how the military regularly played Congress off the president in the budgetary battles of the 1950s (Huntington 1961a). For Avant, the principal-agent perspective leads to the conclusion that there is no post–Cold War civil-military crisis: "Are the reluctant warriors out of control? Not quite. Their conservatism makes sense as a response to the lack of consensus among the civilian leadership in the United States about the importance of low-level threats" (Avant 1996–97, p. 90).

Although she pitches her argument as an alternative to the "crisis" literature, she differs mainly in the interpretation she gives to military and civilian behavior, not in the nature of the behavior itself. She admits that the military was indeed reluctant to use force in Bosnia, Haiti, and Somalia, and may even have exploited civilian indecisiveness so as to guarantee that its preferences were met, but she dismisses this as a natural—and therefore untroubling—result of the constitutional provision that divided civilian authority between Congress and the executive branch. Thus, at the descriptive level Avant's account of military behavior is not very different from that offered by Weigley, Kohn, and rest of the crisis school; the principal difference is that Avant dismisses any concerns about it on the basis of its structural origins.

At the theoretical level, agency theory presented here subsumes the divided-principal approach offered by Avant. While I have treated the principal as a unitary actor in Chapter 4 for modeling reasons, divisions within the principal are incorporated within the framework via the influence such divisions have on the "expectations of being punished" parameter. As Avant argues, divided principals are weaker relative to military agents, and thus there are more incentives for the military to shirk; when divisions are extreme, military agents have reason to believe that punishment efforts by one civilian principal might be blocked by the other civilian principal. Therefore, particularly where the military holds a preference at odds with one set of civilian principals, the military has a greater incentive to shirk that civilian principal's directives. The Avant approach is useful so far as it goes, but it is readily incorporated into agency theory. Moreover, because it does not develop the microfoundations underlying the logic of civil-military relations as does agency theory, it makes fairly limited predictions about the conduct of civil-military relations on a day-to-day basis. As is evident in the next chapter, agency theory provides a rich heuristic for guiding more detailed case studies, suggesting new interpretations, and making sense of odd developments that might otherwise be perplexing. In this sense, agency theory improves on, rather than rebuts, the insights available from Avant's more basic use of the principal-agent framework.

The second theoretically grounded alternative account of American post–Cold War civil-military relations is Michael Desch's threat-based theory.[35] Desch argues that good civil-military relations, defined as when civilian preferences prevail over military preferences, and bad civil-military relations, defined as when military preferences prevail over civilian, are a function of structure—that is, of the threat environment that the polity confronts (Desch 1999). Desch's emphasis on threat environment resurrects the Huntington and Lasswell tradition, but with a twist that generates predictions quite contrary to those of earlier theories. As I explained in Chapter 2, external threat was Huntington's "functional imperative," and Huntington feared that the high threat of the Cold War would create the conditions for problematic civil-military relations in the United States. The problematic relations Huntington feared, however, were not the "bad" relations in which military preferences prevailed but precisely the opposite: he feared liberal civilians would refuse to let the military function as it needed to to meet the Cold War threat. Lasswell also feared that the increased Cold War threat would create problematic civil-military relations, although his concern of a "garrison state" comes much closer to the Desch definition of bad relations. For both Huntington and Lasswell, however, a transition to peace would not necessarily augur harmonious civil-military relations, because when threats receded, the American public would revert to its traditional liberal antimilitary posture, demanding drastic cuts in the force structure and a "return to normalcy" (Huntington 1957, p. 346; Lasswell 1950). A force drawdown is, of course, unpopular with the military, and by themselves such cuts increase civil-military friction.

Michael Desch significantly builds on this Huntingtonian-Lasswellian model by considering a second dimension, internal threat, which yields four threat configurations: high internal and high external (as existed in the Soviet Union from 1986 to 1991); high internal and low external (as in Argentina from 1976 to 1982); low internal and high external (as in the United States during the Cold War); and low internal and low external (as in the United States during the post–Cold War era) (Desch 1999, p. 20). Whereas both Huntington and Lasswell predicted that the Cold War would produce bad civil-military relations—because the high threat would necessitate large forces that would chafe against the constraints imposed by liberal society—Desch's model makes the opposite prediction: because there was no internal threat to the United States in the Cold War, the military would be entirely oriented outside the state and would pose little hazard to the domestic political establishment.

Desch's model is attractively parsimonious and generalizable. By his own reckoning, the basic structural factors are able to account for shifting patterns of civil-military relations in the United States (from Cold War to post–Cold War), in the Soviet Union (during the same period), in France (through the post-Gaullist period), and in South America (in the modern period). A closer look at his model, however, raises questions about the causal mechanism and points to the need for the kind of microfoundational analysis offered by agency theory.

Desch gets from threat environment to civilian control via a complex and somewhat undertheorized causal mechanism, which he develops out of "some simple assumptions" (Desch 1999, p. 13). Following social cohesion theory, Desch assumes that conflict affects the cohesiveness (unified or divided) and the orientation (external or internal) of institutions.[36] In the absence of threats, institutions will be weak and divided; in the presence of threats, institutions will unify so as to counter the threat more efficiently (ibid., pp. 12–17). When the threat is external, the cohesion is good for civil-military relations because it will augur a more capable military organization directed at a threat to the nation-state. When the threat is internal, however, the more cohesive and capable military organization finds its attention directed inward, where it is a "serious contender for control of society" (ibid., p. 13). Thus, Desch assumes, militaries are easier to control when they are divided or externally oriented. Militaries are harder to control when they are unified or internally oriented.

Desch then develops a series of hypotheses, which collectively constitute the six intervening variables in his model: (1) the experience/attentiveness of civilian leaders; (2) the type of control they pursue; (3) how unified the civilians are; (4) how unified the military is; (5) the orientation of the military; and (6) the divergence of ideas (preferences). Many of these variables, of course, also play a role in agency theory, but Desch's structural model requires a series of ad hoc assumptions to generate specific predictions for how the variables relate.

Invoking Posen and contra Huntington, Desch claims that high external threat brings in an experienced and attentive civilian leadership, whereas low external threat, even with a high internal threat, would mean the civilian leadership would be "less likely to be attentive to national security affairs (Desch 1999, pp. 13–14, quote at 14). Huntington, of course, worried about the opposite—that civilian leaders reflecting the biases of liberal society would not meet the demands of the higher threat. Desch's inference on external threat is reasonable and analogous to agency theory's emphasis on the policy and electoral costs of monitoring. The inference on internal threat seems more ad hoc; would not internal threats be just as dangerous for civilian institutions and so galvanize civilian attention just as much? Is a guerrilla threat really less attention-grabbing than a foreign foe? Desch's version is not impossibly far-fetched, but it does not flow directly from his structural model.

Then, invoking Huntington and contra Posen, Desch claims that in the face of external threats, civilian institutions will rely on Huntington's objective control mechanisms (which make the military more effective), but in the face of internal threats civilian institutions will rely on subjective control mechanisms (because civilians wish to use the military in internal conflicts) (Desch 1999, pp. 14–15). In fact, Huntington himself warned precisely the opposite—that U.S. leaders would *not* use objective control in the heightened external threat environment of the Cold War. Moreover, this hypothesis runs counter to Posen's expectation about the reassertion of civilian control in the face of an adverse balance of power (ibid.). In any case, Desch does not consider problematic aspects of Huntington's objective/subjective typology: the fact that the American military remained "professional" despite the alleged use of subjective control that Huntington claimed precluded professionalization; or the fact that civilians adopted yet a third form, assertive control, for key areas during the Cold War.[37] Agency theory's use of intrusive versus nonintrusive monitoring seems superior, better grounding the policy-costs component that drives Desch's functionalist logic here, and providing a closer match to the empirical record.

Desch's core mechanism, social cohesion theory, *does* lead directly to specific hypotheses about the unity of domestic institutions (higher threat leads to more unified institutions), but because Desch is interested in the interplay of *two* domestic institutions, civilian and military, he must once again invoke undertheorized auxiliary mechanisms to reach the hypotheses he advances. Desch claims external threats should unify the state as a whole—that is, both civilian and military institutions individually and also their bonds to each other. Internal threats can have any number of different effects, depending on which combination of actors, state, society, and the military, is threatened and which is doing the threatening. Essentially, Desch claims, some internal threats weaken the state against the military but all internal threats unify the military (Desch 1999, pp. 12–13). It is not clear, however, why social cohesion theory would not expect the intensified internal threat to unify the government as a whole, thus strengthening *all* governmental institutions, including the civilian ones with which military institutions might vie for political power. After all, civilian institutions are functioning in the same threat environment that military institutions confront, and there is nothing in social cohesion theory to distinguish between the two camps. Moreover, if Desch is correct about the selection-of-control-mechanisms claim he makes earlier, then he is less likely to be correct about the effect of internal threat on the cohesiveness of the military. If internal threat makes civilians adopt subjective control mechanisms, then internal threat should *lower* the cohesion of the military, for subjective control divides and factionalizes the military.

To preserve a basic prediction from threat to likelihood of control, Desch is implicitly departing from social cohesion theory, on which he claims to have built his model, and invoking one of several plausible auxiliary assumptions or hypotheses: that the unifying effect of threat is greater on military institutions than civilian institutions since the organizational essence of the military is to respond to threats; that military institutions, by virtue of their near-monopoly on coercive power, are intrinsically more politically powerful than civilian institutions and, therefore, can be controlled only when they are divided or when their attention is distracted elsewhere; or that the source of the internal threat is the very weakness of the civilian government itself (although this hypothesis skirts a tautology—predicting that internal threats weaken the civilian against the military and defining internal threats as those which weaken the civilian against the military). Some of these auxiliary assumptions could easily be imported from the principal-agent framework, so the concern here is not inconsistency so much as an under-theorized model.[38]

Social cohesion theory seems to have a more direct prediction for the final component of Desch's causal mechanism, the divergence of civilian and military preferences, although it is worth noting that his hypothesis runs directly contrary to Huntington, on whose authority Desch rests his earlier auxiliary assumption concerning the choice of control mechanism. Desch claims that high external threat will harmonize preferences and cultures while internal threat will widen the gap (Desch 1999, pp. 14–15). Huntington, as discussed in Chapter 2, rooted the Cold War crisis precisely in the belief that the high external threat would exacerbate the gap between civilian and military institutions, although he claimed the opposite in fact happened when he viewed the Cold War retrospectively; since Huntington is inconsistent on this point, Desch is free to invoke the Huntingtonian authority that best matches his model. The preference-gap intervening variable may yet introduce a separate problem for Desch's model: if the high external–low internal threat configuration causes civilian and military preferences to converge, then there is no need for anything else in the model to explain why civilian preferences prevail. If civilians and the military agree on what is to be done, then it does not matter whether there are experienced leaders, unified civilians, or objective control: the military simply does what it wants, which also happens to be what civilians want.[39]

Although Desch's empirical test focuses on the front and back ends of his model (threat configurations and obedience), the performance of his intervening variables merits this closer scrutiny precisely because they are the direct predictions of his theory. Indeed, one could argue that his theory's direct predictions (intervening variables) have a tighter logical link to a different dependent variable from the one he claims: civil-military conflict rather than civilian control. To be sure, Desch explicitly rejects conflict as a dependent variable,[40] but it is striking how many of his intervening variables are plausibly better associated with conflict than with control. An inexperienced leader who chooses subjective control mechanisms rather than granting the military-preferred autonomy of objective control can expect much greater friction in civil-military relations. The more factionalized civilian and military institutions are, the more likely there will be crosscutting cleavages that drive disputes into the open and thus increase the perception of civil-military conflict. And, obviously, the more civilian and military ideas diverge, by definition the more times those ideas will conflict. Desch has a compelling theory of civil-military conflict, although he claims not to.

Because he does not examine the performance of these intervening variables, Desch's empirical analysis risks overstating the degree to which the U.S. post–Cold War experience confirms the model. The problem is compounded because, by his own admission, his model is indeterminate for the low-low threat configuration the U.S. confronted with the end of the Cold War. In such a configuration, on its own the Desch model cannot say whether there will be good civilian control because the military will be divided (and thus, presumably, easy to control), or whether there will be bad civilian control because without any threats the military's orientation will be uncertain (or because the divided institutions slip into contentious factionalism). Desch claims the model predicts either good civilian control or good civilian control mixed with some instances of military preferences prevailing over civilian (Desch 1999, pp. 16–17). Which of those outcomes prevails depends, according to Desch, on ideational factors such as organizational culture and clashing views on doctrine—a story that transpires more or less off

Desch's structural stage (ibid., p. 36). Thus, while Desch finds strong evidence that military preferences prevailed over civilian more frequently in the post–Cold War era than in the Cold War era, this is, strictly speaking, no more convincing proof of his pure model than would be evidence that showed no dramatic change—because his theory, absent other mechanisms, is indeterminate.[41] Desch's theory thus works best when put in tandem with another theory that accounts for the microfoundations of the civil-military relationship. Such a theory—indeed, something like agency theory—can provide the grounds for the auxiliary hypotheses that drive his intervening variables.

In sum, the few theoretically grounded alternative explanations available offer important insights but are not completely satisfying. The agency model can subsume or incorporate the best insights of existing explanations of the post–Cold War experience, thus providing a superior account that is theoretically grounded and inferentially consistent.

Conclusion

The agency framework provides a plausible explanation for post–Cold War civil-military relations. Civil-military relations *have* been more conflictual than was seen in the previous period, primarily because of the concurrence of civilian intrusive monitoring with military shirking. Such a concurrence is one of the predicted outcomes of the agency model and, consistent with the model, there are demonstrably strong values on several of the parameters the model identifies as important in producing the monitoring/shirking outcome.

As expected by the model, monitoring costs somewhat declined with the end of the Cold War, thus allowing for more intrusive monitoring, other things being equal. At the same time, the gap between the military agent and the civilian principal remained wide and may even have widened in some important ways, and this increased incentives for military shirking. Most important, the military expectation of punishment for shirking dropped precipitously with the election of a commander in chief who was in an equivocal position with respect to the military. The Clinton administration compounded this personality-based weakness with vacillating leadership, most obviously on the gays in the military issue but also in the key post–Cold War uses of force. The inherent weakness of the Clinton administration was then exacerbated by an absence of consensus across the legislative and executive branches more generally, thus further weakening civilian principals vis-à-vis military agents

Agency theory provides a systematic causal mechanism for linking dramatic exogenous developments—especially the end of the Cold War, the divergence between civilian and military elites, President Clinton's personal history, the rise of the chairman of the Joint Chiefs of Staff—to changes in patterns of civil-military relations. The model suggests that these factors have had a profound effect in reducing the perceived costs of monitoring, in reducing the perceived expectation of punishment, and in increasing the gap between what civilians ask for and what the military would prefer to do.

APPENDIX: Post–Cold War Civil-Military Gaps Presented Graphically

In this appendix are figures that illustrate the differences of opinion between civilian and military elites during the post–Cold War era in several areas: political ideology and partisanship (Figures 6.5 and 6.6); social policy (Figures 6.7 and 6.8); foreign policy goals (Figures 6.9 through 6.11); and the use of force (Figures 6.12 through 6.18). The figures present in graphical form how civil-military gaps presented in Appendix 2.2 have continued into the post–Cold War era. While each question represents a slightly different dynamic, an overall pattern emerges consistent with the interpretation presented in the text: that the gap between civilians and the military that characterized the Cold War era continued into the post–Cold War era.

Each figure represents the difference in means between the response of civilian elites and the response of military elites in the Foreign Policy Leadership Project quadrennial surveys and then the Triangle Institute for Security Studies survey of 1998–99. The wider the shaded area, the wider the gap in preferences.

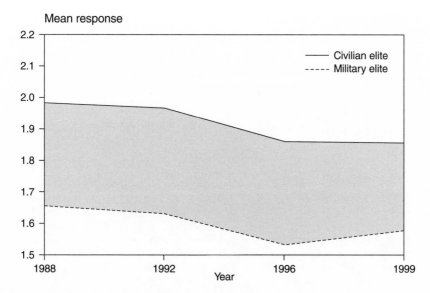

Figure 6.5 Post–Cold War civil-military gap on party identification

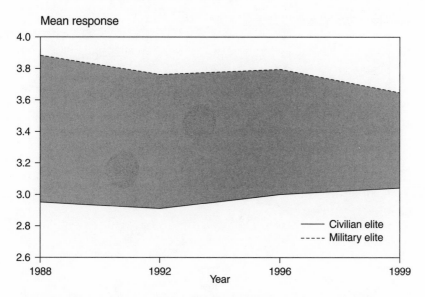

Figure 6.6 Post–Cold War civil-military gap on political ideology

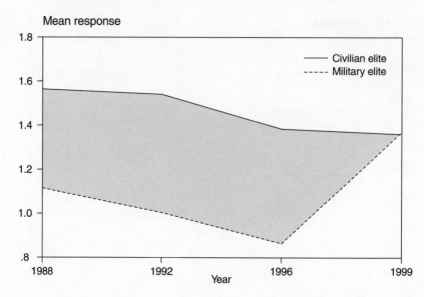

Figure 6.7 Post–Cold War civil-military gap on racial integration by busing

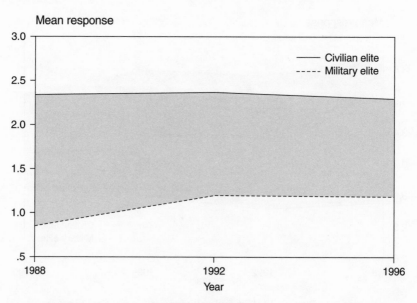

Figure 6.8 Post–Cold War civil-military gap on truth of press over government

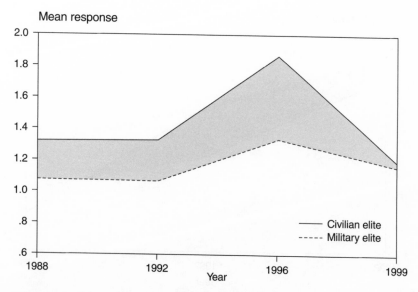

Figure 6.9 Post–Cold War civil-military gap on importance of human rights

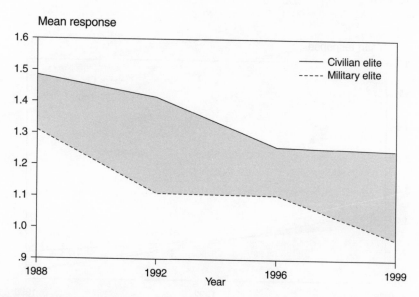

Figure 6.10 Post–Cold War civil-military gap on improving standard of living of less developed countries

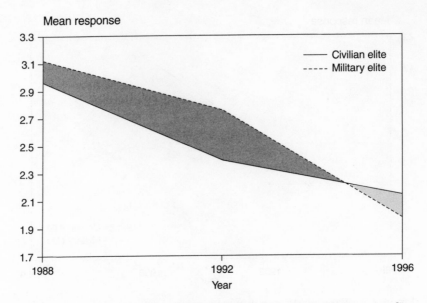

Figure 6.11 Post–Cold War civil-military gap on congressional-executive disagreement

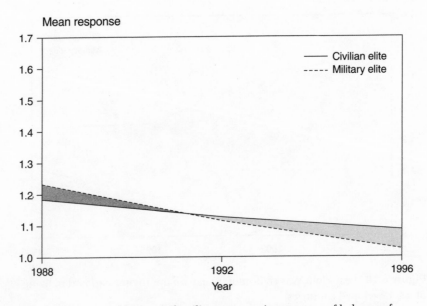

Figure 6.12 Post–Cold War civil-military gap on importance of balance of power

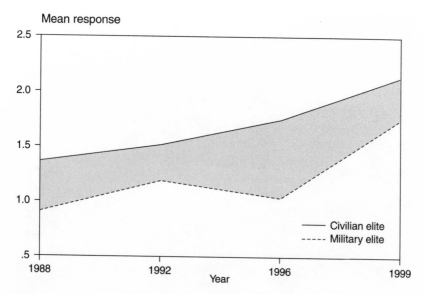

Figure 6.13 Post–Cold War civil-military gap on military goals determining force

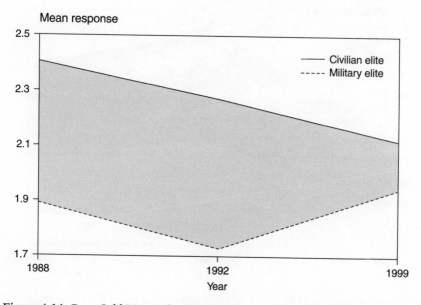

Figure 6.14 Post–Cold War civil-military gap on efficiency of military power declining

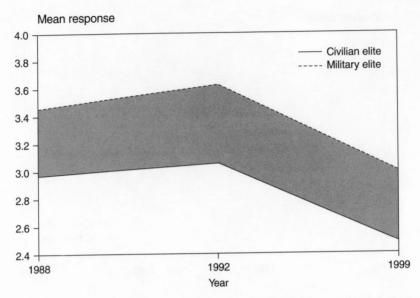

Figure 6.15 Post–Cold War civil-military gap on intervention should be short

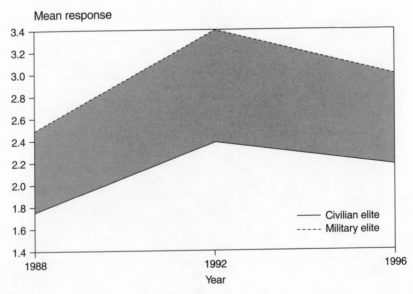

Figure 6.16 Post–Cold War civil-military gap on striking at heart of opponent's power

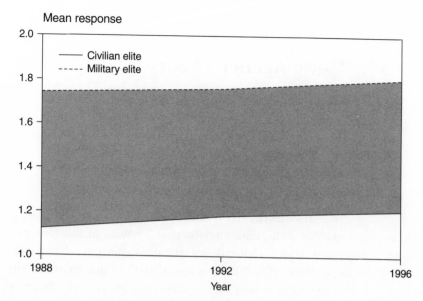

Figure 6.17 Post–Cold War civil-military gap on pursuing victory in Vietnam (early stages)

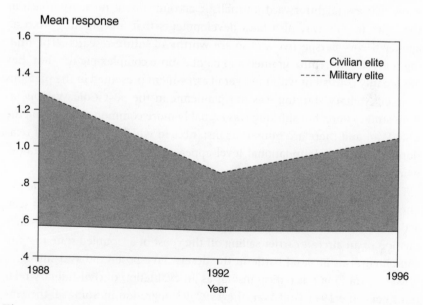

Figure 6.18 Post–Cold War civil-military gap on pursuing victory in Vietnam (late stages)

CHAPTER 7

Using Agency Theory
to Explore the Use of Force
in the Post–Cold War Era

The previous chapter outlined the agency theory interpretation of post–Cold War civil-military relations as a whole. In this chapter, I use agency theory to explore civil-military relations in one crucial domain of activity, the use of force. This chapter is less a "test" of the agency theory than it is a demonstration of how agency theory might serve as a heuristic for guiding the interpretation of recent events. Agency theory cues us to look for certain things and to ask certain questions in a case study and thereby illuminates the give and take of day-to-day civil-military relations in ways that a straightforward journalistic account might miss. Approaching the cases in this way also flags developments that are puzzling from an agency theory perspective and so are worthy of future research. The findings here are more fine-grained and paint a more complex picture, but they are broadly consistent with the overall assessment presented in the previous chapter. Military shirking was not pandemic in the post–Cold War operations studies here, but shirking was arguably more common than during the Cold War, and there are numerous instances in which the patterns of relations at the microfoundational level appear to conform to agency framework expectations.

The end of the Cold War did not end the utility of military force, as the frequency and variety of military deployments can attest. The military has seen action in an extraordinarily wide range of settings, from the simple presence mission of an aircraft carrier sailing off the coast of a troubled state to a full combined-arms air-land battle in the desert. Five post–Cold War missions, however, stand out as critical insofar as an evaluation of civil-military relations goes: the 1991 Gulf War, the 1992–93 operation in Somalia, the embargo and ultimate 1994 "invasion" of Haiti, the five year lead-up to the Dayton peace accords and the ongoing mission in Bosnia, and the 1999 war in Kosovo. These five cases are especially important because they constitute the three pillars of the conventional wisdom on U.S. civil-military relations. First, the Gulf War has been cited as an exemplar of civil-military cooperation; second, the reluctance of senior military officers, especially then-chairman of the JCS Colin Powell, to embrace the missions in Somalia, Haiti, and Bosnia was in fact the precipitating factor that convinced at least some observers that U.S. civil-military relations were out of control (Weigley 1993); and third, the Kosovo war, coming at the close of the Clinton administration, seemed to fit somewhere in between—it was neither a debacle nor a triumph but rather, as the title of one treatment has it, a case of "winning ugly" (Daalder and O'Hanlon 2000).

Given space and scope constraints, it is not possible to present an exhaustive study of each conflict. It is possible, however, to present mini–case studies that bring to the fore aspects that best illustrate the utility of agency theory, and the limits thereof.

The Gulf War, 1990–91

Conventional wisdom holds that President Bush enjoyed the Huntingtonian ideal of civilian control during the Gulf War. The president and his senior civilian leaders established the broad strategic objectives, delegated authority to the military commanders, and then resisted the temptation to monitor intrusively the ongoing operation. The shadow of Vietnam hung conspicuously over the planning and execution of the Gulf War, and the principal players were at pains publicly to claim that President Bush would not pick bombing targets from the White House (Benedetto 1991). Faced with such civilian forbearance, the senior military submitted, as Huntington would expect, and delivered.

Whether this idealized version is accurate is debatable. The available evidence suggests that civilians monitored far more intrusively than was generally believed at the time. From the start, Cheney used back channels into the service and joint staffs to generate a wider range of military options than might have been forthcoming if he had relied on General Powell's JCS staff alone (Woodward 1991, pp. 234–235, 238–239; Gordon and Trainor 1996, pp. 141–152). Cheney did this deliberately because he was dissatisfied with the quality of the early war options generated by the JCS and saw in this kind of intrusion a way to "[light] a fire under the military" (Gordon and Trainor 1996, p. 152). Such involvement was met by military resistance, and according to some analysts, the military responded so as to regain an upper hand; in their insider look at the planning behind the Gulf War, Michael R. Gordon and Bernard E. Trainor describe Generals Powell and Schwarz-kopf as responding to Cheney's option-creation exercise thus: "Now Schwarzkopf and Powell needed to get their heads together and form a united front. Otherwise, the civilians would try telling them what to do" (Gordon and Trainor 1996, p. 147).

The attention to detail extended all the way to the top of the civilian chain of command. In one section of *The Commanders*, Bob Woodward describes Bush as being very detail oriented: "Bush had spent eight years watching Reagan operate, and delegate. Unlike Reagan, Bush wanted the details, all the details. He wanted to be the player, the guy who made as many of the calls as possible." Barely a hundred pages later, however, Woodward paints Bush as highly delegative: "The President has said he does not want another Vietnam, Cheney reminded Schwarzkopf. The administration was commit-ted. The military commanders would not have their hands tied. The Presi-dent, Cheney and Powell had to sign off on the plan, but once it was ap-proved, it would for the most part be in Schwarzkopf's hands." And yet still elsewhere, Woodward details that President Bush, Secretary Cheney, and Secretary Baker each personally vetted the target list and that President Bush personally removed some targets, such as statues of Saddam Hussein (Woodward 1991, pp. 225, 347, 364–365, 368; Betts 1991, p. 223; Cooper 2001). This intrusive monitoring was resisted by the military, and Wood-ward documents General Powell's efforts to keep the civilians out of the op-erational planning by refusing to hold up-to-date lists of targets at the Penta-gon (Woodward 1991, p. 368). Similarly, Rick Atkinson documented that Cheney "took an active role in operations." Despite never having served in uniform, the secretary of defense delved into the operational details of the war, pressing the navy to move aircraft carriers into the Gulf and drawing up an alternative war plan to handle the Scud-hunting problem (Atkinson 1993, pp. 94–96; Woodward 1991, pp. 329–330; Gordon and Trainor 1996, pp. 233–234). John Mueller documented several more examples of civilian interference in operational details: restrictions on where and when recon-naissance aircraft could be flown over Iraq; restrictions on targeting, espe-cially after the bombing of a shelter in Baghdad; restrictions on whether the Iraqi planes that sought sanctuary in Iran could be hit; and the insistence on diverting resources to hunt the militarily insignificant Scuds. Mueller claimed that the explicit limits on the amount of American casualties that would be tolerated—no more than "three companies per Coalition brigade"—constituted a more severe restriction than any imposed during the Vietnam War (Mueller 1995, p. 81 n. 16).

As to whether the military shirked, the evidence is at best suggestive. Certainly there was more debate behind the scenes over how to respond to Iraq's invasion. The broad outlines of the debate followed a familiar pattern found in other Cold War and post–Cold War uses of force: civilians (initially Secretary of Defense Cheney and National Security Advisor (NSA) Brent Scowcroft, and later Secretary of State Baker) pushed for the offensive option to dislodge Iraq from Kuwait, while the military, in the form of the chairman of the JCS and the theater commander, Generals Powell and Schwarzkopf, opposed the offensive option, preferring a containment strategy of sanctions plus a robust deterrent to prevent the Iraqis from continuing on to invade Saudi Arabia (Holland 1999; Gordon and Trainor 1996, pp. 33, 130, 149, 349). General Powell initially resisted the idea of making the liberation of Kuwait a mission goal and was apparently dismayed when President Bush in an impromptu press conference on 5 August appeared to do just that (Woodward 1991, p. 260; Gordon and Trainor 1996, p. 33). Even when the liberation of Kuwait became an unambiguous mission goal, at least one account has General Powell preferring ultimata to an actual use of force as late as early January 1991 (Glad 1993, p. 66).

According to several reports, Secretary Cheney was dissatisfied with the quality of the military advice he was getting. He felt the advice was tainted by political judgments and that the military resistance was so great that the JCS was dragging its heels in preparing viable military options in the immediate aftermath of Iraq's invasion of Kuwait (Woodward 1991, pp. 241–242; Atkinson 1993, p. 122; Gordon and Trainor 1996, pp. 141, 151, 233–234).[1] There is also tantalizing evidence that some civilians believed that the military was shading its estimates so as to constrain the civilian choice in the direction preferred by the military. Gordon and Trainor report that "White House officials were struck by the size of the force that Powell was requesting. Was the military proposing such a large reinforcement in the hope that the president would balk? Was it Saddam Hussein or Bush that Powell was trying to scare?" (Gordon and Trainor 1996, p. 154). General Schwarzkopf himself lifted the veil a bit further in his autobiography, describing his efforts to thwart the "civilian hawks" who wanted to move quickly against Iraq (Schwarzkopf 1992, pp. 325–326, 361–662, 441–445). Moreover, in the early days of the Desert Shield phase of the operation, there were leaks and counterleaks by the military (and by civilians), some perhaps designed to tie the hands of the administration to one course of action or the other (Woodward 1991, p. 279; Gordon and Trainor 1996, pp. 130, 149).

The conventional wisdom thus probably overstates the degree of comity and understates the degree of leaking that bordered on shirking. Woodward's gossipy account of deliberations behind the scenes includes an extraordinary level of detail about the players' private thoughts. Especially in the case of General Powell, these private ruminations take the form of derogatory judgments about the effectiveness or quality of leadership exercised by his civilian superiors: President Bush is likened to a cowboy, Secretary Cheney is not adequately briefing General Powell, NSA Scowcroft is ridiculed as the president's "playmate" and as being overly cavalier about casualties, and so on. If Woodward accurately sourced this to General Powell and reported it contemporaneously, such candor might rise to the level of shirking (Woodward 1991, pp. 40–41, 261, 302).

The internal debate over military options did produce one of the few cases of unambiguous shirking and punishment in the American civil-military record: Secretary Cheney's decision to punish air force chief of staff Michael Dugan for comments he made in an interview published in the *Washington Post* on 16 September 1990. The initial *Post* article contained extensive on-the-record quotes from General Dugan, going into considerable detail about decisions and judgments the JCS was purported to have made: to rely on air power instead of ground power in the war; to target cultural and psychological "centers of gravity," including Saddam Hussein's family and his mistress, in any air campaign; that the operation could be conducted without political constraints, except for efforts to limit collateral damage to civilians; that the Iraqi forces were not nearly as formidable as some press accounts had suggested; and details about how Stealth aircraft and standoff missiles could be integrated into the air campaign (Atkinson 1990). General Dugan later claimed to have been speaking about a purely hypothetical war, but no one was sympathetic to this claim (Gordon and Trainor 1996, pp. 100–101). In fact, the JCS had not adopted the positions identified by General Dugan, and General Powell was furious about what he considered to be a preemptive strike in the interservice rivalry over service roles in the Gulf mission (Woodward 1991, p. 292). Secretary Cheney and NSA Brent Scowcroft were even more angry, and Scowcroft gave something of a rebuke to General Dugan in a television interview that morning. Although President Bush was not reported to be as upset with the article, he gave Secretary Cheney a green light to punish General Dugan however Cheney saw fit (Woodward 1991, p. 293). The next day, Secretary Cheney fired General Dugan for his "inappropriate" remarks and "poor judgment" (Smith 1990).

Civil-military relations during the Gulf War thus were characterized by bargaining, tradeoffs, and strategic interaction, much as agency theory would expect. There was more shirking than the conventional wisdom remembers—perhaps even more than agency theory would expect, given the relative intrusiveness of the monitoring and especially how dramatically Cheney demonstrated a willingness to punish shirking early on. However, compared with the later cases of Haiti, Somalia, and Bosnia, which transpired under a weaker presidency when the expectations of punishment were lower, there was probably a better degree of civil-military cooperation during Desert Storm. No doubt the fact that Desert Storm was a "real" war whereas the others were something less—operations other than war—also played a role, although the contrast with Kosovo shows that even during high-intensity combat, the strategic interaction expected by agency theory can still emerge.

Somalia

Next to the gays in the military imbroglio, the Somalia episode probably had the greatest long-term impact on post–Cold War civil-military relations. Both cases scalded the Clinton administration and have shaped the way civil-military relations have been conducted ever since. The Somalia case cast a particularly long shadow over future decisions on the use of force, delaying U.S. involvement in Haiti and Bosnia and essentially precluding U.S. involvement in Rwanda.[2] For purposes of analysis, it is useful to break up the Somalia case into four decision points: the initial fall 1992 decision under President Bush to intervene; the spring 1993 decision, under the Clinton administration, to expand the scope of the mission with a second phase of the UN Operation in Somalia, UNOSOM II; the summer 1993 decision to launch the manhunt for General Mohammed Farah Aideed; and the decision to retreat after the costly Ranger raid on 3 October 1993.

The Somalia operation grew out of the chaos and civil disorder of the clan fighting that had gripped the country after the long-time dictator, Mohammed Siad Barre, was forced out of power in January 1991. While there was initial reluctance from the JCS to get involved in any fashion, President Bush was under some campaign pressure to "do something" and overrode that reluctance to authorize in mid-August 1992 a limited emergency airlift of food and supplies into northern Kenya and Somalia, Operation Provide Relief.[3] The airlift did little to meet the growing need, however, and Bush was unwilling to do more during the presidential campaign (Rowe 1992, Sahnoun 1994).

The Bush electoral defeat, however, paradoxically freed up the administration to consider more drastic action. President Bush himself reports that he was stimulated to intervene by watching the news accounts of the starving children. He phoned Secretary of Defense Cheney and General Powell and said, "Please come over to the White House . . . I—we—can't watch this anymore. You've got to do something" (Hines 1999). The JCS was still reluctant, but less so than prior to the August airlift; the airlift had fostered an "activist consensus" in the military, and firsthand encounters with the starving masses had profoundly affected Admiral David Jeremiah, vice chairman of the JCS (Hirsch and Oakley 1995, p. 40; Menkhaus and Ortmayer 1995, p. 6). Sometime in November, General Powell seems to have shifted his views, and at one interagency meeting he encouraged consideration of more direct military involvement; he also directed General Hoar, commander of Central Command (CENTCOM) and the senior U.S. military officer with responsibility for the region, to draw up a preliminary plan involving ground troops (Menkaus and Ortmayer 1995, p. 25; Hirsch and Oakley 1995, p. 42). Intriguingly, it was the military, in the person of Admiral Jeremiah, who first suggested the use of ground troops to protect the distribution of humanitarian aid; the proposal apparently caught the civilian members of the interagency planning committee off guard, and only then did civilians begin advocating direct military involvement (Menkaus and Ortmayer 1995, p. 26; Hirsch and Oakley 1995, pp. 42–43).

The shift in JCS opinion is puzzling. A source close to General Powell attributed the change to "'mounting evidence' of the dimensions of the tragedy in Somalia, some of it validated by U.S. military officials on the ground" (Oberdorfer 1992a). But while conditions in Somalia did worsen over the fall of 1992, the situation had been dire during the summer as well. It is hard to argue that a new development on the ground justified so dramatic a change in the JCS position, from resistance to promotion (not mere acquiescence, as would be the case in Bosnia three years later). Certainly at least one senior Bush civilian official expressed surprise at the reversal in an interview with a reporter but indicated that he was "not inclined to question an initiative that surprised and delighted him" (Oberdorfer 1992a).

To solve the puzzle, agency theory suggests putting the Somalia case in the context of the growing pressure to do something in Bosnia. The military had reason to believe that the incoming Clinton administration would press forward with a more activist policy in the Balkans that it strongly opposed; Clinton had campaigned on the promise of lifting the arms embargo against the Muslims and striking Serb targets. It is possible that the military saw in Somalia a "doable" mission that would meet a real need but also be sufficiently absorbing that it would tie the hands of the Clinton administration and make a Bosnian intervention less palatable. The Bosnia-Somalia link is made explicit in Jon Western's probing analysis of the Somalia decision. Western argues that "Bush and his advisors concluded that Clinton would likely alter public attitudes toward Bosnia and launch some form of military action there. In response to these events, Bush and Powell concluded that if the United States was going to intervene in response to a humanitarian crisis, it would be in Somalia and not Bosnia."[4] Western bases his argument on extensive on-the-record interviews with many of the key participants, including Powell's deputy, Admiral Jeremiah, and National Security Advisor Brent Scowcroft, both of whom explicitly linked the two issues and appeared to hint at such a motive (Western 2000, pp. 323–325; Barry and Thomas 2001, p. 38). In the strategic interaction envisioned by agency theory, precisely these sorts of calculations and negotiated deals are expected. While the behavior would not rise to the level of pure shirking—after all, the military in this case was endorsing a proposal advanced by the civilian principals—it is not pure working either, because it is working in such a way as to limit the freedom of action of the civilian principal.

With the decision *whether* to intervene in Somalia made, a civil-military consensus quickly emerged over *how* to intervene. The Deputies Committee developed several options and recommended one at the lower end of the scale, the "Ball-Peen Hammer" option: 5,000 U.S. troops sent in, followed by a much larger UN force. Instead, the president chose the "Sledgehammer" option: roughly 28,000 U.S. troops plus 9,000 more allied troops (Menkhaus and Ortmayer 1995, p. 7; Barnes 1992). But in overruling the Deputies Committee, President Bush was heeding the advice of the JCS and particularly General Powell, who favored using more decisive force so as to enjoy an overwhelming advantage on the ground (Menkhaus and Ortmayer 1995, p. 8; Oberdorfer 1992b, 1992b). The military expressed dismay that the plan set a 20 January 1993 deadline as the date for finishing the operation. One Pentagon official dismissed this as "utterly ridiculous." But since

Secretary Cheney publicly denied the existence of any deadline, it is possible that the deadline was never meant to be enforced anyway. Moreover, a close reading of newspaper accounts suggests that it was mentioned by White House staff, not the result of a policy decision by President Bush (Gordon 1992b, Oberdorfer and Gellman 1992). The military asked for and received permissive rules of engagement to allow the first use of deadly force, and so the on-scene commander enjoyed maximum flexibility (Hirsch and Oakley 1995, p. 46).

The 20 January deadline proved unrealistic, but the initial detachment of U.S. forces did begin their withdrawal in May 1993, by which time some modicum of order had been restored in Somalia. In May the UN officially began the second phase of the Somalia operation, UNOSOM II, which consisted of some 18,000 troops under Turkish commander General Bir, backed up by a U.S. Quick Reaction Force of some 1,300 combat troops under the separate command of Bir's deputy, General Thomas Montgomery, who in turn reported through his U.S. chain of command to CENTCOM. The UN gave a mandate for UNOSOM II that was more expansive and included the disarmament of the rival clans and the promotion of political reconciliation, goals that the new Clinton administration was more willing to embrace than had been the Bush team (Warner and Levin 1995, p. 16). However, UNOSOM II was not given a capacity commensurate with its expanded mission; it was understaffed, underequipped, and plagued by poorly trained troops and weak command and control (Hirsch and Oakley 1995, p. 106; Warner and Levin 1995, pp. 17–18).

The decision to expand the mandate of UNOSOM II provoked considerable civil-military disagreement. Conservative critics in Congress expressed great concern about the chain of command, especially the prospect of U.S. troops serving under foreign UN command, and had to be assured by the Clinton administration that a U.S. officer in the chain of command could veto inappropriate orders (Doherty 1993). Within the administration, the chain of command was less controversial than the mandate given UNOSOM II. While there was a common appreciation for the need for some kind of expansion, the military expressed skepticism about the scope envisioned by civilians in the Clinton administration. The military was anxious to get the troops out of Somalia, and General Powell later disavowed any involvement in the UN's decision to make disarming the factions a UNOSOM II mission (Warner and Levin 1995, p. 19). Although General Hoar, CENTCOM commander in chief, endorsed the notion that the long-term solution in Somalia would involve some kind of nation building, the U.S. military did not view this as an appropriate mission for U.S. forces (Hoar 1993, p. 63). The presence of the U.S. combat troops in the Quick Reaction Force may have been necessary to persuade other countries to contribute troops to UNOSOM II, but from the military's perspective they were not intended to perform the nation-building mission—that U.S. forces *did* conduct nation-building activities was taken as a sign of "mission creep," a gradual loss of control over the operation (Hirsch and Oakley 1995, p. 109; Evans 1994, pp. 131–132). However, compared with similar disputes in Bosnia, military resistance at this point was modest and civilians prevailed in giving UNOSOM II the ambitious mandate, if not the wherewithal to fulfill the mandate.

The ends-means gap that characterized UNOSOM II was exploited by the Somali factions, especially by one of the more powerful warlords, General Aideed. Tensions mounted, and on 5 June 1993, Aideed's forces ambushed a Pakistani patrol, killing twenty-eight Pakistani troops. The UN ordered the U.S. Quick Reaction Force to retaliate with an 11 June strike against Aideed's weapons storage centers and his radio station. A series of skirmishes followed over the next several weeks, culminating in a costly attack on Aideed's enclave in which a Moroccan contingent took heavy casualties. Aideed's intransigence provoked the UN envoy (who was the senior civilian political authority on the ground), retired U.S. Admiral Jonathan Howe, to order Aideed's arrest on 17 June. UN forces were slow to move to arrest Aideed, however, and when they finally attacked Aideed's command center on 12 July they managed to kill many Aideed senior lieutenants but did not get Aideed himself (Hirsch and Oakley 1995, pp. 119–121).

The 12 July 1993 raid did, however, put the UN squarely in the manhunt business and thus set up the most serious civil-military conflict in the Somalia case. The manhunt was approved by the White House—indeed, the White House had pressed the UN to pass the Security Council resolution authorizing Aideed's arrest—and the manhunt was closely monitored by Richard Clarke, a senior member of the National Security Council staff (Gordon and Cushman 1993). It also enjoyed support by the field commanders; in fact, General Montgomery thought the reward for Aideed's arrest should have been larger, and gave hopeful interviews about the manhunt as late as August (Warner and Levin 1995, p. 23; Richburg 1993). The strongest champions of the manhunt were UN envoy Howe and UN secretary general Boutros Boutros-Ghali, and Howe in particular pressed for deployment of Rangers and the Delta Force, U.S. Special Forces specifically trained in "snatch-and-grab" missions (Warner and Levin 1995, p. 24; Gordon and Cushman 1993). Senior State Department officials also strongly pushed for Delta Force. National Security Advisor Tony Lake was more ambivalent, preferring that the British send their commandos; Secretary of Defense Aspin was opposed. Although he sought to distance himself from the policy later, President Clinton personally made the decision to send in the Delta Force on 22 August 1993 (Sloyan 1994). At the same time, however, opposition to the Somalia operation grew in Congress, and in early September the Senate passed a resolution requiring the president to clarify the mission by 15 October and face a formal vote by 15 November (Krause 1993, Ifill 1993).

The rest of the U.S. military strongly opposed the mission. For the first time in the Somalian operation, leaks criticizing current policy, a prominent characteristic of shirking, began to appear. Major David Stockwell, the army officer serving as UN spokesman in Somalia, publicly questioned the mission, and in not-for-attribution interviews military officials were even more direct about criticizing a policy that put "U.S. forces under the control of un-elected officials like Admiral Howe and Boutros-Ghali" (Strobel and Gertz 1993, Richburg 1993). Although the JCS apparently did not participate in the debate leading up to the UN resolution authorizing Aideed's arrest, the chiefs did participate in interagency debates about how to implement the arrest and registered strong opposition to sending the Special Forces requested by Howe, and in this they were supported by Secretary Aspin (Warner and Levin 1995, p. 26; Gordon and Cushman 1993). Likewise, General Powell had expressed public reservations about the manhunt immediately after Howe issued the arrest warrant (Gordon 1993b). Finally, General Hoar expressed strong objections to the manhunt policy and urged in classified cables that the United States government reassess the entire mission in Somalia (Warner and Levin 1995, pp. 24–25). After several U.S. troops died in unsuccessful raids in August, however, General Powell changed his mind on the matter of sending the Rangers and Delta Force, arguing, "We have to do something or we are going to be nibbled to death." Hoar continued to oppose it but was overruled (Gordon 1993b).

Ambivalence about the mission persisted even after the Rangers were sent in. On the one hand, although he was skeptical of the mission, General Powell went so far as to urge against precipitous withdrawal even after several unsuccessful Ranger raids in August and September (Krause 1993). Likewise, Powell passed along to Secretary Aspin a mid-September request from General Montgomery for M1A1 tanks and Bradley fighting vehicles to provide support for the Rangers; normally Rangers deploy without such heavy weapons, but General Montgomery believed they were needed as backup to rescue the Rangers should a raid ever bog down. On the other hand, there is some ambiguity as to whether General Powell advised Secretary Aspin to approve the request and perhaps even asked him to reconsider his initial refusal, or merely forwarded the request without endorsement (Gellman 1993a). For the record, Powell himself claims he endorsed the request and recommended that Aspin support the commander in the field (Warner and Levin 1995, p. 35). Nevertheless, Secretary Aspin rejected the request as inconsistent with the policy to lower the military profile of the mission and focus efforts on a diplomatic track (Marcus and Devroy 1993, Gordon and Cushman 1993, Gellman 1993b). Faced with congressional criticism after the disastrous 3 October raid, Secretary Aspin would later assume full responsibility for the decision; Marcus and Devroy 1993). But earlier, Generals Powell and Hoar had withheld other heavy weaponry, the AC-130 gunships that normally deploy with a Ranger task force, on the same grounds. Moreover, other military commanders agreed with Powell and Hoar that the AC-130s were not needed for the limited manhunt mission although, in hindsight, they might have proved valuable in providing covering fire for the rescue attempts during the 3 October 1993 raid (Warner and Levin 1995, pp. 28–32).

The military ambivalence was matched by civilian ambivalence. In later interviews, President Clinton claimed that he pushed for a deescalation of the manhunt, citing his 27 September 1993 speech to the United Nations in which he called for a renewed diplomatic effort to find a political solution in Somalia (Clinton 1993). The White House excuse was that President Clinton was simply not paying enough attention—in agency theory terms, the civilians were not monitoring intrusively—and so was unaware that the manhunt was ongoing; this is hard to square with the close monitoring done by Clinton's personal National Security Council staff and may be an attempt at ex post exculpation (Smith and Devroy 1993).

From the official White House perspective, however, there *was* shirking; the president claimed he had authorized a shift from the military option to the diplomatic track but the shift was not implemented on the ground. The best evidence for this interpretation is press reports in late September that the United States had moved away from the goal of capturing Aideed as a result of the deaths of three American soldiers shot down in a helicopter by

Aideed's forces (Sciolino 1993c). The move seemed aimed at deflecting pressure from Congress, which was threatening to vote a unilateral pull-out from Somalia that administration officials feared would plunge that country back into total chaos. But the administration never explicitly ordered the halt of the manhunt, and the policy change is merely described as a shift in goals. Moreover, there was no commensurate effort at the UN or elsewhere to rescind the arrest warrant or to shut down the operation. And in his response to the Clinton administration's proposed late-September shift, Boutros-Ghali was explicit in directing that so far as he was concerned the manhunt for Aideed would continue (Sciolino 1993e). Had there been such a decision to stop the manhunt, it strains credulity to say that the military would have resisted implementing it; indeed, except for the local commanders, the military chain of command generally disliked the manhunt and would have seized on a policy reversal to shut it down. While President Clinton professed ignorance of the ongoing manhunt, his NSC staff certainly knew that it continued. More likely, while no decision to *halt* the military mission had been made, the fruitless manhunt had produced a vague unease that translated into a desire to reinvigorate the diplomatic track (Gellman 1993a). Thus, in mid-September 1993, President Clinton talked about a new "political initiative" in Somalia but did not link it to an abandonment of the manhunt (Ifill 1993). Tellingly, administration officials later described the new policy as a "two track" plan, in which the manhunt would continue, in the hope of getting lucky, but the political negotiations would intensify (Sloyan 1994). The shirking, if there was any, was done among the civilian principals themselves.[5]

On 3 October 1993, the Somalia mission fell apart. Acting on a tip, the Rangers and Delta Force launched a raid against a suspected Aideed stronghold that turned into an ambush; by the end of the day, some eighteen American soldiers had died. Although Aideed was not captured, several of his senior lieutenants were, and Aideed's forces suffered terrible losses (Bowden 1999). But the enduring images of the raid were the video clips of dead U.S. soldiers dragged through the streets of Mogadishu by dancing Somalis. In political terms, the costly raid broke the will of the Clinton administration to continue the mission (Apple 1993). Although President Clinton resisted congressional pressure for an immediate withdrawal of all U.S. forces from Somalia, he also resisted pressure from Boutros-Ghali to continue the manhunt. On 7 October, Clinton announced a new compromise policy: the United States would greatly beef up its military presence in Somalia but would unilaterally suspend operations against Aideed and set an early date for a U.S. exit, regardless of whether the negotiations track bore fruit (Jehl 1993). While the administration presented the new policy as consistent with the overall goals of UNOSOM II—indeed, it traced it to the alleged September tilt toward the diplomatic track—the policy amounted to a U.S. retreat and a victory for Aideed (Hirsch and Oakley 1995, p. 128; Friedman 1993e). Indeed, Clinton advisors knew they were choosing the "cut and run" strategy and the only question was how to make the policy look like it was not pure cut and run (Halberstam 2001b, p. 264).

The U.S. retreat bore some fruit in the form of a cease-fire with Aideed and return of U.S. prisoners, but it was bitter fruit for the U.S. military, which barely two months later was obliged to chauffeur to the peace negotiations the very man they had hunted and who had killed their comrades (Serrano and Pine 1993, Lorch 1993). When the last U.S. troops left Somalia in 25 March 1994, the remaining UN force confronted much the same political situation that had led to the expanded UNOSOM mission nearly a year before (Lorenz 1996; Hirsch and Oakley 1995, pp. 131–144).

On balance, compared with Haiti and Bosnia, there was relatively little military shirking in the Somalia operation, but there was perhaps more than in Desert Storm. There was fairly extensive leaking but only scant evidence of the slow rolling, end runs, and inflated estimates that characterize military shirking. Indeed, the intramilitary dispute between Montgomery and Powell/Hoar was as significant as any direct civil-military conflict. Moreover, the vacillation in direction from the civilian principals surely matched or exceeded any resistance by the military. And it is important to note that the pell-mell retreat from Somalia was dictated by the political leaders, not by the military reaction to the tragic Mogadishu raid. Yet Somalia remains significant as a shaper of post–Cold War civil-military relations.

Somalia became synonymous with debacle, and civilian principals emerged from it far weaker and from then on confronted stronger resistance from military agents to any involvement in similar operations. The civilian principals were weakened because they themselves recognized that the debacle had been due largely to errors made by the Clinton administration. In the words of one Clinton confidante, "Somalia was the one thing where we were really responsible for what went wrong" (Sloyan 1994). Moreover, the Somalia experience was especially painful for President Clinton because of his own personal record during Vietnam. He had loathed the tactics then that had resulted in civilian deaths, and now he himself was responsible for authorizing snatch-and-grab missions that resulted in civilian deaths; he had taken extraordinary steps to avoid serving in the military, and now he had ordered men to their death in a mission that had ultimately failed (Sloyan 1994). The shock of the Somalia tragedy continued to haunt the president personally and even threatened to cast a shadow on Clinton's triumphant turn at the celebrations around the fiftieth anniversary of D-Day (Adams 1994). From an agency theory perspective, one of the most important consequences of Somalia was that it undermined the confidence of the civilian principals in their moral competence on decisions to use force.

Ironically, the Somalia case yielded a rare instance of explicit punishment by Clinton, but in this case the agent that was punished for shirking was a civilian agent, Secretary of Defense Les Aspin. Although there were several incidents leading to his removal—one of the last being Secretary Aspin's decision to cross a picket line to make a flight for a weekend vacation—most accounts treated the Somalia debacle, and in particular Aspin's decision not to approve the field commander's request for armor, as the primary factor leading the president to ask for Aspin's resignation (Friedman 1993h). From an agency theory perspective, Aspin's decision was perhaps unfortunate but hardly rose to the level of shirking, and so the punishment seems excessive. Because Clinton himself claimed to have urged a shift *away* from the manhunt, Aspin's decision and rationale (that sending the armor would have been an escalation rather than a deescalation) were fully in keeping with the principal's stated intent. If, however, Aspin was punished for other reasons—perhaps because he was not effective in defusing congressional fury over the Somalia case, or perhaps simply because the Clinton administration needed to project a new beginning—then the decision makes more sense. Whether justified or not, however, Aspin's resignation was remembered as punishment for not accommodating requests from the military rather than for shirking orders from the president. Thus it almost certainly stiffened the resolve of his successor, William Perry, to defer to military agents on such matters and did nothing to increase *military* expectations of punishment.[6]

Haiti

There are three decision points of interest for agency theory in the Haiti case: (1) the debate during the first few months of the Clinton administration over whether to honor candidate Clinton's promise to reverse the Bush policy and install President Aristide by force; (2) the controversial decision in

October 1993, in the face of threatened riots in the Haitian capitol, to turn around the U.S.S. *Harlan County*, a naval vessel carrying lightly armed soldiers sent to Haiti to implement one of several compromises negotiated among the Haitian parties; and (3) the final decision during late summer 1994 to send troops to Haiti, whether or not a last-minute diplomatic overture succeeded (which it did). In each case, the internal debate was fractious and, with prominent exceptions, had a decided civil-military slant that is illuminated well by agency theory.

The Bush administration was more or less united in its opposition to the 1991 coup by General Cedras that deposed President Aristide, the first (relatively) freely elected leader in Haiti's history.[7] Support for Aristide was hardly enthusiastic—he had condoned horrible torture and human rights abuses perpetrated by his supporters, and he had shown little desire and less ability to build a stable ruling coalition in the government. But he had been unambiguously elected by a landslide, and so the Bush administration agreed with the denunciations of the junta issued by the Organization of American States (OAS) and the United Nations and the global embargo that followed. The embargo was devastatingly effective in destroying Haiti's formal economy, but it had little effect on the junta's willingness to step down. Instead, the embargo led to thousands of Haitian refugees attempting to flee Haiti for Florida in rickety boats. By spring 1992, in the middle of the campaign season, the Bush administration had a major political disaster on its hands. The dilemma was how to restore Aristide without keeping the embargo in place and how to stop the flow of refugees without lifting the embargo. On 24 May 1992, President Bush issued the Kennebunkport Order, which authorized U.S. naval vessels to intercept refugee boats and return all undocumented refugees (the vast majority) to Haitian shores. The policy came under strong criticism abroad and especially at home from then-candidate Clinton, but it was very popular with the U.S. military and reflected a fairly wide consensus within the Bush administration (Engelberg 1994; Kamen and Goshko 1992; Goshko 1992; Ballard 1998, p. 28).

The real civil-military conflict over Haiti emerged when the civilian principal changed with the election of Bill Clinton in November 1992. Clinton had made the Bush policy on Haiti a major campaign issue, castigating Bush for his "cruel policy of returning Haitian refugees to a brutal dictatorship without an asylum hearing" (Sciolino 1993b). Clinton had promised to pursue a different policy, and this pledge was taken seriously by one important constituency, the Haitian would-be refugees, who embarked on a massive boat-building project shortly after the election; they built some 1,000 boats, enough to send as many as 150,000 refugees toward Florida as soon as Clinton was inaugurated as president (Sciolino 1993b). Faced with the prospect of the inauguration's being eclipsed by a flood of Haitian refugees, the Clinton transition team made the fateful decision to abandon its campaign promise and instead continue the Bush policy of repatriation, at least until it could put a more comprehensive solution in place (Kirschten 1994). Because the Clinton team essentially adopted the Bush policy, the new policy continued to reflect the preferences of the military; but because the reversal was more an emergency response to developments on the ground in Haiti than a product of bureaucratic wrangling, it cannot be considered shirking. The policy reversal put the administration on the defensive publicly, however, and pressure mounted with the spectacle of Clinton's deputy solicitor general justifying the repatriation policy before the Supreme Court with a brief nearly identical to the one presented by the Bush administration a year earlier (Ortmayer and Flinn 1997, p. 19; Biskupic 1993).

In response to that pressure, the Clinton administration launched a major diplomatic effort seeking a negotiated solution that would allow Aristide's return. The effort bore fruit in the form of the so-called Governor's Island agreement signed 3 July 1993, which provided for President Aristide's return to Haiti under a power-sharing agreement with the military. The attempted implementation of this agreement is the second—and, from a civil-military perspective, most consequential—decision point in the Haitian case study.

The agreement was a classic diplomatic compromise—Aristide's side loathed the concessions that left the Haitian military major power brokers, and the Haitian military loathed the return of a popular and potentially destabilizing political figure. Significantly, the agreement was also not very popular within the military segments of the U.S. government, because the agreement provided for a UN deployment of a complement of some 600 American military engineers and trainers to assist in restructuring the Haitian armed forces. Senior Pentagon and military officials strongly opposed the military mission on the grounds that neither Aristide nor the junta could be trusted to meet their obligations under the agreement, which meant that the lightly armed forces would be left in a volatile situation without the means to defend themselves.

The forces were scheduled to leave for Haiti aboard the U.S.S. *Harlan County* on 7 October 1993. As the date drew near, Pentagon resistance grew, strengthened by the 3 October disaster in Mogadishu that called into question the viability of all such peace-keeping missions. The debate intensified with leaks from the Pentagon about a list of "conditions" presented to Secretary of State Warren Christopher outlining "prerequisites" that had to be in place before the UN deployment could take place.[8] The list, which normally would have been handled at a much lower level, caught Secretary Christopher off guard, and some suspected that the Pentagon was trying to sabotage the *Harlan County* mission with last-minute demands. The conditions were finessed, although not without further confusion. Secretary of Defense Aspin announced on TV that the U.S. soldiers would be armed with M-16s for personal security, but this is not what Anthony Lake had negotiated with Cedras (who had agreed only to "pistols," which is the Creole word for side arms) (Riehm 1997; Shacochis 1999, p. 31; Ortmayer and Flinn 1997, p. 24). Even as the *Harlan County* was sailing into the Port-au-Prince harbor, civil-military conflict was resulting in contradictory statements and a confused policy from the administration.

When the *Harlan County* arrived in Port-au-Prince, it was met by a band of pistol-waving thugs on the dock chanting slogans and calling to mind the disaster in Mogadishu of barely a week prior (French 1993). More troubling still were the actions of Haitian boats inside the port. The *Harlan County* was first approached by small "bum boats" carrying the insignia of the Haitian secret police and then by Haitian gunboats armed with twin .50 caliber machine guns; each time, the Haitian boats retreated when the *Harlan County* mounted its own machine guns and warned the Haitians that the U.S. naval vessel would open fire. This was not the benign environment outlined by the Pentagon as a requirement for mission success. As night fell, the captain of the vessel, Commander Butcher informed his commanding officer that he would pull out of the port (Riehm 1997, pp. 31–36).

The decision to pull back was treated as a major setback in the press and a major embarrassment to the American military. Clinton's own special envoy for Haitian policy, Lawrence Pezzulo, excoriated the decision within the bureaucracy and later in print (after he left the administration) (Pezzullo 1994). However, coding this episode as working or shirking is complicated by the confusion that existed within the Clinton administration over what the policy really should have been . The extensive involvement of the senior civilians in the Department of Defense in the effort to block U.S. participation in this use of force means that it was not pure shirking by the military. Indeed, the military defended the decision and blamed the civilians for not securing the benign environment as negotiated. Some accounts charged civilian factions within the Clinton administration of sabotaging the agreement for fear that it gave too much power to Aristide. According to this view, the protests in the harbor may have been organized by a CIA operative who was in regular contact with the CIA station chief; in addition, the embassy appeared to have had advance warning that the Haitian boats would harass the *Harlan County* (Shacochis, 1999, p. 29; Dupuy 1997, p. 152). All the same, the Pentagon clearly had been resisting the mission and, in the wake of the Mogadishu disaster, was insisting on an unreasonable zero-casualty standard for the Haitian operation (Riehm 1997, pp. 35–36). Although Clinton took ultimate responsibility for the pull-back decision, his White House national security team had pushed strenuously to salvage the *Harlan County* mission (Clinton 1993, Duffy 1994). At least one senior civilian in the Pentagon, Deputy Under Secretary of Defense Walter Slocombe, bragged that he had personally stopped the mission, and military opposition to the operation obviously stymied the efforts of the White House to implement the Governor's Island accord (Sciolino 1994c). The episode hardly counts as pure working; rather, it underscores the extraordinary weakness of Clinton administration civilian principals vis-à-vis the military.

After the retreat from Port-au-Prince, the Clinton Haiti policy was paralyzed for nearly ten months. The administration stepped up enforcement of the UN economic sanctions and secretly initiated planning on invasion scenarios (Morley and McGillion 1997, p. 6; Ballard 1998, p. 65). But critics from the right excoriated the Clinton administration for the *Harlan* fiasco, and former President Bush gave a rare on-the-record interview directly chastising President Clinton for fumbling his use-of-force responsibility as commander in chief (Friedman 1993a). Congressional critics, led by Senator Robert Dole, sought to limit what the administration could do in Haiti, twice attempting to pass amendments precluding any invasion of Haiti without explicit congressional approval (Friedman 1993g, Doherty 1994). Still the situation deteriorated steadily in Haiti, and the administration came under heavy pressure from liberal critics, culminating in a spring 1994 protest hunger strike by Randall Robinson, a prominent civil rights activist, that profoundly unnerved the administration. National Security Advisor Lake called Robinson nearly daily, Deputy NSA Sandy Berger visited him, and even the president endorsed the protest strike saying, "We need to change our policy" (Barnes 1994b).

In response, civilian hawks in the administration (including President

Clinton) began to talk openly of a military intervention. The talk provoked an angry backlash from the Pentagon, which still strongly opposed any use of force in Haiti. The debate was carried out in public, with Secretary Christopher and Deputy Secretary of State Strobe Talbott representing the hawks and Secretary of Defense William Perry representing the doves (Sciolino 1994d). Secretary Perry resisted placing a deadline on an invasion and advocated instead trying to bribe the junta to leave in lieu of invasion.

As agency theory would expect, one way the resistance manifested itself was in a dramatic increase in military estimates of the costs of the mission; the leaked estimates of how many peacekeeping troops would be needed represented a fourfold increase (from roughly 1,250 to 6,000) over the force envisioned to implement the Governor's Island accords barely a year before (Robinson and Klarreich 1994). Although there was a clear civilian-versus-military undertone to the debate, the dividing lines were not perfectly drawn. At least one prominent military figure, General Shalikashvili, seemed to give contradictory signals, on the one hand exhibiting a resigned acceptance to the inevitability of an invasion and on the other hand, resisting the invasion behind the scenes.[9] In any case, the military did embark on preinvasion maneuvers, including on-the-ground surveillance by civilian-clothed special operation forces (Robinson and Klarreich 1994; Masland and Waller 1994; Ballard 1998, p. 125).

Nevertheless, by mid-August the internal debate over *whether* to go was resolved in favor of going and the debate shifted to *how* to go. While no convincing explanation has been given for why the military gave up resisting the Haiti mission after doing so for nearly four years, agency theory suggests one plausible reason: the military was trading off the Haiti mission for the Bosnian mission. During the summer of 1994 the meandering Bosnian crisis seemed to be lurching toward a turning point that would greatly increase U.S. involvement. At the behest of Senator Dole, the Senate passed an amendment unilaterally lifting the arms embargo on the Muslims by 15 November 1994, and the Clinton administration responded by promising to seek a UN resolution that would lift the embargo generally by October (Goshko 1994, Greenhouse 1994). In either case, the move might have precipitated U.S. military involvement in Bosnia, if only to rescue the UN peacekeepers from nearly certain Serb reprisals. Indeed, the prospect of just such a backdoor entry into a Bosnian mission loomed large a year later and led to the initiatives that eventually produced the Dayton peace accords (Holbrooke 1998, pp. 66–68). From an agency theory perspective, it seems

reasonable to expect the military to calculate that "doing" Haiti would reduce the likelihood that it would have to "do" Bosnia. Haiti, though distasteful to the military, was not as unpalatable as Bosnia, and so trading one
for the other would have been a reasonable bargain. Beyond the coincidence of timing, there is no smoking gun to prove this interpretation, but
the speculation is at least not rebutted, since events transpired more or less
in accordance with it.

While the military conceded on *whether* to do Haiti, it prevailed on *how* the
Haiti operation would be done. The military's preferred approach had U.S.
forces deployed in a zero-casualties mode, which involved a very large invasion force (requiring maximum investment of political capital) and extremely restrictive mission goals (ensuring minimum political objectives).
As it happened, last-minute negotiations over the weekend of 17–18 September 1994 by former president Carter, Senator Sam Nunn, and General
Powell persuaded the Haitian junta to step down, thus allowing the U.S. invasion force to reconfigure as a 20,000-person peacekeeping force (fully
three times larger than estimates leaked barely two months earlier) and deploy without firing a shot.

In effect, as would be the case in Bosnia and in contrast to Somalia, the
military traded off acquiescence in carrying out the mission to get wide latitude in how the mission would be conducted (Fineman and Pine 1994).
The military did not get one of its demands—a clear exit strategy—and
this would be a renewed source of contention in Bosnia the following year
(Walsh, Auster, and Zimmerman 1994). But on other matters, particularly
rules of engagement, it was given far greater flexibility than it had enjoyed
in Somalia. Such horse trading is expected by agency theory, with the agent
in effect negotiating the terms under which it will work for the principal.

The military's relatively free hand, however, gave rise to concerns of operational shirking, or at least of the military's conducting the mission in such a
way that the underlying political and humanitarian objectives could not be
satisfactorily achieved. In peacekeeping mode, for example, the military's
tolerance for casualties was even lower than it was for a forceful entry. Force
protection became elevated to a mission goal: the mission was not simply
to minimize casualties while accomplishing the goal of restoring Haiti's democracy, the mission was not to take casualties, period (Gordon 1994b,
Shacochis 1999, p. 254). The military interpreted its rules of engagement
fairly narrowly and in one instance early on stood by while Haitian thugs
beat an Aristide supporter to death (Cockburn 1995). For this the military

was roundly criticized, and some of this criticism may have been unjustified. After the beating death, the military did revise its interpretation of the rules of engagement to allow for more robust policing that could prevent Haitian-on-Haitian violence, and more nation building than a military purist would endorse (Ballard 1998, p. 112). And the military did, after some resistance, agree to use reservists to train the local police—a mission originally assigned to the Department of Justice, which dropped the ball because of resource constraints (Shacochis 1999, p. 254; Ballard 1998, p. 123; Kretchik, Baumann, and Fishel 1999, p. 27).

The Haiti mission also presented an interesting, albeit low-level, episode of shirking: the case of Captain Rockwood, who was court-martialed and convicted for "conduct unbecoming an officer." Rockwood had been nominally assigned to develop informants among the Haitian people, but he expanded his actions to gathering intelligence on human rights abuses more generally. Rockwood claimed to be faithfully implementing President Clinton's stated mission goal of "stopping brutal atrocities," and he filed a formal complaint against his boss, the commander of the Tenth Mountain Division, General David C. Meade, for failing to address these matters and for narrowing the mission to force protection only (Shacochis 1999, pp. 144–145). In effect, Rockwood claimed to be working for the ultimate principal and accused his superior officers of shirking the president's orders. Rockwood disobeyed Meade's orders and conducted an unauthorized inspection of a Port-au-Prince prison, and for this he was convicted. Ironically, Rockwood's unit was replaced by the Twenty-fifth Infantry Division under General James Hill, who made cleaning up that prison a mission priority. In addition, the commander of a Special Forces unit had ordered his troops to do what Rockwood had been ordered *not* to do. Had Rockwood been in either of these other units, he would not have been shirking, and from this perspective, General Meade *may* have been shirking. As it happens, General Meade retired prematurely, perhaps an implicit punishment for shirking (Husarska 1995).

On balance, the Haiti operation was a mixed success in policy terms and a mixed case in civil-military terms. In policy terms, the mission was successful in that the junta stepped down with minimal loss of American lives. But the broader goal of the mission, stability for Haiti, had not been met when the mandate for the original mission expired in late 1997, and by mid-2000 the United States was once again decrying violations of civil rights in Haiti and calling for respect for the electoral process (Fineman 2000, Graham

1997). In the words of one critic, "When the post–Cold War book of rules for global intervention is written, the lesson of the Haiti chapter will be this: define your goals so minimally that it will be easy to meet them, declare victory and go home" (McGreary 1996).

From a civil-military perspective, Haiti falls somewhere between Somalia and Bosnia: less shirking than in the Bosnian case, but strong resistance nonetheless. Desch codes Haiti as one of the rare cases in which civilian preferences prevailed over military during the Clinton era, although he acknowledges that this came about only "eventually" (Desch 1999, pp. 31, 138). Likewise, Avant acknowledges the greater military reluctance but emphasizes that the civilian preferences for invasion were "not widely supported, but were nonetheless carried out" (Avant 1996–97, p. 77). Avant emphasizes the divisions within the civilian principal and how they strengthened the hand of the reluctant military. But agency theory would lay greater stress on how the military's hand was also clearly strengthened by how events had unfolded in Somalia; this shaped what President Clinton could ask of the military and thus gave the agent opportunity, if not exactly to shirk, then to constrain the kind of work asked of it.

Bosnia

The Bosnian case looms large in the debate over post–Cold War civil-military relations. Concern over General Colin Powell's prominent role in the public debate about U.S. involvement in Bosnia was an impetus for Russell Weigley's seminal article that first alleged a general civilian control problem and drew the direct parallels between Powell and Civil War general George McClellan. Desch codes the Bosnia case as a clear instance of military shirking, and certainly the case provides ample evidence of unhealthy civil-military relations, but a close reading of events shows the degree of working or shirking varying across administrations and across aspects of the use-of-force decision.

For the purposes of analysis, it is helpful to disaggregate the Bosnian case into four phases. The first concerns the transition from the original consensus *not* to intervene militarily to the full debate during the summer and fall of 1992 over whether to establish a no-fly zone in Bosnia as a way of tilting the balance of power away from the Serbs. The second period covers the first several months of the Clinton administration, and in particular President Clinton's gradual retreat from his avowed support for the lift and strike option. The third phase is the run-up to the actual Dayton accords in late 1995. The period after Dayton marks the fourth phase, during which the United States actually was "doing" Bosnia.

During the earliest days of the Yugoslavian crisis, there was a civil-military consensus in the United States that the American role should be diplomatic not military. Even in the diplomatic realm, there was a consensus that the breakup of Yugoslavia was first and foremost Europe's problem to solve. Although the fighting received prominent play in the media, accompanied by occasional calls from the left wing of the American political spectrum for a more vigorous response, there was no stomach in the Bush administration for more involvement beyond the UN-imposed arms embargo (Lewis 1991; Western 2000, pp. 284–285). The administration was distracted first by the Gulf War and then by the aftershocks of the war, particularly the question of how to deal with the Kurdish refugees in the north, and finally by the flareup of the Indo-Pakistan Kashmir crisis. Area experts understood that Yugoslavia's civil war would not stop with Croatia, and it was generally agreed that Bosnia's volatile ethnic makeup made it the real Balkan tinderbox. Nevertheless, the consensus plan was to contain the conflict through the arms embargo, vigorous pursuit of a diplomatic resolution under the auspices of the UN and European Union (EU) negotiators, and, above all, avoidance of more direct military involvement. The consensus was tested as the Yugoslavian situation deteriorated throughout the spring of 1992. Armed hostilities broke out after the 1 March 1992 referendum in which the Bosnian Muslims voted overwhelmingly for independence, and the tide quickly turned against the out-manned and out-gunned Muslim forces. By June, the situation was quite dire, leading to the emergence of a real debate within the U.S. government over how to respond.

The first civilian leaders to express significant public support for a more vigorous American military response were Democrats in Congress, who became increasingly vocal as the summer of 1992 unfolded. The argument, as advanced by Senator Biden, was simple (Friedman 1992). A hands-off approach to the Bosnian crisis effectively sided the United States with the Bosnian Serbs. The global arms embargo had little constraining effect on the Bosnian Serbs, who were amply supplied by the rump Yugoslavian army (which was dominated by ethnic Serbs), and they used this advantage to devastating effect. Moreover, the Bosnian Serbs engaged in widespread atrocities, including rape camps, ethnic cleansing, and brutal siege tactics, making the Bosnian Muslim position all the more worthy of U.S. help. The arguments resonated within the Bush administration. According to Secretary of State James Baker, the internal debates over Bosnia policy in June 1992 were as "spirited" as any in the entire Bush tenure (Baker 1995, p. 649). Nevertheless, the cautionary wing within the Bush administration had the upper hand, fearing a "quagmire" or a "tar baby" if limited measures were taken (Newhouse 1992; Western 2000, pp. 284–287).

The Bosnian situation deteriorated sharply over the summer, and the domestic political pressure on the Bush administration increased. Presidential candidate Clinton, seeking to shed his draft-dodger image and also wishing to inoculate himself against the charge that he had little foreign policy experience, used the Bosnian issue to outflank the Bush campaign (Halberstam 2001b, p. 23). He urged that U.S. and NATO forces enforce a naval blockade to stop contraband from reaching Serb forces and accused the United States of failing to show leadership on the issue (Rosenthal 1992b). At the same time, support for a military response was growing within the Bush State Department and the interagency debate over options was becoming more intense. In late August, George Kenney, the State Department official with day-to-day policy management responsibilities for the Balkans, resigned in protest over the feebleness of the administration's response to the Bosnian civil war (Schmitt 1992b).

While the dividing lines were not sharply drawn, the debate over Bosnia nevertheless developed a distinctively civil-military cast. The Defense Department, but especially the Joint Chiefs of Staff, remained adamantly opposed to any increased U.S. military role (Corddry 1992). To insiders, President Bush seemed very reluctant to get involved in the middle of Balkan ethnic fighting (Halberstam 2001b, p. 44); the White House, however, was gradually reconsidering the issue and showed some signs of beginning to tilt in favor of the State Department wing that was demanding more forceful action. In August, President Bush called on the United Nations to authorize the use of force, should it be necessary, to ensure the safe delivery of food and medicine in Bosnia; since most of the would-be recipients were Muslim, such an effort would tilt the UN even further in the direction of supporting the Bosnian Muslim side in the civil war. Bush stopped short of advocating U.S. involvement, and the move could be interpreted as a way of deflecting congressional pressure for direct military action against the Bosnian Serb positions, but in retrospect the gradual slide in the White House position is evident (Rosenthal 1992a).

Civilians who favored intervention, however, were stymied by the estimates presented by the JCS that to "do" Bosnia would involve extraordinarily high numbers of U.S. troops. These controversial estimates constitute the first behavior that might be seen as rising to the level of shirking. In a subsequent interview, Brent Scowcroft suggested that the JCS "probably" inflated the estimates so as to make the costs of doing Bosnia seem prohibitive (Western 2000, pp. 286–287). Halberstam likewise claims that Powell's inflated estimate was a deliberate attempt to test civilian resolve.[10] If Scowcroft and Halberstam are right, this could indeed be considered military shirking.

At the same time, the Bosnian problem emerged as a potent campaign issue, and pressure mounted within the Bush administration to "do something" in the face of unrelenting media coverage of the atrocities visited upon the Muslims in concentration camps (Western 2000, pp. 296–305). The debate intensified throughout September, and the issue became one of whether to establish a no-fly zone in Bosnia, a move that could potentially bring the Western allies in direct conflict with the Bosnian Serbs.

By late September the internal debate had spilled over to the front page of the *New York Times*. In an extraordinary on-the-record interview, General Powell outlined the case against using force in Bosnia, offering an all-or-nothing rationale in rejecting the idea of a no-fly zone. Powell argued that limited measures such as air strikes to deter the Serbs from using artillery against the out-gunned Muslims were unlikely to work and that there was no political will behind a decisive use of force. According to the reporter, Powell "spoke angrily as he complained about the impetuousness of civilians, who he said had been too quick to place American forces in jeopardy" (Gordon 1992c). The same news story underscored the fact that White House and State Department officials, along with influential members of Congress, were supportive of an air-exclusion zone, while the Pentagon (implying both civilian and military leaders) opposed the move. Powell's interview earned him a caustic response in the media, led by a *New York Times* editorial comparing him to General McClellan, the infamously reluctant Civil War general. The rebuke evidently stung General Powell, for he revisited the issue a few days later in an op-ed and then fleshed out his rationale for how force should be used in a subsequent lengthier *Foreign Affairs* article (No author 1992; Powell 1992, 1992–93).

Did Powell's public advocacy of the military point of view constitute shirking? Some analysts think so. Weigley considered Powell's comments to have "raised questions about his conformity to the code that under the principle of civil control over the military, the civilians make United States policy and the military execute it." Weigley disagreed not with the content of Powell's critique—he appears to have shared Powell's doubts about the efficacy of limited force in Bosnia—but rather with the way that Powell added nonmilitary judgments to it. In particular, Weigley accused Powell of claiming a "certainty of knowledge that military expertise could not supply, in order to use his uniform as an instrument of advantage in a policy debate that, because there existed no applicable military certainty, should have been left to the civilians if the idea of civilian control remains meaningful" (Weigley 1993, pp. 28–31). Kohn likewise chastises Powell for "[taking] it upon himself to be the arbiter of American military intervention overseas, an unprecedented policy role for a senior military officer, and the most explicit intrusion into policy since MacArthur's conflict with Truman" (Kohn 1994, p. 12).

Others disagree. Avant notes that the position Powell espoused in the interview was "consistent with the Bush Administration's position" and that in the absence of a clearly unified civilian position to the contrary, military hesitancy was understandable (Avant 1996–97, p. 79). General Powell himself was at pains to emphasize that he cleared his activities with his civilian boss, Secretary Cheney, and that he had cleared the text of his opinion editorial with both Secretary Cheney and the National Security Council (Powell et al. 1994, p. 23; Powell 1995, p. 544). William Odom considers Powell's assertiveness on strategy unexceptional, compared with the Civil War benchmark (Powell et al. 1994, p. 26). And Samuel Huntington gives General Powell a free pass, arguing that Powell was just like other professional military officers who are "properly hesitant about committing their forces to war" (Powell et al. 1994, p. 29).

Given the absence of a clearly articulated administration policy, General Powell was not openly defying civilian control in his interview. But from an agency perspective there are several aspects of the episode that are troubling. Individually, no single feature would make the behavior count as shirking, but collectively they indicate that something short of the idealized relationship prevailed. First, whether this was intended or not, General Powell's public interview gave him greater leverage over the White House by carrying an internal debate into the public. Registering his views on the record avoided the unseemliness of unattributed leaks, but it also greatly raised the political costs of deciding against the JCS-preferred policy. It did not raise the bar too high, of course, because President Bush in fact *did* decide to authorize precisely the kind of limited option General Powell argued against in the interview. On 2 October 1992, unnamed White House sources indicated that President Bush had decided to support establishing a no-fly zone in Bosnia; the decision was treated as an explicit rejection of General Powell's advice (Gordon 1992c). The next day President Bush made the decision official with a written statement; when asked about the policy reversal, General Powell stated that "he [had] no problem with the White House announcement" (Gordon 1992a). Bush's decision was thus both an implicit acknowledgment that Powell was somewhat out of step with civilian authorities and an indication that he was within some broader zone of acceptable debate; in this sense, Powell's actions were not as bad as, say, Ridgway's efforts to thwart Eisenhower's New Look policy (as discussed in Chapter 5), but did fall short of idealized working.

Second, far from absolving General Powell without any reproach, the fact that President Bush ultimately decided against the JCS position raises questions about the timing and content of the follow-on opinion piece Powell published. The *New York Times* ran Powell's op-ed on 8 October 1992, fully a week after the decision to engage in a limited air operation in Bosnia was made. Powell wrote the piece after he "exploded" upon reading the *Times'* own editorial comparing Powell's reluctance to use force to General McClellan's (Powell 1995, p. 544). Powell's op-ed is careful not to criticize directly the decision to pursue a no-fly zone in Bosnia—a step that would easily rise to the level of shirking. Since the op-ed was vetted by the NSC, it is extremely doubtful that such a public break would have been allowed, even if Powell had wanted to include it, which itself is unproven.[11] The op-ed's treatment of Bosnia is suggestive, however: "The crisis in Bosnia is especially complex . . . The solution must ultimately be a political one. Deeper military involvement beyond humanitarian purposes requires great care and a full examination of possible outcomes. That is what we have been doing. Whatever is decided on this or the other challenges that will come along, Americans can be sure that their armed forces will be ready, willing and able to accomplish the mission" (Powell 1992). The op-ed, therefore, criticizes limited uses of force but is strangely silent on the fact that the president had already decided to use limited force. It refers to Bosnian decisions as ongoing ("whatever is decided"), which they surely were, but does not acknowledge that some fateful decisions had already been taken. The op-ed did not escalate the interagency battle on the limited use of airpower in Bosnia, but neither did it signal a clear endorsement of the president's position. Viewed in hindsight, one might wish that the op-ed had not been published or, if published, that it had reflected more awareness of the civil-military equities associated with the episode. Powell has been adamant that there were no civil-military equities involved in the episode, and thus he probably would argue that there was no need to restate what he considered to be obvious: that he would not resist the president's decision to use limited air power in Bosnia. Reasonable people can give conflicting interpretations, but the agency perspective would conclude that Powell missed an opportunity to reflect plainly the agent's clear limits on how to treat a principal's decision, once made.

Third, agency interpretation speaks to the broader context of the debate over the air exclusion zone. Proponents of the limited use of force, such as then-congressman Aspin, dismissed Powell's doctrine of decisive force as an "all-or-nothing" approach that tied the hands of the U.S. national command authorities. Insisting on decisive force raised the political costs of any use of force. Indeed, this was an explicit purpose behind the Powell doctrine: require that leaders mobilize the political support up front before committing U.S. prestige in an operation; otherwise the desire to recoup losses from earlier half-measures will suck the country into a war no one would have signed up for in the first place. This was the thesis of Powell's *Foreign Affairs* article, which can be read as a warning to the incoming president, with the subtle and perhaps not unintended effect of tying Clinton's hands to a particular approach to the use of force (Powell 1992–93). In case anyone missed the point, General Powell reinforced it when he gave a valedictory for President Bush on his last visit to the Pentagon: "Mr. President, you have sent us in harm's way when you had to, but never lightly, never hesitantly, never with our hands tied, never without giving us what we needed to do the job" (Halberstam 2001b, p. 247). But manipulating the cost-benefit calculation of the principal is not an appropriate activity for an agent. The agent can advise on what the true costs and benefits of any decision might be—the agent can suggest, for instance, that half-measures like an air-exclusion zone are unlikely to work—but the agent should not artificially raise the costs of a policy by insisting that it cannot be carried out without being accompanied by other costly military measures. Warren Zimmermann, the last U.S. ambassador to Yugoslavia, appears to have alleged that military advisors did just that:

> The Pentagon's tactic was never to say no, as that would undercut its "cando" approach. Rather it simply raised objections that would make the pro-

posals unworkable. The military argued that it would take fifty thousand ground troops to protect the relief routes from Split to Sarajevo. When its opposition to a Sarajevo airlift was overridden, it tried to limit the amount of goods to be flown in. It ridiculed air drops as infeasible in view of Bosnia's mountainous terrain and uncertain weather. It opposed putting U.S. military observers on the ground in Bosnia to support a no-fly zone, recommending instead foreign service officers or retired military personnel. (Zimmermann 1996, p. 219)

The fact that the military ultimately conducted those missions with a smaller military force than advised suggests that the military had been exaggerating the costs so as to foreclose an option, which would count as shirking from the agency perspective. Even if the military did not exaggerate the costs, the military must be careful not to advance a position disposing on whether the costs are worth the benefits. In other words, the military expert can speak to the pros and cons and riskiness of limited measures, but he cannot declare a limited measure a "mistake," because the judgment of whether the risk is acceptable is a political one. The agency perspective thus is sympathetic to the view that military estimates about the costs of the Bosnian mission were tainted and also to Weigley's concerns that Powell's public (albeit prior) critique of President Bush's limited air policy put the general in the position of delivering political rather than military judgments.

The second phase of the Bosnian operation covers the early part of Clinton administration, during which time the president gradually retreated from his campaign promise of more robust involvement. As in Haiti, the new Clinton team found that the same Bush policy on Bosnia that candidate Clinton had criticized began to look like the best possible compromise position for President Clinton to adopt. The administration arrived committed to pursuing international support for a "lift and enforce" policy—lifting the arms embargo on the parties, which effectively meant arming the Muslims, and enforcing the air exclusion zone, which the Serbs routinely violated. But it did so against a backdrop of second-guessing from within, with aides to General Powell expressing great skepticism about the wisdom of such a policy even as Secretary of State–designate Warren Christopher defended it in confirmation hearings (Gordon 1993c). The administration quickly abandoned the use-of-force option and focused on finding an alternative to the peace plan developed by the UN and the EU, which they regarded as rewarding the Serbs for aggression (Sciolino 1993f, Friedman 1993d). When the administration announced its alternative, however, it differed little from earlier versions and was no more successful in ending the conflict, which continued, albeit at a slower pace, while Bosnians and Croats regrouped (Sciolino 1993g). When negotiations stalled in April 1993 the Clinton team again threatened to use force, but when Secretary Christopher went to Europe to lobby for support for a get-tough policy, he was rejected by the allies. The spectacle of the secretary of state of the most powerful country in the world getting pushed around by his putative allies proved a public relations disaster and, in agency theory terms, was to foreign policy what the gays in the military fiasco was to defense policy: a dramatic demonstration that you could cross President Clinton with impunity (Halberstam 2001b, pp. 224–231). When the Serbs voted down the peace plan in May 1993, effectively killing the diplomatic option for years, Clinton did not carry through on any threats (Cohen 1993, Friedman 1993b).

Unquestionably, the military was advising against Clinton's April 1993 flirtation with actually using force in Bosnia,[12] but it is not obvious that the military was shirking. The civilian principals seemed just as reluctant, publicly advancing very stringent criteria virtually identical to the Powell doctrine—"the goal must be clearly stated to the American people, there must be a strong likelihood of success, there must be 'an exit strategy' and the action must win sustained public support" (Sciolino 1993a)—and privately giving the Europeans de facto veto power over any use (Whitney 1993). In fact, the military did not need to resist very much to turn President Clinton from the use-of-force track. President Clinton was deeply ambivalent about the Bosnia issue, and this made him easier to deflect on those occasions when he seemed to be leaning in favor of more vigorous action (Halberstam 2001b, p. 225). With the gays-in-the-military issue inflicting fresh wounds in the form of the late April 1993 analyses of the president's first 100 days, President Clinton was hardly in a position to take a strong position against his military advisors (Devroy and Marcus 1993). Moreover, President Clinton confronted a formidable obstacle in the form of Powell's adamant opposition; Powell in his memoirs was at pains to detail how he worked hard in meetings of the National Security Council to "patiently explain" to the civilian team that force was not a viable option in the Bosnian case. It was during one of these sessions that Powell had his famous "near-aneurysm" debate with UN ambassador Madeleine Albright (Powell 1995, pp. 561–562). At least one White House staffer evidently thought Powell was undercutting the president's position in briefings with members of Congress and might use the Bosnian situation to politically damage the president (Blumenthal

1993a). Of course, fear of possible shirking is not evidence of actual shirking, but the president's weakened political position vis-à-vis his supposed subordinate is noteworthy nonetheless. And the fact that the U.S. did not commit troops until Powell was replaced by his successor, General Shalikashvili, who was just as famously more willing to contemplate force in Bosnia, underscores the point.

During 1993 and 1994, the Bosnian operation slipped into a desultory pattern of lackluster diplomacy coupled with frequent but effectively unpunished violations of the safe havens, including an infamous shelling of the Sarajevo marketplace in February 1994 (Burns 1993; Sciolino 1994a, 1994b; Cohen 1994; Gordon 1994a; Randal 1994; Gompert 1996). The vacillation in the Clinton policy during this period continued to reflect underlying civil-military tensions, which at times bordered on the kind of shirking captured by the agency model. Secretary of State Christopher and National Security Advisor Tony Lake's efforts to use military threats to pressure the Serbs into a diplomatic resolution of the Gorazde issue were undercut by Secretary of Defense William Perry and Chairman of the JCS John Shalikashvili's public blanket rejection of any use of force (Gordon 1994d, 1994c; Sciolino 1994e; Williams and Devroy 1994; Lippman and Lancaster 1994). Since the debate played out on the front pages of the major newspapers and the grousing concerned ongoing military operations, with unattributed references to senior military officers complaining about the "pinprick" bombing, military behavior approximated shirking. The point bears emphasis: the military was not wrong *about* its critique—the policy of pinprick bombing *was* ineffective—but it was wrong to undercut the civilian policy anyway; agency theory incorporates the democratic principle that civilians have a right to be wrong, and in this instance they probably were. Besides, it was not as if military shirking was needed to bring otherwise hidden problems with Bosnia policy to the surface; the military did not need to undercut the president, because the Congress was plenty willing to do it on its own.

The third phase of the Bosnian case comes in the summer and fall 1995 run-up to the Dayton accords, in which the United States actually committed to deploying ground troops in the region.[13] During this period, the tide decisively turned against the Serbs, both in a diplomatic sense and tactically on the ground. Diplomatically, the Serbs lost a key ally when the hawkish Jacques Chirac replaced the pro-Serb Francois Mitterand at the French helm; the Serb's aggressive treatment of French peacekeepers galvanized

French opposition and lifted a NATO barrier to effective action. Around the same time, the U.S. Congress seized the initiative by passing (by veto-proof majorities) a resolution unilaterally overturning the arms embargo. Serb atrocities in Srebrenica and Zepa shocked even a world dulled by years of Balkan violence. But the key development was the unexpected success of a Croat offensive in early August in Krajina, which meant that for the first time the Bosnian Serbs faced a serious ground threat in addition to the NATO pinprick air strikes. The change in fortunes emboldened the Clinton administration to issue an ultimatum to the Serbs: either they accepted a compromise peace plan or NATO would lift the arms embargo and allow soldiers from Islamic nations to replace UN peacekeepers on the ground. The Serbs agreed to negotiate on those terms in mid-August 1995, but the negotiations were interrupted by the tragic death of a team of three U.S. policymakers, Joseph Kruzel, Robert Frasure, and Nelson Drew, whose armored personnel carrier slid off a Sarajevan road while on a negotiating trip. This tragedy further stiffened the spine of the Clinton administration, and when Serbian mortar fire once again killed civilians in a Sarajevo marketplace, NATO responded massively with a sustained bombing campaign named Operation Deliberate Force. This drove the Serbs back to the negotiating table culminating in the Dayton peace accords, signed on 21 November 1995. Under the Dayton accords, U.S. ground forces were committed to Bosnia for the first time as part of the Implementation Force (IFOR).

Civil-military tensions intensified in direct correlation to the increased involvement of U.S. military forces, and the most serious charges of shirking in the Bosnian case have been levied against military behavior during this period. The civil-military conflict turned less on whether the United States should be involved in Bosnia at all (although the military generally judged the national interests at stake to be lower than did civilians), and more on how to use the military to advance U.S. interests in the region. Until the developments in August 1995, the military had remained strongly opposed to air strikes, and even more strongly opposed to ground forces. But the Pentagon understood that under NATO agreements, and because of President Clinton's promises to the allies, ground forces would be committed whether the Bosnian peace process succeeded or fell apart completely; in the former instance, ground troops would be involved in implementing any agreement, in the latter instance, the troops would be needed for any emergency rescue of the besieged UN peacekeepers. Apparently this double bind caught the State Department and White House by surprise, and contributed to a sense that the military option was inevitable and the only question was under what circumstances (Holbrooke 1998, pp. 66–68).

A major issue in dispute throughout this period was the cumbersome "dual-key" arrangement whereby the United Nations representative held veto power over any NATO retaliatory strike against the Serbs. The UN had regularly used its authority to hold up or modify proposed air strikes, and NATO forces, and especially U.S. officers, chafed against this perceived micromanagement (Owen 1997). Under intense U.S. pressure, the UN veto authority was effectively lifted in July 1995, and at the same time NATO secretary-general Willy Claes delegated the NATO strike authority to the NATO military commanders, General George Joulwan and Admiral Leighton Smith. At that point, the two American officers had sole decision authority to authorize air strikes (Holbrooke 1998, p. 99). As a result, when the Operation Deliberate Force air strikes began on 30 August, the intensity was far greater than any previous Bosnian operation.

The senior U.S. negotiator on the Bosnia issue, Richard Holbrooke, reports that civil-military tension came to a peak during Operation Deliberate Force over how to integrate the bombing with the diplomatic efforts. Holbrooke pressed for tighter integration, which would have meant in effect greater control by Holbrooke over the operation. Admiral Smith strongly resisted this and, according to Holbrooke, went so far as to order his air commander, General Michael Ryan, to have no contact with the negotiating team.[14] Admiral Smith was eager to halt the bombing as soon as possible, and was reluctant to resume bombing after a pause during which the United Nations attempted to negotiate a resolution, while Holbrooke insisted that the bombing resume and continue. Holbrooke accuses Admiral Smith of being at least duped—and seems to imply that Smith may have been willingly misled—by a token concession from Bosnian Serb general Mladic, who was trying to prevent the resumption of bombing. According to Holbrooke, Smith and the UN commander, General Janvier, hastily accepted an "insolent proposal" from Mladic because they did not want the bombing to resume anyway, perhaps also because, as Smith had told Holbrooke privately before, the United States really did not have "a dog in this fight" anyway (Holbrooke 1998, pp. 118–120). Holbrooke and his aides also suspected that the military dissembled to the senior national security policymaking team about whether it was running out of approved Serbian targets to strike (Holbrooke 1998, pp. 101–168, especially pp. 118 and 145–146).

Since Holbrooke was not in the chain of command, Smith's direct confrontations with him cannot exactly be called shirking. If Holbrooke is correct about the military biasing its advice about what targets could be hit, however, the conflict did rise to the level of shirking. Holbrooke may have misinterpreted the military statements about running out of targets; the air force was considering additional targets, and other options were available (Owen 1997). Moreover, in an interview before Operation Deliberate Force commenced, Admiral Smith indicated that his concern was that the *civilian politicians* in NATO would limit any use of force, not that civilians would pressure him to continue bombing when he wanted to stop (Rainbow and Miller 1995). Indeed, one of the reasons why NATO was running out of first-tier targets is that NATO forces were bombing at an accelerated pace because they feared the politicians would halt the bombing before the strikes achieved their desired effect (Owen 1997). However, President Clinton, who obviously *was* in the chain of command, evidently did think that Admiral Smith was shirking and said as much to his closest aides (Halberstam 2001b, p. 349). Importantly, from the standpoint of an agency theory interpretation, Clinton apparently let this shirking go unpunished.

The agency perspective also provides insight into the arrangement under which the U.S. military dropped its opposition and accepted an IFOR role. Military agents traded off a willingness to do the mission in exchange for greater autonomy in setting the rules of engagement governing how they would actually implement the mission. Holbrooke goes into considerable detail in his memoirs about the extensive involvement and stubborn negotiating position of the U.S. military in the period leading up to Dayton (Holbrooke 1998, pp. 215–312, especially 215–227; Perry and Shalikashvili 1995). Some critics have argued that some of the military conditions, for instance insisting that IFOR stay perfectly neutral between Serb, Croat, and Muslim forces, amounted to *political* not military judgments—that is, they were not within the military's purview, even under a classic Huntingtonian understanding of civil-military relations—and if so should count as shirking (Perle 1995). Compromises were reached on most of these, but the intra-U.S. negotiations almost reached an impasse over whether the IFOR would be responsible for assisting in refugee relocation and pursuing war criminals. The resolution took the form of a subannex to the military annex, Annex 1-B, that gave the IFOR "the authority but not the obligation" to undertake tasks like these. Then, to make it clear, the military representatives at Dayton drafted what became known as the "silver bullet" clause: "The Parties understand and agree that the IFOR Commander shall have the authority, without interference or permission of any Party, to do all the Commander judges necessary and proper . . . The violating Party shall be subject to military action by the IFOR, including the use of necessary force to ensure compliance with the Annex (Holbrooke 1998, p. 223).

Such permissive rules of engagement gave U.S. commanders wide latitude and considerable autonomy in interpreting their orders, considerably more than they had enjoyed in Somalia. According to several contemporaneous accounts, the "silver bullet" clause was included at General Shalikashvili's insistence and was the military's requirement for supporting the mission (Smith and Priest 1995, Schmitt 1995, Priest 1995). As one report described it, "Some administration officials say the military, as a price for its support, has basically gotten anything it wanted in the last three months" (Strobel 1995). In any case, it was precisely the kind of flexibility that Admiral Smith had listed as a mission essential requirement in an interview published in September 1995 and closely matched the military preference for how to carry out the Bosnia mission (Rainbow and Miller 1995). With this autonomy, the military could resist civilian-led efforts to expand the mission, a phenomenon derided as mission creep, and thereby strictly control the nature and extent of the use of force. From the agency perspective, Bosnia became "doable" once civilian principals traded off autonomy for the agent in exchange for the agent's promise to work.

The post-Dayton period can be considered the fourth phase, the actual conduct of the military operation. From the start, the civil-military tensions that had given rise to the pre-Dayton compromises were evident in the post-Dayton operation. In a remarkable account of a White House meeting immediately after the peace treaty was signed, Holbrooke describes how Vice President Gore and President Clinton essentially accused the military of undercutting efforts to build support for the operation on Capitol Hill. Holbrooke reports that Gore looked at the Defense Department representatives and said: "I want to make an important practical point regarding the JCS and the Pentagon . . . I've had lots of conversations with the Congress. They have told me that our military representatives on the Hill usually leave their audience more uncomfortable than when they arrived. I'm not saying they are trying to undercut our policy, but they are losing us votes up there." President Clinton then added, "It's not a question of being dishonest, but we can't close the deal without the Pentagon's support . . . I know there has been ambivalence among some of your people—not you, Shali, but some of your people—about Bosnia . . . but that is all in the past. I want everyone here to get behind the agreement." While Clinton and Gore took pains to claim that they were *not* explicitly accusing the military of shirking, that was in fact what they were doing. Holbrooke seems to agree that the military had been shirking, because he claims the dual warning from the top civilian principals had "substantial effect" (Holbrooke 1998, p. 316).

On the ground in Bosnia, the U.S. military commanders interpreted their mission orders narrowly and used the silver bullet autonomy to avoid activities that the civilians involved in the operation wanted them to pursue (Pomfret 1996a, 1996b; Barber 1996). The military's insistence on using its autonomy to restrict rather than expand its implementation of the accords occasionally led to disaster, as when it dragged its heels in stopping the looting, arson, and rape inflicted by Bosnian Serbs as they left Sarajevo in March 1996—only relenting when Christopher and Perry personally intervened, by which time millions of dollars of damage had been done (Holbrooke 1998, p. 337).

The most contentious civil-military issue during the implementation phase was the pursuit and arrest of war criminals. NATO and IFOR military commanders made it clear that they would not actively pursue the individuals indicted by the International Criminal Tribunal for war crimes, although such activity was within the scope of their authority under the Dayton accords (Hedges 1996). The apparent "timidity" of the military was sharply criticized by the civilians on the U.S. team, and Holbrooke, in particular considered that Admiral Smith's reluctance to arrest indicted war criminal Radovan Karadzic rose to the level of shirking (Holbrooke 1998, pp. 328–339; Hedges 1996). According to Holbrooke, the silver bullet clause was meant to enable the IFOR to do things (like arrest war criminals) when feasible, but not to *obligate* them and thus set the military up for failure should the IFOR be stretched too thin on the ground (Holbrooke 1998, p. 328). General Shalikashvili evidently had had the same idea in mind, as he suggested during the pre-Dayton intra-U.S. negotiations that "if there is an incident and the police are overwhelmed, then the IFOR commander has the authority to assist. But there could be days when he can't do this because his resources are stretched too thin" and "we do not wish to be obligated to arrest war criminals . . . but we will accept the authority *to arrest them if we get the chance*" (Holbrooke 1998, p. 222, italics added). When Admiral Smith refused to arrest Karadzic unless specifically ordered to by President Clinton, he was, in the minds of some civilian officials, shirking the original understanding of the arrangement. Smith's rationale was not that the military was

stretched too thin—indeed, the primary challenge of the mission was boredom (Pomfret 1996b)—but rather that any attempt to arrest Karadzic, even
when Karadzic passed through a military checkpoint, would be met with
Serb reprisals and result in U.S. casualties (Holbrooke 1998, pp. 338–339).
For his part, Admiral Smith claimed that he was willing to arrest Karadzic
and merely wanted the politicians to give the order to do so (Bonner 1996).

The military reluctance in Bosnia prevailed until summer 1997, when the
newly invigorated Clinton civilian team was able to put in place different
military commanders in NATO and locally in Bosnia. Secretary Christopher
was replaced with an even more hawkish Secretary Madeleine Albright, and
she teamed with new National Security Advisor Sandy Berger—himself as
hawkish as his predecessor Anthony Lake but far closer to the president and
so a more potent player in civil-military squabbles—to convince President
Clinton to back a more vigorous pursuit of war criminals in Bosnia (Smith
1996, Dobbs 1997, Erlanger 1997, Drozdiak 1997, Harris and Priest 1997,
Hedges 1997, Hockstader 1997). The change in the Clinton approach to
Bosnia was facilitated by the replacement of NATO commander general
Joulwan with General Wes Clark, who had earlier been Holbrooke's military
aide in the negotiations leading up to the Dayton accords; Admiral Smith,
who had insisted on interpreting the IFOR rules of engagement narrowly,
was also gone, and the new commander, General Shinseki, was less adamant about opposing mission creep. Clark's views of the military mission
matched the civilian views much more closely and the result was a dramatic
drop-off in military resistance to enforcing the provisions of the Dayton accords (Shenon 1997). Opposition did not end altogether, however, and the
issue of how much to involve the military in these aspects of the Bosnian
mission remained contentious (Pomfret and Hockstader 1997).

A more detailed analysis of the Bosnian case is beyond the scope of this
project.[15] But enough detail has been presented here to render a summary
judgment on civil-military relations in Bosnia mission. There was far more
negotiation and bargaining between the civilian principal and military agent
than a Huntingtonian theory would suggest. While the civil-military conflict
rarely if ever rose to the level of open insubordination, there were numerous instances of behavior that could constitute shirking. Recall that the
agency perspective counts a variety of behaviors short of open revolt as
shirking: military advice that is corrupted by inflated risk estimates, unauthorized public protest and end runs to the public or to Congress to block a
policy that civilians inside the executive branch are pursuing, and general

administrative foot-dragging. The Bosnian case has examples of each. The estimates of how many troops it would take to carry out a mission in Bosnia were far in excess of the number the U.S. ultimately committed (36,000 at its peak), and this wide disparity suggests that earlier military estimates were intended partly to raise the price of the mission beyond what civilian leaders were willing to pay. Significantly, Brent Scowcroft came to the same conclusion about the military estimates (Western 2000, pp. 286–287, 314). Likewise, the military's opposition to the mission prior to 1995 was extraordinarily public and hard to square with the military's merely fulfilling its advisory role. Finally, the reluctance of the military, particularly in the early stages of IFOR to enforce key provisions of the Dayton accords at times elevated foot-dragging to the level of shirking. All the same, the turning points in the Bosnian operation followed the expectations of the agency model. Military resistance intensified in the wake of the gay-ban fiasco and Christopher's abortive trip to Europe in the spring of 1993, all demonstrations of obvious civilian weakness that undermined expectations of punishment. The military dropped its reluctance to a Bosnian mission when the military leadership changed (Shalikashvili replaced Powell, so the gap between s and w narrowed) and when it could trade autonomy in the operation for acquiescence. Likewise, the military stopped shirking the assignment of arresting war criminals when the gap between s and w again narrowed because the military leader changed from someone who strongly opposed that mission, Admiral Smith, to someone who embraced it, General Clark.

Compared with coup-ridden countries, the outcome of the Bosnian case for the United States was an obvious civil-military success: democratically elected officials, once they made up their mind, were able to order the military to do something it opposed strongly. But the tortuous course of events covers far more fits and starts, and at least some shirking, than is supposed to be possible with military subordination to civilian control—and thus the case follows the expectations of agency theory more than the classical model of civil-military relations.

Kosovo

In the spring of 1999, the long series of Balkan conflicts culminated in a war between NATO and Serbia over the fate of ethnic Albanians in Kosovo, a province in rump Yugoslavia.[16] The U.S. stake in Kosovo was greater than in any other corner of the Balkan tinderbox—indeed, even as the Bush administration was saying it did not have a dog in Balkan Wars in 1992, it gave a "Christmas warning" to Slobodan Milosevic, president of Yugoslavia, that any action in Kosovo would precipitate a U.S. response (Daalder and O'Hanlon 2000, p. 9). Kosovo was a quasi-autonomous province of Serbia— but importantly, from the Serb perspective, never a full republic in the former Yugoslavia. While the majority of Kosovars are ethnic Albanian, Kosovo itself had the status of something like the historical cradle of Serbia, too important to the Serbian national identity for Serbia to let it go without a fight. The gradual breakup of Yugoslavia, accelerated by the implementation of the Dayton peace accords, gave impetus to a guerrilla Kosovar independence movement, and a cycle of attacks-reprisals-counterreprisals escalated throughout 1998. In October 1998, U.S. threats of air strikes led to a temporary cease-fire to be monitored by the Organization for Security and Co-operation in Europe "observers." The cease-fire progressively broke down with a series of atrocities, and in February all parties assembled in Rambouillet, France, for a last-ditch effort at a negotiated settlement. Representatives of the ethnic Albanians accepted, albeit grudgingly, terms hammered out by the NATO hosts, but the Serbs rejected them and walked out on 23 March. NATO air strikes against Serb targets commenced the following day and continued until 10 June, when the Serbs effectively capitulated.

Civil-military tensions were extraordinarily high in the Kosovo operation, and agency theory helps illuminate some, though perhaps not all, of the dynamics involved. In particular, agency theory suggests six key windows into the Kosovo case: (1) the debate and bargaining over whether to take any military action in Kosovo; (2) the debate and bargaining over how to take military action; (3) the degree of intrusive monitoring (micromanagement) that continued throughout the operation; (4) the shirking and "working-with-conflict" during the operations; (5) the multiple divisions among the civilian principals and military agents, and especially the contest over whether the United States or NATO should be the ultimate civilian principal; and (6) the punishment inflicted on the NATO commander General Clark, even though NATO prevailed in the conflict. Although the numerous cross-cutting cleavages and the sketchiness of the historical record preclude a dogmatic conclusion, the evidence suggests that weak civilian leadership again produced more shirking than the classical theory of civil-military relations would admit.

To begin with, the debate over whether to get involved militarily in Kosovo followed a variant of the now-familiar hawk-dove pattern. Hawks favored using the threat of military action to coerce Serbian concessions; if threats were not enough, hawks backed the use of military power to enforce a peace, effectively bombing Serbia to the negotiating table. The hawks tended to be the key civilian actors: Vice President Gore, Secretary of State Albright, Prime Minister Blair of Britain, UN Ambassador Holbrooke, and, to a lesser extent, National Security Advisor Berger and, more uncertainly still, Clinton himself; the hawks included, however, one key military figure, NATO commander in chief General Wesley Clark. The doves considered the Serbs uncoercable without an unacceptable level of military commitment from NATO and included the JCS chairman, General Shelton, along with most of the other chiefs; the doves included, however, several key civilian players, including Secretary of Defense Cohen as well as the other NATO political leaders, especially the French and Italians, who were reluctant to use force for a variety of reasons (Halberstam 2001b, p. 409; Clark 2001, pp. 135, 168; Ricks 1999).

The debate played out in particularly vigorous bureaucratic wrangling that just skirted shirking. In January 1999 the JCS met and decided to recommend against military involvement in Kosovo for two reasons, first, because any involvement in Kosovo would be detrimental to "military readiness," throwing in doubt the ability of U.S. forces to fulfill the obligations of the national military strategy; and second, because the Kosovo issue was not in the "national interest" anyway (Clark 2001, p. 167). The first reason, of course, is a military judgment, well within the competency of the military to make. It is not a dispositive judgment, however. The military could advise civilians that a Kosovo entanglement would tie up forces dedicated to other national security missions and thereby increase the risk that the national military strategy could not be readily executed; the civilians could trump this military advice merely by judging the risk worth taking, a judgment that is exclusively the prerogative of the civilian leaders. Because of this, the second reason is *not* a judgment the military is competent to make; civilian principals are the ones who decide what is and is not in the national interest, and the chiefs stepped beyond the bounds of their proper role in arrogating that judgment for themselves. In February, even after the president had said he would use force, if necessary, to get a peace agreement, senior figures in the Defense Department were telling the Government Accounting Office that they were "no longer willing to use air or ground forces to get an agreement" (Scarborough and Cain 1999). Eventually, of course, the civilian hawk preference prevailed, so these are at worst fairly low-level instances of shirking.

The second issue, the debate over how to use force, is of course integrally linked to the decision whether to use force. There were three broad options: limited air strikes; relatively unrestricted air strikes; and a full ground invasion coupled with massive air strikes. The military doves opposed the use of force in Kosovo because they reasoned that nothing short of a full ground invasion would cause the Serbs to concede and such a massive operation was too costly to contemplate. Interestingly, once the decision to go was made, the logic of the military doves' position confronted them with a choice: they could seek victory, which by their own logic probably required ground troops; or they could stick to the judgment that Kosovo was not "worth" a ground invasion, and, following their own logic, accept something less than victory. For the most part, the military doves continued to argue against ground troops as a matter of policy, even when forced to admit that air power would not likely suffice (Burns 1999; Graham 1999b; Schmitt and Myers 1999; Harris and Graham 1999; Myers 1999a; Daalder and O'Hanlon 2000, p. 96). The hawks, however, tended to favor the limited bombing options. General Clark, virtually alone among the top advisors, wanted to use the full range of NATO power, including explicitly preparing for the use of ground troops (Clark 2001, p. 119). Secretary Albright argued that air power alone would suffice, going so far as to predict that Milosevic would fold after three days of bombing, and NSA Berger continued to resist the idea of using ground troops (Daalder and O'Hanlon 2000, pp. 97, 130, 290). The NATO allies strongly opposed both the ground invasion and the massive air campaign and agitated strenuously for the most restrictive air strikes. The most important actor, President Clinton, shared the reservations of his principal advisors on the use of ground troops. He had assured the Senate in 1998 that he would not use ground troops in Kosovo (Schweid 1998), and he readily accepted the consensus position (excepting Clark) that Kosovo was either not worth a ground invasion (the military doves) or doable without it (the civilian hawks). Consequently, Clinton made the fateful and controversial step to foreclose the ground option from the very start, saying, "I do not intend to put our troops in Kosovo to fight a war," even as he announced the commencement of hostilities on 24 March (Halberstam 2001b, p. 423).

At first glance, Clinton's no ground troops pledge looks suspiciously like the kind of grand bargain concession that agency theory would expect a weak civilian principal to make on *how* to intervene in order to prevail over the prior decision *whether* to intervene. In fact, however, the pledge of no ground troops seems to derive more from three other factors: (1) Clinton's

own personal reluctance to contemplate the casualties that a ground invasion would entail, reinforced by (2) naively optimistic thinking on the part
of his civilian advisors, itself shaped in response to (3) adamant opposition
to any ground war on the part of the NATO allies and congressional opponents (Daalder and O'Hanlon 2000, pp. 96–100). Military reluctance about a
ground war was not, it appears, decisive in convincing Clinton to make the
pledge. Indeed, Halberstam traces the pledge to the kibbitzing of Ivo Daalder,
a former midlevel NSC staffer who was a prominent media pundit on Balkan issues; according to Halberstam, Daalder was consulted in advance on
the president's remarks and suggested that the original wording, "we have
no plans to put in ground troops," be replaced with "we have no intention
of using ground troops."[17] From the point of view of military strategy, the
pledge was almost certainly bad policy. It reinforced in the enemy's mind the
notion that NATO was casualty phobic, thus giving Milosevic reason to hold
out far longer—NATO might be defeated, not by the hopelessly impossible
task of prevailing over NATO on the battlefield but by killing enough NATO
troops to break its political will. It was also bad policy from the broader view
of civil-military relations, reinforcing all the Vietnam-era images of an uncertain civilian leadership hoping for military victories at little cost and
unwilling to spend the necessary political capital to guarantee victory
(Halberstam 2001b, pp. 424–425). But from the point of view of agency theory itself, the decision was not military shirking because it was dictated *by* civilians and not *to* civilians; civilian principals have the right to be wrong, and
in this case they probably were.

President Clinton and his NATO allies thus decided to intervene in
Kosovo, but to "do it on the cheap." This meant highly restricted bombing of
Serb targets, necessitating an extraordinary degree of civilian intrusive monitoring of military operations, the third major civil-military issue of concern
here. Air force General Charles Wald said the rules of engagement were "as
strict as any I've seen during 27 years in the military" (Priest and Drozdiak
1999). The restrictions were aimed at minimizing any chance of civilian collateral damage in Serbia or Kosovo and also minimizing any chance that
NATO pilots would be killed. The net result was that many likely targets
could not be hit under the rules of engagement, thus greatly limiting the effectiveness of the military operation in the early stages.

Consistent with agency theory logic, the military did trade off support for
the mission in exchange for at least some initial civilian concessions on
monitoring. Civilian leaders, especially in the NATO allies, wanted the mil-

itary to seek approval for every individual target, whereas the military wanted a free hand but traded down to the requirement of civilian approval for classes of target sets (for example, phase 1: anti-aircraft and Serb military hardware; phase 2: communication facilities in Serbia; and so on) (Priest and Drozdiak 1999). The military got this compromise preference, at least at the outset, but when errant strikes that hit civilians on 12 and 14 April raised fears of rampant collateral damage, civilians tightened the reins and insisted on micromanagement of the targeting process, with many more layers of cross-checking; when the Chinese embassy in Belgrade was bombed accidentally on 7 May (blamed on faulty targeting information), the intrusive monitoring intensified further. Indeed, in an obvious if awkward echo of the Vietnam War, the JCS daily brought targeting lists to the White House for specific approval, including even direct supervision by the president himself (Graham 1999b; Priest 1999a, 1999b, 1999c). Even Secretary of Defense Cohen, who was among the most reluctant of the Kosovo doves, later conceded that the multiple layers of restraint placed on the military impeded the progress of the war.[18] It is striking that the military commander in charge of the bombing, General Short, considered the bombing so purposefully ineffective that he believed it could be explained only by an elaborate conspiracy plot: that perhaps an explicit deal had been cut between Milosevic and the senior-most NATO officials for only token bombing, after which point Milosevic would back down, having saved face by standing up to NATO (Halberstam 2001b, p. 450).

The civilians' close micromanagement and tentative "stumbling into war" naturally meant that the operational conduct of the war itself was fraught with civil-military conflict, the fourth issue to be highlighted by the agency theory perspective.[19] From the outset the war did not go well for NATO, and the Serbs showed far more resilience than NATO leaders had expected— what is worse, Milosevic used the NATO bombing as a pretext for engaging in massive ethnic cleansing in Kosovo, thus ensuring that the plight of ethnic Albanian Kosovars actually significantly worsened as a result of NATO action (Daalder and O'Hanlon 2000, pp. 101–136). Barely two weeks into the war, the war's poor fortunes were obvious enough that the JCS was emboldened to engage in an unambiguous display of shirking, captured in a graphic *Washington Post* headline: "Joint Chiefs Doubted Air Strategy" (Graham 1999b). The *Post* story was full of not-for-attribution quotes from "senior officers" about how the chiefs considered ongoing operations to be disastrous and had, in fact, argued against the war from the beginning. The quotes tried to convey the impression that the chiefs had agreed to go along only out of respect for proper civil-military relations: according to one senior officer, "But you know, you make your case, and that's why we have civilian control over the military." Far from showing a respect for civilian control, however, the very existence of the article indicated just how little fear of punishment the senior military officers actually had—they were willing to undermine the current policy with leaks calculated to embarrass and handicap the commander in chief while the operation was still unfolding; the unnamed military officers evidently assessed the likelihood of punishment correctly, for there is no record of the Clinton administration's making any response to these subversive leaks.

Although the war was going badly, the military continued strenuously to object to the use of ground troops. The lack of progress from the air campaign was beginning to convince senior civilian leaders that a ground option might be necessary. General Clark had never wavered in his support for the ground option, and arguably his relentless pressure to involve ground troops constituted shirking. The president had expressly ruled out ground troops and, though a foolish strategic move, it was nonetheless official policy. Some of Clark's gambits were interpreted as backdoor efforts to undo the no-ground-troops decision (Halberstam 2001b, pp. 464–465); if so, they constituted shirking, which was the final judgment some of Clark's successors reached. At the same time, Clark was able over time to change civilian minds; Prime Minister Blair was his first true convert, but as early as 28 March, NSA Berger was refusing to rule out ground troops (Halberstam 2001b, p. 462; Berger 1999).

By the time of the NATO summit held on 23–25 April to celebrate the organization's fiftieth anniversary, civilians in Washington (with the exception of Secretary of Defense Cohen) were beginning to see a ground invasion, or at least the credible threat of a ground invasion, as necessary for victory (Daalder and O'Hanlon 2000, pp. 155–157). Congress, however, was not convinced, and in late April the House voted to block funding for the use of ground troops without congressional approval (Babington and Eilperin 1999). Clinton, for his part, publicly reversed himself on the no ground troops pledge in mid-May, announcing that all options were on the table (Halberstam 2001b, p. 475). From that point on, the locus of any shirking shifted from Clark to the Pentagon. The senior military officers back in the Pentagon continued to oppose ground troops and floated remarkably high estimates of required troops, such as 200,000, as against the 45,000 to

50,000 requested by the commander in chief himself (Schmitt and Myers 1999, Myers 1999b). Moreover, in another remarkable display of open subversion of civilian policy during war time, the chiefs leaked again to the *New York Times* their adamant opposition to ground troops, even as the White House clearly signaled a desire to at least credibly threaten the use of ground troops (Myers 1999a). From an agency standpoint, these leaks are in and of themselves evidence of shirking, but what is even more striking is the rationale reflected in the report: "The senior commanders, including the Chairman and Vice Chairman of the Joint Chiefs of Staff, believe there is insufficient domestic and international political support for sending ground troops into Kosovo." The sufficiency of political support is, of course, a quintessentially political judgment on which military advisors may certainly have an opinion but which lies beyond their professional competence to judge dispositively. To be sure, the military appears to have been joined by Secretary of Defense Cohen in opposing ground forces, and it is possible that the source of the leak was Cohen himself. In this case, it would be Cohen who was shirking. No one, however, was punished.

The efforts to thwart the use of ground troops culminated in the affair of Task Force Hawk, the Apache helicopter force requested by Clark in late March as a way of improving close air support capabilities inside Kosovo. After some delay, and in the face of obvious reluctance by senior military advisors, Clinton approved the request (Daalder and O'Hanlon 2000, p. 125; Halberstam 2001b, p. 466). From that point on, however, the Pentagon dragged its feet, slow rolling on site selection and delivery of the Apaches, sending fewer helicopters than requested, and going to extraordinary lengths to block any approval for actually using the Apaches (Richter 1999; Halberstam 2001b, p. 466). One method used to block approval was inflation of the estimates of how many U.S. casualties could be expected if the helicopters were used. The field commanders reported a 5 percent estimate; senior military leaders in the Pentagon claimed they heard and passed on a 6 to 15 percent estimate; and the White House claimed it was given a 50 percent estimate, the latter being, of course, prohibitively high and effectively vetoing the operation (Halberstam 2001b, pp. 466–467; Clark 2001, p. 291). Even while Clark was privately pushing for authority to use the Apaches, the army was leaking to the press that the Apaches were primarily in Kosovo as a bluff (Scarborough 1999). Again, the JCS had one key civilian ally in its effort—Secretary Cohen himself apparently opposed the deployment and use of the Apaches, and this doubtless affected any expectations of punishment for slow rolling on the delivery of a critical weapon system during wartime or inflating the estimates of casualties (Gordon and Schmitt 1999). From an agency viewpoint, however, it is curious that the obvious parallels to the Somalia debacle—in which Secretary Aspin was fired for blocking the delivery of weapons requested by the field commander—were not sufficient to alter the strategic calculations of the actors.[20] In any case, a more confident judgment about the strategic interaction behind the scenes is not possible without a fuller account from all of the parties, including Secretary Cohen and Chairman Shelton.

The foregoing suggests yet a fifth issue of concern both from and for the agency perspective. The cross-cutting cleavages produced extraordinary levels of bargaining and double-dealing within the NATO side; civilians within the alliance and within the Clinton administration fought among each other, and each found factions within the U.S. military or allied militaries with which to conspire. The stylized model of civil-military relations presented in Chapter 4 is hard-pressed to incorporate all these cleavages, although the underlying agency logic of strategic interaction and monitoring/shirking certainly obtains. A staple of principal-agent theories is precisely the expectation that the more unified the principal is the stronger it is against the agent; determined agents can play divided principals against each other. Likewise, the more divided the agent is, the stronger the hand of the principal (Avant 1994). When the cleavages are as deep and as cross-cutting as they were in the case of Kosovo, and when the ultimate principal, the president, is either unable or unwilling to exert authority, the agency perspective would lead to the generalized if imprecise expectation of quasi-paralysis—and something very close to that obtained in the Kosovo case. The extraordinary effort by NATO allies to constrain the bombing targets presented, in agency terms, an especially debilitating challenge because it constituted a contest over who would be the principal.[21] Would Clark answer to NATO political leaders or to President Clinton? Clark, of course, answered to both, and the fact that NATO was itself a divided principal allowed him to form a tactical alliance with Prime Minister Blair and through that relationship shape his interactions with his other civilian bosses. Indeed, Clark's chain of command suspected him of doing just that (Halberstam 2001b, p. 462). Moreover, Clark's immediate bosses, Cohen and Shelton, suspected Clark of regularly going behind their backs to appeal directly to *their* bosses in the White House (Halberstam 2001b, p. 456–457; Clark 2001, p. 129). At the same time, Clark was wrestling with his own insubordinate subordinate,

General Short, who greatly resented the restrictions placed on the bombing.[22] Agency theory can shed some light on this tangled mess, but it defies easy modeling.

Finally, it is worth noting that the Kosovo case did end with a punishment for shirking: in late July General Clark was informed that he would not be allowed to complete his first tour, let alone be given the customary second tour as SACEUR, but was instead forced into retirement to make a four-star slot available for the vice chairman of the JCS, Joseph Ralston. Technically President Clinton at least gave formal approval since all four-star billets are vetted at the White House, but he privately told Clark that he had nothing to do with the decision (Clark 2001, pp. 416–417); indeed, he claimed that he had been "snookered" and did not realize that the decision to award the slot to Ralston meant a de facto early retirement for Clark—tantamount to punishment of a senior military officer (Halberstam 2001b, p. 478; Babington 1999). Clinton's alleged anger is hard to credit because there was no effort made to reverse the decision, let alone punish anyone for embarrassing the president in this way; Halberstam speculates that Clinton was afraid to cross the chiefs on something like this (Halberstam 2001b, p. 480). That the decision was intended by Cohen and Shelton to be a punishment is clear from the way the message was delivered: Clark was summarily informed of the decision, without warning, and roughly at the same time that the decision was leaked to the press, thereby ensuring that Clark could not reverse it on appeal (Clark 2001, pp. 413–416). This is, moreover, how the press treated the move, and it had ample not-for-attribution quotes to substantiate the interpretation (Graham and Priest 1999, Graham 1999a). In agency terms, Clark was punished by his immediate principals for what they considered to be shirking: pressing to use ground troops and doing end runs to the White House. The same agency perspective, however, would raise questions about the degree of working and shirking higher up the chain, especially between the Pentagon and the White House. And, ironically, the punishment of Clark only deepened military distrust of the president without materially enhancing its estimation of the likelihood of punishment.

Above all, however, the Kosovo case underscores just how difficult it is to have healthy civil-military relations, even or especially in wartime, when the commander in chief is as weakened as was Clinton after the lengthy Lewinsky and impeachment scandals. Clinton was the first impeached commander in chief to lead the nation in war, and this undoubtedly contributed to his equivocal position. To be sure, the Senate voted not to convict him before the war started, but the damage to the president, at least in terms of his ability to dominate a civil-military contest, was already done. Agency theory emphasizes that the quality of the principal is a vitally important ingredient in civil-military relations.

Conclusion

Agency theory treats day-to-day civil-military relations as an ongoing game of strategic interaction, in which civilian principals vary the intrusiveness of their monitoring of military agents and military agents vary their compliance with civilian preferences. The particular pattern of strategic interaction is influenced by such exogenous factors as the costs of monitoring and the military expectations of punishment. Determined military actors can and will exploit the weakness of civilian principals at crucial points, and will do so without launching a formal coup or precipitating a full-blown crisis in civil-military relations. Civilian principals, however, can manipulate the cost-benefit calculations even of very reluctant military agents and thus prevail if they are sufficiently determined.

All of these dynamics are evident in the "minicases" presented here, and the collective picture that emerges is of a much messier civil-military relationship than traditional theory admits, although perhaps not the full-blown crisis that is prominent in the conventional wisdom on the post–Cold War era. The Gulf War was not the idealized civil-military consortium that the official rhetoric of the war claimed; indeed, the pull and haul of civil-military bargaining was more or less what agency theory would expect. At the same time, Somalia, Haiti, and Bosnia certainly had examples of shirking—which conventional wisdom remembers and agency theory explains. In particular, the bargaining over whether and how to do those missions, with tradeoffs within and between missions, fits the expectations of agency theory when a strong military is led by a weak civilian principal. Nevertheless, the shirking that did go on was more nuanced than some accounts relate. The Kosovo war illustrated that conflicts are messy and that at the nitty-gritty level one should not expect all civilians to line up on one side and all military agents to line up on the other. This complicates the use of agency theory but does not invalidate it, for the same basic strategic interactions are evident across the various cleavages. Civil-military relations in the United States, above all in Kosovo but also in every other case examined, are about bargaining, monitoring, and strategic calculations over whether to work or shirk.

CHAPTER 8

Conclusion

This book explores how civilians control the military in theory and how that theory plays out in practice in the United States. In this concluding chapter, after summarizing the main argument of the book and the basic outlines of agency theory, I briefly consider what agency theory has to say about civil-military relations after the Clinton era and then suggest avenues for future research that would build on the argument and findings I have presented. The agency model is intended to be only a first cut at a general institutional theory of civil-military relations. While the simplified model presented here yields interesting results, there are obvious ways to expand on the research. Finally, I wish to consider a normative question that my empirical and theoretical analysis has left begging: although civilian control of the military is the distinguishing hallmark of democratic politics, is it necessarily a good thing for the polity? Put another way, what are the costs of maintaining civilian control?

Agency Theory's Contribution

Agency theory is a worthy alternative to the reigning institutional paradigm of civil-military relations, Huntington's model of civilian control. Huntington's theory confronts a puzzle: the United States violated Huntington's model and yet did not suffer the consequences predicted by the model. As explained in Chapter 2, at the outset of the Cold War Huntington derived prescriptions for the United States from his model of civil-military relations, warning that if the United States did not follow those prescriptions it would risk losing the Cold War. With the Cold War over, it is clear that the United States prevailed even though it did not follow Huntington's prescriptions of a conservative shift in civilian values coupled with objective civilian control over the military. This central empirical challenge calls into question Huntington's general model of civil-military relations and opens the door for alternative explanations, including agency theory.

As explained in Chapter 3, agency theory treats civil-military relations as a special case of the more general phenomenon of political principals seeking to monitor and influence the behavior of their political agents. The phenomenon is ubiquitous in politics, but is especially important in democracies. Democratic theory establishes that the citizen is the ultimate political principal—as a body, the citizenry chooses its leaders, who in turn establish the government to fulfill the wishes of the electorate. Faithful political agents work and do not shirk. Just as voters seek to ensure that the politicians they elect follow their wishes, so too do politicians seek to ensure that the subordinate arms of the government—bureaucracies or, in this case, the military—follow their wishes. The political agents, for their part, have preferences of their own, and these preferences can diverge from those of their political masters, leading them to consider shirking instead of working. The day-to-day business of civil-military relations, then, is a game of strategic interaction, with civilians monitoring their military agents and military agents determining whether to work or shirk based on expectations the agents have about the likely consequences: will shirking be discovered and, if so, will it be punished?

This interaction can be represented in a simplified formal game, explained more fully in Chapter 4. Civilians choose the monitoring mechanisms, relatively intrusive or relatively nonintrusive, and the military chooses whether to work or shirk, based in part on expectations of an exogenously determined likelihood of punishment. Under different conditions, then, the civil-military relationship can yield one of four basic outcomes: military working under civilian nonintrusive monitoring; military working under civilian intrusive monitoring; military shirking under nonintrusive monitoring; and military shirking under intrusive monitoring. Viewed this way, the agency model subsumes Huntington's theory, which yields only the "military working under civilian nonintrusive monitoring" outcome. Since Huntington, however, does *not* explain well the actual Cold War record of U.S. civil-military relations, it begs the question whether the United States followed one of the other possible outcomes anticipated by agency theory (but not by Huntington).

In fact, as I argue in Chapter 5, the Cold War pattern of U.S. civil-military relations is best understood as a case of "military working under civilian intrusive monitoring." Agency theory expects that this will be the outcome when the costs of monitoring are relatively low and when the military's expectation of punishment is relatively high. Although these factors are difficult to measure precisely, the evidence presented in Chapter 5 seems to confirm that these conditions were met for most of the Cold War. Importantly, the few instances of shirking seem to be correlated with a significant case-specific change either in the costs of monitoring or the expectations of punishment.

Finally, as demonstrated in Chapters 6 and 7, agency theory explains the early post–Cold War friction in U.S. civil-military relations as an instance of "military shirking under civilian intrusive monitoring." Agency theory thereby subsumes the factors highlighted by other explanations of the post–Cold War friction, such as the changed threat environment, the persistent gap between the preferences of military agents and civilian principals, and the idiosyncratic weakness of the Clinton administration vis-à-vis the military. Moreover, agency theory provides a rich heuristic by which to interpret civil-military relations in the most important post–Cold War uses of force.

Agency theory, then, makes several distinctive contributions to our understanding of civil-military relations. First and foremost, it reconceptualizes civil-military outcomes beyond the stale coup/no-coup dichotomy and replaces it with a working-shirking continuum that captures rich variation in patterns of civil-military interaction even in the absence of coups. In so doing, it turns U.S. civil-military relations into a variable rather than a constant.

Second, agency theory brings material incentives back into the story and in particular highlights military expectations of punishment. In retrospect, it is rather surprising that strategic interaction and cost-benefit calculations were essentially absent in the literature before agency theory. The idea that the military may adjust its behavior based on material incentives has great intuitive appeal and resonates with anyone who has worked in day-to-day U.S. civil-military relations at a responsible level. And yet that basic insight is at best implicit and more often totally ignored in existing theoretical treatments. Huntington and Janowitz make essentially no allowance for military shirking and, consequently, for civilian-imposed punishment. Other theories that do admit of shirking, for example Avant's principal-agent account and Desch's structural-threat theory, give scant attention to civilian responses to military behavior. Civil-military relations theory has always emphasized that the quality of the civilian principal and the quality of the military agent are crucial to preserving a proper civil-military balance. Thus, an early Cold War analysis concluded, "civilian supremacy is going to depend essentially (as trite as it may sound) on the quality of the Government's civilian leadership" (Sapin and Snyder 1954, p. 57). And although Huntington did not use the jargon, his emphasis on the norm of professionalism was essentially consistent with the claim from the principal-agent literature that adverse selection (picking the right agent) trumps moral hazard (the quality of efforts to monitor the agent) (Brehm and Gates 1997). Agency theory does not rebut the importance of these factors but suggests that material incentives be added (or retained) for consideration. Thus, it matters what types of punishments military agents can expect. It matters how monitoring mechanisms function—whether fire alarms like the free press are adequate or not and whether technological constraints limit the kinds of intrusive monitoring that are possible. Even noble political actors are sensitive to the likely costs and benefits of their actions.

Third, agency theory provides a logically coherent way of grounding observations that have prominence in historical accounts of civil-military relations, such as President Clinton's idiosyncratic relations with the military, into a systematic theory. There has been something of a theory-practice gap in the U.S. civil-military relations literature to the effect that what matters for the theoretician does not seem to matter for the practitioner. To be sure, a practitioner will find the jargon of agency theory off-putting, but the core logic should not be foreign. Agency theory provides a bridge between the academic theoretical understanding of civil-military relations and the observations of experts who watch those relations unfold on a day-to-day basis.

Fourth, agency theory suggests a conclusion that there are multiple solutions to the civil-military problematique and that there is no such thing as perfect civilian control. The challenge for democratic civil-military relations is thus to minimize what civilian principals must concede to the military agent, recognizing that this decision is revisited and tested every day in multiple dimensions and issues.

Finally, the deductive rationalist core of agency theory allows for ready expansion, revision, or contrast with other theories. Agency theory is thus more flexible than existing alternatives. Indeed, agency theory explains a large portion of basic civil-military relations in the United States and does so even though it uses a spare model. But the spareness of the model points to obvious ways of adding complexity to get still richer explanations. The rationalist baseline, resting primarily on material factors, can also be used as a foil for future explanations that depend on nonrationalist factors or relax rationalist assumptions. I sketch out several such promising avenues for future research below.

At the same time, the civil-military relationship constitutes an especially interesting case for the principal-agent framework. First, and most obviously, this is a case in which the agent can sometimes overtake the principal. The U.S. focus of this book has put this aspect of civil-military relations into the background, but follow-on work could take this up more explicitly. Nevertheless, even within the context of generalized military subordination to civilian rule, shirking at the margins is still possible. This leads to a second important insight exported from the study of civil-military relations to the principal-agent literature: shirking is multifaceted and must encompass more than merely disobeying orders. The military can engage in behavior that constitutes shirking even if it is technically following the explicit orders of a civilian principal. The military can shirk by shading its advice so the civilian principal chooses to give an order contrary to the one that he would have given had the military advice been more sincere—the "Washington monument" tactic in which underlings inflate cost estimates to dissuade a principal from adopting an unwanted course of action. And the military can shirk while obeying if it ties the hands of civilians for follow-on decisions, or practices excessive foot-dragging or other dilatory tactics that undermine the civil-military relationship. Moreover, civil-military relations make clear that the principal can also shirk, by giving inadequate direction or uncertain guidance. These aspects of agency have not been as prominent in the principal-agent literature as they should be.

Civil-Military Relations and Agency Theory after Clinton

President Clinton obviously played a central role in post–Cold War civil-military relations, and this begs the question of the significance of his departure from office.[1] If President Clinton were the entire problem, then one would expect a return to civil-military comity, especially under an avowedly pro-military president like George W. Bush. However, many prominent assessments of post–Cold War civil-military relations identify long-term factors—such as the changed threat environment and a decades-long erosion of professional norms in the military—that should continue to shape relations in much the same way long after Clinton (Desch 1999, Kohn 2002).

Agency theory suggests a middle-ground view: civil-military relations after Clinton will improve, but some of the structural factors and contexts mean the corrosive effects will linger. On the one hand, Clinton's personal baggage conspired to give extreme values to factors that shape the relationship. It is hard to imagine a president with a weaker hand vis-à-vis the senior military leadership than President Clinton; that weakness translated into extremely low expectations of punishment and, consequently, strong incentives for shirking. Replacing a weak commander in chief with a potentially stronger one should change the expectations of military agents and result in stronger incentives for the military to work. On the other hand, agency theory suggests that over time the principal can shape the outlook of the military by preferentially promoting some officers over others and creating a cadre of like-thinking military leaders. Thus, when the White House changes hands, and especially when it changes parties, the gap between the senior-most civilian and military ranks can widen, at least until the promotion process brings about a natural readjustment. At the same time, there is no reason to believe that the departure of President Clinton per se had any discernible effect on another key variable in the agency model, the costs of monitoring; nevertheless, the slowness of the transition, an unintended consequence of the way the 2000 election played out, temporarily hampered the efforts of the incoming Bush administration to assert intrusive control in the Pentagon. The 2000 election, therefore, produced cross-cutting changes to several key factors in the agency model: the arrival of a potentially stronger civilian principal who has broad support among the ranks, but one whose agenda will diverge at points from that of the established military leadership.

Once the electoral mess of 2000 was resolved,[2] the initial transition from Clinton to Bush followed something like an agency theory script, as if the new team were determined to correct what were identified by the theory as mistakes in the previous administration. President Bush and his team arrived with an explicit and expressed contempt for the quality of civilian control under President Clinton (Gertz and Scarborough 2002). Bush appointed Donald Rumsfeld, an especially strong and experienced insider, to be secretary of defense. Rumsfeld gave particular stress to the need to "restore" strong civilian control, and this was a prominent theme in his "Rumsfeld's Rules," a list of maxims he had assembled from his years in government service (Rumsfeld 2001). The "Rules" were promoted throughout the early days of his tenure, and the implications of the change in leadership were not lost on the military. According to press reports, early in the Bush tenure the senior air force staff were concerned that Secretary of Defense Rumsfeld might peremptorily fire an air force general to send a message that disobedience would not be tolerated (No author 2001b). Even so, senior civilians in the Pentagon believed that still more drastic measures were needed to correct for "eight years of no discipline." According to one official: "If you think of a generation of officers as coming along every three years then we are in our third-generation of officers who experienced no discipline" (Gertz and Scarborough 2001). Another report led with a quote attributed to "one of President Bush's top advisors," who said that the only way to reform the Pentagon was "to fire a few generals" (Richter 2001, p. A1). The invocation of agency theory logic could hardly be more explicit.

The arrival of a Republican president probably had cross-cutting effects on the gap between military and civilian preferences. On the one hand, the gap narrowed in the sense that there was now a Republican administration presiding over a largely Republican officer corps. On the other hand, the Clinton administration had had eight years to narrow the gap, at least at the very top. Even an administration that is weak in civil-military terms can have a significant effect over time just by handpicking officers for promotion to the senior-most slots. The fact that Rumsfeld was dealing with Clinton-picked generals was given high prominence throughout the first year of the Bush administration (Whitworth and Watson 2001, Waller 2001, Gertz and Scarborough 2001).

On the one hand, the effect of this dynamic was in fact an early honeymoon for the Bush team that even outlasted initial reports of a lower-than-expected increase in defense spending (Curl and Scarborough 2001). During this period there was great enthusiasm among even the senior military for the Bush arrival; in the words of one observer, even the Clinton-picked chiefs of staff "were dying to have these guys back" (Duffy 2001).

On the other hand, the same dynamic probably ended the honeymoon. Rumsfeld was determined to push reforms in force structure and strategy, loosely lumped together under the heading of "transformation," and, in so doing, overturn the interservice compromises that had been extracted from the civilians over successive reviews dating back to the Base Force. While there were proponents for this within the military, they were not by and large at the senior-most ranks, and within months Rumsfeld's reviews were bogged down by extensive leaks and congressional criticisms about the chaotic and poorly coordinated nature of the effort.[3] The rancor was qualitatively different from what had transpired eight years earlier under Clinton. For instance, President Bush was largely above the fray, and the military's resistance was never as open nor as bitterly personal—almost certainly due to changed expectations of punishment. Nevertheless, it was serious enough to qualify as shirking, and certainly this was how Rumsfeld and his team viewed the military's end runs to Congress (No author 2001b, Calmes 2001). It also made Rumsfeld a prominent target of speculation about whether he would be the first Bush cabinet official to be sacked (Duffy 2001, Donnelly 2001). Frustrated civilian leaders in the Pentagon, borrowing a page from agency theory, traced the problem directly back to military leaders who had come of age under weak civilian control (Gertz and Scarborough 2001, Waller 2001).

From the standpoint of agency theory, what was surprising was not military opposition to the Rumsfeld reviews that threatened the status quo, but rather that, on several dimensions, the military seemed to prevail over Rumsfeld. In late August 2001, Rumsfeld announced that, contrary to hints emanating for months from the DoD, he would not seek deep cuts in the force structure. This move was treated as surrendering—as in "Rumsfeld sued for peace" (Duffy 2001)—"retreating" (Shanker 2001), or simply deferring to the military (Loeb 2001, Weisman 2002). Of course Rumsfeld himself insisted that no such reversal had taken place, that he had merely conducted a review with an open mind and come to the conclusion that more modest reform was the appropriate course of action. If this is an accurate depiction, it is easier to square with agency expectations. If not, it is puzzling why a strong civilian could not prevail over the military. One answer is that Rumsfeld ran afoul of Congress, thus his problems were partly the old divided-principal challenge. But his biggest problem on the Hill was with his fellow Republicans, which raises the question of why the principals had such difficulty reaching a consensus. The most common explanation focuses on Rumsfeld's style, which emphasized making decisions and giving orders over consulting and building coalitions of support. Ironically, in an effort to undo the perceived weaknesses of earlier civilian leadership, Rumsfeld may have overcompensated and provoked a backlash that produced a comparable paralysis in civilian control.

The civil-military relations picture, as with so many other things, changed dramatically on September 11. For the first time since the end of the Cold War, the vital national interest was threatened, and the Department of Defense immediately moved to a war footing. In terms of the agency model, the heightened national interest lowered the policy costs of monitoring. The early reporting suggested that the traditional hawk-dove debate over how to respond militarily played out with some distinctive twists. The debate over what to do in Afghanistan was not that rancorous, and President Bush quickly approved the use of extensive military force to destroy Al-Qaeda and bring down its Taliban sponsors. In so doing, Bush explicitly sought to distance himself from his predecessor, whose excessive caution in the use of military force had contributed to the terrorists' image of the United States as a paper tiger (Woodward and Balz 2002c). The debate over whether to go beyond Afghanistan and perhaps attack Iraq, in contrast, did provoke more of a schism, this time with Secretary of State Powell teaming with the military against the civilian leadership in the Pentagon (Kagan and Kristol 2001a, 2001b; Woodward and Balz 2002a, 2002b, 2002c; Balz, Woodward, and Himmelman 2002; Ricks 2002a, 2002b). According to one report, Powell even approached General Shelton and urged Shelton to restrain his civilian superiors and somehow "get these guys back in the box" (Balz, Woodward, and Himmelman 2002). Of course, the fact that the secretary of state was Colin Powell, the famously cautious former general, is probably not irrelevant.

Reports are contradictory as to whether the war in Afghanistan was micromanaged or not, although the lowered costs of monitoring (because of higher stakes) would suggest that civilians had greater incentive to monitor. On the one hand, President Bush clearly delegated considerable authority to his deputies, both military and civilian (Waller 2002). On the other hand, Secretary of Defense Rumsfeld used very intrusive monitoring mechanisms to manage the war; however, the assertive civilian control produced little backlash from the military operators, and Rumsfeld was even credited with letting the senior military "run the war."[4] In some areas, for instance ensuring that collateral damage was minimized, the available evidence suggests that the war in Afghanistan was every bit as micromanaged as any preceding use of force (Schrader 2002). There were few reports of operational shirking, although it appears that some civilian leaders were frustrated by the caution of General Franks, the senior military commander (Hersh 2001; Kaplan 2001; Ricks 2001c; Kagan and Kristol 2001a, 2001b).

The war certainly changed the conventional wisdom on how civilian control was faring in the Bush administration. Rumsfeld even became a cult hero, enjoying some of the most flattering press coverage of the entire war and sparking discussions about his sex appeal (Donnelly 2001, Nordlinger

2001, Mazzetti and Newman 2001). Nevertheless, the war only delayed some of the tough choices that confront the post–Cold War United States, and so challenges certainly remain (Waller 2002). Moreover, the debate over Iraq has followed a very familiar civil-military script (Ricks 2002a, 2002b). Above all, there is no evidence that September 11 repealed the basic working of agency theory. Civil-military relations in the United States continued to reflect the strategic interaction of civilian principals and military agents, each playing out a role, pursuing preferences, and responding to the shifting costs of monitoring and expectations of punishment. The new war on terrorism altered the stakes but did not otherwise constitute a fundamental change in the logic of how civilians and the military interact to provide for the common defense.

Avenues for Future Research

The most obvious avenue for future research is to explore the generalizability of the argument by expanding the cases considered—looking at civil-military relations in other countries altogether and looking at more civil-military issue areas in the U.S. case. Although developed in the context of the American case, agency theory should be useful in comparative contexts, especially for other advanced democracies where civil-military relations are no longer primarily a matter of avoiding coups d'état. Much of the literature in comparative politics on civil-military relations concerns coup prevention and the transition from military-led regimes to functioning democracies (Feaver 1999). That literature, in other words, ends where agency theory begins, and so as democratic institutions take root in those countries, the previous theoretical paradigms may lose their analytical utility.

Agency theory may even make some contributions to the study of civil-military relations in countries where the threat of coups is real. After all, a coup represents the ultimate in shirking—reversing the principal-agent relationship so that the old agent (the military) becomes the new principal (the dictator). Pathological civil-military interactions within the agency framework could end up in a coup. Of course, once a military has seized power, the agency problems immediately reemerge, only this time the intragovernment agency relationship has both principals and agents wearing uniforms and the extragovernment agency relationship has the civilian polity as agents. It is likely, however, that modifications to the principal-agent framework are necessary in studying coup-ridden states. Agency interactions cannot be analyzed within the principal-agent model unless the principal can commit in advance to "buying" what the agent produces; if the agent has no way of developing an expectation of how the principal will act, then the selection, monitoring, and punishment qualities of the principal-agent framework cannot function (Bendor 1988). Does the model obtain when the *agent* cannot commit in advance because he has the ability to reverse the relationship?

Agency theory could also be used to flesh out U.S. civil-military relations, only this time looking at other issue areas, including force structure and strategy. For instance, one could code shirking as the fate of "orphan missions," the things that are necessary for combat but which fall outside of the services' organizational essence and so are traditionally unfunded. The more orphaned these missions are, the more clearly services are pursuing their own agenda rather than the broader civilian one. The better the missions are cared for, the more the agent is faithfully fulfilling the principal's desires. Other topics, such as personnel and training policy (policies on race, gender, and sexual orientation, for example) are also obvious places where the agency dynamic of monitoring, working or shirking, and punishment come into play.

In this vein, the agency model could be employed in a more detailed look at civil-military relations during combat, which this book considered in broad-brush strokes. When a military force deploys in combat, its behavior is determined by literally thousands of standard operating procedures (SOPs) governing everything from how to dig a foxhole to how to destroy vital equipment before surrendering. In theory, if civilians want to direct unequivocally how the military will function in combat, they must determine each of these procedures. Collectively, the SOPs are known as doctrine, and civilian control over at least general features of doctrine is an enduring theme in the study of civil-military relations (Posen 1984, Van Evera 1984, Snyder 1984, Avant 1994, Kier 1997).

Certain SOPs, however, are especially significant for civilian control over the conduct of military operations: rules of engagement. Rules of engagement "are written to provide guidance to military commanders in the field on appropriate action under peacetime circumstances, in crises, and in the event of war" (Sagan 1991, p. 80). The agency theory model developed in Chapter 3 suggests that rules of engagement serve three sometimes contradictory functions: (1) as means of constraining military agents with more explicit orders (also anticipated by traditional theory); (2) as an enhanced information-gathering mechanism for civilian principals to monitor military agents even on the chaotic battlefield, because requests to change the rules of engagement alert civilians to how the battle is progressing; and (3) as an "interest in the residual," an incentive to reluctant military agents to go along with missions they might otherwise not want to carry out. Which role the rules are actually playing may itself be a function of the different monitoring-cost environments. Thus, when information from the battlefield is essentially impossible to get, rules of engagement cannot be used as an information source; even if the civilians want to glean information from requests to change the rules, the communications technology will not allow it. In those cases, the only function for rules of engagement is to make orders more explicit. When communications technology allows some limited reporting from the field, the rules may serve to enhance the quality of information, allowing civilians to understand whether the conflict is expanding or not. When communications technology is fully advanced, rules of engagement may no longer be needed in the information-gathering role, and the other functions of constraint and incentive may come to the fore. Follow-on studies could assess this argument by comparing how rules of engagement functioned in three different monitoring-costs environments: (1) the pre-telegraph era, when timely information from the battlefield was largely nonexistent; (2) the early telegraph and radio era, when some timely reporting was possible but limited; (3) the current era, when communication is so good that it leads almost to a surfeit of information from the battlefield.[5]

The simple model presented in Chapter 4 made numerous assumptions that could be revised in future extensions of agency theory. Most obviously, reducing civil-military relations to a two-actor game abstracts from the reality that, in the American case, civilian principals and military agents are in fact numerous and diverse. Indeed, a key aspect of American civil-military relations is the explicit decision, enshrined in the Constitution, to divide the civilian control responsibility between the executive and the legislative branches, creating at a minimum two competing principals. In practice, the executive and legislative branches do not always disagree and do not always compete directly for day-to-day control of the military, but in important cases they can—as for instance when Congress opposed President Clinton's efforts to lift the ban on gays serving openly in the military—and this can have obvious implications for the conduct of civil-military relations. Most treatments of American civil-military relations (mine included) privilege the executive branch because of the primacy of the president as commander in chief, but the legislative branch is important as well. In the empirical applications of agency theory presented in Chapters 5, 6, and 7, this central fact was incorporated into the model as one of the exogenous factors that affect the likelihood of civilian punishment: when civilian principals are in agreement, the military has a higher expectation of punishment for shirking but when civilian principals disagree, the military has the opportunity to play one principal off the other and thereby get away with behavior that, from the perspective of one of the principals, would constitute shirking.

Future extensions of the agency model might incorporate more directly the idea of split principals. The unified-principal assumption could be relaxed in future versions to consider strategic interaction among more players, although such a step might make the model intractable to formal analysis. There might be ways to differentiate systematically between the various preferences of the civilian players. For instance, executive civilians might care more about efficient delegation when it comes to the use of force than do members of Congress, thus making the legislative players less concerned about civilian monitoring that would sabotage an operation. Once differentiated, the constellations of civilian preferences could be aggregated (which would be the functional equivalent of replicating the unitary-principal assumption) or perhaps be modeled as a prior game in a larger, nested principal-agent game.

Another simplifying assumption that could be relaxed in future research is the game's requirement that the military agent consider only pure strategies (shirk or not shirk) for any given monitoring condition. In practice, the military agent probably considers a mixed strategy, shirking part of the time and working part of the time, for instance as a way of testing a new president. Although the formal analysis in Chapter 4 considered only pure strategies, the empirical applications in Chapters 5, 6, and 7, allowed for something of a mixed strategy by way of a loose coding system for working and shirking. Thus *instances* rather than generalized patterns of shirking were considered; when the military was said to shirk, for example, on gays in the military, the coding was limited to that issue area even though in strict terms the formal model would expect generalized shirking. Future extensions of agency theory may want to formalize the mixed strategy option to see what analytical insights result.

Future analysis might also revisit the simplifying assumption that civilians never punish working. A further assumption is embedded within this: that civilians always know when the military has worked, but when the military does not work, the civilian does not know whether this is (punishable) shirking or some other (nonpunishable) behavior. In this way, the agency model assumes away a plausible outcome that may deserve closer scrutiny in follow-on work: the possibility that the civilian will punish the military even though it is working. One could treat the game as if the uncertainty over unobservable behavior were even more profound. The civilian might not be sure whether the military worked *or* shirked. This would leave open the possibility that the civilian might think the military had shirked and so punish even though in fact the military had not. It is not clear what the implications for agency theory would be in expanding the players' uncertainty in this way, but it could capture the well-known political phenomenon of scapegoating—punishing an actor when something bad happens, regardless of whether it is clear that the unfortunate actor deserves the punishment.[6]

The use of economics jargon encourages thinking of the civil-military relationship at least partly in economic market terms, and this suggests other interesting extensions of the model. Is the military agent really a monopoly supplier, and is the principal really a monopsony buyer? If so, does this change the bargaining relationship? In fact, traditional civil-military relations theory has noted that the military is not a monopoly supplier; military services compete with each other, and service rivalry has the advantage of avoiding what Huntington called strategic monism, or undue reliance on one narrow military approach to national security (Huntington 1961a, pp. 369–381). When civilians want to do something, they can let the market of services bid for the mission. This helps explain why Special Forces are more popular with civilians than they are with the regular military. Special Forces usually underbid the regular forces for military missions, offering to do the job with fewer troops, fewer casualties, and thus lower political capital at risk. Likewise, changes in the threat environment—which have the effect of changing the demand for military services—along with changes in the supply of military services—through the presence of other agencies like the CIA, the Drug Enforcement Agency, and the like—may increase market pressure on the military to adapt. The regular military has an incentive to control the "pricing" of missions. To what extent are civilians and military aware of these latent market forces in what is often assumed to be a non-market relationship?[7]

The foregoing suggests considering other costs of delegation in future extensions of the model. In Chapter 3, I treated the costs of delegating more or less in terms of "intentional" disobedience on the part of the military. Drawing on the transaction-cost analogy, it is also instructive to consider the costs of inefficient outcomes that result not from disobedience but rather from market conditions. The economics literature has shown that the costs of bargaining (and therefore the costs of buying on the market) are a function of coordination costs—that is, the difficulty actors have in coming to a mutually acceptable contract (Milgrom and Roberts 1990). These costs, in turn, increase when there is less competition in the market; the less competitive the market, the greater the likelihood that mutually self-interested actors will settle on a contract that is suboptimal in terms of overall economic efficiency. In the civil-military context, competition is a function of service rivalry. The more the military is unified, the less service rivalry or "competition" there is before the civilian decisionmaker. Thus, the more unified the military, the more likely delegating to the military (buying the policy rather than making the policy) will produce a suboptimal outcome, hence the greater the costs of delegating; the greater the costs of delegating, the less likely it is that civilians will delegate. This produces the counterintuitive hypothesis that the more joint the U.S. military is, the less civilians will delegate to the military (or at least the greater the incentive civilians will have *not* to delegate). Of course a more unified military is able to act more strategically and so is better able to resist assertions of civilian control. Empirically, it could produce the same de facto level of delegation, although it would be a result of greater military resistance to greater efforts by civilians *not* to delegate. *Ceteris paribus,* this means greater jointness could lead to greater civil-military friction.

Still another extension to the game would involve making punishment endogenously derived in the model. Currently, the likelihood of punishment is determined by exogenous factors such as the relative strength of the civilian leader and the salience of the issue at stake. The punishment move could be made endogenous to the game, perhaps as a function of the type of monitoring adopted by civilians. For instance, choosing intrusive monitoring could be an indication that the civilians are more likely to punish any shirking detected—civilians who bear the costs of conducting this intrusive monitoring are signaling that they are particularly sensitive to shirking. Alternatively, intrusive monitoring by Congress may simultaneously increase the likelihood that shirking is exposed but decrease the likelihood that the shirking is punished. The public nature of congressional oversight increases the likelihood that the punishment process will be politicized. This, in turn, could modify our expectations of the conditions under which the military will work or shirk.

In sum, one of the virtues of the method on which agency theory rests is that the assumptions that drive the model are more explicit than would be the case in an informal or inductively derived argument. Thus, it is easy to see how to build on the argument through normal social-scientific procedures: tweaking assumptions, exploring the logical implications of those changes, testing those implications against historical evidence, and returning to the model to revisit the assumptions and internal logic. I hope that the agency model will be developed and improved upon in this fashion.

Normative Concerns: Revisiting the Problematique

The application of agency theory I have presented focuses on just one side of the problematique, namely the mechanisms for implementing civilian control over the military, and has paid relatively less attention to the other side, how civilian control might affect the ability of the military to carry out its functional role to defend and advance the national interest. One must begin somewhere, and this is a reasonable place to begin the development of a new theory of civil-military relations. Moreover, this focus has the virtue of hewing to one of the bedrock foundations of democratic theory: voters should get the leaders they elect, even if the leaders they elect are less desirable than the alternatives they rejected. Civilian principals are to be obeyed even when they are wrong about what is needed for national security. Civilians have the right to be wrong. But in what ways can the civilians turn out to be wrong, and how wrong are they likely to be? What are the costs of civilian control?

The principal-agent literature has long understood the perverse aspects of any agency relationship. Agents have incentives to try to waste time influencing or even manipulating decisionmakers rather than doing the job asked of them (Milgrom and Roberts 1988). These efforts can be costly and can lower the overall utility achieved by the political enterprise. But these are largely costs imposed by recalcitrant agents. At least in the civil-military context, there are also potential costs imposed by foolish principals. And even nominally wise principals impose costs because of potentially perverse side effects of civilian control measures.

One of the goals of healthy civil-military relations is providing adequate security for the polity. As discussed in Chapter 3, however, working means doing what civilians ask, and this is not synonymous with meeting the security needs of the polity. Foolish civilian principals can ask for things that will have the ultimate effect of undermining national security. A prime debate during the early post–Cold War era was over whether President Clinton's avowed desire to lift the ban on gays serving openly in the military would harm national security by undermining military cohesion and military effectiveness. It was relatively clear what the president wanted, that is, what was working and what was shirking. It was less clear whether what the president wanted was good for the military and for national security. Indeed, just such a rhetorical defense could probably underlie every instance of military shirking—"We must not do what civilians want because that would be bad for the country." Every coup leader frames his seizure of political control as an effort to rescue the state from the predations of an inept government. And even relatively wise requests and faithful working can come a cropper if some external enemy is lucky or somehow more capable.

The means by which civilians exercise control can influence the likelihood of ultimate success or failure in the provision of adequate national security. Concerns on this point were the motivating force behind Huntington's theory of civilian control. The "requisite" for national security in the Cold War, Huntington argued, was a change in America's national ideology that would allow for objective civilian control (Huntington 1957, p. 464). Huntington understood that there is a perverse side to control mechanisms. Intrusive civilian monitoring can become micromanagement, interfering with the military function perhaps at a crucial time. Shirking and working have several different components, both functional, concerning what civilians want, and relational, concerning the preservation of the civilians' prerogative to decide for themselves what they want. Control measures aimed at one might adversely affect others. Thus, the intrusive monitoring may create an incentive for the military to obey but may interfere with its ability to obey. Nonintrusive monitoring can become so delegative, ceding so much autonomy to the military, that basic civilian prerogatives are undermined. More fundamental even than these concerns is the fact that control mechanisms must balance what I have elsewhere called the always/never dilemma—the need for the military to function both safely and reliably (Feaver 1992, pp. 12–28). Measures designed to make the military operate more safely may undermine the reliability of the military, and vice versa.

These problems are in some sense unavoidable, but what Eliot Cohen has called the "normal theory of civil-military relations" goes a step further and claims that these problems are more likely when civilians monitor intrusively (Cohen 2000, 2001). Civilians, it is argued, are less knowledgeable about military matters than are the uniformed military experts, and so more likely to be wrong about military affairs. The civil-military challenge, from this point of view, is for military experts to educate civilian amateurs before civilian ignorance damages national security—and to do so without undermining the role of the civilian as principal.

Are civilians more likely than the military to be wrong on the important matters of national security? This is an article of faith, at least among American military officers and possibly even in the traditional literature on civil-military relations. One can trace the theme from Emory Upton through Samuel Huntington to recent literature on the Vietnam War and the Gulf War (Upton 1917, Huntington 1957, McMaster 1997, Johnson 1996).[8] The normative implication is clear: delegative control, nonintrusive monitoring, gives the military the necessary free hand to translate civilian orders into successful national security (and if necessary, to improve on them so as to achieve it). Cohen shows, however, that delegative control is not always the best model for battlefield success. Moreover, the proper limits of delegation are best determined not by military expertise but by political calculation (Cohen 2001; Brodie 1973, pp. 416–419, 456–457). Civilians are better positioned to judge the political underpinnings of military policy. Even in areas of obvious military expertise, tactics and operations, the best performance on the battlefield may come as the result of the very questioning, probing, auditing, and even hectoring that an intrusive monitoring regime would entail. Civilians ought to listen to military advice and weigh it, but military advice will improve with a vigorous give-and-take led by activist civilian principals.

This truth may not be sufficiently well appreciated even in relatively healthy civil-military systems like the one the United States enjoys. Yes, the principle of civilian control is well established in the United States, but what that principle means may be contested (Feaver and Kohn 2000a). We may be seeing the emergence of a norm among American military officers that civilian control does not mean that civilians have the right to be wrong. At least concerning decisionmaking on the use of force, officers see no inconsistency between endorsing civilian control and endorsing an "insist" role for the military, where "insist" implies "accept our advice or else we will shirk or resign in protest." The reason for this is not contempt for the principle of civilian control but rather concern that to do otherwise would be to risk national security.[9] But the effect is pernicious for the principle of civilian control and, if history is any guide, is not a more sure path to better national security. Shirking undermines democracy. Even resigning in protest, if generalized, is a troubling reaction, for it threatens to hold the civilian principal hostage to the preferences of the military agent. On the battlefield and at the tactical level, resigning in protest is called mutiny, and it is punished severely. At the strategic-political level, would not mass or highly salient resignations in protest be almost as poisonous for civil-military relations?

This does not mean that the military obligation to work is absolute. The military has an obligation to shirk illegal orders. But this is exceedingly narrowly circumscribed. The military has only very limited competence to adjudicate the legality of civilian orders. There must be a very strong presumption that an order from the national command authority is legal.[10] And the military has an obligation to advise strenuously against legal but foolish orders—in fact, at some point individual military agents may be compelled by conscience to offer up their resignation if they can no longer faithfully execute a policy. But this action should be rare and very carefully circumscribed, lest it undermine the ability of civilians to be the principals in the civil-military relationship.[11]

In yet another way, agency theory suggests that the military's ability to avoid shirking faces some structural limits, at least in a democracy. In a democracy, the ultimate principal, the voter, relies on various political agents—the executive branch, the legislative branch, and the judiciary—to monitor each other and also to monitor the military. The checks and balances are built into the American system of civilian control, requiring the military to answer to all three branches but, on a day-to-day basis, especially to the executive and legislative branches. The historical record suggests that this divided-principal arrangement may be a necessary part of *democratic*, as opposed to merely *civilian*, control of the military. Likewise, in a healthy democracy the media play a vital watchdog role that involves investigating and reporting on the doings of all these agents. If the foregoing is accepted, then it may be impossible to eliminate entirely the opportunity for shirking.[12] Shirking involves end runs around the chain of command to Congress, but at some level this may be an inevitable consequence of democratic control. Shirking involves leaks to the media, but the media are hard-pressed to perform their watchdog function without leaks. This paradox is not a problem for agency theory as an explanation, but it does point to a limit to agency theory as a prescription. From an agency perspective, the military may at times find itself trapped in a dirty-hands dilemma in which any choice amounts to shirking.

Of course, the more ably the principal performs its function, the fewer of those instances there are likely to be. If the military has an obligation to work, civilians have even more of an obligation to fulfill their role responsibly. If civilian leaders are not responsibly managing the military, then the ultimate civilian principal, the electorate, has an obligation to punish its agents, the elected officials. This requires that voters monitor how civilian leaders are conducting civil-military relations and vote accordingly. Unfortunately, in the U.S. case, neither civilian leaders nor, especially, voters are likely to give civil-military relations the attention it deserves (Kohn 1997). Sometimes the system works, albeit imperfectly, late, and at great cost; the voters punished President Lyndon Johnson, forcing him to forgo a run for reelection, because of Johnson's Vietnam policies. A special challenge in recent civil-military relations in the United States was the feeling on the part of many military agents that their civilian principal, President Clinton, was not held responsible for his civil-military mismanagement by *his* principals, the electorate and public opinion. Civil-military relations will undoubtedly improve with better civilian leaders and deteriorate with worse leaders. A priority for observers of civil-military relations must be an effort to hold civilians accountable with the same or greater vigor with which military agents are held accountable.

But in the final analysis, the health of the democracy depends as much on the health of the institutions as it does on the quality of the people running the institutions—as much on respect for the process of democratic politics as on the substance of the policies that process yields. Civilian control of the military is a crucial democratic institution, and agency theory shows how that process works in practice. History shows that the military is not as "right" in civil-military disputes as the military triumphalists might suppose. But even when the military is right, democratic theory intervenes and insists that it submit to the civilian leadership that the polity has chosen. Let civilian voters punish civilian leaders for wrong decisions. Let the military advise against foolish adventures, even advising strenuously when circumstances demand. But let the military execute those orders faithfully. The republic would be better served even by foolish working than by enlightened shirking.

NOTES

REFERENCES

INDEX

Abbreviations

Notes

1. Introduction

1. There are already numerous primarily historical works that cover these periods. See Kolodziej 1966, Yarmolinsky 1971, Russett and Stepan 1973, Brodie 1973, Cohen 1985, Petraeus 1987, Hendrickson 1988, Betts 1991, Millett and Maslowski 1994, Gacek 1994, Friedberg 2000, Halberstam 2001a, Roman and Tar 2001. Elsewhere I have made more explicitly empirical investigations of U.S. civil-military relations. See Feaver 1992, Feaver and Kohn 2001, Feaver and Gelpi forthcoming.

2. The literature is too vast to summarize here, but some influential ones include Finer 1962, Lyons 1961, Stepan 1971, Perlmutter 1977, and Rouquie 1982.

3. Two important exceptions are Avant 1994 and Desch 1999. Both are institutional in their orientation, like Huntington (not sociological like Janowitz), and both are making similarly sweeping theoretical claims. I address these alternative theories more directly in Chapter 6.

4. This is adapted from Feaver (1996b, 1999). Previously published material is used with the permission of the copyright holders.

5. Of course, the military may not be established solely to protect the polity against external threats. Other motivations—for instance, to preserve the regime's power over the masses or to create the trappings of the modern state for symbolic purposes—may also come into play. Nevertheless, regardless of the motivation for creating the institution, once created, the military raises the same control problematique described in the text.

6. It also arises in authoritarian regimes and even military dictatorships. The very existence of political power creates the delegation-agency problem. In military regimes, even though political leaders and the fighting groups alike wear uniforms, responsibility is nevertheless divided between those who do the fighting and those who remain behind to wield political power. Wearing the same uniform does not prevent those who stay behind from worrying about whether the fighters are adequate to defend them or whether the fighters are liable to turn

around and unseat them, as the many coups and countercoups in military dictatorships attest. This is what Stepan (1971) has called the distinction between the
"military as an institution" and the "military as government." It even arises
when the civilians in question are not yet a state but a transnational organization. See Bar-Or (1995).

7. I will focus on the officer-civilian interface because that is the most important
for civilian control. For stylistic reasons, I use "soldier," "sailor," and "officer" as
synonymous for military. Where necessary for the argument, I will distinguish
between enlisted and officers.

8. Picking Huntington as a foil begs the question of which Huntington to select. I
use his major theoretical exposition (Huntington 1957) even though there were
others that show a slightly different model. Huntington seemed to retreat from
his *Soldier and State* framework a bit in Huntington 1963, where he addressed
two dominant trends: (1) the military's increasing need for expertise (suggesting
an expertise gap favorable to civilians that surely was shaped by the fact that he
was writing during the McNamara years) and (2) the declining power and influence of the military. This treatment showed more of the pulling and hauling
among competing interest groups of the kind contemplated in agency theory
than one finds in *The Soldier and the State*. Nevertheless, when assigned to evaluate explicitly the Huntington model of civil-military relations, Huntington himself reverted to the more restrictive treatment of *The Soldier and the State*. See
Goodpaster and Huntington 1977.

9. See Janowitz 1971, pp. xiii–liv, and contrast him with more severe critiques like
Lyons (1961) or Miles (1968).

10. I myself have made this observation with respect to nuclear weapons, in Feaver
1992.

11. Consider recent efforts to subcontract out military functions to private firms. See
Avant manuscript.

12. Contrast the remarkably similar conclusions of the following diverse group of
writings: Sapin and Snyder 1954, Barrett 1965, Russett and Stepan 1973, Lovell
1974, Slater 1977, Sarkesian 1981, Bland 2001, Roman and Tarr 2001, Nelson
2001.

13. The principal-agent approach is rare but not entirely absent in studies of American foreign and defense policy. See Avant 1994, Richards et al. 1993, Lindsay
1994a, Downs and Rocke 1995, Zegart 1996, Weiner 1997, Goemans 2000.

2. Huntington's Cold War Puzzle

1. Lebow and Stein 1994. Despite their provocatively titled book, *We All Lost the
Cold War*, Lebow and Stein in fact argue only that the strategies of deterrence
and compellence were more dangerous than is generally accepted, and that reliance on such confrontational strategies may have precipitated some crises while
prolonging the superpower contest beyond when it otherwise might have
ended. This is a far cry from losing the Cold War. And, in any case, Lebow and

Stein are not suggesting that the Cold War produced the Huntingtonian nightmare of the Soviet Union prevailing over an underdefended United States.

2. This is the solution offered by Aaron Friedberg (2000) and Josef Joffe (1993) for
an analogous civil-military puzzle: why Harold Lasswell's (1941, 1950, and
1962) predictions that the United States would become a "garrison state"
proved false. Friedberg and Joffe conclude that Lasswell's logic was correct, but
that nuclear weapons provided security on the cheap. See also the evaluation of
Lasswell's model in Clotfelter 1969.

3. Goodpaster and Huntington 1977, pp. 11–15. Huntington cited surveys reviewed in Russett 1974b.

4. He cited the Yom Kippur War, the problems with SALT II, the collapse of South
Vietnam, and the Soviet-Cuban operation in Angola as precipitating factors for
renewed support for military spending. Goodpaster and Huntington 1977, p. 16.

5. There is a disconnect between the way Huntington coded the 1950s in the two
works cited here. *Soldier and the State* was far less sanguine about how favorable
the climate of the 1950s was for Huntington's prescriptions than was the 1977
reconsideration of his theory. In general, *Soldier and the State* treated the emergence of a favorable ideological climate as a future possibility while the 1977 article treated it as a past reality. In the final pages of *Soldier and the State*, Huntington was at best guardedly optimistic: "While liberalism continued to dominate
the American approach to civil-military relations in the postwar decade, some
evidence also existed of the beginnings of a fundamental change which might
herald the emergence of a new, more sympathetically conservative environment
for military institutions. These beginnings by no means constituted a major revolution in the American intellectual climate. But, if continued and enlarged
upon, they would facilitate the establishment of a new equilibrium in civil-military relations compatible with the security demands of the Cold War" (Huntington 1957, p. 457). Looking back in 1977, however, Huntington identified the
1950s as the high-water mark for the kind of public attitudes to the level and
use of military force his theory prescribed (Goodpaster and Huntington 1977,
p. 11).

6. While I am focusing on the links between the earlier and the later steps in Huntington's theory, others have criticized the empirical validity of the crucial inter-
mediary stage in Huntington's argument: the link between professionalism and
unwavering military obedience. S. E. Finer (1962, pp. 24–27) was perhaps Huntington's sternest critic on this point, arguing that his model reduces to the claim
that armies that accept civilian control will not reject civilian control. Subsequent comparative treatments have emphasized that military organizations that
look professional by most measures have nevertheless conducted coups or otherwise subverted civilian authorities. See also, Janowitz 1971, Abrahamsson
1972, Welch 1976, Stepan 1971, and Rouquie 1982. Even if his critics are right
on this point, however, Huntington might still be correct in claiming that his
form of professionalism is a necessary condition for adequate defense.

7. Janowitz 1971, p. 227. These data are not very reliable indicators of public es-

teem, however, since they appear to reflect the respondents' desire to pursue that career, as opposed to how positively they regard people who have chosen the military profession as a career. Clotfelter (1969, pp. 124–125) found similar results in a 1947 and a 1965 poll but did not interpret them as negatively as did Janowitz. Although analysts rarely comment on the other side of the equation, it is interesting to note that there is some evidence from the early Cold War period to suggest that the military likewise held civilians in low esteem. Huntington (1963, p. 802) cited an unpublished 1954 survey that showed that "32 percent of high-ranking Pentagon staff officers attributed the differences between civilians and military to the professional virtues of the military and the absence of those virtues among the civilians." (Cited to Brown, Henry, and Masland, 1958.) And, of course, the military was quite vocal in expressing its contempt for the McNamara "whiz kids," whom one general dismissed as "pipe-smoking, tree-full-of-owls type[s] of defense intellectuals" (White 1963, pp. 10–12).

8. Note, however, that the data are sparse for the early and mid-1960s. Only one survey, taken in October 1964, had a relevant question. Russett 1974b, pp. 61, 79.

9. Russett later admitted that he was wrong about presuming that the opposition to increased defense spending in the early 1970s represented a "semipermanent change" (Russett 1990, p. 98). Moreover, Russett's 1974 description of public opinion during the late 1960s—"unprecedented" levels of opposition to increases in defense spending ("approximately half the populace")—was partially a function of his choice of opinion surveys. He cited the American Institute of Public Opinion (AIPO) survey result for this time period in 1974, and this particular survey did reflect a dramatic level of opposition. In a later analysis, Hartley and Russett (1992) used an average of several polls and found that the average percentage of respondents who thought the United States was spending too much on defense during the 1965–1975 time period never climbed above 37 percent. The later analysis was more complete, but it did not change substantially the general claim that civilian opposition to greater defense spending peaked in the early 1970s.

10. The point is made even more starkly by considering public attitudes immediately after the end of the Cold War. The public supported a decrease in defense spending by large margins, even while the military as an institution enjoyed unprecedentedly high levels of public respect. Gallup 1991, pp. 5 and 100.

11. Joffe's rebuttal of Lasswell's prediction applies *a fortiori* to Huntington: "To list these developments [the expansion of political participation and individual rights during the Cold War] is merely to belabor the obvious" (Joffe 1993, p. 111). See also Putnam 1995.

12. Ironically, Huntington made a similar observation concerning leftist worries about the military-industrial complex, and his explanation could rationalize his own timing problem. In observing that public and elite concern about the power of the military-industrial complex came on the heels of the decline in force levels of the early 1970s, rather than a decade earlier, when Eisenhower warned of

a coming crisis, Huntington opined: "In American society, whenever the power of an organization or group is being exposed, it is also in the process of being reduced." Perhaps Huntington's own concern for the negative side-effects of American liberalism was precipitated by—rather than precipitated—its temporary decline. Goodpaster and Huntington 1977, p. 15.

13. Elite polling would be preferable to mass polling because it would more closely reflect the viewpoints of the relevant political actors in the civil-military relationship, the governmental policymakers. Censoring the data in this way probably overstates any convergence, if other arguments about an elite-mass divergence in opinions have merit. Since the data presented in the text do not support the convergence hypothesis, this possible bias lends greater weight to the findings. See Mills 1956 for arguments about an elite-mass gap in policy preferences, especially on matters relating to national security. See Russett 1990 for an argument that the elite-mass gap has been overstated.

14. The compilers of a massive annotated bibliography on civil-military relations published in 1973 concluded that "many of our entries reflect the declining popularity in recent years of military institutions and values." Douglas H. Rosenberg and Maj. Raoul H. Alcala, "The New Politics of National Security: A Selected and Annotated Research Bibliography," in Russett and Stepan 1973, p. 199.

15. Russett and Hanson conducted a survey of business elites drawn from a sample of high-level vice presidents from Fortune 500 firms, and military elites, relatively senior officers (lieutenant colonel/commander and colonel/navy captain) enrolled in the five war colleges (The Air War College, Army War College, Naval War College, National War College, and the Industrial College of the Armed Forces). Russett and Hanson then compared their business-military results to another 1971–72 survey of other civilian elites. Russett and Hanson (1975).

16. Note that this interpretation of the polling data is somewhat different from the one Russett himself offered. When he directly addressed Huntington's "military mind" thesis, Russett concluded: "Together these findings suggest that the political relevance, and even the distinctiveness, of any special 'military mind' is not very great, certainly no greater than that of businessmen themselves" (Russett 1974a, p. 97). Although he intended this to be a criticism of Huntington's 1957 theory, it might be at least partial confirmation of Huntington's interpretation of the Cold War. However, as explained in the text, the divergence of opinion even between the military and the relatively conservative business elite was rather greater on defense-oriented items and was pronounced across the range of issues with civilian elites as a whole (business plus other civilian groups), Russett 1974a, p. 93. Indeed, Russett concluded with an observation that directly undermined the Huntington interpretation of the Cold War: "On many matters that *might* be construed as in the sphere of professional military expertise, but where constitutional authority is vested in civilians, the civilian-military differences in policy preferences are great" (p. 98).

17. Russett and Hanson also found strong support for one of Huntington's implicit claims: that domestic ideology on a broad social conservative-liberal dimension

correlates with narrow foreign policy preferences. In predicting a foreign policy preference, one's domestic ideology, as reflected in views on civil rights and civil liberties, carried greater explanatory weight than one's economic material interest. Russett and Hanson 1975, pp. 248–249.

18. The survey was conducted as part of the Foreign Policy Leadership Project (FPLP), which has conducted surveys of elite opinion on foreign policy in 1976, 1980, 1984, 1988, 1992, and 1996. Each survey year, questionnaires were mailed to roughly 4,000 opinion leaders drawn from general sources such as *Who's Who in America* and *Who's Who in American Women*. To reach leaders in occupations that were underrepresented in *Who's Who*—for example, media figures, politicians, military officers, labor leaders, State Department personnel, and academic foreign policy experts—Holsti and Rosenau also pulled names from specialized directories. In the 1976 survey, the military sample consisted of some 500 respondents drawn from officers serving as students at the Naval Post-Graduate School as well as a smaller number of senior uniformed military officers serving in the Pentagon whose names were drawn randomly from the *Congressional Directory*. I am grateful to Ole Holsti for providing me access to the raw data on which the analyses presented in the text and the tables are based.

19. In his own analysis of civil-military divergence, Holsti used an index to categorize attitudes to the modality of American involvement in world affairs. He found that during the Cold War those in the military were consistently more "internationalist" or "hard-liner" than civilians, who were primarily "accommodationist." Internationalists support cooperative (e.g., UN) and military international involvement, hard-liners support only military international involvement, and accomodationists support only cooperative international involvement. Neither the civilian nor the military group had more than 10 percent of the respondents appearing as isolationists, who support neither military nor cooperative international involvement. See Holsti 1997.

20. The FPLP followed the same basic survey design throughout this period. The military sample, however, changed. In 1976, the survey was administered to officers serving as students at the Naval Post-Graduate School. In every subsequent survey, the officer sample consisted of students serving at the National War College. The National War College samples were smaller and ranged between 115 and 177 officers.

21. Indeed, Vietnam was explicitly invoked in the preamble to the question in the 1976, 1980, and 1984 surveys. The specific reference was dropped in 1988 and replaced with "past experiences abroad."

22. Whether the Weinberger doctrine is, in fact, Clausewitzean is debatable. Gacek (1994, pp. 262–272) argues that it is Jominian because the criteria have the net effect of establishing an "all or nothing" threshold for the use of force, whereas a Clausewitzean approach would allow for more political uses.

23. There is only sketchy evidence on whether the American public *wanted* this kind of civilian control. A World War II survey found that 64 percent of the public

thought military and naval leaders, not Roosevelt and Churchill, should have "the final decision on the military and naval plans of the war." Similarly, a Vietnam-era poll found that 52 percent agreed and 34 percent disagreed with the statement, "In wartime, civilian government leaders should let the military take over running the war." In the same poll, however, 58 percent agreed and 29 percent disagreed with the statement, "The President is the Commander-in-Chief, and all important military orders should come from him." Clotfelter 1973, p. 126. Even if the apparent contradiction in the Vietnam poll could be explained away, it is not clear whether this was capturing support for objective control as Huntington envisaged it or reflecting the kind of spasmodic and pathological abdication of civilian control that Huntington considered characteristic of liberal societies in a war, especially in World War II.

24. In his 1977 update, Huntington did not discuss objective control and its relationship to professionalism, adopting instead the Janowitzean language of congruence/convergence. For Huntington, congruence with civilian institutions—measured in terms of personnel, function, and structure—varied negatively with professionalism: the greater the congruence the less professional was the military. During the early Cold War, Huntington saw greater congruence (hence less professionalism), but he claimed the trends reversed in the early 1970s with the abandonment of the draft and the decline of the Reserve Officers' Training Corps (ROTC) at elite schools. Goodpaster and Huntington 1977, pp. 22–25.

25. James S. Dickey, "A Personal Statement," in Russett and Stepan 1973, p. 18. To be fair, Huntington did note that the desirability of the traditional division of labor was very much in dispute during this period and so Dickey's assessment can be discounted as part of this debate. Goodpaster and Huntington 1977, p. 24.

3. The Informal Agency Theory

1. Peterson 1992 reverses the causal arrow and has the military inventing outside enemies to create the civilian state. Peterson's argument is a highly implausible general explanation of military politics, but even if it were true, it does not amount to a qualitative change in the civil-military problematique. At most, if true, it might intensify the difficulties associated therewith.

2. For an overview of the literature see: Hammond, Hill, and Miller 1986; Bendor 1988; and Spence (no date). For an introduction to the now-standard applications see: Altfeld and Miller 1984; Ferejohn and Shipan 1990; Kiewet and McCubbins 1991; McNollgast 1987, 1989, 1990a, 1990b; McCubbins and Schwartz 1984; Mitnick 1975, 1994; Moe 1984, 1987; and Weingast and Moran 1983. (Note that McNollgast is a pseudonym for Mathew D. McCubbins, Roger G. Noll, and Barry R. Weingast.)

3. For a representative account of the abdication thesis, which constitutes the chief foil of most political applications of the principal-agent framework, see Schoenbrod 1993. Bendor points out, however, that economic applications of

the principal-agent framework tend to conclude the opposite point: that even if the principal knows a great deal, control inefficiencies can still emerge (Bendor 1988).

4. Thus, the principal-agent framework stands between two extreme forms of analysis, one that concludes bureaucracies are hopelessly uncontrollable and one that concludes democratic institutions work nearly perfectly. For a provocative example of the latter approach, see Wittman 1995.

5. There are still other applications of the principal-agent framework to security questions. Jervis (1976, pp. 332–342) uses a similar metaphor to understand the difficulty of reliable crisis management. Lindsay (1994a) evaluates the congressional dominance hypothesis and Congress's role in foreign policymaking. Richards et al. (1993), Goemans (2000), and Downs and Rocke (1995) use a principal-agent argument to examine leaders' incentives to initiate external conflicts or to continue fighting. These are the only security applications of which I am aware.

6. Of course, there is an anomaly in applying the principal-agent framework to the civil-military setting. There is not really a market of agents; the civilian cannot hire from many different militaries to do its work. The principal can create new military agents, and does so from time to time, but there is something of a monopoly in providing security. At the same time, the government enjoys a monopsomy in purchasing security. See Brenner 2001 for a further exploration of these features. The increasing use of private security firms by governments and large multinational corporations may represent a fundamental change in this traditional feature of civil-military relations; see Avant manuscript.

7. I am not trying to give the history of the evolution of civilian control in Western society. I am describing a notional evolution that would establish the kind of agency relationship we have today. A useful survey of the evolution of the military is Lynn 1996.

8. The range of civilian choices could be expanded further. When facing a security issue, the principal's first choice is whether to deal with it himself or to delegate it to the agent. On the one hand, the more that is delegated to the military the less the burden on civilians. On the other hand, delegation carries with it risks that the will of civilians will be flouted. The decision to start war, for instance, has rarely been delegated to the military, while the preparation for war has. The next choice is whether to delegate the security issue to an existing agent or to create a new agent. On the one hand, delegating to an existing agent has fewer transaction costs because the relationship is already established. On the other hand, delegating too much, or too often, to one agent may make that agent too powerful—and if the mission is sufficiently novel, the old agent may not be qualified to handle it. In the earliest days of the Cold War, civilian principals clearly felt that the nuclear mission was too novel and important to be delegated in toto to the traditional defense establishment so they created a new agent, the Atomic Energy Commission. Only after all these choices have been settled does the principal face the question of how to monitor the agent. For the game-theo-

retic analysis developed here, I collapse the delegation and the "which agent" choices into the monitoring decision. As discussed in the text, restrictive delegation and creating new agents are treated as special forms of monitoring. In an earlier decision-theoretic cut at the problem (Feaver 1996c), I analyzed the delegation and the monitoring decisions separately, but my analysis showed that with rationalist assumptions these decisions should closely correlate. Zegart (1999), Avant (1994), and (Feaver 1992) all looked at the decision to create new agents. In future work, it may prove fruitful to build an expanded principal-agent game that includes all of these decisions sequentially.

9. Deborah Avant (1994, p. 12) lays particular stress on this phenomenon, arguing that the inertia built into an organization is its "institutional bias." When civilians ask the military to innovate in ways contrary to this original delegation, in other words to lean against the institutional bias, military organizations will resist more vigorously than when civilians press them to accept doctrinal innovations that are consistent with this original delegation.

10. The monitoring-shirking interaction continues down the chain of command as senior military commanders wrestle with the problem of how to delegate authority to junior commanders. Micromanagement by senior military officers is as prevalant, perhaps more so, than micromanagement by civilian leaders. Likewise, the interaction continues higher within the civilian branch as well. For instance, Lebow argues forcefully that Kissinger shirked extensively (committed "political sabotage," in Lebow's terms) during the 1973 Middle East crisis: ignoring direct orders and resisting the implementation of others so as to pursue a strategy favored by Kissinger himself. Lebow 1988, pp. 52–58. I focus on the civil-military interface because it is central to democratic theory, but the approach could be profitably extended to examine agency within other parts of the national security establishment.

11. Brehm and Gates (1997) distinguish between two types of nonworking: sabotage, or actively undermining the policy objective of the principal, and shirking, or directing effort to nonpolicy goals like leisure. Sabotage is "negative work," since it directly works against production of the outcome desired by the principal; shirking simply introduces inefficiencies, such as excessively long coffee breaks. The authors hint at an even finer-grained typology including "go slow" behavior, "work-to-rule," "leisure-shirking" (not working because one does not feel like it), "dissent-shirking" (not working because one is opposed to the policy), and so on. For my basic treatment, I follow the standard convention and lump all forms of noncompliant behavior into the general category of shirking. Most of the examples of military shirking examined here are what Brehm and Gates call sabotage and dissent-shirking.

12. The assumption of an industrious military is not universally valid, of course. In some countries, the military commitment to state security is almost certainly disingenuous. In those settings, a more colloquial understanding of working/shirking may be acceptable. For the U.S. case this is clearly *not* appropriate, but that does not mean shirking is absent. One does not need to question the com-

mitment of the civilians or the military to the common goal of national security to find considerable disagreements over how to achieve it. In either case, the logic of the agency model works the same.

13. This is a subset of what Bouchard (1991) calls "coupled" action, where tactical military operations are consonant with political strategic directives. Shirking is therefore "decoupled" action: "the extent that operational decisions on the employment of military forces made at the strategic and tactical levels differ from the operational decisions political-level decisionmakers would have made to coordinate those military actions with their political-diplomatic strategy for resolving the crisis" (p. 43). Bouchard considers both accidental and deliberate decoupling, and further distinguishes between constructive and malicious unauthorized action. As I use the term, *shirking* refers only to deliberate actions, whether constructive or malicious, that deviate from what civilians wanted (Bouchard 1991, pp. 25–30).

14. This is analogous to Oliver Williamson's distinction between consummate cooperation and perfunctory cooperation. See Williamson 1992, p. 385. Working does not mean going beyond the call of duty to perform supererogatory feats. Moreover, a principal could always contract with an agent to work at half-speed, in which case the agent would be working if he worked at half-speed, even if he was physically able to work much faster or harder.

15. These first two relational goals are consistent with Kemp and Hudlin's thesis that civilian supremacy is not achieved unless the civilian decides both the ends of policy and the dividing line between ends and means. See Kemp and Hudlin 1992; and Kohn 2002.

16. Zisk 1993. This assumption flows directly from a principle tenet of traditional civil-military relations: that there is something called the "military mind." See Sapin and Snyder 1954, pp. 19–20. While the exact content of the military's preferences is debatable—and stereotypes about "military rigidity" and "insensitivity to political factors" may be overblown—their existence is not. This is akin to what Brehm and Gates (1997) call functional preferences. Wilson (1989, pp. 54–55) suggests that the linkage between beliefs (in my usage, policy preferences) and behavior among bureaucrats is marginal. However, as his subsequent discussion makes clear, he is really making two different claims. First, he shows that there are multiple sources for the beliefs of bureaucrats. Organizational cultural norms and other factors contribute to the beliefs of bureaucrats; it is not simply personal political ideology that determines a preference. Second, Wilson notes that these beliefs are not translated *directly* into behavior but are filtered through other factors including the control mechanisms in place to govern the bureaucracy. Wilson clarifies this confusion on p. 156 by noting that "bureaucrats have preferences and these include definitions of how the job *ought to be done* as well as how much it ought to pay." This is entirely consistent with my argument in the text.

17. This goes against an older literature on militarism that caricatures the military as glory seeking and hence war prone, as typified in Vagts 1937.

18. This is akin to what Brehm and Gates (1997) call solidary preferences.

19. It is the hallmark of what Wilson means by "professional"—one who receives important occupational rewards from the other members of a narrowly defined reference group—and it also forms an important part of what he means by "organizational culture"—a "persistent, patterned way of thinking about the central tasks and human relationships within an organization" (Wilson 1989, pp. 60, 91).

20. Bouchard notes that navy regulations specifically authorize "unauthorized actions" if the commanding officer believes he must act contrary to orders to save his ship. In such a case, the officer must immediately report his actions, which can then be reversed (and punished) as superior commanders decide. Bouchard 1991, pp. 30–31.

21. As we shall see, however, the distance between what is asked for and the ideal point can be affected by the cost variables incorporated in the agency model.

22. Petraeus 1987, pp. 286–288. Summers 1982, pp. 33–44. This is part of a more general shirking tactic in which the military resists drawing up contingency plans so that the civilian leadership will not be able to select choices and give orders that the military finds distasteful. The military sought to resist option generation in nuclear war planning and sought to resist contingency planning for Central America during the early 1980s, and even during the build-up phase of the Gulf War in 1990. On nuclear weapons, see Nolan 1989, pp. 54–57; on the Central American case, see Petraeus 1987, pp. 209–223; on the Gulf War case, see Rowen 1995.

23. Even some army officers concur with this estimation; Johnson 1996, p. 36. An army apologist might demur, noting that civilian leaders had ample opportunity to propose alternative force structures. That sets the bar for military insubordination too high to be meaningful in a democracy. The fact that the U.S. Army was able to get civilian leaders to bless individual decisions whose collective effect was to weaken civilian authority is testimony to the army's political savvy. But it does not change the fact that the army leadership set out to undermine the ability of civilians to take a course of action that they might otherwise adopt, just as a civilian figurehead does not change the reality of a military coup.

24. At the same time, military performance on the battlefield does provide civilians with after-the-fact information on how adequate the military is for the tasks assigned to it. Thus, while monitoring the military during a battle may be more difficult, monitoring the military after operations is easier, or at least is facilitated by the information generated by the operation itself. Of course, the basic information asymmetry continues to disadvantage civilians against the military, because the military will have a better awareness of how well it performed and civilians will still be somewhat dependent on reporting from the military or other third-party actors. Wilson distinguishes between monitoring outputs, what the military is doing, and outcomes, what results from that activity. He claims that the military during peacetime is "procedural," meaning you can observe outputs but not outcomes; in wartime it becomes "craft," where outputs are hard to ob-

serve but outcomes are clear. Wilson 1989, pp. 163–171. I would instead argue that, at least during the conflict, the military is in Wilson's typology a "coping" organization, where neither outputs nor outcomes are easily observable. It is not until the dust has settled that the outcome, success or failure, becomes apparent.

25. Andrew Goodpaster states the idea particularly forcefully: "It is not that all wisdom resides in the military; far from it. Civilian students of strategy, operations, procedures, intelligence methods, procurement practices, educational methods, and training techniques have offered much in the past and continue to do so, though such contributions, be it noted, have not come without effort or intensive application to the facts. But it is the test of combat, or the perceived probable results of the test of combat—the unique domain of the military professional—that ultimately and fundamentally establishes the validity of military posture and action." Goodpaster 1977, p. 32. I would not press this point too far, however, because many civilian officials in the defense arena are combat veterans. The gap between civilian and military is almost certainly more narrow than Goodpaster allows. Civilian expertise grew considerably during the Cold War, whereas combat experience, except among a very small number of officers, did not.

26. Hence this is an even harsher form of agency than Mitnick's "closed agency," where both the information and the action is hidden to the principal. In the civil-military relationship, some information is hidden from the military agent as well. Mitnick 1994.

27. Moe 1984, pp. 754–755. The term *adverse selection* comes from the economics of insurance literature, which has found that insured populations have a higher propensity to experience the adverse consequences insured against than do uninsured populations. In other words, unhealthy (or reckless) people are more likely to want insurance and also more likely to need insurance. From the point of view of a profit-maximizing insurance company, this is adverse selection.

28. The term again comes from the economics of insurance literature. Once insured, individuals have less incentive to take care of their property, since any losses will be covered by the insurance.

29. This section modifies Kiewet and McCubbins's (1991) typology of control mechanisms. They speak of four sets of controls: contracts, screening mechanisms, reporting requirements, and institutional checks. Under reporting requirements, they further distinguish between monitoring through "police patrol" (principal-led inspections) and "fire alarm" (third-party reporting). I collapse these four classes into one intrusive/nonintrusive scale with police patrol referring to all the more intrusive measures and fire alarms referring to all the less intrusive measures.

30. Bouchard refers to these as "indirect mechanisms of control." Bouchard 1991, pp. 32–34.

31. Indeed, Brehm and Gates (1997, p. 18, n. 15) explicitly dismiss this feature: "It is quite evident that the notion of a residual cannot be effectively applied to a governmental bureaucracy." I agree that the concept cannot be translated from

the economic to the political setting easily, but I argue in the text that a plausible analog, autonomy, does play a similar role in political bureaucracies.

32. Smith 1951, p. 3. Likewise, before the rise of professional armies, the military was customarily "given an interest in the economic residual" through the privileges of booty. This is consistent with Andreski's basic claim that obedience of the army to the government is largely a function of whether the government is responsible for equipping and remunerating the army. Andreski 1968, pp. 34–35.

33. According to the Folk Theorem, certain games, including the iterated principal-agent problems of interest in this study, have many equilibria, some involving cooperation (or working) and some involving defection (or shirking). Formal analysis cannot say which particular outcome will obtain or even how players can influence the game to move to their desired outcome. Kreps (1990) and Miller (1992) treat organizational culture as focal points, strategies that naturally draw the attention of players and that distinguish salient equilibria as likely outcomes. Even Alchian and Demsetz (1972), in their original introduction of the principal-agent contract-based approach to the firm, acknowledged that what they called "team spirit and loyalty" could play an important role in reducing shirking.

34. I am indebted to Katherine Brennan, who suggested this idea to me.

35. Huntington (1957, pp. 418–423) disapproves of interservice rivalry but notes that it does prevent strategic monism. In a subsequent work, however, Huntington assigns to interservice rivalry a far more beneficial role in preserving civilian control (Huntington 1961b). He even calls interservice rivalry "a key aspect in the maintenance of civilian control" (1961b, p. 378); and later he says that "the single most significant factor abetting the rise of civilian influence [since World War II] was the continued division of the military against itself" (Huntington 1963, p. 800). These are not necessarily contradictory observations, if the latter two are viewed as accepting an inevitable condition that the former disparaged.

36. These arguments were advanced by the military services themselves, although perhaps for instrumental reasons. Zegart 1996, pp. 129–151.

37. I am indebted to Lauren Aronson for suggesting this idea to me.

38. Kiewet and McCubbins 1991, pp. 33–34. Belkin (1998) speculates that another danger of institutional checks, at least in coup-prone states, is that they foster an aggressive foreign policy, as the civilian principal seeks to distract each of the submilitary components with foreign adventures.

39. They argue, in other words, that adverse selection trumps moral hazard. Solve the adverse selection problem and you do not need to worry about moral hazard. Fail to solve adverse selection, they argue, and no reasonable amount of monitoring can prevent moral hazard. Brehm and Gates 1992b, 1997. Chayes and Chayes (1995) extend this claim to the field of international law.

40. Even Brehm and Gates concede this point (1997, p. 200–201).

41. Taylor 1996, Weber 1996. The classical/neoclassical debate is explained in Shafritz and Ott 1996, pp. 96–99. See also Bachman, Bowers, and Marcus 1968.

42. Larson 1974, p. 57. See also Janowitz's explicit "rejection of economic self-interest theories" that emphasize coercive control, Janowitz 1991, pp. 73–74. The often underappreciated similarities in the role norms play in Huntington's and
Janowitz's theories is explained in Feaver (1996b). In this way, Brehm and
Gates's conclusion that the key to ensuring that agents work lies in the recruit-
ment of the right sort of agents, and in on-the-job education to turn wrong sorts
into the right sort, is consistent with a long-held tenet of the civil-military relations literature. Brehm and Gates 1997, pp. 201–202.

43. Barker and Wilson (1997, p. 244) acknowledge a weakness with the survey
method: "Asking senior civil servants about working against their ministers is a
little like asking Roman Catholic clergy about their sexual conduct; it is supposed not to happen and almost certainly does so only rarely." Brehm and Gates
(1997) make extensive use of survey responses but also examine data on the
way police officers spend time as reported by ride-along observers.

44. Brehm 1996; Bachman, Bowers, and Marcus 1968; Rahim and Buntzman 1989.
Interestingly, in the one case where shirking is measured independently of self-
reports, Brehm and Gates found that workers who were more satisfied with
their superiors *shirked more frequently.* This finding appears to undercut the validity of survey responses as a measure of shirking (Brehm and Gates 1997,
p. 145). Note that, because of a typesetting error, the text reads "the more satisfied the officer is with his superior the more likely that officer is to work." However, the context and the regression tables make it clear that Brehm and Gates
meant to say "more likely that officer is to shirk." The authors have confirmed
that this is an erratum. Private correspondence with author, 10 June 1997.

45. However, this punishment was weakened in the late 1990s when recruiting and
retention problems made it more likely that even twice-passed-over middle-
rank officers (army, air force, and marine majors and navy lieutenant commanders) would be able to stay in the service for the full twenty years.

4. A Formal Agency Model of Civil-Military Relations

1. Huntington 1957, pp. 70–74; Clausewitz 1976, pp. 605–606. Deciding what exactly is "civilian" and what is "military" was difficult when Clausewitz wrote; it
is decidedly more so today. Feaver 1993.

2. My approach basically treats the monitoring decision as a transaction costs problem. Coase 1988. This grounding was suggested to me by Hamilton and
Schroeder's analysis of an EPA administrator's decision to use informal rules
(that is, to decide a matter internally) or formal rules (to post the rules and involve the public and other actors, as required by statute). Hamilton and
Schroeder 1994, p. 128. See also Milgrom and Roberts 1990.

3. Of course, if the policies prove disastrous or deviate widely from the views of
constituents, there will be an electoral connection. Lindsay (1994b) argues,
however, that defense policy issues have only a very marginal electoral impact.
See also Fenno 1973. Mayhew (1974, p. 122) claims that congressional princi-

pals (at least) are essentially (even solely) electorally motivated and so do not get involved with those policies, like most military issues, that bring little electoral benefit.

4. For example, it is possible that some communications improvements resulted from defense contracts that were partly an effort to preserve civilian control over the military. The Internet's origins as an effort to devise a postnuclear continuity-of-government mechanism illustrates the point. Future modifications to agency theory may involve endogenizing the costs of monitoring in this way.

5. The model runs the risk of overstating military shirking by not including an advisory stage. The story could include the following additional bargaining stages. Civilians make an offer *(W)*, and the military can accept or counteroffer *(W')*. Civilians can accept counteroffer *(W')* or insist on original offer *(W)*. If the civilians do not accept the military counteroffer *(W')*, the military may choose whether to implement *(W)* faithfully or shirk, which at that point would include continuing to push counteroffer *(W')*. Future extensions of the model could involve additional moves to explore this dynamic. The model also abstracts out another factor that plays a key role in the real world, the Clausewitzean notion of "friction." This is the natural slippage between what is intended and what transpires, regardless of the good intentions of the military operator. In all human endeavor, but especially in combat, things will go wrong and the civilian may not get what it asks for even though the military is sincerely trying to work. In terms of the model, Clausewitzean friction would inflate apparent shirking beyond the true level of military shirking.

6. As a first cut to analyzing the agency model, I will not take up several intriguing possibilities suggested by the deductive logic so far. First, as I develop it here, the model assumes that the civilian always knows when the military has worked, but when the military does not work, the civilian does not know whether this is (punishable) shirking or some other (nonpunishable) behavior. In this way, the model assumes away a possible outcome that may deserve closer scrutiny in follow-on work: the possibility that the civilian will punish the military even though it is working. One could treat the game as if the uncertainty over unobservable behavior was even more profound. The civilian might not be sure whether the military worked *or* shirked. This would leave open the possibility that the civilian might think the military has shirked and so punish, even though in fact the military has *not* shirked. Second, the model also considers only one dimension of uncertainty—whether or not punishment will be imposed—and ignores the dimension of uncertainty over the severity of the punishment. As discussed in the previous chapter, there is an almost infinite range of severity, ranging from a mild verbal rebuke to capital punishment. In future work it might be fruitful to explore the question of severity more fully. It is reasonable to expect that the severity of the punishment will be a function of the severity of the shirking. If the desired and actual behavior can each be represented as points in an issue-space, there is probably a zone of acceptance within which divergence between desired and actual behavior, though technically

shirking, will hardly be punished at all. The further the military's actual behavior diverges from the desired behavior, the more severe the punishment.

7. As a first cut at the problem, I am considering only pure strategies. One could extend the analysis by examining mixed strategies in which the military randomizes its response, say by working 75 percent of the time and shirking 25 percent of the time.

5. An Agency Theory Solution to the Cold War Puzzle

1. This stylizes Huntington's theory somewhat. Huntington defines subjective and objective control in terms of intrusive monitoring and in terms of the politicization of the military as reflected in military involvement in nontraditional roles. My model captures the first part of Huntington's argument but not the second. Likewise, Huntington's argument involves changing the content of what civilians asked the military to do by changing the civilian ideological profile. Confusion arises because Huntington makes an auxiliary claim about working and shirking that lies outside of the civilian control issue. Recall that civilian leaders and military leaders both draw conclusions about what is needed for national security and that both preferred policies are only approximations of some unknown "true" ideal policy that would provide optimal security for the state. The civilian approximation is represented by the "work" requested of the military, and the military approximation is represented by the "shirking" it might prefer to do. Huntington claims, in effect, that the military ideal point (shirking) is likely closer to the true point at least in the Cold War crisis of the 1950s than the civilian ideal point (work). Asking the military to deliver the civilian desired point would hurt U.S. national security. He further claims that monitoring the military intrusively (à la subjective control) would produce an outcome even further from the ideal point than the civilian desired point. Civilian micromanagement, in other words, produces negative work that damages the functional goal even more than simply achieving the desired civilian policy mix. As discussed in the text, the model can reflect part of Huntington's causal argument, specifically the claim that as preferences converge, the military is more likely to produce the civilian-desired outcome. What the model does not capture as clearly is the fact that the content of what civilians have asked for *after* a preference convergence has also changed.

2. The military will choose to always work when its payoffs from working exceed the expected payoffs of shirking. Expressed algebraically, the military will choose to always work if the following inequalities are true: $w1 > s1 - agP$ and $w2 > s2 - bgP$. Faced with such a military, the civilian's best choice is not to monitor intrusively so long as $W > W - C1$, in other words, so long as there are some intrinsic costs associated with monitoring intrusively.

3. McNamara 1995, pp. 22–24. McNamara's intrusiveness poses a special problem for Huntington's evaluation of Cold War civil-military relations. On the one hand, McNamara's assertive control would seem to violate the objective control

pattern Huntington recommends. On the other hand, Huntington actually in-
vokes McNamara's Office of the Secretary of Defense reforms favorably, and by
extension his method of civilian control. Goodpaster and Huntington 1977,
p. 10; Huntington 1963, pp. 798–802.

4. I thank John Rattliff for collecting and analyzing these data. Data in the following figures reflect total military and civilian personnel assigned to either the
Joint Chiefs of Staff or the Office of the Secretary of Defense; in preparing these
figures I also examined various permutations, such as reporting just the civilians
within the OSD versus just the military in the JCS. The results did not change,
so I decided to report only the most basic aggregate numbers. The sources for
these data are as follows: OSD military personnel and OSD civilian personnel
(1948–1986) and JCS military personnel and JCS civilian personnel (1948–
1985) are from: Robert W. Downey et al., "A Resource Data Base Covering the
Office of the Secretary of Defense, the Defense Agencies, and DOD Field Activities," Center for Naval Analyses, Research Memorandum CRM 87–213 (October 1987), Appendix A, Table A-3, pp. A-39, A-54, A-69, A-84 and A-99. JCS
Mil and JCS Civ (1986–2001) are from: Lorna Jaffe, Joint History Office, OJCS,
e-mail correspondence to Peter Feaver, 5 November 2001; the original source:
OJCS, J-1 *Manpower and Personnel Directorate,* Personnel Services Division, Staff
Management Branch. Note that the 1986 numbers for the JCS were also available in the Downey et al. memo, but the numbers reported in the figures are as
provided by Lorna Jaffe. OSD military personnel (1988–2000) and OSD civilian
personnel (1988–1994) are from: e-mail correspondence from Bradford Loo,
CIV, OSD-P&R, 2 October 2001; no data were available for 1987. OSD civilian
data (1995–2000) are from: *Monthly Report of Federal Civilian Employment* (Form
SF113-A), Department of Defense, Office of the Secretary of Defense, 31 December of each year, accessed from DoD, WHS, DIOR website http://
web1.whs.osd.mil/mmid/mmidhome.htm and http://web1.whs.osd.mil/mmid/
civilian/fy2000/December1999/osdd.pdf.

5. Some of these declines may be attributable to changes in the way the data were
reported, perhaps to reflect shifts of personnel into new defense agencies and
field activities such as the Defense Security Assistance Agency, the Civilian
Health and Medical Program of the Uniformed Services, and the Washington
Headquarters Services.

6. No data were available for 1987.

7. Data on defense outlays are from the Office of Management and Budget: *Budget
of the United States Government, Fiscal Year 2002,* Historical Tables, Table 8.2—Outlays By Budget Enforcement Act Category in Constant (FY 1996) Dollars: 1962–
2006 ($billions). Online at http://w3.access.gpo.gov/usbudget/fy2002/hist.html.
Data on military strength levels are from: Department of Defense, *Selected Manpower Statistics* (M01), DoD Active Duty Military Personnel Strength Levels, Table
2-11, available online at http://web1.whs.osd.mil/mmid/military/ms9.pdf.//
enottxt//

8. Lindsay 1994b, pp. 165–167. Lindsay argues that these requests are less intru-

sive than they appear and may not rise to the level of micromanagement that some critics charge, but he does not dismiss them as trivial in their totality.

9. Bouchard examines naval operations in four crises—the 1958 Taiwan crisis, the 1962 Cuban missile crisis, the 1967 Arab-Israeli crisis, and the 1973 Arab-Israeli crisis—and distinguishes between four types of control, ranging from intrusive to nonintrusive. His nomenclature is different, thus his "monitored delegated control" would correspond to my nonintrusive monitoring. Bouchard 1991, pp. 29–30.

10. Bouchard codes civilian control during the Cuban missile crisis as relatively nonintrusive monitoring because civilian leaders did not give orders directly to the ships and instead used the chain of command. It is true that the monitoring would have been even more intrusive if President Kennedy and Secretary of Defense McNamara had skipped the chain of command, but the tight reins held via the chain of command would suggest relatively intrusive monitoring. Moreover, Bouchard's own evidence gives ample support to the conventional explanation of the crisis as characterized by close control of operations. Bouchard 1991, pp. 96, and 128.

11. The military's shirking in response to Eisenhower's New Look policy is discussed in Korb 1976, pp. 103–110. There are other examples from later periods. Morton (1964, pp. 136–137) described the effort to reach the public over the head of the president as a "dangerous trend" and "an assault upon civilian supremacy." See also Buzzanco 1996, pp. 16–18; Clotfelter 1973, p. 135–136; and Petraeus 1987, pp. 248–249.

12. Korb 1976, p. 109. See Scroggs 1996 for an intriguing analysis of the army's alleged relative ineptness in exploiting this opportunity for shirking.

13. Desch's terms "compliance" and "noncompliance" are more or less synonymous with work and shirk. Desch 1999, pp. 135–139. On three other issues, he finds the degree of compliance too ambiguous to code: the 1946–47 fights over the reorganization of the War Department and the Department of the Navy, the Reagan administration's aborted efforts to consider military action in Central America in the mid-1980s, and the lead-up to the 1986 Goldwater-Nichols reforms of the Joint Chiefs of Staff. In the analysis of the use of force presented in the text, I code some cases differently, but I do not differ on the baseline assessment about military obedience. For instance, Desch codes the MacArthur incident as a case of military compliance because Truman's preference eventually prevailed over MacArthur's. As I explain in the text, however, that incident is better understood as a case of shirking and punishment.

14. Betts makes a similar observation in the epilogue to the revised edition of his book. Betts 1991, p. 226.

15. The table is the compilation of several sources, principally Betts 1991, Petraeus 1987, Gacek 1994, Perry 1989, Halberstam 1972, Millett and Maslowski 1994, Lowenthal and Goldich 1992, and Zelikow 1987. The cases follow the selection criteria used by Betts (1991, p. 239): "cold war decisions in which the use of American forces in combat was considered by high-level policymakers." Based

on the descriptions of the issues from these sources, my research assistants (thanks to Damon Coletta and Christopher Shulten) and I identified the dominant civilian and dominant military preference and then identified which preference prevailed. If the civilian preference prevailed, the case is coded as working. If the military preference prevailed, a judgment was made as to the reason why: was it because civilians found the military advice persuasive and thus civilian preferences changed, or did the military merely manipulate the civilians' decisionmaking calculus (for instance, by giving inflated cost estimates, or by leaking the dispute to a wider public audience, or by foot-dragging) and so cause the civilians to defer to the military preference? In the former case, the action taken would be coded as working. In the latter case, the incident would be coded as shirking, even if the civilians offered nominal acquiescence to the decision.

16. Petraeus 1987, p. 246. Petraeus says, however, that the military does not regularly inflate estimates.

17. Contrast the civil-military deliberations on Laos in Gacek (1994, pp. 158–178), Betts (1991, p. 178), and Petraeus (1987, pp. 61–71), and on Nicaragua in Petraeus (1987, pp. 209–223) and Gacek (1994, pp. 251–257), with the unfolding of the 1954 Taiwan Straits crisis in Betts (1987, pp. 54–62).

18. Significantly, in both these cases Betts claims that archival material and recent memoirs contradict somewhat other contemporaneous accounts. In the Indochina 1954 case, Betts notes that some scholars believe that Eisenhower may not have strongly favored the use of force anyway. In the EC-121 1969 case, Betts retreats somewhat from his initial estimate that civilians strongly favored, while the military sharply opposed, retaliating for the shoot-down. Betts 1991, pp. 226 and 230.

19. The table is the compilation of several sources, principally Betts 1987, 1991; Petraeus 1987; Zelikow 1987; Perry 1989; Buzzanco 1996; McMaster 1997; Gacek 1994; Divine 1981; Millett and Maslowski 1994; Dupuy and Dupuy 1986; and Lowenthal and Goldich 1992.

20. Sagan describes other near accidents that almost resulted from various concatenations of coincidences and poorly designed procedures, including a U-2's accidental overflight of the Soviet Union during the crisis. These might better fit Clausewitz's category of "friction" rather than shirking as understood by the agency perspective.

21. Sagan notes that civilian authorities worried enough about the Malmstrom incident to direct the JCS to conduct an after-action inspection. The JCS report concluded that no rules were broken, but Sagan concludes otherwise. Sagan 1993, pp. 78–91.

22. Perhaps the most provocative example of this kind of operational sabotage is the story Seymour Hersh tells of air force activities after Soviet air defenses shot down the South Korean passenger jet KAL 007. According to Hersh, subordinate officers tried to provoke an incident with the Soviet Union by filing fraudulent intelligence reports and changing their rules of engagement without autho-

rization. If Hersh's account of military behavior is true, it would be evidence of egregious shirking. Hersh 1986, p. 74.

23. Upton 1917; Huntington 1957, p. 83; Barrett 1983, pp. 82–85; Van Creveld 1985, pp. 258–260; Owens 1990; Crovitz 1990; Bouchard 1991, pp. 218–222. Even Russell Weigley, who is otherwise uncompromising on the obligation of the military to accept civilian meddling, argues that civilian involvement often puts the military at a disadvantage. Weigley 1993.

24. This is the core claim of Eliot Cohen's analysis of presidential leadership in war time, Cohen 2001. This is also one of Posen's conclusions in Posen 1984, pp. 220–236. See also Brodie 1973, pp. 416–419 and 456–457. And Quincy Wright claims that Lloyd George had a superior mastery of World War I compared with General Kitchener, in Kerwin 1948, p. 122.

25. The percentage of civilians agreeing with the statement, "press is more likely than the government to report the truth about the conduct of foreign policy," in the 1976, 1980, 1984, and 1988 surveys was 64 percent, 54 percent, 55 percent, and 62 percent, respectively. The surveys showed an even stronger military distrust of the press, however; military respondents agreeing with the statement dropped from a 41 percent high in 1976 to 35 percent, 16 percent, and 16 percent in the subsequent polls.

26. Huntington references MacArthur eighteen times, not an untoward count given General MacArthur's significance and the scope of *Soldier and the State*. But only half of those references are to his dismissal, which is arguably one of the pivotal events in U.S. civil-military history. See index (Huntington 1957, p. 526).

27. Bacevich 1997, p. 330. One could argue, however, that the very existence of Ridgway's shirking and the fact that it was tolerated for several years is a counterinstance not anticipated by the model. Certainly Eisenhower's status as a military hero empowered him to punish military officers for shirking, and so his subordinates should have had a strong expectation that such shirking would be punished. According to the agency model, Ridgway should have anticipated this and submitted, or at least Eisenhower should have acted earlier to nip Ridgway's campaign in the bud. There is not a completely satisfactory answer to this puzzle, although some speculations are possible. Ridgway evidently viewed his behavior in quasi-religious terms, as a campaign to avoid what he considered to be the "spiritual bankruptcy" of Eisenhower's policies; it was, therefore, the kind of issue on which Ridgway was evidently prepared to accept punishment, a cause worthy of a martyr's fate. Moreover, consistent with the model's logic, Ridgway's shirking intensified once he could not be punished any more, that is, once he was notified that he would not get a second term as chief of staff. Eisenhower's slowness to punish is harder to square with the agency model and remains worthy of further research.

28. The rationale behind such a move is explored using the principal-agent framework in Weiner 1997.

29. This is precisely the fear of contemporaneous critics of the reforms. See Previdi 1988.

30. Janowitz 1971, pp. 44–45; Lurie 1992, especially pp. 128–149. Huntington decried the trend as the "civilianization of the military," Huntington 1957, pp. 460–461.

31. For instance, the Womble Committee investigating military performance during the Korean War criticized the post–World War II reforms and recommended a restoration of commanders' prerogatives in punishing military infractions. Janowitz 1971, p. 50.

32. Herring (1994, pp. 30–36) gives a similar interpretation of military manipulation during the Vietnam War, although he explicitly rejects the claim that the military deliberately deceived Johnson.

33. Betts 1991, pp. 49–50, and 262–263, fn. 30. Uncertainty over the complicity of superior officers continues, with some suggesting that senior air force officers condoned the shirking and others alleging that they "sold" him out to civilian authorities. See Summers 1997 and Ryan 1997.

34. Gelb and Betts 1979, pp. 309–310. President Kennedy apparently so distrusted military reports from Vietnam that he relied on the newspapers for accurate accounts of what was going on. Herring 1994, p. 30.

35. I was cued to this episode in Buzzanco 1996, pp. 354–355. It is described in greater detail in Colodny and Gettlin 1991, pp. 3–68; Zumwalt 1976, pp. 369–376; Kissinger 1982, pp. 806–809; Hersh 1983, pp. 465–479; and Isaacson 1992, pp. 380–386. Colodny and Gettlin see the spy ring as part of a larger effort by military officers, with Al Haig at the helm, to control an unruly president. Zumwalt insists that the clerk acted on his own initiative. Intriguingly, Isaacson (1992, pp. 385–386) maintains that Nixon downplayed the incident because Nixon claimed that "it had been traditional that the JCS spied on the White House. They wanted to know what was going on." I have no further evidence that the JCS regularly spied on the White House in this fashion.

36. Janowitz 1974, p. 495. He does not, however go on to discuss how such an action would square with his theory of civilian control.

37. The most recent and emphatic exponent of this view is McMaster (1997, especially pp. 323–334). The "dereliction of duty" to which his book title alludes was the failure of the military to work hard enough to subvert civilian policies.

38. Had they done so, Buzzanco asserts, it "might have become the gravest crisis in civil-military relations in modern U.S. history." Buzzanco 1996, p. 300.

39. Herring's chapter on civil-military relations during the Vietnam War is entitled "No More MacArthurs." Herring 1994, pp. 25–62, see especially p. 48–49.

40. Herring 1994, p. 29; McMaster 1997, p. 331. This conclusion directly contradicts Avant's interpretation of agency problems in the Vietnam War. In her account, the military successfully resisted integration with civilian grand strategy (shirked) precisely because divisions between the executive and congressional components of the civilian principal prevented Presidents Kennedy and Johnson from advancing their favored candidates. Avant 1994, p. 50.

41. This may be an enduring feature of American public opinion, for similar poll results can be found from World War II. Clotfelter 1973, pp. 124–126. Elite opin-

ion, however, was more mixed. The Foreign Policy Leadership Project polling data show that the military far more than civilian elite respondents consistently supported the statement that a very or moderately important factor explaining the U.S. failure in Vietnam was the fact that "the use of American air power was restricted," although the gap narrowed over the years that the question was asked. In 1976, 81 percent of military respondents agreed, compared with 47 percent of civilian respondents; in 1980 the gap was a bit narrower: 81 percent of military respondents and 54 percent of civilian respondents; and by 1984 it was narrower still: 70 percent for the military and 46 percent for civilians.

42. Pape dismisses as a "myth" the charge that micromanagement undermined bombing effectiveness. Pape 1996, p. 186. See also Cooper 2001.

43. This, framed another way, is the central thesis of Gelb and Betts 1979.

6. Explaining the Post–Cold War "Crisis," 1990–2000

1. This chapter is adapted from material first published in Feaver 1998 and 1995. The material is used with the permission of the copyright holders, Transaction Publishers and the Center for Strategic and International Studies, respectively.

2. The article was published in *Parameters*, an influential journal within military circles but relatively obscure in the broader community. Part of the influence of this article derived from the fact that it won first prize in the National Defense University's Chairman of the Joint Chiefs of Staff Strategy Essay Competition. Although the terms of the contest explicitly state that the winners do not bear the imprimatur of the JCS or its chairman, the award gave the article a quasi-official air. Dunlap 1992–93, Ricks 1993.

3. Campbell's analysis, in turn, echoed the arguments of those (especially in the navy) who resisted Goldwater-Nichols in the first place. See Previdi 1988.

4. At the end of the chapter, I consider another line of criticism levied at the crisis school of thought, namely that the strife, though evident, is merely the naturally expected result of disagreements between civilians in Congress and the executive branch over the proper role for the military in the post–Cold War world.

5. One observer of the end-of-Vietnam phase openly worried that civilian control was "a good deal less than a generally prevailing reality." Yarmolinksy 1974, p. 654.

6. See Slater 1977, p. 117, fn. 32. Also Hanks 1970, an award-winning essay that argued the military had a role in fighting problems on the domestic front, and Miles 1968, which argued that the military should act to save the democratic process.

7. My list differs from other catalogs of post–Cold War civil-military relations offered in the literature, notably Deborah Avant's threefold typology of "excessive influence," "military representativeness," and "civil-military tension." Avant's list conflates descriptions of the problem, such as "the military are not sufficiently responsive to civilian direction," with explanations of root causes, namely that "the military is increasingly unrepresentative of society." Avant

1998. My list is a slight variant of Desch's review of candidate descriptions of "good" civil-military relations: absence of coups, extent of military influence, frequency of conflict, degree of mutual respect, effectiveness of military policies, and whose preferences prevail. Desch 1999, pp. 1–7.

8. This is the most extreme form that has been credibly claimed. A still more drastic charge would be that the military has usurped political power more generally. This is the endpoint warned about in Dunlap and at least hinted at in Kohn and Weigley, but no responsible observer has claimed that this catastrophe is already upon us.

9. This is what Huntington in an earlier era called the gap between the Establishment and the fundamentalists. Huntington wrote, "It is not the 'unwarranted' power of the military which is cause for concern, but rather the feelings of resentment and frustration which develop when the military believes that it is unaccountably and unjustifiably losing power." Huntington 1963, p. 803.

10. McMaster's (1997) prose is a tad purple, reflecting the still-raw emotions surrounding the Vietnam War. For instance, his index contains twenty references to President Johnson's "deceptions/lies" and twenty-one references to McNamara's "deceptions and lies." It is noteworthy that McMaster's publication coincided with an equally bombastic account by Robert Buzzanco (1996), who covers essentially the same historical terrain but concludes that the lies and deception were largely perpetrated by the military.

11. Source information for these figures is presented in Chapter 5, note 4.

12. Data from Committee on Post Office and Civil Service, House of Representatives, *United States Government Policy and Supporting Positions* (Washington, D.C.: GPO): quadrennial 1968–1988; Committee on Governmental Affairs, United States Senate, *United States Government Policy and Supporting Positions* (Washington, D.C.: GPO): quadrennial 1962–1996; and Department of Defense, *Selected Manpower Statistics* (Washington, D.C.: GPO): 1980–1996.

13. Data from Larry Curry, director of correspondence and directives, Office of the Executive Secretary, Department of Defense, 10 March 1997 and 13 April 2000. These data are different from the numbers of "written inquiries" referenced in Chapter 5. There I use the numbers as reported in Lindsay 1994, p. 166. Lindsay reports much higher numbers for both periods (although in relative terms they fit the pattern of an increase at the end of the Cold War compared with the Reagan years). His source is the Office of the Comptroller of the Department of Defense and the U.S. Government Accounting Office, which may be using more expansive counting rules. The numbers I report here are those logged by the Office of the Executive Secretary, which would involve matters of higher import and political or policy sensitivity.

14. By the end of July 1993, for instance, nearly half of the senior DoD jobs (twenty-three) remained empty. No author 1993b; Dowd 1993; LeSueur 1993.

15. Of course, some defense policy issues will have a larger electoral payoff than others, regardless of whether the threat is high or low. For instance, deciding whether to close a base in a home district will almost always be electorally more

significant for a representative than deciding whether to base a strategy on preparing to fight two or just one and one-half small wars nearly simultaneously.

16. Gordon 1992a; Schmitt 1993e; Jaffe 1993; Weiner 1996; Wilson 2000, pp. 38–
44. In other cases, the rancor was so great that it is difficult to assess blame. Such
might be the case with the debate over military readiness, with its bitter recrimi-
nations back and forth between the legislative and executive branches, criss-
crossing the civil-military divide.

17. By the end of the Clinton administration, the policy was unraveling and the issue became a hot political football in the 2000 presidential campaign. Feaver
2000a.

18. Not-for-attribution interview with the author, 3 June 1994.

19. Ricks 1996. For a comprehensive review of this literature, see Cohn 1999.

20. The results of the TISS project are reported in Feaver and Kohn (2000a, 2000b,
2001). The agency perspective does not directly address *why* the gap might
change. Consistent with Huntingtonian logic, the gap could in part be a function
of the external threat. Arguably, the divergence in preferences should *increase* as
the threat increases and narrow as the threat decreases. Traditional
Huntingtonian theory assumed that preferences diverged as external threat increased. The conservative realist military would desire to respond to the increased threat while the liberal civilian polity would resist, hence Huntington's
"crisis" in the 1950s. Interestingly, the gap between civilian and military preferences has changed in the past decade in spite of, rather than because of, the decrease in external threat. The more plausible explanation for the move is the remarkable change in the sociological makeup of the two sets of political elites,
civilian and military, due to the transition from conscription to an all-volunteer
force at the end of the Vietnam War. The trend probably began earlier with the
rise of selective service, which provided many ways for wealthier families to
avoid military service through college deferments and so on. Over time a strong
selection effect has taken root; those who would volunteer are a distinctive subset of the larger population. For other explanations of the changes, see Desch
2001, Burk 2001, and the articles in Feaver and Kohn 2000b.

21. In the 1998–99 TISS survey, the civilian self-identification according to party
preference was as follows: elite respondents were 36 percent Republican, 36
percent Democrat, and 28 percent Independent, no preference, or other; mass
respondents were 31 percent Republican, 33 percent Democrat, and 37 percent
Independent, no preference, or other. See also Cochran and Malone 1995.

22. Figures from the 1985 and 1999 *Defense Almanac,* respectively, published by the
Department of Defense.

23. Gibson and Snider 1999. Note that I interpret Gibson and Snider's data differently than they do. Although they purport explicitly to reject the idea that military preferences have prevailed over civilian preferences, they in fact make the
case that military influence relative to civilian influence has greatly increased
during the post–Cold War era.

24. As one editorial opined, "Administration policies on key issues—ranging from
changes in force structures to women in combat—have run into unnecessary

trouble because civilians whose jobs it would be to implement them were not in place." No author 1993e, p. C6.

25. As discussed in the next chapter, it is perhaps also the case that Bush himself was uncertain about the wisdom of the lift-and-strike option in Bosnia. Powell, for his part of course, claimed he was merely fulfilling his statutory responsibilities as advisor in chief and, had civilian principals made a decision to bomb, he would have carried out the orders unequivocally. Thus, if we code this as shirking we must recognize that it is a far cry from the most egregious forms of shirking imaginable in a civil-military context. Powell et al. 1994.

26. The efforts of Clinton and his team to spin away the draft story is covered in some detail in Halberstam (2001b), pp. 110–120.

27. Halbsertam 2001a, p. 230. Clinton's self-doubt extended to the entire arena of foreign policy; after the Kosovo war he remarked to one senator who was calling to congratulate him, "Remember I came in as a governor and I didn't have any experience in foreign policy?" Halberstam 2001b, p. 480.

28. On Clinton's steps to improve relations with the military, and General Powell's complementary activity, see Gellman 1993a and Schmitt 1993b.

29. For instance, when President Clinton in December 1995 visited the troops bound to implement the Bosnian peace treaty known as the Dayton Accords, reporters were at pains to spot protestors and to cull quotes from military spouses skeptical of the president's moral authority in the role of commander in chief. See Devroy 1995.

30. War records never played a big part in the 1996 campaign, even though the comparisons with Dole, as a wounded veteran, could have been even more invidious for the Clinton team. The general sense was that the voters had come to terms with President Clinton's avoidance of service in Vietnam and, in any case, the president now had four years of foreign policy and national security experience under his belt. See, for example, Maraniss 1996, p. W8. The Clinton campaign team did prepare a counterattack on the draft-dodging issue. They were ready to present a story that depicted Dole himself as desperately seeking to avoid first the draft and then combat during World War II, thus implying that he was no braver than Bill Clinton, just more unlucky. Because the issue never gained any salience, the campaign did not have to use this particular spin and the election ended without a significant exchange between the candidates on their fitness to serve as commander in chief. Private interview with senior White House official, 18 October 1996.

31. Perlez 2000. For example, Clinton's queasiness about ordering the military into harm's way was a major theme in the discussion surrounding his decision to send ground troops to enforce the Bosnian peace accords. Cannon 1995; Summers 1995, 1996; Atkinson 1996; Komarow 1996.

32. The existence of confusion is all too easy to document. In addition to the obvious confusion surrounding whether and whom to punish for the terrorist bombing of the air force base in Dharan, discussed in the text, consider the treatment of Admiral Macke, who was summarily fired for making insensitive remarks in the 1995 Okinawa rape case (No author 1995b). See also the turmoil

following Admiral Boorda's suicide (Charles 1996 and Lehman 1996). Nowhere is the problem more evident than in the military's halting attempts to adjust to the presence of women in the ranks and changing social mores. The presence of women has intensified the military's effort to regulate sex between consenting adults, and this has undoubtedly exacerbated confusion over what sorts of behavior will result in punishment. Jones 1996a, 1996b.

33. For details of the Khobar Towers case, see Kifner 1996 and Schmitt 1997. For a vigorous defense of Schwalier, see Labash 1997.

34. Kohn 2001, p. 16. Fogleman explicitly, if half-heartedly, exempts President Clinton from this charge. "This really did not involve the president; frankly, my dealings with the president, both as a CINC and as a service chief, led me to conclude that he executed his commander-in-chief responsibilities pretty well, at least his interface with the military." Ibid.

35. This section draws on a review of Desch published elsewhere, Feaver 2000b.

36. Desch 1999, p. 13. Desch is relying here on the work of Georg Simmel (1955).

37. Feaver 1996a. There is some support from the empirical record in the United States for a causal link between threat and type of control mechanism adopted, at least insofar as control over nuclear weapons is concerned, but the relationship is ambiguous and complicated by equivocal tradeoffs that leaders must confront as they move from a peacetime-but-high-threat environment through crisis to wartime. Feaver 1992.

38. I am grateful to Michael Desch for pointing this out to me. Private correspondence with the author, 5 January 2002.

39. Of course, a similar problem could attend agency theory, which is why I emphasize that some divergence is inevitable, though the *relative* convergence or divergence of preferences can shape patterns of relations.

40. Conflict, he argues, is not a good dependent variable because "some conflict is inevitable and perhaps even desirable in a pluralistic political system." Desch 1999, p. 4.

41. Interestingly, his evidence from the U.S. case provides a muddier picture if his theory is recast to focus on civil-military conflict, the dependent variable he claims to eschew but which, I argue, his model more directly predicts. During the Cold War there were some thirty-three "major" civil-military conflicts. This would seem a fairly large number of conflicts, given that this was with the high external–low internal threat configuration under which Desch predicts there should be a civil-military convergence of views. According to Desch's reckoning, however, the frequency of conflict did increase with the end of the Cold War, as would be predicted by his model. Desch 1999, pp. 136–138.

7. Using Agency Theory to Explore the Use of Force in the Post–Cold War Era

1. The charge of shirking, although not with that terminology, is also made explicitly by Record 2000.

2. Although it is beyond the scope of the analysis here, the Somalia case also gave

rise to one of the more pernicious civil-military myths: that the American public is reflexively averse to casualties. This myth continues to shape how policymakers handle tradeoffs on decisions to use force, despite its weak empirical foundation. See Dauber 2001 and Feaver and Gelpi forthcoming.

3. For more on the civil-military dynamic during this early phase, see Western 2000, pp. 289–295; Menkhaus and Ortmayer 1995, p. 3; Oberdorfer 1992a; and Stevenson 1996, p. 523.

4. Western 2000, p. 264. Halberstam (2001b, pp. 251–252) makes a similar claim. Other analysts explain the linkage as a way for President Bush and General Powell to deflect criticism from their handling of the Bosnian conflict, or simply to relieve the tensions of the failed reelection campaign. Glynn 1992, 1993; Luttwak 1993; Blumenthal 1992, 1993b.

5. In interviews at the end of his administration, President Clinton appeared to go even further in shifting the blame for the Somalia disaster onto General Powell. He implied that he had misgivings early on about the hunt for Aideed but that he simply followed Powell's advice on the matter. Although he claimed not to be "blaming" Powell, Clinton pointed out that shortly after the mission fell apart, Powell retired. Klein 2000, p. 200.

6. For a telling account of how Secretary Perry understood the Somalia lesson, see Gertz 1995.

7. For general background on the Haiti case see: Ortmayer and Flinn 1997; Morley and McGillion 1997; Shacochis 1999; Ballard 1998.

8. Sciolino (1993d). The list included questions about the following: "whether American troops would have the airfield and port access they needed, whether the rules of engagement for the American and foreign forces had been resolved with the United Nations, and whether the Haitian government had signed a formal agreement defining the mission . . . whether Haiti's Parliament had passed a law creating an independent police force, why Father Aristide had not formally granted amnesty for political crimes and whether the United Nations had sent a formal note to the United States requesting the troops."

9. Contrast Sciolino 1994d with Ricks 1994. Also Post et al. 1994.

10. Halberstam 2001b, p. 42. He also implies (and this is not seconded by any other source) that Powell actually supported the compromise position of lifting the arms embargo during the summer of 1992 and was simply waiting for the State Department to initiate the policy change. Ibid., p. 141. See also Martin 1993, p. 153.

11. According to one account, President Bush *wanted* General Powell to write the op-ed, hoping the piece would keep public pressure on the president to avoid an open-ended commitment to Bosnia. Thomas Langston attributes this interpretation to a personal interview with Lorne Jaffe, a historian in the office of the chairman of the JCS, cited in Langston draft. If true, this undercuts a coding of shirking.

12. The one optimistic assessment of air strikes by air force chief of staff Merrill McPeak was largely drowned out by the louder chorus of naysayers. Sciolino 1993h.

13. This section draws heavily on the memoirs of the senior U.S. negotiator, Richard Holbrooke. Holbrooke 1998, pp. 60–79.

14. This is separately confirmed in Owen 1997, pp. 10, 14.

15. Such an effort could profitably explore an angle only lightly touched upon here, namely Congress's role in the process. Deborah Avant (1996–97), emphasizes that congressional opposition to the Bosnian mission greatly contributed to the civil-military challenge. By threatening at points to unilaterally lift the arms embargo against the Muslims, Congress pressured civilians in the executive branch to consider more aggressive action than they or the military wanted; but by expressing grave reluctance to involve any U.S. forces in the mission, Congress greatly emboldened military officers to resist the mission as well.

16. The overall story of the Kosovo tragedy is well told in Daalder and O'Hanlon 2000; the best analysis of the military aspects of the campaign is Arkin 2001.

17. Halberstam 2001b, pp. 423–424. In his own coauthored book on Kosovo, Daalder does not claim credit for the pledge, which he roundly criticizes. Daalder and O'Hanlon 2000, pp. 96–100.

18. Warner 1999. For a more sanguine account see Cooper 2001.

19. This characterization is from Daalder and O'Hanlon 2000, p. 103.

20. To be sure, Cohen gave at least public lip service to the lesson of Somalia and promised that Clark would receive whatever he needed. No author 1999.

21. See the analysis of coalition warfare in Cohen 2001, pp. 46–52, and 57.

22. The judgment that Short shirked comes from Arkin 2001, pp. 28–29. It is supported by Halberstam (2001b), pp. 447–451. Clark himself does not quite make that charge, although he acknowledges the friction; Clark 2001, pp. 245–247.

8. Conclusion

1. Space and scope constraints require only cursory treatment of this issue here. For more, see Cohn and Feaver draft.

2. Civil-military relations were remarkably prominent in the 2000 campaign. Both Gore and Bush sought to distance themselves from Clinton by playing up their military credentials, and both platforms made direct appeals to the pro-defense wing and thereby implicit indirect appeals to the military as an interest group: Gore by promising large increases in the defense budget and Bush by promising to eschew nation-building and restore respect for the office of commander in chief. To be sure, both platforms also contained elements that were threatening to entrenched military interests: Gore promised to expand opportunities for gays in the military, and Bush promised to make dramatic, transformational changes in defense roles and force structure. The endgame in Florida turned in part on the Republicans' successful appeal to the large bloc of military voters there—and the Democrats' unsuccessful bid to invalidate as many absentee military votes as possible. The closeness of the final count means that there were numerous small constituencies who "cast the decisive vote," but few enjoyed the media prominence of the military voter. Moreover, at least some Republican operatives cred-

ited the margin of victory to the military vote. Bedard 2001. Thus, in agency theory terms, the 2000 election brought us as close as we have come in modern times to a situation in which the military agents picked their civilian principal. See Kohn 2002 for a different take on the civil-military implications of the Florida saga.

3. A representative account is Ricks 2001a. For a more extensive bibliography and review of this, see Kohn 2002.

4. Quote to Mazetti and Newman (2001). Compare with Schmitt 2001; Kaplan 2001; Ricks 2001b, 2001c; and Balz and Woodward 2002.

5. This is explored further in Coletta and Feaver draft.

6. Intriguingly, the unpredictability of punishment can be an explicit strategy of control. For instance, it is possible that the army deliberately imposed very inconsistent punishments on "troublemakers" during the Vietnam War as a means of keeping the war protesters in the army off balance. See Sherrill 1970, pp. 62–65.

7. For a first cut at expanding agency theory in this way, see Brenner 2001.

8. Of course, there is a long-standing revisionist literature that makes more or less the opposite claim, that military influence leads to militarism, and that this is the more pernicious root of problems. See, for example, Vagts 1937 or Buzzanco 1996.

9. See, for example, Admiral Crowe's rationale, as relayed by Bob Woodward, for challenging and perhaps circumventing the president on military-to-military contacts with the Soviet Union. Woodward describes Crowe's reasoning thus: "The simple truth was that the Chairman could not be a player unless he disagreed at times and fought the White House . . . [Crowe and his Soviet counterpart set up a secret back channel for military-to-military communication because both] believed it was too easy for politicians to let a misunderstanding throw the superpowers over the brink to nuclear war." Woodward 1991, p. 40.

10. Dunlap 2002. A uniformed professor of military ethics challenged me on this point, and gave as an example the assertion that the military should have resisted the decision to put Japanese Americans in internment camps during World War II. However regrettable that policy was, it was nevertheless deemed legal by no less an authority than the Supreme Court. To have the military second guessing the Supreme Court would be to reverse the principal-agent relationship further than democratic theory could allow.

11. Osiel (1999) argues that the military should have more room for exercising judgment about which orders to obey or not. If the goal is to avoid illegal orders, this recommendation is largely moot in the U.S. case because the ubiquity of military legal counsel ensures that virtually every order receives careful legal scrutiny. If the goal is to avoid unwise orders, this recommendation is problematic because it asks the military to make judgments it is not, in a democracy, given the competence to judge.

12. I am indebted to James Burk for suggesting this line of reasoning to me.

References

Abercrombie, Clarence L., and Raoul H. Alcala. 1973. "The New Military Professionalism." In Bruce M. Russett and Alfred Stepan, eds., *Military Force and American Society*. New York: Harper and Row. 34–58.

Abrahamsson, Bengt. 1972. *Military Professionalization and Political Power*. Beverly Hills: Sage.

Adams, James. 1994. "Dead Hero's Father Tears into Clinton." *Sunday Times* (London), 29 May, 18.

Alchian, Armen, and Harold Demsetz. 1972. "Production, Information Costs, and Economic Organization." *American Economic Review* 62, no.5: 777–795.

Aldrich, John H., John L. Sullivan, and Eugene Borgida. 1989. "Foreign Affairs and Issue Voting: Do Presidential Candidates 'Waltz before a Blind Audience?'" *APSR* 83, no. 1 (Mar.): 123–141.

Allard, C. Kenneth. 1990. *Command, Control, and the Common Defense*. New Haven: Yale University Press.

Allison, Graham T. 1971. *Essence of Decision: Explaining the Cuban Missile Crisis*. Boston: Little, Brown.

Alter, Jonathan. 1994. "A Tough Act to Follow." *Newsweek*, 23 May, 39.

Altfeld, Michael F., and Gary J. Miller, 1984. "Sources of Bureaucratic Influence: Expertise and Agenda Control." *Journal of Conflict Resolution* 28, no. 4 (Dec.): 701–730.

Andreski, Stanislav. 1968. *Military Organization and Society*. Berkeley: University of California Press.

Apple, R. W. 1993. "Clinton Sending Reinforcements after Heavy Losses in Somalia." *NYT*, 5 Oct., A1.

———. 1994. "Clinton, in Rome, Starts Tour of Europe to Burnish Image." *NYT*, 2 June, A1.

Appleby, Paul. 1948. "Civilian Control of a Department of National Defense." In Jerome Kerwin, ed., *Civilian-Military Relationships in American Life*. Chicago: University of Chicago Press.

Arkin, William. 2001. "Operation Allied Force: 'The Most Precise Application of Air Power in History.'" In Andrew J. Bacevich and Eliot A. Cohen, eds., *War over*

Kosovo: Politics and Strategy in a Global Age. New York: Columbia University Press. 1–37.

Arthur, Stanley. 1996. "The American Military: Some Thoughts on Who We Are and What We Are." In *Civil-Military Relations and the Not-Quite Wars of the Present and Future.* Carlisle Barracks, Pa.: Strategic Studies Institute.

Aspin, Les. 1992. "The Use and Usefulness of Military Forces in the Post–Cold War, Post-Soviet World." Speech before the Jewish Institute for National Security Affairs, Washington, D.C., 21 Sept.

Atkinson, Rick. 1990. "U.S. to Rely on Air Strikes If War Erupts." *WP,* 16 Sept., A1.

———. 1993. *Crusade: The Untold Story of the Persian Gulf War.* Boston: Houghton Mifflin.

———. 1996. "GI's on Clinton's Bosnia Visit: "He's Coming . . . It's Great." *WP,* 12 Jan., 17.

Avant, Deborah D. 1993. "The Institutional Sources of Military Doctrine: Hegemons in Peripheral Wars." *International Studies Quarterly* 37, no. 4: 409–430.

———. 1994. *Political Institutions and Military Change: Lessons from Peripheral Wars.* Ithaca: Cornell University Press.

———. 1996–97. "Are the Reluctant Warriors Out of Control? Why the U.S. Military Is Averse to Responding to Post–Cold War Low-Level Threats." *Security Studies* 6, no. 2 (Winter): 51–90.

———. 1998. "Conflicting Indicators of 'Crisis' in American Civil-Military Relations." *AFS* 24, no. 3 (Spring): 375–388.

———. Manuscript. "The Market for Force."

Avant, Deborah D., and James Lebovic. 2000. "U.S. Military Attitudes toward Post–Cold War Missions." *AFS* (Fall): 37–56.

Babington, Charles. 1999. "Clark Announcement Disturbing to Clinton." *WP,* 31 July, 16.

Babington, Charles, and Juliet Eilperin. 1999. "Clinton Signals Raids May Last 3 More Months; House Votes to Require Assent for Ground Troops." *WP,* (29 April, A1.

Bacevich, Andrew J. 1993. "Clinton's Military Problem—And Ours." *National Review* 45, no. 24: 36–40.

———. 1994–95. "Civilian Control: A Useful Fiction." *Joint Forces Quarterly,* no. 6 (Autumn/Winter): 76–83.

———. 1997. "The Paradox of Professionalism: Eisenhower, Ridgway, and the Challenge to Civilian Control, 1953–1955." *Journal of Military History* 61, no. 2 (April): 303–333.

Bachman, Jerald G., John D. Blair, and David R. Segal. 1977. *The All-Volunteer Force.* Ann Arbor: University of Michigan Press.

Bachman, Jerald G., David G. Bowers, and Philip M. Marcus. 1968. "Bases of Supervisory Power: A Comparative Study in Five Organizational Settings." In Arnold S. Tannenbaum, ed., *Control in Organizations.* New York: McGraw-Hill. 229–239.

Bachman, Jerald G., Lee Sigelman, and Greg Diamond. 1987. "Self-Selection, Socialization, and Distinctive Military Values: Attitudes of High School Seniors." *AFS* 13, no. 2: 169–187.

Baker, Gerard. 1998. "Cynical View from Clinton Opponents." *Financial Times*, 17 Dec., 12.

Baker, James A. 1995. *The Politics of Diplomacy: Revolution, War, and Peace, 1989–1992.* New York: Putnam's.

Ballard, John R. 1998. *Upholding Democracy: The United States Military Campaign in Haiti, 1994–1997.* Westport, Conn.: Praeger, 1998.

Balz, Dan, and Bob Woodward. 2002. "A Day to Speak of Anger and Grief." *WP*, 30 Jan., 1.

Balz, Dan, Bob Woodward, and Jeff Himmelman. 2002. "Afghan Campaign's Blueprint Emerges." *WP*, 29 Jan., 1.

Barber, Ben. 1996. "'Mission Creep' Could Hinder Bosnia Goals." *WT*, 5 Jan., 1.

Barker, Anthony, and Graham K. Wilson. 1997. "Whitehall's Disobedient Servants? Senior Officials' Potential Resistance to Ministers in British Government Departments." *British Journal of Political Science* 27, pt. 2 (April): 223–246.

Barnard, Chester. 1938. *The Functions of the Executive.* Cambridge, Mass.: Harvard University Press.

Barnes, Fred. 1992. "White House Watch: Last Call." *TNR*, 28 Dec., 11–13.

———. 1994a. "Oh, All Right Then." *TNR*, 10 Oct., 11–12.

———. 1994b. "Viva Haiti." *TNR*, 30 May, 17.

Bar-Or, Amir. 1995. "Military Force without a State: Sources for Patterns of Political Supremacy over Military Organization in a Transition Period." Paper presented at the Inter-University Seminar Biennial Conference on Armed Forces and Society.

Barrett, Archie D. 1983. *Reappraising Defense Organization.* Washington, D.C.: National Defense University Press.

Barrett, Raymond J. 1965. "Partners in Policymaking." *Military Review* 45, no. 10 (Oct.): 84–88.

Barry, John, and Evan Thomas. 2001. "Colin Powell: Behind the Myth." *Newsweek*, 5 Mar., 34–38.

Bawn, Kathleen. 1995. "Political Control versus Expertise: Congressional Choice and Administrative Procedures." *APSR* 89, no. 1: 62–73.

Bedard, Paul. 2001. "Washington Whispers." *U.S. News and World Report*, 10 Sept.

Belkin, Aaron. 1998. "Performing the National Security State: Civil-Military Relations as a Cause of International Conflict." Ph.D. diss., University of California at Berkeley.

Bendor, Jonathan. 1988. "Review Article: Formal Models of Bureaucracy." *British Journal of Political Science* 18: 353–395.

Benedetto, Richard. 1991. "For the Most Part, Bush Lets Military Do Its Job." *USA Today*, 23 Jan., 42.

Bennett, W. Lance, and David L. Paletz, eds. 1994. *Taken by Storm: The Media, Public Opinion, and U.S. Foreign Policy in the Gulf War.* Chicago: University of Chicago Press.

Berger, Sandy. 1999. Interview on *ABC News This Week*, 28 Mar.

Betts, Richard K. 1987. *Nuclear Blackmail and Nuclear Balance.* Washington, D.C.: Brookings.

————. 1991. *Soldiers, Statesmen, and Cold War Crises,* rev. ed. New York: Columbia University Press.

Bianco, William T., and Robert H. Bates. 1990. "Cooperation by Design: Leadership, Structure, and Collective Dilemmas." *APSR* 84, no. 1: 133–149.

Bianco, William, and Jamie Markham. 2001. "Vanishing Veterans: The Decline in Military Service in the U.S. Congress." in Peter D. Feaver and Richard H. Kohn, eds., *Soldiers and Civilians: The Civil-Military Gap and American National Security.* Cambridge, Mass.: MIT Press.

Bird, Julie. 1996. "Orders: Why the Chief of Staff Is So Concerned." *Air Force Times,* 24 June, 12–14.

Biskupic, Joan. 1993. "Administration to Defend Bush Haitian Policy in Court." *WP,* 1 Mar., A9.

Blair, Bruce G. 1985. *Strategic Command and Control: Redefining the Nuclear Threat.* Washington, D.C.: Brookings.

————. 1993. *The Logic of Accidental Nuclear War.* Washington, D.C.: Brookings.

Bland, Douglas L. 2001. "Patterns in Liberal Democratic Civil-Military Relations." *AFS* 27, no. 4 (Summer): 525–540.

Blechman, Barry. 1990. *The Politics of National Security: Congress and U.S. Defense Policy.* New York: Oxford University Press.

Blechman, Barry, and Stephen S. Kaplan. 1978. *Force without War.* Washington, D.C.: Brookings.

Blight, James G., and David A. Welch. 1995. "Risking 'The Destruction of Nations': Lessons of the Cuban Missile Crisis for New and Aspiring Nuclear States." *Security Studies* 4, no. 4 (Summer): 811–850.

Blumenthal, Sidney. 1992. "All the President's Wars." *New Yorker,* 28 Dec., 62.

————. 1993a. "Lonesome Hawk." *New Yorker,* 31 May, 38–39.

————. 1993b. "Why Are We in Somalia?" *New Yorker,* 25 Oct., 53–58.

Boene, Bernard. 1990. "How 'Unique' Should the Military Be? A Review of Representative Literature and Outline of a Synthetic Formulation." *European Journal of Sociology* 31, no. 1: 3–59.

Bonner, Raymond. 1996. "U.S. Fears Bosnian Serb Chiefs Won't Be Ousted." *NYT,* 6 July, 1.

Bouchard, Joseph F. 1991. *Command in Crisis: Four Case Studies.* New York: Columbia University Press.

Bowden, Mark. 1999. *Black Hawk Down: A Story of Modern War.* New York: Atlantic Monthly Press.

Bowers, Jean M. 1993. *The Presidential Use of American Troops in U.N. Actions: Selected References.* Congressional Research Service. 93–1066 LSD, Dec.

Bracken, Paul. 1983. *The Command and Control of Nuclear Forces.* New Haven: Yale University Press.

Brehm, John. 1996. "Steps toward a Political Science of Compliance: Common Insights and Recurring Problems." Paper presented at the annual meeting of the Midwest Political Science Association, Chicago.

Brehm, John, and Scott Gates. 1992a. "Policing Police Brutality: Evaluation of Principal-Agent Models of Noncooperative Behavior." Paper presented at the annual meeting of the Midwest Political Science Association, Chicago.

———. 1992b. "Supervision and Compliance." Papers in American Politics, Working Paper 159, Duke University Program in Political Economy.

———. 1993. "Donut Shops and Speed Traps: Evaluating Models of Supervision on Police Behavior." *American Journal of Political Science* 37, no. 2: 555–581.

———. 1997. *Working, Shirking, and Sabotage: Bureaucratic Response to a Democratic Public.* Ann Arbor: University of Michigan.

Brenner, Carl N. 2001. "An Expanded Agency Theory Explanation for American Civil-Military Relations." Paper presented at the annual meeting of the American Political Science Association, San Francisco.

Brodie, Bernard. 1973. *War and Politics.* New York: Macmillan.

Brooks, Risa. 1996. "Political-Military Relations, Endogenous Institutions, and Grand Strategy: The Political Origins of Oversight and Policy Coherence." Paper presented at "A Crisis in Civilian Control? Contending Theories of American Civil-Military Relations." John M. Olin Institute for Strategic Studies, 11–12 June, Cambridge, Mass.

———. 2000. "Institutions at the Domestic and International Nexus: The Political-Military Origins of Strategic Integration, Military Effectiveness and War." Ph.D. diss., University of California, San Diego.

Brown, MacAllister, Andrew F. Henry, and John W. Masland. 1958. "Some Evidence on the 'Military Mind.'" Unpublished paper, Dartmouth College, June.

Bryant, Clifton D. 1979. *Khaki-Collar Crime: Deviant Behavior in the Military Context.* New York: Free Press.

Brzezinski, Zbigniew, and Samuel P. Huntington. 1964. *Political Power: USA/USSR.* New York: Viking.

Bueno de Mesquita, Bruce, and Randolph M. Siverson. 1995. "War and the Survival of Political Leaders: A Comparative Study of Regime Types and Political Accountability." *APSR* 89, no. 4 (Dec.): 841–855.

Burk, James. 1993. "Morris Janowitz and the Origins of Sociological Research on Armed Forces and Society." *AFS* 19, no. 2: 167–186.

———. 1994. "Major Trends in Civil-Military Relations." Paper presented at "Sociology and War" conference sponsored by the Triangle Universities Security Seminar, Chapel Hill, N.C., 18 Nov.

———. 2001. "The Military's Presence in American Society." In Peter D. Feaver and Richard H. Kohn, eds., *Soldiers and Civilians: The Civil-Military Gap and American National Security.* Cambridge, Mass.: MIT Press.

Burns, John F. 1993. "NATO Planes Fly Sarajevo Sorties: Low-Level Runs Considered Warning to Serbs Not to Renew Their Shelling." *NYT,* 18 Oct., A5.

Burns, Robert. 1999. "Reimer Reveals His Views on Kosovo Strategy." *European Stars and Stripes,* 27 May, p. 1.

Buzzanco, Robert. 1996. *Masters of War: Military Dissent and Politics in the Vietnam Era.* Cambridge: Cambridge University Press.

Calmes, Jackie. 2001. "Washington Wire" *WSJ,* 13 April.

Campbell, Kurt. 1991. "All Rise for Chairman Powell." *National Interest* 23 (Spring): 51–60.

Cannon, Carl M. 1995. "Failure to Serve Shadows Clinton." *Baltimore Sun,* 10 Dec., 1.

Cannon, Lou. 1991. *President Reagan: The Role of a Lifetime.* New York: Simon and Schuster.

Carter, Ashton B., John D. Steinbruner, and Charles A. Zraket, eds. 1987. *Managing Nuclear Operations.* Washington, D.C.: Brookings.

Cerami, Joseph R. 1996–97. "Presidential Decisionmaking and Vietnam: Lessons for Strategists." *Parameters* 26, no. 4 (Winter): 66–80.

Charles, Roger. 1996. "It's a War for Soul of U.S. Military." *Baltimore Sun,* 2 June, 1.

Chayes, Abram, and Antonia Handler Chayes. 1995. *The New Sovereignty: Compliance with International Regulatory Agreements.* Cambridge, Mass.: Harvard University Press.

Clark, Asa A., et al. 1987. "Did Vietnam Make a Difference? No! Conclusions and Implications." In George Osborn et al., *Democracy, Strategy, and Vietnam: Implications for American Policymaking.* Lexington, Mass.: D. C. Heath. 319–350.

Clark, Wesley. 2001. *Waging Modern War.* Oxford: Public Affairs.

Clausewitz, Karl Von. 1976. *On War,* ed. and trans. Michael Howard and Peter Paret. Princeton: Princeton University Press.

Clinton, William Jefferson. 1993. *Remarks by President Clinton and Prime Minister Ciller of Turkey in Press Availability,* 15 Oct. White House, Office of the Press Secretary, p. 17.

———. 1994a. *A National Security Strategy of Engagement and Enlargement.* July.

———. 1994b. "Press Conference by the President," 15 Oct. White House, Office of the Press Secretary.

Clotfelter, James. 1969. "The Garrison State and the American Military: Public Attitudes and Expectations." Ph.D. diss., University of North Carolina.

———. 1973. *The Military in American Politics.* New York: Harper and Row.

Coase, Ronald. 1988. *The Firm, the Market, and the Law.* Chicago: University of Chicago Press.

Cockburn, Alexander. 1995. "Beat the Devil." *Nation,* 3 April, 443.

Cochran, Charles L., and Eloise F. Malone. 1995. "A Comparison of Naval Academy Plebes and College Freshmen over Twenty Years Using the Ace's Student Information Form." Paper prepared for the 1995 Inter-University Seminar on the Armed Forces and Society, Baltimore, 20–22 Oct.

Cohen, Eliot A. 1984. "Constraints on America's Conduct of Small Wars." In Steven E. Miller and Sean M. Lynn-Jones, eds., *Conventional Forces and American Defense Policy: An International Security Reader.* Cambridge, Mass.: MIT Press. 325–355.

———. 1985. *Citizens and Soldiers: The Dilemmas of Military Service.* Ithaca: Cornell University Press.

———. 2000. "Why the Gap Matters." *National Interest* 61 (Fall): 38–48.

———. 2001. "The Unequal Dialogue: The Theory and Reality of Civil-Military Relations and the Use of Force." In Peter D. Feaver and Richard H. Kohn, eds., *Soldiers and Civilians: The Civil-Military Gap and American National Security.* Cambridge, Mass.: MIT Press.

———. 2001. "Kosovo and the New American Way of War." In Andrew J. Bacevich and Eliot A. Cohen, eds., *War over Kosovo: Politics and Strategy in a Global Age.* New York: Columbia University Press. 38–62.

Cohen, Roger. 1993. "Europeans Reject U.S. Plan to Aid Bosnia and Halt Serbs." *NYT,* 11 May, A1.

———. 1994. "NATO Gives Serbs a 10-day Deadline to Withdraw Guns." *NYT,* 10 Feb., A1.

Cohn, Lindsay. 1999. "The Evolution of the Civil-Military 'Gap' Debate." Paper prepared for the Triangle Institute for Security Studies (TISS) Project on the Gap between the Military and Civilian Society.

Cohn, Lindsay, and Peter D. Feaver. Draft. "American Civil-Military Relations: Challenges and Opportunities." In Stephen Cimbala, ed., *Over the Horizon: U.S. Defense Issues for the Twenty-first Century.*

Coletta, Damon, and Peter D. Feaver. Draft. "Civilian Control of Operations: Agency Theory and Rules of Engagement."

Collier, Ellen C. 1993. *Instances of Use of United States Armed Forces Abroad, 1798–1993.* Congressional Research Service. 93–890 F, 7 Oct.

Colodny, Len, and Robert Gettlin. 1991. *Silent Coup: The Removal of the President.* New York: St. Martin's.

Colton, Timothy. 1979. *Commissars, Commanders, and Civilian Authority: The Structure of Soviet Military Politics.* Cambridge, Mass.: Harvard University Press.

———. 1990. *Soldiers and the Soviet State: Civil-Military Relations from Brezhnev to Gorbachev.* Princeton: Princeton University Press.

Cooper, Scott A. 2001. "The Politics of Airstrikes," *Policy Review,* no. 107 (June): Accessed by Internet at www.policyreview.org/jun01/cooper_print.html

Corddry, Charles. 1992. "Cautious Officials Fear Intervention in Bosnia." *Houston Chronicle,* 12 July, A16.

Crovitz, L. Gordon. 1990. "Micromanaging Foreign Policy." *Public Interest* 100 (Summer): 102–115.

Curl, Joseph, and Rowan Scarborough. 2001. "Bush Takes Troop Pledge to Front Line." *WT,* 13 Feb., A1.

Cushman, John (USA-Ret). 1994. "Bungling the Informal Contract." *USNI* (Jan.): 10–13.

Daalder, Ivo, and Michael O'Hanlon. 2000. *Winning Ugly: NATO's War to Save Kosovo.* Washington, D.C.: Brookings

Dahl, Robert. 1985. *Controlling Nuclear Weapons.* Syracuse: Syracuse University Press.

Dauber, Cori. 1998. "The Practice of Argument: Reading the Conditions of Civil-Military Relations." *AFS* (Spring): 205–231.

———. 2001. "Image as Argument: The Impact of Mogadishu on U.S. Military Intervention." *AFS* 27 (Winter): 205–229.

Davidson, Michael W. 1987. "Senior Officers and Vietnam Policymaking." In Lloyd J. Matthews and Dale E. Brown, eds., *Assessing the Vietnam War: A Collection from the Journal of the U.S. Army War College.* Washington, D.C.: Pergamon-Brasseys.

Debenport, Ellen. 1992. "GOP Will Hound Clinton on Draft." *St. Petersburg Times,* 30 Sept., 1A.

Desch, Michael. 1995. "Losing Control? The End of the Cold War and Changing U.S. Civil-Military Relations." Paper presented at the annual meeting of the American Political Science Association, Chicago.

———. 1999. *Civilian Control of the Military: The Changing Security Environment.* Baltimore: Johns Hopkins Press.

———. 2001. "Explaining the Gap: Assessing Alternative Theories of Divergence of Civilian and Military Cultures." In Peter D. Feaver and Richard H. Kohn, eds., *Soldiers and Civilians: The Civil-Military Gap and American National Security.* Cambridge, Mass.: MIT Press.

Devroy, Ann. 1994. "Clinton Salutes Carrier Crew—and Vice Versa." *WP,* 6 June, A14.

———. 1995. "Clinton Reassures Bosnia-Bound Forces Mission Is 'Safe as It Can Be.'" *WP,* 3 Dec., A32.

Devroy, Ann, and Ruth Marcus. 1993. "President Clinton's First 100 Days: Ambitious Agenda and Interruptions Frustrate Efforts to Maintain Focus." *WP,* 29 April, A1.

Devroy, Ann, and R. Jeffrey Smith. 1994. "A Split Administration Debated Invasion Risks." *WP,* 25 Sept., A1.

Diamond, Larry, and Marc F. Plattner, eds. 1996. *Civil-Military Relations and Democracy.* Baltimore: Johns Hopkins Press.

Divine, Robert A. 1981. *Eisenhower and the Cold War.* New York: Oxford University Press.

Dobbs, Michael. 1996. "Fewer Doubts about Clinton as Commander." *WP,* (6 Sept., 28.

———. 1997. "In Bosnia, A Dubious Peace Process." *WP,* 2 May, 1.

Doherty, Carroll J. 1993. "U.S. Is Warily Welcoming a Beefed-up United Nations." *St. Louis Post-Dispatch,* (14 Mar., B8.

———. 1994. "Senate Defeats GOP Proposal to Limit Clinton on Haiti." *Defense and Foreign Policy,* 2 July, 1814.

Donnelly, John M. 2001. "Rumsfeld Makes War." *Chicago Tribune,* 22 Oct.

Donovan, Robert J. 1982. *Tumultuous Years: The Presidency of Harry S. Truman, 1949–1953.* New York: Norton.

Dowd, Ann Reilly. 1993. "Hello, Washington, Anybody There?" *Fortune,* 26 July, 18.

Dowd, Maureen. 1994a. "Commander in Chief in the Role of Protégé." *NYT,* 7 June, A8.

———. 1994b. "Retracing History: Clinton's 20-Something Aides." *NYT,* 6 June, A10.

Downs, George W., and David M. Rocke. 1995. *Optimal Imperfection? Domestic Uncer-*

tainty and Institutions in International Relations. Princeton: Princeton University Press.

Downs, George W., David M. Rocke, and Peter N. Barsoom. 1996. "Is the Good News about Compliance Good News about Cooperation?" *International Organization* 50, no. 3 (Summer): 379–406.

Drew, Elizabeth. 1994. *On the Edge: The Clinton Presidency.* New York: Simon and Schuster.

Drozdiak, William. 1994. "Veterans See Commander in Chief in New Light." *WP,* 7 June, A1.

———. 1997. "Call for Pursuit of Bosnian War Criminals Resisted." *WP,* 13 June, 36.

Duffy, Brian. 1994. "A Question of Options." *U.S. News and World Report,* 23 May, 30.

Duffy, Michael. 2001. "Rumsfeld: Older but Wiser?" *Time,* 27 Aug.

Dunlap, Charles. 1992–93. "The Origins of the American Military Coup of 2012." *Parameters* (Winter): 2–20.

———. 1994. "Welcome to the Junta: The Erosion of Civilian Control of the U.S. Military." *Wake Forest Law Review* 29, no. 2: 341ff.

———. 1996. "Melancholy Reunion: A Report from the Future on the Collapse of Civil-Military Relations in the United States." Institute for National Security Studies Occasional Paper 11, Oct.

———. 2002. "International Law and Terrorism: Some Q's and A's for Operators." Unpublished manuscript.

Dupuy, Alex. 1997. *Haiti in the New World Order: The Limits of the Democratic Revolution.* Boulder: Westview.

Dupuy, R. Ernest, and Trevor N. Dupuy. 1986. *The Encyclopedia of Military History from 3500 B.C. to the Present.* New York: Harper and Row.

Eagleton, Thomas T. 1974. *War and Presidential Power: A Chronicle of Congressional Surrender.* New York: Liverright.

Edmonds, Martin. 1988. *Armed Services and Society.* Boulder: Westview.

Ekirch, Arthur A., Jr. 1956. *The Civilian and the Military.* New York: Oxford University Press.

Engelberg, Stephen. 1993. "Inman has a Careful Career of Unexpected Moves." *NYT,* 21 Dec., A9.

———. 1994. "A Haitian Leader of Paramilitaries Was Paid by CIA." *NYT,* 8 Oct., A1.

Enthoven, Alain C., and K. Wayne Smith. 1971. *How Much Is Enough? Shaping the Defense Program, 1961–1969.* New York: Harper and Row.

Erlanger, Steven. 1997. "On Bosnia, Clinton Supports Albright against Cohen View." *NYT,* 12 June, A1.

Etzioni, Amitai. 1961. *A Comparative Analysis of Complex Organizations: On Power, Involvement, and Their Correlates.* New York: Free Press.

Evans, David. 1994. "The U.S. Marine Corps in Review." *USNI* 120, no. 5 (May): 131–138.

Fearon, James. 1995. "Rationalist Explanations for War." *International Organization* 49, no. 3: 379–414

Feaver, Peter D. 1992. *Guarding the Guardians: Civilian Control of Nuclear Weapons in the United States*. Ithaca: Cornell University Press.

———. 1993. "Discords and Divisions of Labor: The Evolution of Civil-Military Conflict in the United States." Paper presented at the annual meeting of the American Political Science Association, Washington, D.C.

———. 1995. "Civil-Military Conflict and the Use of Force." In Donald Snider and Miranda A. Carlton-Carew, eds., *U.S. Civil-Military Relations: In Crisis or Transition?* Washington, D.C.: Center for Strategic and International Studies.

———. 1996a. "An American Crisis in Civilian Control and Civil-Military Relations? Historical and Conceptual Roots." *Tocqueville Review* 17, no. 1: 159–184.

———. 1996b. "The Civil-Military Problematique: Huntington, Janowitz, and the Question of Civilian Control." *AFS* 23, no. 2 (Winter): 149–178.

———. 1996c. "Delegation, Monitoring, and Civilian Control of the Military: Agency Theory and American Civil-Military Relations." John M. Olin Institute for Strategic Studies, Project on U.S. Post Cold-War Civil-Military Relations, Working Paper no. 4.

———. 1998. "Crisis as Shirking: An Agency Theory Explanation of the Souring of American Civil-Military Relations." *AFS* 24, no. 3 (Spring): 407–434.

———. 1999. "Civil-Military Relations." *Annual Review of Political Science* 2: 211–241.

———. 2000a. "Gore Steps on a Land Mine." *WP,* 10 Jan., 19.

———. 2000b. Review of *Civilian Control of the Military: The Changing Security Environment,* by Michael C. Desch, *APSR* 94, no. 2 (June 2000): 506–507.

Feaver, Peter D., and Christopher Gelpi. Forthcoming. *American Civil-Military Relations and the Use of Force*. Princeton: Princeton University Press.

Feaver, Peter D., and Richard H. Kohn. 2000a. "The Gap: Soldiers, Civilians, and Their Mutual Misunderstanding." *National Interest* 61 (Fall): 29–37.

———. 2000b. "Media and Education in the U.S. Civil-Military Gap." of *AFS,* special ed. (Winter 2000): 177–182.

Feaver, Peter D., and Richard H. Kohn, eds. 2001. *Soldiers and Civilians: The Civil-Military Gap and American National Security*. Cambridge, Mass.: MIT Press.

Fenno, Richard F. 1973. *Congressmen in Committees*. Boston: Little, Brown.

Ferejohn, John, and Charles Shipan. 1990. "Congressional Influence on Bureaucracy." *Journal of Law, Economics, and Organization* 6: 1–43.

Fineman, Mark. 2000. "As Tallying Drags On, Haiti Election Is Called Unfair." *LAT,* 27 May, A5.

Fineman, Mark, and Art Pine. 1994. "In Contrast to Somalia, White House Is Letting Military Call Shots in Haiti." *LAT,* 29 Sept., 11.

Finer, S. E. 1962. *The Man on Horseback: The Role of the Military in Politics*. London: Pall Mall Press.

Flint, Roy K. 1991. "The Truman-MacArthur Conflict: Dilemmas of Civil-Military Relations in the Nuclear Age." In Richard Kohn, ed., *The United States Military under the Constitution, 1789–1989*. New York: New York University Press. 223–267.

Frazer, Jendayi E. 1994. "Sustaining Civilian Control in Africa: The Use of Armed Counterweights in Regime Stability." Ph.D. diss., Stanford University.

Freedman, Jonathan L., and Scott C. Fraser. 1966. *Journal of Personality and Social Psychology* 4, no. 2: 195–202.

French, Howard. 1993. "Haitians Block Landing of U.S. Forces." *NYT,* 12 Oct., A1.

Friedberg, Aaron L. 1992. "Why Didn't the United States Become a Garrison State?" *International Security* 16, no. 4 (Spring 1992): 109–142.

———. 2000. *In the Shadow of the Garrison State.* Princeton: Princeton University Press.

Friedman, Thomas L. 1992. "Baker Hints at the Use of American Forces to Supply Sarajevo." *NYT,* 24 June, A9.

———. 1993a. "A Broken Truce: Clinton vs. Bush in Global Policy." *NYT,* 17 Oct., A1.

———. 1993b. "Chiefs Back Clinton on Gay-Troop Plan." *NYT,* 20 July, A1.

———. 1993c. "Clinton, Saluting Vietnam Dead, Finds Old Wound Is Slow to Heal." *NYT,* 1 June, A1.

———. 1993d. "Clinton Seeking Negotiated Path to Bosnia Pact." *NYT,* 4 Feb., A1.

———. 1993e. "Clinton Sending More Troops to Somalia." *NYT,* Oct. 19, A1.

———. 1993f. "Clinton, Short of Support, Puts Bosnian Issue on Hold." *NYT,* 11 May, A7.

———. 1993g. "Clinton Vows to Fight Congress on His Power to Use the Military." *NYT,* 19 Oct., A1.

———. 1993h. "Others Tottered Earlier but Aspin Fell." *NYT,* 17 Dec., B13.

Friedrich, Carl J. 1935. *Problems of the American Public Service.* New York: McGraw-Hill.

———. 1941. "The Nature of Administrative Responsibility." In Carl Friedrich, ed., *Public Policy.* Cambridge, Mass.: Harvard University Press.

Gacek, Christopher. 1994. *The Logic of Force: The Dilemma of Limited War in American Foreign Policy.* New York: Columbia University Press.

Gallup, George. 1991. *The Gallup Poll: Public Opinion 1990.* Wilmington: Scholarly Resources.

Gelb, Leslie H., and Richard K. Betts. 1979. *The Irony of Vietnam: The System Worked.* Washington, D.C.: Brookings.

Gellman, Barton. 1992. "Clinton Says He'll 'Consult' on Allowing Gays in Military." *WP,* 13 Nov., A1.

———. 1993a. "Turning an About-Face into a Forward March." *WP,* 1 April, A1.

———. 1993b. "U.S. Rhetoric Changed, but Hunt Persisted." *WP,* 7 Oct., A37.

———. 1993c. "The Words behind a Deadly Decision." *WP,* 31 Oct., A1.

George, Alexander, and Richard Smoke. 1974. *Deterrence in American Foreign Policy: Theory and Practice.* New York: Columbia University Press.

Gertz, Bill. 1995. "Perry Talks of Somalia Lessons: Says Peacekeepers Must Be Well Armed." *WT,* 4 Oct., A9.

Gertz, Bill, and Rowan Scarborough. 2001. "Inside the Ring." *WT,* 10 Aug., 10.

———. 2002. "Inside the Ring." *WT,* 1 Feb., 8.

Gibson, Christopher P., and Don M. Snider. 1997. "Explaining Post–Cold War Civil-Military Relations: A New Institutionalist Approach." John M. Olin Institute for

Strategic Studies, Project on U.S. Post Cold-War Civil-Military Relations, Working Paper no. 8.

———. 1999. "Civil-Military Relations and the Potential to Influence: A Look at the National Security Decision-Making Process." *AFS* 25, no. 2 (Winter): 193–218.

Glad, Betty. 1993. "Figuring Out Saddam Hussein." In *The Presidency and the Persian Gulf War*, ed. Marcia Lynn Whicker, James P. Pfiffner, and Raymond A. Moore. Westport, Conn.: Praeger.

Glynn, Patrick. 1992. "Why Africa? Anywhere but Bosnia." *TNR*, 28 Dec., 20.

———. 1993. "Somalia vs. Bosnia. Now. The 'Doable' War." *TNR*, 16 Aug., 15–18.

Goemans, Henk. 1996. "War and Punishment: War Termination and the Fate of Political Leaders." Paper presented at the annual meeting of the American Political Science Association, San Francisco.

———. 2000. *War and Punishment: The Causes of War Termination and the First World War*. Princeton: Princeton University Press.

Goldman, Nancy L., and David R. Segal, eds. 1976. *The Social Psychology of Military Service*. Beverly Hills: Sage.

Goldstein, Judith, and Robert Keohane. 1993. *Ideas and Foreign Policy: Beliefs, Institutions and Political Change*. Ithaca: Cornell University Press.

Gompert, David C. 1996. "The United States and Yugoslavia's Wars." In *The World and Yugoslavia's Wars*, ed. Richard H. Ullman, New York: Council on Foreign Relations. 121–124.

Goodpaster, Andrew J., and Samuel P. Huntington. 1977. *Civil-Military Relations*. Washington, D.C.: American Enterprise Institute.

Gordon, Michael R. 1992a. "Bush Backs a Ban on Combat Flights in Bosnia Airspace, Rejects Powell's Advice." *NYT*, 2 Oct., A1.

———. 1992b. "Bush Would Use Force to Ban Serbs' War Flights." *NYT*, 3 Oct., A1.

———. 1992c. "Powell Delivers a Resounding No on Using Limited Force in Bosnia." *NYT*, 28 Sept., A1, A5.

———. 1992d. "Report by Powell Challenges Calls to Revise Military." *NYT*, 31 Dec., A1, A10.

———. 1992e. "UN Backs Somalia Force; Bush Promises Quick Exit but Pentagon Is Less Sure." *NYT*, 4 Dec., A1.

———. 1993a. "Joint Chiefs Warn Congress against More Military Cuts." *NYT*, 16 April, A8.

———. 1993b. "A Limited Mission: Sidestepping the Issue of Aidid's Capture, U.S. and UN Can Claim Complete Success." *NYT*, 18 June, A7.

———. 1993c. "Military Officials Say U.S. Role in Bosnia Would Help Little." *NYT*, 30 Jan., I4.

———. 1994a. "NATO Craft Down 4 Serb Warplanes Attacking Bosnia." *NYT*, 1 Mar., A1.

———. 1994b. "Pentagon's Haiti Policy Focuses on Casualties." *NYT*, 6 Oct., A5.

———. 1994c. "Secretary of Defense Wins Few Points for Candor, Liz." *NYT*, 8 April, A10.

———. 1994d. "U.S. Rules Out Using Force to Save Muslim Town." *NYT,* 4 April, A1.

Gordon, Michael R., and John H. Cushman. 1993. "U.S. Supported Hunt for Aidid." *NYT,* 18 Oct., A8.

Gordon, Michael R., and Eric Schmitt. 1999. "Pentagon Withholds Copters from Battlefields in Kosovo." *NYT,* 16 May, A1.

Gordon, Michael R., and Bernard E. Trainor. 1996. *The General's War: The Inside Story of the Conflict in the Gulf.* Boston: Little, Brown.

Goshko, John M. 1992. "U.S. Seeks New Ways to Prod Haitian Military." *WP,* 26 Mar., A37.

———. 1994. "Reaction to Lifting Ban on Bosnia Muslim Arms Worries Administration." *WP,* 13 Aug., A14.

Graham, Bradley. 1996. "Army Leaders Feared Aberdeen Coverup Allegations." *WP,* 11 Nov., A1.

———. 1997. "Clinton Decides to Maintain U.S. Military Presence in Haiti." *WP,* 6 Dec., A26.

———. 1998. "Military Leaders Worry Privately about Impact: Some Troops Offended by Double Standard." *WP,* 15 Sept., A10.

———. 1999a. "Cohen Takes Flak for Clark Decision." *WP,* 29 July, A4.

———. 1999b. "Joint Chiefs Doubted Air Strategy." *WP,* 5 April, 1.

———. 1999c. "US Analysts Misread, Relied on Outdated Map." *WP,* 11 May, 17.

Graham, Bradley, and Dana Priest. 1999. "NATO Commander to Leave: Clark Had Strains with Pentagon over Kosovo." *WP,* 28 July, A1.

Greenhouse, Steven. 1994. "Clinton Proposes Deadline to End Bosnia Arms Embargo." *NYT,* 12 Aug., A3.

Greig, Geordie. 1992. "Republicans Take Heart as Slick Willy Fails to Dodge Vietnam Flak." *Sunday Times* (London), 27 Sept., 17.

Grundstein, Nathan D. 1961. *Presidential Delegation of Authority in Wartime.* Pittsburgh: University of Pittsburgh Press.

Hackworth, David H. 1993. "Rancor in the Ranks: The Troops vs. the President." *Newsweek,* 28 June, 24–25.

Hadley, Arthur T. 1986. *The Straw Giant: Triumph and Failure: America's Armed Forces.* New York: Random House.

Hahn, Robert F. 1997. "Politics for Warriors: The Political Education of Professional Military Officers." John M. Olin Institute for Strategic Studies, Project on U.S. Post Cold-War Civil-Military Relations, Working Paper no 12.

Halberstam, David. 1972. *The Best and the Brightest.* New York: Random House.

———. 2001a. "Clinton and the Generals." *Vanity Fair,* Sept., 230.

———. 2001b. *War in a Time of Peace: Bush, Clinton, and the Generals.* New York: Scribner.

Halloran, Richard. 1988. "What Terrifies the Toughest Soldiers? A Civilian Military Plan." *NYT,* 14 April, 1.

Halperin, Morton. 1972. "The President and the Military." *Foreign Affairs* 50, no. 2 (Jan.): 310–324.

———. 1974. *Bureaucratic Politics and Foreign Policy*. Washington, D.C.: Brookings.

Hamilton, James T., and Christopher H. Schroeder. 1994. "Strategic Regulators and the Choice of Rulemaking Procedures: The Selection of Formal vs. Informal Rules in Regulating Hazardous Waste." *Law and Contemporary Problems* 57, nos. 1–2: 111–165.

Hammond, Thomas H., Jeffrey S. Hill, and Gary J. Miller. 1986. "Presidents, Congress, and the 'Congressional Control of Administration' Hypothesis." Paper presented at the annual meeting of the American Political Science Association, Washington, D.C.

Hanks, Robert J. 1970. "Against All Enemies." *USNI* 96, no. 3 (Mar.): 22–29.

Harris, John F. 1994. "Military's Rapid Switch in Haiti a Tactical Winner for Joint Force Planner." *WP*, 28 Sept., 21.

Harris, John, and Bradley Graham. 1999. "Clinton Is Reassessing Sufficiency of Air War." *WP*, 3 June, 1.

Harris, John F., and Dana Priest. 1997. "Alliance Gets Aggressive on Arrests." *WP*, 11 July, A1.

Hartley, Thomas, and Bruce Russett. 1992. "Public Opinion and the Common Defense: Who Governs Military Spending in the United States." *APSR* 86, no. 4: 905–915.

Hedges, Chris. 1996. "Diplomats Fault Bosnia NATO Chief." *NYT*, 28 April, 19.

———. 1997. "NATO Troops Raid Serb Hard-Liners in Bosnian City." *NYT*, 21 Aug., 1.

Henderson, William Darryl. 1985. *Cohesion, the Human Element in Combat: Leadership and Societal Influence in the Armies of the Soviet Union, the United States, North Vietnam, and Israel*. Washington, D.C.: National Defense University Press.

Hendrickson, David. 1988. *Reforming Defense: The State of American Civil-Military Relations*. Baltimore: Johns Hopkins University Press.

Henkin, Louis. 1972. *Foreign Affairs and the Constitution*. Mineola, N.Y.: Foundation Press.

Herken, Gregg. 1985. *Counsels of War*. New York: Knopf.

Herring, George C. 1994. *LBJ and Vietnam: A Different Kind of War*. Austin: University of Texas Press.

Hersh, Seymour M. 1983. *The Price of Power: Kissinger in the Nixon White House*. New York: Summit.

———. 1986. *The Target Is Destroyed: What Really Happened to Flight 007 and What America Knew about It*. New York: Random House.

———. 1998. "The Missiles of August." *New Yorker*, 12 Oct., 34–41.

———. 2001. "Escape and Evasion," *New Yorker*, 12 Nov.

Hicks, Louis Ephraim. 1991. "From Coercion to Persuasion: Social Control in the U.S. Army from 1917 to 1989." MA thesis, University of Virginia.

———. 1994. "The Effect of Technology on Social Control in U.S. Military Organizations: Trends in Court-Martial Rates from 1917–1991." Ph.D. diss., University of Virginia.

Hillen, John. 1998. "The Civilian-Military Gap: Keep It, Defend It, Manage It." *USNI* 124 (Oct.): 2–4.

———. 1999. "Must U.S. Military Culture Reform?" *Orbis* 43 (Winter): 43–57.

Hines, Cragg. 1992. "Clinton's Vow to Lift Gay Ban Is Reaffirmed." *Houston Chronicle,* 12 Nov., A1.

———. 1999. "Pity, Not U.S. Security, Motivated Use of GIs in Somalia, Bush Says." *Houston Chronicle,* 24 Oct., A11.

Hirsch, John L., and Robert B. Oakley. 1995. *Somalia and Operation Restore Hope: Reflections on Peacemaking and Peacekeeping.* Washington, D.C.: United States Institute of Peace Press.

Hoar, Joseph P. 1993. "A CINC's Perspective." *Joint Force Quarterly* 2 (Autumn): 56–63.

Hockstader, Lee. 1997. "Bosnian Serbs Again Attack U.S. Troops." *WP,* 2 Sept., 1.

Hofstetter, C. Richard, and David W. Moore. 1979. "Watching TV News and Supporting the Military: A Surprising Impact of the News Media." *AFS* 5, no. 2: 261–269.

Holbrooke, Richard. 1998. *To End a War.* New York: Random House.

Holger, Robert, and Stephen LeSueur. 1994. "JCS Chairman's Rising Clout Threatens Civilian Leaders." *Defense News,* 13–19 June, 29.

Holland, Lauren. 1999. "The U.S. Decision to Launch Desert Storm: A Bureaucratic Analysis." *AFS* 25, no. 2.: 219–242.

Holmes, Richard. 1985. *Acts of War: The Behavior of Men in Battle.* New York: Free Press.

Holsti, Ole. 1996. *Public Opinion and American Foreign Policy.* Ann Arbor: University of Michigan Press.

———. 1997. "A Widening Gap between the Military and Society? Some Evidence, 1976–1996." John M. Olin Institute for Strategic Studies, Project on U.S. Post–Cold War Civil-Military Relations, Working Paper no. 13.

———. 1998–99. "A Widening Gap between the U.S. Military and Civilian Society? Some Evidence, 1976–96." *International Security* 23, no. 2 (Winter 1998–99): 5–42.

———. 2001. "Of Chasms and Convergences: Attitudes and Beliefs of Civilians and Military Elites at the Start of the New Millenium." In Peter D. Feaver and Richard H. Kohn, eds., *Soldiers and Civilians: The Civil-Military Gap and American National Security.* Cambridge, Mass.: MIT Press.

Hoopes, Townsend. 1954. "Civilian-Military Balance." *Yale Review* 43 (Winter): 218–234.

Horowitz, Donald. 1985. *Ethnic Groups in Conflict.* Berkeley: University of California Press.

Huntington, Samuel P. 1956. "Civilian Control of the Military: A Theoretical Statement." In Heinz Eulau, Samuel J. Eldersveld, and Morris Janowitz, eds., *Political Behavior: A Reader in Theory and Research.* Glencoe, IL: Free Press.

———. 1957. *The Soldier and the State: The Theory and Politics of Civil-Military Relations.* Cambridge, Mass.: Harvard University Press.

———. 1961a. *The Common Defense: Strategic Programs in National Politics.* New York: Columbia University Press.

———. 1961b. "Interservice Competition and the Political Roles of the Armed Services." *APSR* 55, no. 1 (Mar.): 40–52.

———. 1963. "Power, Expertise and the Military Profession." *Daedalus* 92, no. 4 (Fall): 785–807.

———. 1968. *Political Order in Changing Societies*. New Haven: Yale University Press.

Husarska, Anna. 1995. "Fort Drum Diarist: Military Music." *TNR*, 10 July, 42.

Ifill, Gwen. 1993. "President Defends American Presence in Somalia." *NYT*, 18 Sept., A5.

Ingram, Samuel P. 1968. "Civilian Command or Civilian Control," *USNI* 94, no. 5: 26–31

Irvine, Dallas D. 1938. "The Origin of Capital Staffs." *Journal of Modern History* 10, no. 2 (June): 161–179.

Isaacson, Walter. 1992. *Kissinger: A Biography*. New York: Simon and Schuster.

Jacobs, James B. 1978. "Legal Change within the United States Armed Forces since World War II." *AFS* 4, no. 3 (May 1978): 391–421.

Jaffe, Lorna. 1993. *The Development of the Base Force, 1989–1992*. Washington, D.C.: Joint History Office, Office of the Chairman of the Joint Chiefs of Staff.

James, D. Clayton. 1985. *The Years of MacArthur*, vol. 3: *Triumph and Disaster, 1945–1964*. Boston: Houghton Mifflin.

Janowitz, Morris. 1971. *The Professional Soldier: A Social and Political Portrait*, 2nd ed. New York: Free Press.

———. 1974. "Toward a Redefinition of Military Strategy in International Relations." *World Politics* 26, no. 4 (July): 473–508.

———. 1991. *On Social Organization and Social Control*, ed. James Burk. Chicago: University of Chicago Press.

Javits, Jacob K. 1973. *Who Makes War: The President vs. Congress*. New York: Morrow.

Jehl, Douglas. 1993. "U.S. Shifts Troops to Defense Role in Somalia Mission." *NYT*, 20 Oct., A1.

Jervis, Robert. 1976. *Perception and Misperception in International Politics*. Princeton: Princeton University Press.

Joffe, Josef. 1993. "Democracy and Deterrence: What Have They Done to Each Other?" In Linda B. Miller and Michael Joseph Smith, eds., *Ideas and Ideals: Essays on Politics in Honor of Stanley Hoffmann*. Boulder: Westview.

Johnson, David E. 1996. "Wielding the Terrible Swift Sword: The American Military Paradigm and Civil-Military Relations." John M. Olin Institute for Strategic Studies, Project on U.S. Post Cold-War Civil-Military Relations, Working Paper no. 7.

Johnson, Douglas V. II, and Steven Metz. 1995. "American Civil-Military Relations: New Issues, Enduring Problems." Strategic Studies Institute, Carlisle, Pa., 24 April.

Jonas, David S., and Hagen W. Frank. 1993. "Basic Military Leadership." *WP*, 4 April, C7.

Jones, Tamara. 1996a. "The Pilot's Cloudy Future." *WP*, 29 April, D1.

———. 1996b. "U.S. Military Takes Aim at Adultery: In the Wake of Sex Scandals, Services Mete out Harsh Penalties for Illicit Romance." *WP*, 28 April, 1.

Kagan, Robert, and William Kristol. 2001a. "Getting Serious." *Weekly Standard*, 19 Nov.

———. 2001b. "A Winning Strategy." *Weekly Standard,* 26 Nov.

Kamen, Al, and John Goshko. 1992. "U.S. Plans to Ease Embargo on Haiti." *WP,* 5 Feb.

Kaplan, Fred. 1983. *Wizards of Armageddon.* New York: Simon and Schuster.

Kaplan, Lawrence. 2001. "Ours to Lose." *TNR,* 12 Nov.

Kaufman, Burton I. 1986. *The Korea War: Challenges in Crisis, Credibility, and Command.* Philadelphia: Temple University Press.

Kearns, Doris. 1976. *Lyndon Johnson and the American Dream.* New York: Harper and Row.

Kemp, Kenneth W., and Charles Hudlin. 1992. "Civil Supremacy over the Military: Its Nature and Limits." *AFS* 19, no. 1 (Fall): 7–26.

Kennedy, Robert. 1971. *Thirteen Days: A Memoir of the Cuban Missile Crisis.* New York: Norton.

Kernell, Samuel, and Samuel Popkin. 1986. *Chief of Staff.* Berkeley: University of California Press.

Kerwin, Jerome G. 1948. *Civil-Military Relationships in American Life.* Chicago: University of Chicago Press.

Kier, Elisabeth. 1997. *Imagining War: French and British Military Doctrine between the Wars.* Princeton: Princeton University Press.

Kiewet, D. Roderick, and Mathew D. McCubbins. 1991. *The Logic of Delegation: Congressional Parties and the Appropriations Process.* Chicago: Chicago University Press.

Kifner, John. 1996. "In Saudi Base Bombing, Debate on Placing Blame." *NYT,* 6 Dec., 1.

Kirkpatrick, Samuel A., and James L. Regens. 1978. *Journal of Political and Military Sociology* 6, no. 1 (Spring): 29–47.

Kirschten, Dick. 1994. "Off Shore, Bill Clinton's at Sea." *National Journal,* 30 April, 1040.

Kissinger, Henry. 1982. *Years of Upheaval.* Boston: Little, Brown.

Kitfield, James. 1998. "Standing Apart." *National Journal,* 13 June, 1350–1358.

Klein, Joe. 2000. "Eight Years: Bill Clinton and the Politics of Persistence." *New Yorker,* 16 and 23 Oct., 188–209.

Kohn, Richard. H. 1994. "Out of Control." *National Interest* 35 (Spring): 3–31.

———. 1997. "How Civilians Control the Military." *Journal of Democracy* 8: 140–153.

———. 2002. *The Erosion of Civilian Control of the Military in the United States Today.* Harmon Memorial Lecture in Military History no. 42. Colorado Springs: U.S. Air Force Academy.

———, ed. 2001. "The Early Retirement of Gen. Ronald R. Fogleman, Chief of Staff, United States Air Force." *Aerospace Power Journal* (Spring): 6–23.

Kohn, Richard. H., and Joseph P. Harahan, eds. 1988. "U.S. Strategic Air Power, 1948–1962: Excerpts from an Interview with Generals Curtis E. LeMay, Leon W. Johnson, David A. Burchinal, and Jack J. Catton." *International Security* 12, no. 4 (Spring): 83–85.

Kolodziej, Edward. 1966. *The Uncommon Defense and Congress, 1945–1963.* Columbus: Ohio State University Press.

Komarow, Steve, 1994. "Clinton Carrying Extra 'Baggage.'" *USA Today,* 31 May, 8.

———. 1996. "Clinton on Good Footing in Bosnia." *USA Today,* 15 Jan., 1.

Komer, Robert. 1986. *Bureaucracy at War: U.S. Performance in the Vietnam Conflict.* Boulder: Westview.

Korb, Lawrence. 1976. *The Joint Chiefs of Staff: The First Twenty-Five Years.* Bloomington: Indiana University Press.

——. 1996a. "The Military and Social Change." John M. Olin Institute for Strategic Studies, Project on U.S. Post Cold-War Civil-Military Relations, Working Paper no. 5.

——. 1996b. "The President, the Congress, and the Pentagon: Obstacles to Implementing the 'Don't Ask, Don't Tell' Policy." In Gregory M. Herek, Jared B. Jobe, and Ralph M. Carney, eds., *Out in Force: Sexual Orientation and the Military.* Chicago: University of Chicago Press. 290–301.

Kranish, Michael. 1992. "In Florida, Bush Attacks Clinton on Draft Issue." *NYT,* 4 Oct., A18.

Krause, Clifford. 1993. "House Vote Urges Clinton to Limit American Role in Somalia Conflict." *NYT,* 29 Sept., A1.

Krepinevich, Andrew F. 1986. *The Army in Vietnam.* Baltimore: Johns Hopkins University Press.

Kreps, David M. 1990. "Corporate Culture and Economic Theory." In *Perspectives on Positive Political Economy,* ed. James E. Alt and Kenneth A. Shepsle. New York: Cambridge University Press.

Kretchik, Walter E., Robert F. Baumann, and John T. Fishel. 1999. *Invasion, Intervention, Intervasion: A Concise History of U.S. Operations in Haiti.* Fort Leavenworth, Kans.: U.S. Army Command and General Staff College Press.

Labash, Matt. 1997. "The Scapegoat: How the Secretary of Defense Ended the Career of an Exemplary Air Force General." *Weekly Standard,* 24 Nov., 20–29.

Lancaster, John. 1993a. "Accused of Ridiculing Clinton, General Faces Air Force Probe." *WP,* 8 June, A1.

——. 1993b. "Air Force General Sets Retirement." *WP,* 19 June, A1.

——. 1993c. "Army Challenges Clinton Defense Cuts as Security Threat." *WP,* 13 Nov., A16.

——. 1993d. "Clinton and the Military: Is Gay Policy Just the Opening Skirmish?" *WP,* 1 Feb., A10.

——. 1993e. "Crowe Discounts Military Objection to Homosexuals." *WP,* 11 April, A16.

Lancaster, John, and Ann Dewey. 1993. "Storming the Pentagon." *WP,* 9 April, A1.

Lane, Charles. 1995. "The Legend of Colin Powell." *TNR,* 17 April, 20–32.

Langston, Thomas. Draft. "In the Shadow of War: Military-Society Relations and the Transition to Peace."

Larson, Arthur D. 1974. "Military Professionalism and Civil Control: A Comparative Analysis of Two Interpretations." *Journal of Political and Military Sociology* 2, no. 1 (Spring): 57–72.

Lasswell, Harold D. 1941. "The Garrison State and Specialists on Violence." *American Journal of Sociology* 46: 455–468.

——. 1950. *National Security and Individual Freedom.* New York: McGraw-Hill.

————. 1962. "The Garrison-State Hypothesis Today." In Samuel P. Huntington, ed., *Changing Patterns of Military Politics*, New York: Free Press of Glencoe. 51–70.

Lebow, Richard Ned. 1987. *Nuclear Crisis Management: A Dangerous Illusion*. Ithaca: Cornell University Press.

————. 1988. "Clausewitz, Loss of Control, and Crisis Management." In Gilbert R. Winham, ed., *New Issues in International Crisis Management*. Boulder: Westview. 37–66.

Lebow, Richard Ned, and Janice Gross Stein. 1994. *We All Lost the Cold War*. Princeton: Princeton University Press.

Lehman. John. 1996. "The Navy's Enemies." *WSJ*, 21 May, 22.

LeSueur, Stephen C. 1993. "Women Find Easy Acceptance in DoD Male Bastion." *Defense News*, 6 Dec., 14.

Lewis, Anthony. 1991. "Where Is the Outrage?" *NYT*, 4 Nov., A19.

Lind, William S., John F. Schmitt, and Gary I. Wilson. 1994. "Fourth Generation Warfare: Another Look." *Marine Corps Gazette* (Dec.): 34–37.

Lindsay, James M. 1994a. "Congress, Foreign Policy, and the New Institutionalism." *International Studies Quarterly* 38, no. 2: 281–304.

————. 1994b. *Congress and the Politics of U.S. Foreign Policy*. Baltimore: Johns Hopkins University Press.

Lippman, Thomas W., and John Lancaster. 1994. "Clinton Team Is Committed to Airstrikes." *WP*, 12 April, A1.

Loeb, Vernon. 2001. "Rumsfeld May Let Military Branches Decide Cutbacks." *WP*, 17 Aug., A5.

Lorch, Donatella. 1993. "U.S. Flies Faction Leader, An Ex-Foe, to Somalia Talks." *NYT*, 3 Dec., A7.

Lorenz, F. M. 1996. "Non-Lethal Force: The Slippery Slope to War?" *Parameters* (Autumn): 52–62.

Lovell, John P. 1974. "The Agonies of Adjustment to Post-Vietnam Realities." In John P. Lovell and Philip S. Kronenberg, eds., *New Civil-Military Relations: The Agonies of Adjustment to Post-Vietnam Realities*. New Brunswick: Transaction.

————. 1987. "Vietnam and the U.S. Army: Learning to Cope with Failure." In George Osborn et al., eds., *Democracy, Strategy, and Vietnam: Implications for American Policymaking*, Lexington, Mass.: D. C. Heath. 121–154.

Lovell, John P., and Philip S. Kronenberg, eds. 1974. *New Civil-Military Relations: The Agonies of Adjustment to Post-Vietnam Realities*. New Brunswick: Transaction.

Lowenthal, Mark M., and Robert L. Goldich. 1992. *Use of Force by the United States: Case Studies, 1950–1991*. Congressional Research Service. 92–757 F, 14 Oct.

Lupia, Arthur, and Mathew D. McCubbins. 1994. "Designing Bureaucratic Accountability." *Law and Contemporary Problems* 57, nos. 1–2: 91–126.

Lurie, Jonathan. 1992. *Arming Military Justice*. Princeton: Princeton University Press.

Luttwak, Edward. 1993. "Unconventional Force." *TNR*, 25 Jan., 22.

————. 1994. "Washington's Biggest Scandal." *Commentary* (May).

Lynch, Maj. Gen. J. D. 1997. "All Volunteer Force Is in Crisis." *USNI* 123, no. 9 (Sept.): 30–34.

Lynn, John A. 1996. "The Evolution of Army Style in the Modern West, 800–2000."
International History Review 18, no. 3 (Aug.): 505–545.

Lyons, Gene M. 1961. "The New Civil-Military Relations." *APSR* 55, no. 1 (Mar.):
53–63.

MacArthur, Douglas. 1964. *Reminiscences.* New York: McGraw-Hill.

Maraniss, David. 1996. "First and Last: Bill Clinton Gets Places before His Peers. Bob
Dole Has Outlasted a Generation." *Washington Post Magazine,* 27 Oct., W8.

March, James. 1978. "Bounded Rationality, Ambiguity, and the Engineering of
Choice." *Bell Journal of Economics* 9 (Autumn): 587–608.

March, James, and Johan Olsen. 1984. "The New Institutionalism." *APSR* 78, no. 3:
734–739.

Marcus, Ruth, and Ann Devroy. 1993. "Clinton to Double Force in Somalia." *WP,* 8
Oct., A1.

Marshall, S. L. A. 1947. *Men against Fire.* Toronto: McClelland and Stewart.

Martin, David. 1993. "Landing the Eagle." *Vanity Fair* (Nov.).

Masland, John W., and Laurence I. Radway. 1957. *Soldiers and Scholars: Military Education and National Policy.* Princeton: Princeton University Press.

Masland, Tom, and Douglas Waller. 1994. "Should We Invade Haiti?" *Newsweek,* 18
July, 40.

Mathis, Nancy. 1992a. "Clinton Douses Flames of Perot Campaign, Bush Attack."
Houston Chronicle, 13 Oct., A12.

———. 1992b. "Clinton Launches Damage Control." *Houston Chronicle,* 13 Feb. A1.

Matthews, Christopher. 1993. "Clinton, Drop Military Salute." *Arizona Republic,* 22
Mar., A11.

May, A. L. 1992. "Election '92: Clinton Says Draft Rules Favored People like Him."
Atlanta Constitution, 20 Sept., A6.

Mayer, William G. 1992. *The Changing American Mind: How and Why American Public
Opinion Changed between 1960 and 1988.* Ann Arbor: University of Michigan Press.

Mayhew, David. 1974. *Congress: The Electoral Connection.* New Haven: Yale University
Press.

Mazetti, Mark, and Richard J. Newman. 2001. "Rumsfeld's Way." *U.S. News and
World Report,* 17 Dec.

McCaffrey, Lt. Gen. Barry. 1993. "Good Vibes between White House, Military." *NYT,*
6 April, A15.

McClosky, Herbert, and John Zaller. 1984. *The American Ethos: Public Attitudes toward
Capitalism and Democracy.* Cambridge, Mass.: Harvard University Press.

McCubbins, Mathew D., and Thomas Schwartz. 1984. "Congressional Oversight
Overlooked: Police Patrols versus Fire Alarms." *American Journal of Political Science*
2: 165–179.

McDonough, James R. 1998. "Clinton's Contempt for U.S. Soldiers." *WSJ,* 28 Sept.,
A28.

McGarvey, Patrick J. 1969. *Visions of Victory: Selected Vietnamese Military Writings, 1964–
1968.* Stanford: Hoover Institution Press.

McGrory, Brian. 1998. "U.S. Military, Clinton Achieve Wary Truce." *Boston Globe,* 22
Feb., 1.

McGreary, Joanna. 1996. "Did the American Mission Matter?" *Time,* 12 Feb., 36.

McMaster, H. R. 1997. *Dereliction of Duty: Lyndon Johnson, Robert McNamara, the Joint Chiefs of Staff, and the Lies that Led to Vietnam.* New York: HarperCollins.

McMichael, William H. 1997. *The Mother of All Hooks: The Story of the U.S. Navy's Tailhook Scandal.* New Brunswick: Transaction.

McNamara, Robert, with Brian VanDeMark. 1995. *In Retrospect: The Tragedy and Lessons of Vietnam.* New York: Times Books.

McNollgast. 1987. "Administrative Procedures as Instruments of Political Control." *Journal of Law, Economics, and Organization* 6: 243–277.

———. 1989. "Structure and Process, Politics and Policy: Administrative Arrangements and the Political Control of Agencies." *Virginia Law Review* 75: 431–482.

———. 1990a. "Positive and Normative Models of Procedural Rights: An Integrative Approach to Administrative Procedures." *Journal of Law, Economics, and Organization* 6: 307–332.

———. 1990b. "Slack, Public Interest, and Structure-Induced Equilibrium." *Journal of Law, Economics, and Organization* 6: 203–212.

Menkhaus, Ken, and Louis Ortmayer. 1995. "Key Decisions in the Somalia Intervention." Pew Case Studies in International Affairs, no. 464. Washington, D.C.: Institute for the Study of Diplomacy.

Miles, Jack L. 1968. "The Fusion of Military and Political Considerations: Threat or Challenge to the Military." *Marine Corps Gazette* 52, no. 8 (Aug.): 22–29; no. 9 (Sept.): 45–52.

Milgrom, Paul, and John Roberts. 1988. "An Economic Approach to Influence Activities in Organizations." *American Journal of Sociology* 94 (Supplement): S154–S179.

———. 1990. "Bargaining Costs, Influence Costs, and the Organization of Economic Activity." In James E. Alt and Kenneth A. Shepsle, eds. *Perspectives on Positive Political Economy,* Cambridge: Cambridge University Press. 57–89.

Miller, Gary J. 1992. *Managerial Dilemmas: The Political Economy of Hierarchy.* New York: Cambridge University Press.

Miller, Laura, and Jay Allen Williams. 2001. "Combat Effectiveness vs. Civil Rights? U.S. Military Culture, Cohesion, and Personnel Policies in the 1990s." In Peter D. Feaver and Richard H. Kohn, eds., *Soldiers and Civilians: The Civil-Military Gap and American National Security.* Cambridge, Mass.: MIT Press.

Millett, Alan R. 1979. *The American Political System and Civilian Control of the Military: A Historical Perspective.* Columbus: Mershon Center, Ohio State University.

Millett, Allan R., and Peter Maslowski. 1994. *For the Common Defense: A Military History of the United States of America,* 2nd ed. New York: Free Press.

Millis, Walter. 1956. *Arms and Men: A Study of American Military History.* New York: Putnam.

Millis, Walter, H. Mansfield, and Harold Stein. 1958. *Arms and the State: Civil-Military Elements in National Policy.* New York: Twentieth Century Fund.

Mills, C. Wright. 1956. *The Power Elite.* New York: Oxford University Press.

Mitnick, Barry M. 1975. "The Theory of Agency: The Policing 'Paradox' and Regulatory Behavior." *Public Choice* 25: 27–42.

————. 1994. "The Hazards of Agency." Paper presented at the annual meeting of the American Political Science Association, New York.

Moe, Terry M. 1984. "The New Economics of Organization." *American Journal of Political Science* 28, no. 4.

————. 1987. "An Assessment of the Positive Theory of 'Congressional Dominance.'" *Legislative Studies Quarterly* (Nov.): 475–520.

————. 1990. "The Politics of Structural Choice: Toward a Theory of Public Bureaucracy." In Oliver Williamson, ed., *Organizational Theory: From Chester Barnard to the Present and Beyond.* New York: Oxford University Press.

Morley, Morris, and Chris McGillion. 1997. "'Disobedient Generals and the Politics of Re-Democratization: The Clinton Administration and Haiti." *Political Science Quarterly* 112, no. 3 (Fall): 363–384.

Morton, Louis. 1964. "Civilians and Soldiers: Civil-Military Relations in the United States." In William H. Nelson, ed., *Theory and Practice in American Politics.* Chicago: University of Chicago Press. 123–138.

Moskos, Charles C. 1970. *The American Enlisted Man: The Rank and File in Today's Military.* New York: Russell Sage Foundation.

————. 1974. "Foreword." In John P. Lovell and Philip S. Kronenberg, eds., *New Civil-Military Relations: The Agonies of Adjustment to Post-Vietnam Realities.* New Brunswick: Transaction.

————. 1977. "From Institution to Occupation: Trends in the Military Organization." *AFS* 4, no. 1: 41–50.

————, ed. 1971. *Public Opinion and the Military Establishment.* Beverly Hills: Sage.

Moskos, Charles C., and Frank R. Wood, eds. 1988. *The Military: More Than Just a Job?* Washington, D.C.: Pergamon-Brassey's.

Moss, J. 1992. "Clinton Vows to Allow Gays in Military." *WT,* 12 Nov., A1.

Mueller, John. 1995. "The Perfect Enemy: Assessing the Gulf War." *Security Studies* 5, no. 1 (Autumn): 77–117.

Myers, Steven Lee. 1999a. "Military Chiefs Firm: No Ground Force for Kosovo." *NYT,* 3 June, A16.

————. 1999b. "NATO Leaders Reject Plan to Fire on Ships That Defy Oil Embargo." *NYT,* 5 May, 11.

Nelson, Daniel N. 2001. "Definition, Diagnosis, Therapy: A Civil/Military Critique." Paper presented at the conference "Taking Stock on Civil-Military Relations," sponsored by the Centre for European Security Studies, The Hague.

Newhouse, John. 1992. "The Diplomatic Round (Yugoslavia)." *New Yorker,* 24 Aug., 60–71.

Niskanen, William. 1971. *Bureaucracy and Representative Government.* Chicago: Aldine-Atherton.

No author. 1963. "Adm. Anderson Is Given a Medal by President." *NYT,* 31 July, 4.

————. 1984a. "New Pentagon Stand on When to Fight." *U.S. News and World Report,* 10 Dec., 8.

————. 1984b. "Shultz vs. Weinberger: When to Use U.S. Power." *U.S. News and World Report,* 24 Dec., 21.

———. 1992. "Our 'No Can Do' Military." *NYT,* 4 Oct., D12.

———. 1993a. "Bush, in West Point Valedictory, Offers Principles on Use of Force." *NYT,* 5 Jan., A6.

———. 1993b. "Clinton's Picks Faster than Bush's, Lag Reagan's." 1993. *WP,* 25 July, A8.

———. 1993c. "Clinton's Quick Steps to Better Relations; After Summit Jog, General Snubbed at White House Has Warm Words for President." *WP,* 6 April, A7.

———. 1993d. "The Military and the Commander-in-Chief." Transcript of *ABC News Nightline,* 30 Mar.

———. 1993e. "The Pentagon's Missing Civilians." *WP,* 27 June, C6.

———. 1993f. "Who's in Charge of the Military." *NYT,* 26 Jan., A18.

———. 1994a. "Bill Clinton at Normandy." *WP,* 7 June, A18.

———. 1994b. "Pentagon's Haiti Policy Focuses on Casualties." *NYT,* 6 Oct., A5.

———. 1994c. "Wars and Generations." *NYT,* 7 June, A22.

———. 1995a. "Colin Powell as JCS Chairman: A Panel Discussion on American Civil-Military Relations." John M. Olin Institute for Strategic Studies, Project on U.S. Post Cold-War Civil-Military Relations, Working Paper no. 1.

———. 1995b. "U.S. Seeks to Defuse Controversy over Admiral's Remarks." Reuters, 19 Nov.

———. 1999. "Clark's Firepower Requests for Kosovo Prompt Anxiety among Chiefs." *Inside the Pentagon,* 15 April, 1.

———. 2001a. "Military Brass Wondering Whether Heads Will Roll Again under Bush." *Chicago Sun-Times,* 3 Mar., 12.

———. 2001b. "Rumsfeld Upset by Joint Chiefs' $10B Supplemental Plan." *Congress Daily,* 24 Jan.

Nolan, Janne E. 1989. *Guardians of the Arsenal: The Politics of Nuclear Strategy.* New York: Basic Books.

Nordlinger, Eric. 1977. *Soldiers in Politics: Military Coups and Governments.* New York: Prentice-Hall.

Nordlinger, Jay. 2001. "Rumsfeld Rules." *National Review,* 31 Dec.

Oberdorfer, Don. 1992a. "The Path to Intervention: A Massive Tragedy 'We Could Do Something About.'" *WP,* 6 Dec., A1.

———. 1992b. "U.S. Moves to Protect Somalia Food Aid." *WP,* 25 Nov., A1.

Oberdorfer, Don, and Bart Gellman. 1992. "U.S. Plans Short Stay for Forces in Somalia; Bush's Goal Is Return of Troops by Jan. 20." *WP,* 2 Dec., A29.

Oberdorfer, Don, and John Lancaster. 1992. "Security Council to Consider Options for Protecting Relief Supply Lines." *WP,* 27 Nov., A1.

O'Meara, Andrew P. 1978. "Civil-Military Conflict within the Defense Structure." *Parameters* 8, no. 1 (Mar.): 85–92.

Ortmayer, Louis, and Joanna Flinn. 1997. "Hamstrung over Haiti: Returning the Refugees." Pew Case Studies in International Affairs. Washington, D.C.: Institute for the Study of Diplomacy.

Osiel, Mark J. 1999. *Obeying Orders: Atrocity, Military Discipline, and the Law of War.* New Brunswick: Transaction.

Owen, Robert C. 1997. "The Balkans Air Campaign Study: Part I." *Airpower Journal* 11, no. 2 (Summer 1997): 4–24.

Owens, Mackubin Thomas. 1990. "Micromanaging the Defense Budget." *Public Interest* 100 (Summer): 131–146.

Palmer, Bruce. 1984. *The 25-Year War: America's Military Role in Vietnam.* New York: Simon and Schuster.

Palmer, David R. 1978. *Summons of the Trumpet: US-Vietnam in Perspective.* Novato, Calif.: Presidio Press.

Pape, Robert A. 1996. *Bombing to Win: Air Power and Coercion in War.* Ithaca: Cornell University Press.

Perle, Richard N. 1995. "'Neutrality' Won't Protect Our Troops." *NYT,* 7 Dec., 31.

Perlez, Jane. 2000. "For 8 Years a Strained Relationship with the Military." *NYT,* 28 Dec., A13.

Perlmutter, Amos. 1977. *The Military and Politics in Modern Times: On Professionals, Praetorians, and Revolutionary Soldiers.* New Haven: Yale University Press.

Perry, Mark. 1989. *Four Stars.* Boston: Houghton Mifflin.

Perry, William J. 1994. Speech to the National Defense University, Fort McNair, 15 June.

Perry, William, and Gen. John Shalikashvili. 1995. "U.S. Involvement Underwrites Bosnian Peace Bid." *Defense Issues* 10, no. 90.

Peterson, V. Spike, ed. 1992. *Gendered States: Feminist (Re)Visions of International Relations Theory.* Boulder: Lynne Rienner.

Petraeus, David H. 1987. "The American Military and the Lessons of Vietnam." Ph.D. diss., Princeton University.

———. 1989. "Military Influence and the Post-Vietnam Use of Force." *AFS* 15, no. 4 (Summer): 489–505.

Pezzullo, Lawrence A. 1994. "Our Haiti Fiasco." *WP,* 3 May, A23.

Pfiffner, James P. 1996. *The Strategic Presidency: Hitting the Ground Running,* 2nd ed. Lawrence: University Press of Kansas.

Philpott, Tom. 1993. "Blue Mood Rising." *Army Times,* 14 June, 14–20.

Pine, Art. 1996. "Clinton Begins to Win over Military." *LAT,* 5 Feb., 1.

Pollack. Mark A. 1997. "Delegation, Agency, and Agenda Setting in the European Community." *International Organization* 51, no. 1 (Winter): 99–134.

Pomfret, John. 1996a. "Bosnia's Beat Police: U.S. MPs Fight Boredom to Keep Peace in Role More Patrolman Than Military." *WP,* 13 May, 13.

———. 1996b. "Perry Says NATO Will Not Serve as 'Police Force' in Bosnia Mission." *WP,* 4 Jan., 18.

Pomfret, John, and Lee Hockstader. 1997. "In Bosnia, a War Crimes Impasse." *WP,* 9 Dec., 1.

Posen, Barry R. 1982. "Inadvertent Nuclear War? Escalation and NATO's Northern Flank." *International Security* 7, no. 2 (Fall): 28–54.

———. 1984. *The Sources of Military Doctrine: France, Britain, and Germany between the World Wars.* Ithaca: Cornell University Press.

Post, Tom, et al. 1994. "Mixing the Signals." *Newsweek,* 16 May, 41.

Powell, Colin L. 1992. "Why Generals Get Nervous." *NYT,* 8 Oct., A35.

————. 1992–93. "U.S. Forces: Challenges Ahead." *Foreign Affairs* 71, no. 5 (Winter): 36–41.

————. 1995. *My American Journey.* New York: Random House.

Powell, Colin L., et al. 1994. "Exchange on Civil-Military Relations," with Colin Powell, John Lehman, William Odom, Samuel Huntington, and Richard Kohn. *National Interest* 36 (Summer): 23–31.

Previdi, Robert. 1988. *Civilian Control versus Military Rule: Has Congress Surrendered Control of the Armed Forces by Passing the Goldwater-Nichols Act?* New York: Hippocrene.

Priest, Dana. 1995. "1,400 U.S. Troops Part of Advance Group." *WP,* 28 Nov., 9.

————. 1998. "Military Reiterates Ban on 'Contemptuous Words' against President." *WP,* 21 Oct., A6.

————. 1999a. "The Battle inside Headquarters; Tension Grew with Divide over Strategy." *WP,* 21 Sept., A1.

————. 1999b. "Bombing by Committee; France Balked at NATO Targets." *WP,* 20 Sept., A1.

————. 1999c. "Target Selection Was Long Process; Sites Were Analyzed Again and Again." *WP,* 20 Sept., A11.

Priest, Dana, and William Drozdiak. 1999. "NATO Struggles to Make Progress from the Air." *WP,* 18 April, 1.

Putnam, Robert. 1995. "Bowling Alone: America's Declining Social Capital." *Journal of Democracy* 6, no. 1, 65–78.

Putzel, Michael. 1992. "Draft Questions Continue to Swirl around Candidates; Clinton's Response Has Stirred Doubts." *Boston Globe,* 21 Sept., 1.

Rabinowitz, Dorothy. 1994. "Normandy's Lessons for Clinton." *WSJ,* 13 June, A16.

Radine, Lawrence B. 1977. *The Taming of the Troops: Social Control in the United States Army.* Westport, Conn.: Greenwood.

Rahim, M. Afzalur, and Gabriel F. Buntzman. 1989. "Supervisory Power Bases, Styles of Handling Conflict with Subordinates, and Subordinate Compliance and Satisfaction." *Journal of Psychology* 123, no. 2: 195–210.

Rainbow, Fred, and John Miller. 1995. "An Interview with Admiral Smith." *USNI* (Sept.): 47–51.

Randal, Jonathan. 1994. "U.S. Planes Blast Serb Forces Again." *WP,* 12 April, A1.

Raymond, Jack. 1963. "Adm. Anderson Is Chosen as Envoy to Portugal." *NYT,* 22 May, 14.

Record, Jeffrey. 1996–97. "Vietnam in Retrospect: Could We Have Won?" *Parameters* 26, no. 4 (Winter): 51–65.

————. 2000. "Force-Protection Fetishism: Sources, Consequences, and (?) Solutions." *Airpower Journal* 14 (Summer): 4–11.

Rice, Condoleeza. 1984. *The Soviet Union and the Czechoslovak Army, 1948–1983: Uncertain Allegiance.* Princeton: Princeton University Press.

Richards, Diana, et al. 1993. "Good Times, Bad Times, and the Diversionary Use of Force." *Journal of Conflict Resolution* 37: 504–35.

Richburg, Keith B. 1993. "UN's Somalia Quandary." *WP,* 8 Aug., A19.

Richter, Paul. 1993. "Clinton's Visit Aboard Aircraft Carrier Makes a Few Waves with Crew." *LAT,* 13 Mar., A20.

———. 1999. "Critics See Idle Gunships as Sign of U.S. Hesitation." *LAT,* 10 April, 1.

———. 2001. "For the Military, Bush Is Not Yet All That He Can Be." *LAT,* 10 Feb., A1.

Ricks, Thomas E. 1993. "Colonel Dunlap's Coup: A Fictionalized Essay That Has Been Circulating within the Pentagon Offers a Blunt Warning on Several Fronts." *Atlantic* 271, no. 1 (Jan.): 23–25.

———. 1994. "As Pressure Mounts for Invasion of Haiti, U.S. Asks Others about Joining a Force." *WSJ,* 8 July, A3.

———. 1996. "On American Soil: The Widening Gap between the U.S. Military and U.S. Society." John M. Olin Institute for Strategic Studies, Working Paper no. 3, May.

———. 1997. *Making the Corps.* New York: Scribner.

———. 1999. "NATO Commander's Job Is Maintaining Support from Members for Airstrikes." *WSJ* (13 April): 10.

———. 2001a. "Review Fractures Pentagon; Officials Predict Major Military Changes Far Off." *WP* (14 July): A1.

———. 2001b. "Rumsfeld's Hands-On War." *WP,* 9 Dec., A1.

———. 2001c. "Target Approval Delays Cost Air Force Key Hits." *WP,* 18 Nov., 1.

———. 2002a. "Some Top Military Brass Favor Status Quo in Iraq." *WP,* 28 July, A1.

———. 2002b. "Timing, Tactics on Iraq War Disputed." *WP,* 1 Aug., A1.

Ricks, Thomas E., and Jeffrey H. Birnbaum. 1994. "Clinton Aides Hope D-Day Trip Will Establish a Beachhead with His Own Uneasy Military." *WSJ,* 1 June, A16.

Riehm, Peter J. A. 1997. "The USS Harlan County Affair." *Military Review* 77, no. 3 (July/Aug.): 31–36.

Ripley, Randall B., and James M. Lindsay, eds. 1993. *Congress Resurgent: Foreign and Defense Policy on Capitol Hill.* Ann Arbor: University of Michigan Press.

Robinson, Linda, and Kathie Klarreich. 1994. "Backing into a Corner." *U.S. News and World Report,* 27 June, 38.

Rogers, Lindsay. 1940. "Civilian Control of Military Policy." *Foreign Affairs* 18, no. 2 (Jan.): 280–291.

Roman, Peter J., and David W. Tarr. 1995. "Soldiers, Presidents, and the Use of Force in the Post Cold War." Paper presented at the annual meeting of the American Political Science Association, Chicago.

———. 2001. "The Military Leadership, Professionalism, and the Policy Making Process." In Peter D. Feaver and Richard H. Kohn, eds., *Soldiers and Civilians: The Civil-Military Gap and American National Security.* Cambridge, Mass., MIT Press.

Rosen, Stephen Peter. 1982. "Vietnam and the American Theory of Limited War." *International Security* 7, no. 2 (Fall): 83–113.

———. 1991. *Winning the Next War.* Ithaca: Cornell University Press.

Rosen, Steven. 1973. *Testing the Theory of the Military-Industrial Complex.* Lexington, Mass.: Lexington Books.

Rosenberg, David Alan. 1981–82. "'A Hulking, Radiating Ruin at the End of Two

Hours': Documents on American Plans for Nuclear War with the Soviet Union, 1954–1955." *International Security* 6, no. 3 (Winter): 3–38.

———. 1986. "Reality and Responsibility: Power and Process in the Making of United States Nuclear Strategy, 1945–68." *Journal of Strategic Studies* 9, no. 1 (Mar.): 35–52.

Rosenthal, Andrew. 1992a. "Bush Urges U.N. to Back Force to Get Aid to Bosnia." *NYT*, 7 Aug., A1.

———. 1992b. "Clinton Attacked on Foreign Policy." *NYT*, 28 July, A1.

Rosenstiel, Thomas. 1991. "American Praise Media, but Still Back Censorship, Postwar Poll Says." *LAT*, 25 Mar., 9.

Ross, Stephen A. 1973. "The Economic Theory of Agency: The Principal's Problem." *American Economic Review* 62, no. 2: 134–139.

Rouquie, Alain. 1982. *The Military and the State in Latin America*, trans. Paul E. Sigmund. Berkeley: University of California Press.

Rowan, Carl. 1997. "Military Has Wavy Rule of Thumb in Sex Cases." *Houston Chronicle* (7 June): A40.

Rowe, Travor. 1992. "UN Officials Weigh Use of Force in Somalia." *WP*, 28 Oct., A26.

Rowen, Henry. 1995. "Inchon in the Desert." *National Interest* 40 (Summer): 34–39.

Rumsfeld, Donald. 2001. "Rumsfeld's Rules." Accessed at *www.defenselink.mil/news/jan2001/rumsfeldsrules.pdf*

Russett, Bruce M. 1974a. "Political Perspectives of U.S. Military and Business Elites." *AFS* 1, no. 1 (Nov. 1974): 79–108.

———. 1974b. "The Revolt of the Masses: Public Opinion on Military Expenditures." In John P. Lovell and Philip S. Kronenberg, *New Civil-Military Relations: The Agonies of Adjustment to Post-Vietnam Realities*. New Brunswick: Transaction.

———. 1990. *Controlling the Sword: The Democratic Governance of National Security.* Cambridge, Mass.: Harvard University Press.

Russett, Bruce M., and Elizabeth C. Hanson. 1975. *Interest and Ideology: The Foreign Policy Beliefs of American Businessmen*. San Francisco: Freeman.

Russett, Bruce M., and Alfred Stepan. 1973. *Military Force and American Society*. New York: Harper and Row.

Ryan, Michael E. 1997. "Air Force Gen. John Ryan Was an Honorable Man." *WT*, 20 July, B2.

Sagan, Scott D. 1989. *Moving Targets: Nuclear Strategy and National Security*. Princeton: Princeton University Press.

———. 1991. "Rules of Engagement." *Security Studies* 1, no. 1: 78–108.

———. 1993. *The Limits of Safety: Organizations, Accidents, and Nuclear Weapons*. Princeton: Princeton University Press.

———. 1994. "The Perils of Proliferation: Organization Theory, Deterrence Theory, and the Spread of Nuclear Weapons." *International Security* 18, no. 4: 66–107.

Sahnoun, Mohammed. 1994. *Somalia: The Missed Opportunities*. Washington, D.C.: United States Institute of Peace Press.

Sapin, Burton M., and Richard C. Snyder. 1954. *The Role of the Military in American Foreign Policy*. Garden City, N.Y.: Doubleday.

Sarkesian, Samuel C. 1981. "Military Professionalism and Civil-Military Relations in the West." *International Political Science Review* 2, no. 3: 283–297.

———. 1975. *The Professional Army Officer in a Changing Society.* Chicago: Nelson-Hall.

———. 1981. *Beyond the Battlefield: The New Military Professionalism.* New York: Pergamon.

Sarkesian, Samuel C., John Allen Williams, and Fred B. Bryant. 1992. "Civilian Graduate Education and U.S. Military Professionalism." Paper presented at the annual meeting of the American Political Science Association, Chicago.

———. 1995. *Soldiers, Security and National Security.* Boulder: Lynne Rienner.

Scarborough, Rowan. 1996. "New Marine Officers Cheated on Field Test." *WT,* 7 June, A1.

———. 1999. "Apaches Were Sent to Scare Serbs." *WT,* 21 May, 1.

Scarborough, Rowan, and Andrew Cain. 1999. "GAO Cites 'Confusion' in Kosovo Policy." *WT,* 8 April, 1.

Schiff, Rebecca. 1992. "Civil-Military Relations: A Theory of Concordance." Paper presented at the annual meeting of the American Political Science Association, Chicago.

———. 1995. "Civil-Military Relations Reconsidered: A Theory of Concordance." *AFS* 22, no. 1 (Fall): 7–24.

Schmitt, Eric. 1992a. "Pentagon Accused of Bias in Enforcing Ban on Booty." *NYT,* 21 Aug., A18.

———. 1992b. "U.S. Aide Who Quit Calls Yugoslav Policy Ineffective." *NYT,* 27 Aug., A10.

———. 1993a. "Air Force General Faces Inquiry on Jab at Clinton." *NYT,* 9 June, A17.

———. 1993b. "Clinton, in Gesture of Peace, Pops in on Pentagon." *NYT,* 9 April, A8.

———. 1993c. "General to Be Disciplined for Disparaging President." *NYT,* 16 June, A20.

———. 1993d. "In Break for Clinton, Nunn Lends Support to Gay-Troop Plan." *NYT,* 21 July, A1.

———. 1993e. "The Top Soldier Is Torn between 2 Loyalties." *NYT,* 6 Feb., A1, A12.

———. 1995. "Commanders Say U.S. Plan for Bosnia Will Work." *NYT,* 27 Nov., 1.

———. 1997. "Air Force Reviewing Exoneration of General in Attack." *NYT,* 18 Feb., 1.

———. 1998. "Joint Chiefs Accuse Congress of Weakening U.S. Defense." *NYT,* 30 Sept., 1.

———. 2001. "Seeking a Blend of Military and Civilian Decision-Making." *NYT,* 24 Oct., B1.

Schmitt, Eric, and Steven Lee Myers. 1999. "U.S. Balkans Effort Points Up Difficulty of Fast Intervention." *NYT,* 28 April, 1.

Schoenberg, David W. 1971. "Loyalty Actions in the Army." *Military Law Review,* no. 51 (Jan. 1972): 249–277.

Schoenbrod, David. 1993. *Power without Responsibility: How Congress Abuses the People through Delegation.* New Haven: Yale University Press.

Schrader, Esther. 2002. "War, On Advice of Counsel." *LAT,* 15 Feb., 1.

Schwarzkopf, H. Norman, with Peter Petre. 1992. *The Autobiography: It Doesn't Take a Hero*. New York: Bantam.

Schweid, Barry. 1998. "NATO Preparing for Bombing Serbs." *Associated Press Headlines*, 8 Oct.

Sciolino, Elaine. 1993a. "Christopher Explains Conditions for Use of U.S. Force in Bosnia." *NYT*, 28 April, A1.

———. 1993b. "Clinton Says U.S. Will Continue Ban on Haitian Exodus." *NYT*, 15 Jan., A1.

———. 1993c. "Pentagon Alters Goals in Somalia, Signaling Failure." *NYT*, 28 Sept., A1.

———. 1993d. "Pentagon and State Department at Odds over Sending Soldiers to Haiti." *NYT*, 8 Oct., A1.

———. 1993e. "U.N. Chief Warning U.S. against Pullout of Force in Somalia." *NYT*, 1 Oct., A1.

———. 1993f. "U.S. Backs Bosnian Peace Plan, Dropping Threats to Use Force." *NYT*, 11 Feb., A1.

———. 1993g. "U.S. Declines to Back Peace Plan as the Balkan Talks Shift to U.N." *NYT*, 2 Feb., A9.

———. 1993h. "U.S. Military Split on Using Air Power against the Serbs." *NYT*, 29 April, A1.

———. 1994a. "Clinton Aides Seek Approval by NATO on Bosnia Air Raids." *NYT*, 8 Feb., A1.

———. 1994b. "Clinton Rules Out a Quick Response to Bosnia Attack." *NYT*, 7 Feb., A1.

———. 1994c. "Haiti Standoff: The U.S. Will Try Again." *NYT*, 28 April, A1.

———. 1994d. "Top U.S. Officials Divided in Debate on Invading Haiti." *NYT*, 4 Aug., A1.

———. 1994e. "U.S. Says Force Is Still a Choice in Bosnia Crisis." *NYT*, 8 April, A1.

———. 1997. "B-52 Pilot Requests Discharge That Is Honorable." *NYT*, 18 May, A1.

Scott, W. Richard, and John W. Meyer. 1983. *Organizational Environments: Ritual and Rationality*. Beverly Hills: Sage.

Scroggs, Stephen K. 1996. "Army Relations with Congress: The Impact of Culture and Organization." Ph.D. diss., Duke University.

Segal, David. 1975. "Civil-Military Relations in the Mass Public." *AFS* 1: 215–229.

Segal, David R. 1986. "Measuring the Institutional/Occupational Change Thesis." *AFS* 12, no. 3 (Spring): 351–376.

———. 1994. "National Security and Democracy in the United States." *AFS* 20: 375–394.

Segal, David R., and John D. Blair. 1976–77. "Public Confidence in the U.S. Military." *AFS* 3, no. 1: 3–11.

Segal, David, et al. 1974. "Convergence, Isomorphism, and Interdependence at the Civil-Military Interface." *Journal of Political and Military Sociology* 2: 157–172.

Serrano, Richard A., and Art Pine. 1993. "Many in Military Angry over Clinton's Policies." *LAT*, 19 Oct., A1.

Sestak, Joseph A. 1984. "The Seventh Fleet: A Study of Variance between Policy Directives and Military Force Postures." Ph.D. diss., Harvard University.

Shacochis, Bob. 1999. *The Immaculate Invasion.* New York: Viking.

Shafritz, Jay S., and J. Steven Ott, eds. 1996. *Classics of Organizational Theory,* 4th ed. Orlando: Harcourt, Brace.

Shanker, Thomas. 2001. "Rumsfeld Says Plans for Military Transformation Are Limited." *NYT,* 18 Aug., A10.

Shenon, Philip. 1997. "NATO General Warns Defenders of Karadzic." *NYT,* 4 Sept., 1.

Sherrill, Robert. 1970. *Military Justice Is to Justice as Military Music Is to Music.* New York: Harper and Row.

Simmel, Georg. 1955. *Conflict and the Web of Group Affiliation,* trans. Kurt Wolff and Rheinhard Bendix. New York: Free Press.

Slater, Jerome. 1977. "Apolitical Warrior or Soldier-Statesman: The Military and the Foreign Policy Process in the Post-Vietnam Era." *AFS* 4, no. 1 (Nov.): 101–118.

Sloyan, Patrick J. 1994. "How the Warlord Outwitted Clinton's Spooks." *WP,* 3 April, C3.

Smith, Hedrick, ed. 1992. *The Media and the Gulf War.* Washington, D.C.: Seven Locks Press.

Smith, Louis. 1951. *American Democracy and Military Power.* Chicago: University of Chicago Press.

Smith, R. Jeffrey. 1990. "Chief of Air Staff Fired by Cheney; Dugan Discussed Targeting Baghdad, Saddam." *WP,* 18 Sept., A1.

———. 1996. "Push on Bosnia War Crimes Pledged; Berger Says U.S. Plans 'More Effective Steps' against Those Indicted." *WP,* 9 Dec., 2.

Smith, R. Jeffrey, and Ann Devroy. 1993. "Handling Global Trouble Spots." *WP,* 17 Oct., A29.

Smith, R. Jeffrey, and Dana Priest. 1995. "Troops Given Wide Range of Authority." *WP,* 23 Nov., 1.

Snyder, Jack. 1984. *The Ideology of the Offensive: Military Decisionmaking and the Disasters of 1914.* Ithaca: Cornell University Press.

Sofaer, Abraham. 1976. *War, Foreign Affairs, and Constitutional Power: The Origins.* Cambridge: Ballinger.

Sorley, Lewis. 1992. *Thunderbolt: General Creighton Abrams and the Army of His Times.* New York: Simon and Schuster.

Spanier, John. 1959. *The Truman-MacArthur Controversy in the Korean War.* Cambridge, Mass.: Harvard University Press.

Spence, David B. No date. "Administrative Law and Agency Policymaking: Rethinking the Positive Theory of Political Control." Unpublished manuscript.

Stepan, Alfred. 1971. *The Military in Politics: Changing Patterns in Brazil.* Princeton: Princeton University Press.

Stevenson, Charles A. 1996. "The Evolving Clinton Doctrine." *AFS* 22, no. 4 (Summer): 511–536.

Stimson, James A. 1991. *Public Opinion in America: Moods, Cycles, and Swings.* Boulder: Westview.

Stockton, Paul. 1996. "Recent Developments in U.S. Civil-Military Relations." Working paper prepared for conference "A Crisis in Civilian Control? Contending Theories of American Civil-Military Relations," John M. Olin Institute of Strategic Studies, Harvard University, June.

Strobel, Warren P. 1995. "This Time, Clinton Is Set to Heed Advice from Military." *WT,* 1 Dec., A1.

Strobel, Warren, and Bill Gertz. 1993. "Admiral Slammed for Giving Priority to Aidid's Capture." *WT,* 7 Oct., 11.

Summers, Harry G. 1982. *On Strategy: A Critical Analysis of the Vietnam War.* Novato, Calif.: Presidio.

————. 1995. "After the Doubts, Salute and Obey." *WT,* 11 Dec., 19.

————. 1996. "President's Military Opening." *WT,* 18 Jan., 16.

————. 1997. "Take One Fit Man." *WT,* 10 July, 12.

Sundquist, James L. 1981. *The Decline and Resurgence of Congress.* Washington, D.C.: Brookings.

Tarr, David W., and Peter J. Roman. 1995. "Serving the Commander-in-Chief: Advice and Dissent." Paper presented at the annual meeting of the American Political Science Association, Chicago.

Taylor, Frederick Winslow. 1996. "The Principles of Scientific Management." In Jay S. Shafritz and J. Steven Ott, eds., *Classics of Organizational Theory,* 4th ed. Orlando: Harcourt, Brace.

Taylor, John H. 1992. "Perspective on the Draft." *LAT,* 21 Sept., B7.

Taylor, Telford. 1952. *Sword and Swastika: Generals and Nazis in the Third Reich.* New York: Simon and Schuster.

Taylor, William J., and David H. Petraeus. 1987. "The Legacy of Vietnam for the U.S. Military." In George Osborn et al., *Democracy, Strategy, and Vietnam: Implications for American Policymaking.* Lexington, Mass.: D. C. Heath. 249–268.

Thomas, Helen. 1993. "Clinton Seeks Improved Image with Military." United Press International, 7 May.

United States Department of Defense. 1993. Office of the Inspector General. *The Tailhook Report: The Official Inquiry into the Events of Tailhook '91.* New York: St. Martin's.

Upton, Emory. 1917. *The Military Policy of the United States,* 4th impression. Washington, D.C.: Government Printing Office.

Vagts, Alfred. 1937. *A History of Militarism: Romance and Realities of a Profession.* New York: Norton.

Van Creveld, Martin. 1985. *Command in War.* Cambridge, Mass.: Harvard University Press.

————. 1989. *Technology and War: From 2000 B.C. to the Present.* New York: Free Press.

Van Evera, Stephen. 1984. "The Cult of the Offensive and the Origins of the First World War." *International Security* 9, no. 1: 58–107.

Waller, J. Michael. 2001. "Rumsfeld: Plagues of a Biblical Job." *Insight Magazine,* 10 Dec.

————. 2002. "Command Performance." *Insight Magazine,* 4 Mar.

Walsh, Kenneth T., Bruce B. Auster, and Tim Zimmerman. 1994. "Good Cop, Bad Cop." *U.S. News and World Report,* 26 Sept., 43.

Warner, John W. 1999. "U.S. Policy and Military Operations Regarding Kosovo." Hearing of the Senate Armed Services Committee, 20 July.

Warner, Senator John H., and Senator Carl Levin. 1995. "Memorandum for Senator Thurmond and Senator Nunn: Review of the Circumstances surrounding the Ranger Raid on Oct. 3–4, 1993 in Mogadishu, Somalia." Washington, D.C.: United States Senate.

Webb, James. 1997. "The War on Military Culture." *Weekly Standard* 2, no. 18 (20 Jan.): 17–22.

Weber, Max. 1996. "Bureaucracy." In Jay S. Shafritz and J. Steven Ott, eds., *Classics of Organizational Theory,* 4th ed. Orlando: Harcourt, Brace.

Weigley, Russel F. 1993. "The American Military and the Principle of Civilian Control from McClellan to Powell." *Journal of Military History* 57, no. 5: 27–58.

Weinberger, Caspar. 1990. *Fighting for Peace.* New York: Warner.

Weiner, Sharon. 1996. "Resource Allocation in the Post–Cold War Pentagon." *Security Studies* 5, no. 4 (Summer): 125–142.

———. 1997. "The Changing of the Guard: The Role of Congress in Defense Organization and Reorganization in the Cold War." John M. Olin Institute for Strategic Studies, Working Paper no. 10, June.

Weingast, Barry R., and Mark J. Moran. 1983. "Bureaucratic Discretion or Congressional Control? Regulatory Policymaking by the Federal Trade Commission." *Journal of Political Economy* 91, no. 5: 765–800.

Weisman, Jonathan. 2002. "Cuts Get Cut from Pentagon Budget," *USA Today,* 8 Jan., 4.

Welch, Claude, ed. 1976. *Civilian Control of the Military.* Albany: State University of New York Press.

———. 1987. *No Farewell to Arms? Military Disengagement from Politics in Africa and Latin America.* Boulder: Westview.

Western, Jon. 2000. "Warring Ideas: Explaining U.S. Military Intervention." Ph.D. diss., Columbia University.

Westmoreland, William C. 1976. *A Soldier Reports.* Garden City: Doubleday.

White, Thomas D. 1963. "Strategy and the Defense Intellectuals." *Saturday Evening Post* 236 (4 May): 10–12.

Whitney, Craig R. 1993. "Europe's Cry: Lead On, U.S." *NYT,* 7 May, A1.

Whitworth, Damien, and Roland Watson. 2001. "Rumsfeld at Odds with His Generals." *London Times,* 16 Oct.

Wicker, Tom. 1963. "President Drops His Naval Chief in Surprise Move." *NYT,* 7 May, 1.

Williams, Dan, and Ann Devroy. 1994. "U.S. Policy Lacks Focus, Critics Say." *WP,* 24 April, A1.

Williamson, Oliver E. 1992. "Understanding the Employment Relation." In Jay M. Shafritz and J. Steven Ott, eds., *Classics of Organization Theory,* 3rd ed. Belmont, Calif.: Wadsworth. 379–395.

Wilson, George. 2000. *This War Really Matters: Inside the Fight for Defense Dollars.* Washington, D.C.: Congressional Quarterly Press.

Wilson, James Q. 1989. *Bureaucracy: What Government Agencies Do and Why They Do It.* New York: Basic Books.

Wines, Michael. 1993. "Law of Wild Prevails in Washington." *NYT,* 19 Dec., A15.

Wittman, Donald A. 1995. *The Myth of Democratic Failure: Why Political Institutions Are Efficient.* Chicago: University of Chicago Press.

Woodward, Bob. 1991. *The Commanders.* New York: Simon and Schuster.

Woodward, Bob, and Dan Balz. 2002a. "At Camp David, Advise and Dissent." *WP,* 31 Jan., A1.

———. 2002b. "Combating Terrorism: 'It Starts Today.'" *WP,* 1 Feb., A1.

———. 2002c. "'We Will Rally the World.'" *WP,* 28 Jan., 1.

Wyly, Michael D. 1995. "Fourth Generation Warfare: What Does It Mean to Every Marine?" *Marine Corps Gazette* (Mar.): 55–58.

Yarmolinsky, Adam. 1971. *The Military Establishment: Its Impact on Society.* New York: Harper and Row.

———. 1974. "Civilian Control: New Perspectives for New Problems." *Indiana Law Journal* 49, no. 4 (Summer): 654–671.

Zagorski, Paul W. 1992. *Democracy vs. National Security: Civil-Military Relations in Latin America.* Boulder: Lynne Rienner.

Zegart, Amy Beth. 1996. "In Whose Interest? The Making of American National Security Agencies." Ph.D. diss. Stanford University.

———. 1999. *Flawed by Design: The Evolution of the CIA, JCS, and NSC.* Stanford: Stanford University Press.

Zelikow, Philip. 1987. "The United States and the Use of Force: A Historical Summary." In Goerge K. Osborn et al., eds., *Democracy, Strategy and Vietnam: Implications for American Policymaking.* Lexington, Mass.: Lexington Books.

Zimmermann, Warren. 1996. *Origins of a Catastrophe: Yugoslavia and Its Destroyers— America's Last Ambassador Tells What Happened and Why.* New York: Times Books.

Zisk, Kimberley M. 1993. *Engaging the Enemy: Organization Theory and Soviet Military Innovation, 1955–1991.* Princeton: Princeton University Press.

Zoroya, Greg. 1996. "He's at the Front Lines Once Again." *LAT,* 6 Mar., E1.

Zumwalt, Elmo R. 1976. *On Watch.* New York: Quadrangle.

Index